Managing Globalization in Developing Countries and Transition Economies

Building Capacities for a Changing World

MOSES N. KIGGUNDU

Westport, Connecticut
London

#49679827

Library of Congress Cataloging-in-Publication Data

Managing globalization in developing countries and transition economies : building capacities for a changing world / Moses N. Kiggundu.

   p. cm.
  Includes bibliographical references and index.
  ISBN 1–56720–615–8 (alk. paper)
   1. Developing countries—Foreign economic relations. 2. Globalization—Economic aspects—Developing countries. 3. Globalization—Social aspects—Developing countries. 4. Globalization—Political aspects—Developing countries. 5. Globalization—Environmental aspects—Developing countries. 6. Developing countries—Economic policy. 7. World Trade Organization—Developing countries. 8. Europe, Eastern—Economic conditions—1989– 9. Former Soviet republics—Economic conditions. I. Title.
HF1413 .K54   2002
337'.09172'4—dc21   2002069694

British Library Cataloguing in Publication Data is available.

Library of Congress Catalog Card Number: 2002069694
ISBN: 1–56720–615–8

First published in 2002

Praeger Publishers, 88 Post Road West, Westport, CT 06881
An imprint of Greenwood Publishing Group, Inc.
www.praeger.com

Printed in the United States of America

The paper used in this book complies with the Permanent Paper Standard issued by the National Information Standards Organization (Z39.48-1984).

10 9 8 7 6 5 4 3 2 1

Dedicated to the memory of Eunice Kiggundu

Contents

Preface

Twenty years ago, the word *globalization* hardly existed in daily use. Today, it is used extensively and evokes strong intellectual and emotional debate and reactions. Globalization has come to characterize the end of the twentieth century and the beginning of the new millennium. It makes and unmakes individuals, families, organizations, communities, and nation–states. Some think it will save the world; others are convinced it will destroy it. It differentiates and integrates. Those who drive it are exalted and at the same time condemned. After more than ten years of breaking walls, liberalization, democratization, increasing international trade and investment flows, and street demonstrations, the message is beginning to sink in: Globalization is here to stay. Those with the capacity to manage it effectively will cope and even thrive; those without will lose, suffer, and stay behind. Those who isolate themselves from the global economy and the global society will remain permanently handicapped. Winners will be those with the capacity and motivation to manage globalization in all its aspects for mutual benefit. It is not a quick fix, therefore winners must also be able to persevere and have the capacity for staying power. World reaction to the events of September 11, 2001, confirm the resilience of globalization in the face of adversity. Governments, corporations, institutions, and individuals will seek ways to protect themselves against terror but will not give up globalization to terror. The socioeconomic logic, governance, and infrastructure that drive globalization have not diminished.

This book is about the opportunities and challenges globalization offers to developing countries and transition economies. Globalization offers these countries the opportunity for economic, political, social, and cultural development. By participating in the global economy, these counties increase their chances of reducing poverty, raising wages and incomes, and accumulating wealth. By interacting with other open societies in the world, they create favorable conditions for democratic development, and by improving the quality of public management, they can mobilize resources and improve services such as health care to their citizens. The central message is that globalization is not a unitary concept. It is not only about trade and investments. Rather, it is complex, dynamic, and multidimensional and needs to be understood by individuals, families, groups, communities, and public and private sector organizations in order to maximize its potential benefits and minimize its inevitable unintended adverse effects. Globalization does not happen by accident; it needs effective leadership, planning, resourcing, and management by both the public and the private sectors working together at all levels of society.

Unfortunately, most developing countries and transition economies do not have the necessary and sufficient resources, capacities, and competencies to manage globalization in order to maximize its potential benefits and minimize its inevitable unintended adverse consequences. To build and sustain these capacities, these countries need to establish public–private partnerships, both domestically and internationally so as to be able to manage the various dimensions of globalization and their interrelationships to mutual advantage. Regardless of current violent opposition and almost insurmountable obstacles, the fortunes and civilization of the twenty-first century are inexplicably linked with the future of globalization.

The international community—individuals, businesses, institutions, the voluntary sector, and governments—in the United States and other industrialized democracies have a role to play in facilitating effective globalization in the rest of the world. Globalization is not only about competitiveness; it is also about collaboration. In December 2001, on the one-hundredth anniversary of the Nobel Prize, one hundred Nobel laureates warned that the world must learn to think and act differently because as never before, the future of each of us depends on the good of all. A global economy needs a global dialogue. Therefore, this book is intended to facilitate informed dialogue among Americans and with citizens of other parts of the world about the opportunities and challenges of globalization and how to build a global economy and global society for the benefit of all. No dialogue on globalization is complete without the active involvement of the United States. Globalization needs America, and America needs globalization. As they say in India, first light the light in your house, and use the light to light the rest of the world.

Whether you run a global organization, earn your living as a small entrepreneur, own stocks or mutual funds, or if you or a member of your family or community owns a pension plan or other retirement benefits, or if you are a child or student lucky enough to have parents or guardians saving or investing for your education, you must support globalization. To do otherwise is to shoot yourself in the foot. Likewise, if you are a political, business, or community leader in any of the developing countries or transition economies, an ambitious young person growing up, a farmer, an unemployed university graduate looking for work, or a young couple raising a family, you must also support globalization. This is because globalization is not a policy option but a fact of life to which we must all adapt. It is also because globalization is not a handout, but a potential hand up. It offers the poor and oppressed people the best hope, opportunity, and prosperity to get out and stay out of poverty and to enjoy freedom.

The anti-globalization movement has been glorified by the media, tolerated by the public, and flirted with by leading world leaders. Yet, in reality, those who are violently opposed to globalization and seek the destruction of the institutional foundation, values, and ideals of the evolving global economy and global society are the blood cousins of the terrorists: They seek to destroy civilization as we know it.

During the last half of the twentieth century, it was believed that foreign aid offered poor countries the best hope for freedom, prosperity, and a better life. After more than fifty years, the results of that benevolent experiment are at best mixed. Experience has shown that while foreign aid, properly targeted and implemented, can stop poor human conditions from getting worse, its ability to create conditions for income generation, wealth creation, growth, local capacity, and sustainable development is very limited indeed. The logic, rationale, passion, and morality that supported foreign aid for the better part of the last century must now be scaled up to support globalization for the twenty-first century. We must not allow emotions to dictate our reactions to globalization's short-term or unintended negative consequences. History offers instructive lessons of experience. For example, while the Industrial Revolution was beneficial to Britain, Europe, and other industrialized countries, millions of citizens paid heavily for the progress and success of industrialization. We can learn from such experiences and draw out important lessons for managing globalization more equitably and with a human face, taking into account the sensibilities and moralities of the twenty-first century. We need to turn the challenges of globalization into opportunities for all, not behave like the Luddites of nineteenth-century Britain (1811–1816) who wanted to destroy the technology arising out of the Industrial Revolution.

I have written this book with several audiences in mind: for the professional men and women in the international community in America, Europe, and elsewhere doing business in these countries and wishing to understand and play an active role in the exciting and challenging journey of globalization; and for professionals working for the United Nations system and other international organizations including churches, nongovernmental organizations, and private consultants such as engineers, aid workers, lawyers, accountants, senior administrators, and security and intelligence officers. This book should also be attractive to the academic community, especially the professional and area studies interested in globalization and international relations. Ordinary Americans wishing to expand their global awareness and knowledge about the evolving relationships between America and the rest of the world also may find the book attractive. Likewise, political, business, and community leaders as well as professionals and academics from developing countries and transition economies should find this book useful in bringing together examples and lessons of experiences from different counties.

This book is especially important for Americans. Since World War II, historical evidence suggests that American engagement with the rest of the world contributes to global peace, hope, and prosperity. This was the case with America's belated participation in World War II, the reconstruction of war-torn Europe, the development of a new world order, and the global fight against Communism and the Cold War. More recently, active involvement and leadership by America in Bosnia, Kosovo, Kuwait, East Timor, and Afghanistan has contributed to a more stable and prosperous world. In contrast, when America remained disengaged in Rwanda, the Democratic Republic of the Congo, Liberia, and Sierra Leone, there were tragic consequences. Although America is the only remaining superpower, Americans as individuals are more local than global. Very few take the trouble to study or read about other countries, cultures, religions, or foreign sociopolitical systems. Fewer still speak foreign languages, and less than 10 percent hold passports or visit other countries. This must change because with globalization America and the rest of the world are inexplicably linked. For globalization to succeed and benefit all of humanity, America must remain engaged. This book provides the basis for informed engagement among Americans and between Americans and the rest of the world.

This book has a number of unique attributes: It is balanced, recognizing the unprecedented opportunities globalization offers to the people in developing countries and transition economies, while at the same time mindful of the potential for unintended negative consequences, especially if these are not effectively managed with proper mitigating contingencies. It is comprehensive in that it does not limit globalization only to economic considerations but includes political (governance), social (for example, labor, employment, health), environmental, and cultural aspects. It is global in that it is not limited to a single country or region but covers all regions of the developing and transition economies. It is practical and managerial in that it provides practical concepts, approaches, frameworks, and tools to help these countries to build a better world for globalization. It is instructional in that it provides a lot of examples from real-life experiences of globalization and draws out lessons of experience for others to learn from. It is simple, written in nontechnical language with illustrations (tables and figures) to let the story speak for itself. It is conceptual in that, when necessary, it briefly explains the theory or conceptual framework applicable to certain aspects of globalization. It is professional because it deals with issues that professionals from different disciplines are confronted with as they work with colleagues from other parts of the world. Finally, it is American because it seeks to establish informed dialogue between Americans (and others in advanced countries) and citizens of newly globalizing countries to develop a common understanding and strategies for the effective and equitable management of globalization.

This book is organized in three parts and twelve chapters. Parts I through III discuss globalization and the state, the economy, and society, respectively. Part I consists of two chapters. Chapter 1 discusses the conceptual and practical meaning of globalization and the translation of these definitions into images and life experiences ordinary people can understand and relate to. The chapter emphasizes the idea that globalization is basically local. Chapter 2 discusses the relationship between globalization and governance. Governments have a critical role to play in creating enabling or disabling environments for the effective management of globalization. It discusses the strategic and structural changes governments and society in general must undertake to equip themselves with the values, institutions, and capacities for managing globalization to advantage. It links the public sector reforms these countries are undertaking to the need to develop institutional capacities and competences for globalization. The chapter concludes with a brief discussion of globalization and national security for select countries in Africa and the Middle East.

Part II, consisting of six chapters, discusses globalization and various aspects of the economy. Chapter 3 discusses the relationship between globalization and a country's macroeconomic and microeconomic conditions. It starts by emphasizing the need for building effective working relationships between the public and the private sectors and the importance of ensuring an effective national integrity and regulatory system to contain corruption and build confidence for private sector participation. Chapter 4 defines entrepreneurship and explains the role it plays in creating a dynamic domestic and innovative environment for global participation, innovation, and competitiveness. It discusses the critical importance of good corporate governance and draws out lessons of experience from Central and Eastern Europe for other newly globalizing countries. Chapter 5, on trade and investment, begins with a brief explanation of trade theory and the idea of comparative advantage. It outlines some of the key impediments to global trade such as protectionism, and export subsidies and the reforms needed by all countries to facilitate freer trade. This is followed by a discussion of foreign direct investment, the factors which determine its flows, and the prospects for newly globalizing countries to attract more and better foreign direct investment.

Chapter 6 turns to the institutional aspects of globalization. Specifically, it describes the history, structure, mission, roles, and responsibilities of the World Trade Organization and the challenges it poses for developing countries and transition economies. It draws out important issues and lessons from Seattle, Washington, and Doha, Qatar, for newly globalizing countries and the need for these countries to develop the necessary national capacities and competencies for effective participation in global trade and investment. It outlines a model for identifying and developing the relevant capacities, drawing on recent methods of international development such as program-based and sectorwide approaches. The chapter emphasizes the need to balance the forces for competitiveness and equity in the process of driving for globalization.

Chapter 7 focuses on banking and financial crises. During the 1990s, many banking and financial crises were blamed on globalization. This chapter discusses the historical evolution of the banking system from the relatively closed and stable days of the Cold War to the more open and competitive 1990s. It describes the anatomy and causes of financial and banking crises and provides lessons of experience from Chile, one of the most active newly globalizing countries. It also describes efforts being made to develop the emerging global institutional architecture for strengthening financial institutions. After discussing the strategies and limitations of regional approaches to managing financial crisis management, the chapter concludes by outlining practical steps countries can take to prepare for these crises and to protect the poor and most vulnerable groups against the effects of these crises.

Chapter 8 discusses the relationship between debt and globalization. Opponents of globalization have argued that it is responsible for worsening the debt burden for developing countries and transition economies. This chapter begins by explaining a country's debt burden and how it is measured. It also discusses the relationship between debt and poverty and the performance of various groups of countries. It gives details of current efforts led by the World Bank to reduce debt, especially for the highly indebted poor countries. The chapter makes a distinction between domestic and foreign debt, and suggests that both types of indebtedness are important and need to be effectively managed. The chapter ends by outlining practical steps countries can take to enhance their capacity and competencies for managing the debt burden from both domestic and foreign debt.

Part III, on globalization and society, consists of four chapters. Chapter 9 is about globalization and health services. Services are among the most important areas of discussion among globalizing countries. The stakes are particularly high for developing countries and transition economies because of the potential comparative advantages they enjoy in some service sectors over the advanced countries. The chapter focuses on health services to highlight key challenges and opportunities these countries face in promoting and benefiting from trade in services. Chapter 10 discusses globalization and culture. Using music as an example, the chapter discusses challenges and opportunities developing countries face in developing commercially profitable cultural products and services with the rest of the world. Key challenges include the need to develop effective copyright and intellectual protection and antipiracy strategies.

Chapter 11 discusses the relationship between globalization, labor, and employment practices, including the problems of child labor and the applications of labor standards for newly globalizing countries. After reviewing the global employment situation for the twenty-year period ending in 2000, the chapter discusses the need for the development of flexible industrial relations systems and practices, especially at the enterprise level so as to maintain competitiveness. The chapter also discusses the skills and competencies globalizing countries need to emphasize in formulating and implementing their education and human resource development policies and strategies. The chapter concludes with a brief discussion of the effects of globalization on the distribution of wages and incomes among various segments of society. Chapter 12 focuses on globalization and the environment. It starts by reviewing the environmental health of the earth as of 2000 and concludes that the earth is in deteriorating ill health. After discussing the impact of the eight big environmentally important countries, including the United States, the chapter examines the effects on the environment of the business sector, both global corporations and indigenous small- and medium-size enterprises, and the relationship between the environment and poverty in the context of globalization. It is observed that most newly globalizing countries experience an imbalance between the speed at which the economy is growing and the local capacity for sustainable development. Therefore, the chapter concludes by outlining strategies these countries can take to build local and national capacities in the public and the private sectors for the effective protection, conservation, and management of the environment.

Acknowledgments

This book reflects my career: a long interest in the development of management theory and practice in developing countries and transition economies. Therefore, it is not possible to acknowledge all the support, advice, and criticisms I have received from individuals and institutions during the book's development and production. Over the years, I have had the opportunity to work with individuals from various local, national, international, and multilateral organizations including the United Nations and its specialized agencies, global corporations, universities, indigenous institutions, and nongovernmental organizations.

In 1994, I was invited by the Nippon Telecommunications Consulting Company of Japan to work on the restructuring and commercialization of Indonesia's telecommunications industry at a time when both the industry and the country were grappling with different aspects of globalization. In 2000, I was invited to be a member and to participate in the Fifteenth Meeting of the Group of Experts on the United Nations Programme of Public Administration and Finance focusing on "Globalization and the State." As well, my association with the United Nations Development Programme, the World Bank, The International Training Center of the International Labour Organization, and the Canadian International Development Agency, has shaped my thinking on matters of development, capacity development, governance and public service reform, public–private partnerships, and globalization. A little-known book entitled *Going Glocal* by a little-known Malaysian Moslem woman, Asma Abdullah, provided insights and stimulated my interest in studying the opportunities and challenges of ordinary citizens of newly globalizing transition societies.

Carleton University, my present employer, provided more than the usual institutional support and intellectual freedom. The research for this book was done when I was on sabbatical leave, and the offices of the dean of public affairs and management and the director of the Eric Sprott School of Business provided administrative and material support during the preparation of the manuscript. Patricia (Trish) O'Flaherty provided useful instruction and tips on how to navigate the various library systems. Bernie Rawlings and Diane Berezowski helped me in the preparation of an earlier draft, and Astrid Hoffmann helped with copyediting and formatting the manuscript.

Hilary Claggett, senior editor, introduced me to Greenwood Publishing Group and guided me through the various stages of proposal development and manuscript preparation. Denise Quimby of A & B Typesetters and Editorial Services provided excellent editorial services. I am grateful to you all.

My family background is a constant reminder of the personal nature of my academic and professional work. With family both in Africa and North America and close friends in Europe, my family and I try to avoid—with a varying degree of success—the temptation of "living in the middle of the Atlantic." My immediate family provides a supportive environment for my largely unstructured but often hectic work both at home and abroad. My son Andrew and my daughter Jacquie are much more understanding and supportive of my work now that they are university students in the process of shaping their own academic and career paths. I am grateful to my partner Dr. Kabahenda Nyakabwa for her love and support. She has constantly drawn my attention to the negative consequences of globalization, especially for refugees and other vulnerable groups in developing countries and transition economies. My sister Lucia Nantongo and Mother Juliet Namukasa, living in a poor neighborhood in Kampala, Uganda, epitomize the challenges and unrealized potentials of a struggling newly globalizing society. Finally, this book is dedicated to the memory of Eunice Kiggundu whose sagacious understanding of the dynamic forces of globalization was instrumental in the transformation of a reluctant immigrant into a self-actualizing and productive "glocal" citizen. Needless to point out, any errors of omission or commission are exclusively mine.

Moses N. Kiggundu

PART I
Globalization and the State

CHAPTER 1

What Is Globalization?

Globalization is easier to describe than to define. This is because, in its present form and usage, it is a new, complex, dynamic, multidimensional, and worldwide phenomenon, which means different things to different people and different things to the same people across time and space. It evokes strong emotions because it is associated, rightly or wrongly, with most of the world's significant challenges and opportunities. It cuts across many academic disciplines—such as economics, political science, history, geography, and environmental science—and many professional practices—such as diplomacy and international relations, management (public and private), journalism, national and global security, and international development. It is also seen through ideological prisms as being associated with capitalism or what George Soros calls "market fundamentalism (laissez-faire), liberalism, and Western democracy."[1] With all this diversity, it is hard to achieve common understanding.

To provide the reader with a broader meaning of globalization, I have done two things: First, I provide lists of select definitions from recent authors and writers. This is what I call "expert definitions." Second, I have collected a list of descriptors from ordinary people as to their understanding of the concept of globalization. This is the citizens' definition. It is expected that these two lists will help the reader broaden his or her understanding of globalization and compare these lists with the understanding of other associates such as policy makers, managers, community leaders, coworkers, or fellow citizens. Globalization is everyone's business.

Exhibit 1.1 provides a list of eight expert definitions. These experts are from different disciplines and organizations as well as from both poor and rich countries. The organizations include the United Nations systems, universities, and leading media outlets. The disciplines include management and journalism. Still, the list must be seen only as a small sample and is not intended to be comprehensive.

EXHIBIT 1.1
Globalization: Select Expert Definitions

"It is the inexorable integration of markets, nation–states and technologies to a degree never witnessed before—in a way that is enabling individuals, corporations and nation–states to reach around the world farther, faster, deeper and cheaper than ever before, and in a way that is enabling the world to reach into individuals, corporations and nation–states farther, faster, deeper, cheaper than ever before."

—Thomas L. Friedman (2000: 9)

"Globalization is the growing interdependence of the world's people . . . a process integrating not just the economy but culture, technology, and governance. People everywhere are becoming connected-affected by events in far corners of the world."

—United Nations Development Program (1999: 1)

"Globalization has become . . . the most important economic, political, and cultural phenomenon of our time. Around the globe the integration of the world economy is not only reshaping business but also reordering the lives of individuals, creating new social classes, different jobs, unimaginable wealth, and, occasionally, wretched poverty. . . . Globalization is neither new nor complete. . . . Globalization has begun to assume mythical overtones. . . . For Bill Clinton and Tony Blair, it is synonymous with modernity; for the French establishment and Asian leaders, it stands for American domination; for Pat Buchanan and some of the blue-collar workers who joined the protest in Seattle, it means the emasculation of America. . . . Globalization stands accused . . . of helping spur growing inequality within companies . . . , within countries . . . , and even between countries. . . . But the world economy remains much less integrated than either the proponents of globalization or its critics admit. . . .

"Globalization offers the chance to fulfill . . . the goals that classical liberal philosophers first identified several centuries ago and that still underpin Western democracy."

—John Micklethwait and Adrian Wooldridge (2000: xvi–xxii)

"Present day globalization is a unique convergence of technological, economic and political forces of daunting power and influence, having a massive impact on all aspects of public and private life in economic, social, political and cultural affairs at global, national and local levels. As it influences states and their partner actors, it is also exploited and shaped both positively and negatively by those with the foresight and resources to appreciate its power. Yet, so diverse and overwhelming is globalization's manifold influences that no one group or sector can control or stop it. As such, it has been responded to and manipulated by a range of actors in the public, private and civil society actors, is instigated in good and bad motives, and has benefited some social and economic

groups, but has hurt others who have become more vulnerable and dis-empowered due to its influence."
—United Nations (2000: 10)

"Globalization has three dimensions: cultural-ideational, politico-institutional, and economic. There are three ordinarily ranked levels of economic integration: existence of global infrastructure, harmonization and convergence of economic policies and institutions, and/or borderless-ness. To understand the policy implications of cross border economic in-tegration, we need to focus on flow of goods and services as well as factors of production-land, labour, capital, entrepreneurship, and technology."
—Aseem Prakash and Jeffery A. Hart (1998: 611)

"All institutions have to make *global competitiveness* a strategic goal. No institution, whether a business, a university, or hospital, can hope to survive, let alone to succeed, unless it measures up to the standards set by the leaders in its field, any place in the world. . . . The world econ-omy is increasingly becoming global. National boundaries are impedi-ments and cost centers."
—Peter F. Drucker (1999: 61, 63)

"Globalization . . . refers to the advancement of a 'global mentality'—a borderless world through the use of information technology to create part-nerships across the globe to deliver value-added services and products. It means a person can be a world citizen in spite of having a national iden-tity. Most countries in the world are currently subjected to this force and have to respond to . . . values to remain globally competitive. . . . The process . . . led to a rapid transformation of both our physical landscapes and the evolution of a competitive work culture. An individual, no matter where he works, is now expected to simultaneously assimilate new values at both the individual and the cultural levels without being given the time to go through the conscious choice. While he sees the physical changes around him, he may not be equipped with the appropriate attitudes, skills, and knowledge to make the mental transformation."
—Asma Abdullah (1996: 176, 178)

"Communism abolished the market mechanism and imposed collective control over all economic activities. Market Fundamentalism seeks to abolish collective decision-making and to impose the supremacy of mar-ket values over all political and social values. Both extremes are wrong. What we need is a correct balance between politics and markets, be-tween rule making and playing by the rules. . . .

"We cannot live as isolated individuals. As market participants, we serve
our self-interest, but it does not serve our self-interest to be nothing but
market participants. We shall need to be concerned with the society in
which we live, and when it comes to collective decisions we ought to be
guided by society as a whole rather than our narrow self-interest. The ag-
gregation of narrow self-interest through the market mechanism brings
unintended adverse contingencies. Perhaps the most severe, at the present moment in history, is the instability of financial markets."
                                    —George Soros (1998: xxvii–xxviii, 96–97)

These experts tell us a lot about the nature of globalization: its causes and consequences.
They tell us that globalization is important for all of us because it is pervasive and global and
is creating deeper interdependencies and interconnectednesses among regions, nations, governments, businesses, institutions, communities, families, and individuals. It is bringing
about fundamental and swift changes in the way we live, work, travel, govern ourselves, and
manage our economic interests and social relations. Openness is its platform, but it is driven
by technology, finance, information, and politics. It is not only an economic phenomenon but
also it affects political, social, cultural, technological, and environmental interests. It imposes
on nations, corporations, institutions, and individuals the burden of universal standards,
rules, rule enforcement, and the pressure to conform to these universal norms, expectations, and requirements. Nobody can hide from globalization and its extreme effects.

Asma Abdullah brings home the real meaning of globalization for organizations, managers, families, and individuals living and working in developing and globalizing countries
such as Malaysia.[2] Globalization is not value free; rather, the pressures to conform to universal standards of conduct and competitive performance force organizations and individuals to assimilate new values, which may be in conflict with local cultural values and
practices. This requires the individuals, organizations, and nations to build the necessary
mind-set, competencies, capabilities, and capacities to manage the transformations associated with globalization.

George Soros, a practicing capitalist and one of the richest men in the world who has
benefited from globalization, has reminded us of the need for balance between self-interest
and social interests; between the needs of the market and the state. He also asserts that the
present system is faulty and needs correction. "We have a global economy without a global
society. The situation is untenable."[3] Consequently, there is an increasing concentration of
income, opportunities, resources, and wealth among people, corporations, and countries.
He calls on the world community to rethink and reform the capitalist global economy on
which globalization is predicated. Of course, Soros does not want to abolish capitalism.
Rather, he criticizes globalization, as currently practiced, in the same way Democrats criti-
cize democracy. The objective is not to throw the baby out with the bath water, but to examine its fundamental premises and practical weaknesses, improve on it, and move it closer
to the ideal benefit of all citizens of the world.

A key lesson we learn from these experts is that globalization can and must be managed.
Since globalization affects all nations, governments, businesses, communities, and individ-

uals, the best we can do is fight back or respond in kind in order to take advantage of its opportunities and to minimize its potential adverse consequences. This requires a strategic approach to globalization. Nations, governments, businesses, institutions, communities, and individuals should not see themselves as helpless victims of globalization; rather, they should actively take the initiative to understand the nature of globalization, its causes, and its consequences on the ground; assess their own opportunities, strengths, and limitations; and develop realistic goals and a plan of action for managing globalization. It is not easy, and there are no guarantees or shortcuts, but the strategic approach is better than isolation or surrender. Doing it in partnership with others increases the chances of success and mitigates against some of the negative consequences.

The management literature is rich with descriptive materials on how businesses can become globally strategic and competitive in the twenty-first century.[4] Nations, government institutions, communities, and individuals can draw on this body of knowledge to develop their own tailor-made strategic directions and action plans for managing globalization. In its 1999 *Human Development Report* on globalization with a human face, the United Nations Development Program (UNDP), one of the U.N. specialized agencies doing extensive work in developing countries, provides a framework and guidelines for managing globalization. Recognizing that globalization is characterized by new markets, new tools, new actors, and new rules, the report challenges governments and the international community to find rules and institutions for stronger governance at the local, national, regional, and global levels. To bring about the kind of balance that Soros was talking about, the UNDP report[5] calls for an approach to globalization that, in addition to global markets and competitive profits (survival of the fittest), governments and private sector organizations should be managed on the basis of:

- Ethics—Less violation of human rights.
- Equity—Less inequality within and among nations.
- Inclusion—Less marginalization of people, organizations, communities, and nations.
- Human Security—Less physical, mental, and psychological harm to citizens and employees.
- Sustainability—Less environmental destruction.
- Development—Less poverty and deprivation.

The report also outlines six elements of a possible agenda for action:

1. Strengthening policies and actions for human development and adapting them to the new realities of the global economy.
2. Reducing the threats of financial volatility.
3. Taking a stronger global action to deal with global threats to human security.
4. Enhancing public action to develop technologies for human development and the eradication of poverty.
5. Reversing the marginalization of poor, small-island countries.
6. Addressing the imbalances in the structures of global governance in the twenty-first century.

Of course, these are ambitious goals, and in the imperfect world we live in, some of them may not be realistic. Yet, the best chance for achieving these goals is for all global actors—international and regional organizations, governments and their institutions, private sector organizations and their managers and employees, communities, leaders, and ordinary citizens—to work together for a better global world. This is particularly important for developing countries, which are much more vulnerable to the vagaries of globalization.

Abdullah describes the complexity of managing globalization in the Malaysian context. In addition to the demands arising out of globalization, Malaysians are subjected to pressures for industrialization, modernization, urbanization, Westernization, Islamization, and Vision 2020—the country's national long-term vision. These forces for change are each associated with a set of values, which in turn require public and private sector organizations, communities, and individuals to acquire corresponding attitudes, skills, knowledge, competencies, and capabilities required to perform in accordance with global competitive standards and expectations. Key required competencies include:

1. Anticipating needs and understanding business opportunities.
2. Using information and other resources strategically.
3. Constantly benchmarking and enhancing productivity, customization, and service delivery.
4. Managing change and being flexible.
5. Using computers and information technology for business improvements.
6. Learning how to learn and being flexible.
7. Relating across cultures, developing interpersonal skills, and managing diversity.[6]

National policy makers and private sector managers are expected to provide resources and leadership for Malaysian organizations, communities, and individuals to develop and enhance these competencies in order to participate fully in the changing global economy.

"The process of reflecting critically on our work styles is one way of achieving our targets of becoming globally integrated and yet be locally in touch."[7] This is what Abdullah calls "going glocal"—a necessary strategy for all globalizing developing countries.

From Abdullah, we move to the understanding of globalization by ordinary citizens. During the summer of 2000, as I was doing research for this book, I asked individuals of different walks of life what comes to mind when they think of the word *globalization*. Reactions varied from total silence for those who could not find a single word to express their cognitive understanding and emotional reaction to globalization to those who provided a torrent of descriptive and evaluative responses. This was an informal survey and no attempts were made to follow standard survey methods. My interest in doing this was to get a clinical appreciation of what ordinary people (nonexperts) know and think about globalization.

The results are summarized in Exhibit 1.2, which contains almost one hundred words and phrases on globalization. Some of the words used are positive (for example, freedom, peace, good government), others are negative (for example, war, crime, fear, anxiety, prostitution, corruption), technical (for example, comparative advantage, trade policy, leapfrogging), ideological (for example, capitalism, neocolonialism, hegemony, Americanization), populist (for example, protest, genetically modified [GM] food, "Big Brother"), and institutional (for example, the World Trade Organization [WTO], the International Monetary Fund [IMF], the World Bank, stock market).

Exhibit 1.2
Globalization: Descriptors from Ordinary Citizens

1. Openness
2. Interdependence
3. Individual freedom, liberty, empowerment
4. Competitiveness
5. Wealth creation
6. Capitalism
7. Partnership
8. Innovation
9. Communication: Internet, E-mail
10. Change, speed
11. Good, smaller government
12. Connectedness, interaction, exchange
13. Development, growth
14. Alliances, mergers
15. Americanization, dollarization
16. Capital flows, markets
17. Privatization
18. Inequalities, extremes
19. Peace
20. War, terrorism
21. Foreign direct investments
22. Comparative advantage
23. Crime, international, organized
24. Neocolonialism
25. Environment: degradation, protection
26. Europeanism
27. *1984:* "Big Brother"
28. Size
29. Fear, anxiety
30. Cultural assimilation
31. Overpopulation
32. Politics, geopolitics
33. Marginalization
34. New world order
35. Hegemony
36. Protest, Seattle, Prague, Genoa
37. Regionalism
38. Imperfection
39. Fund managers
40. Technology
41. Brain drain, gain
42. Networking
43. Boom and bust
44. Unemployment
45. Transformation
46. Westernization
47. Child labor, sweatshops
48. Corruption
49. Stock market, stock options
50. Polarization
51. Complexity
52. Trade, trade policy
53. Multiculturalism
54. Migration, refugees
55. Democratization
56. Human security
57. Rule of law
58. Volatility, risk
59. Poverty
60. GM food
61. Leapfrogging
62. Deregulation

63. Global corporations	68. WTO, IMF, BIS, World
64. Travel, tourism	Bank
65. Prostitution, sex trade	69. Crash, meltdown
66. CNN, MTV, media	70. Industrialization
67. Transparency,	71. Militarism
accountability	72. Civil society, grass roots

Together, the information in Exhibits 1.1 and 1.2 enriches our understanding of globalization from the experts' and the nonexperts' viewpoints. While the experts are more lucid and articulate, the nonexperts have a lot to say about globalization. From both groups, globalization is associated with many things partly because of its complexity, pervasiveness, and multidimensionality but also because people, both experts and nonexperts, tend to mix the concept, its causes, and its consequences. For example, some of the concepts—such as crime, environmental degradation, protest, and even corruption—are not intrinsic to globalization; rather, they are the unintended consequences of a potentially beneficial but imperfect global system. These negative extreme consequences can be controlled or eliminated through proper planning and management.

The challenge for the twenty-first century for both industrialized and developing countries and their citizens is whether a mutually beneficial partnership can be forged to manage globalization, its causes, and its consequences so as to maximize its benefits and minimize or contain its extreme consequences for all humanity instead of a select few. Indeed, the future of globalization may well depend on how successfully the world meets this challenge. Less than twenty years after the collapse of Communism and the end of the Cold War, there is a growing perverse, protectionist, and populist backlash that, left unchecked and unchallenged, could undermine the potential benefits which more open and more globally integrated economies and governments can eventually deliver to all citizens of the world.

A return to the old protectionist ways would hurt developing countries and their people the most because they are least able to fend for themselves. At the moment, globalization, at least as an ideal rather than current practice, offers these countries and their citizens the most realistic opportunity to undertake economic and political reforms necessary for economic growth, democratic development, human security, and improvements in the overall living standards of the majority of their citizens. For some of these developing countries, their own survival as nation–states may well depend on whether they succeed in managing globalization for the betterment of their citizens.

Finally, Exhibit 1.2 is presented with instructional purposes in mind. To get people to develop a deeper and more sophisticated understanding of globalization, it is important to start with where people are, not where you want them to end up. Therefore, a senior government official, corporate manager, community leader, or schoolteacher, working with a group of people on globalization, should start by asking them to write down or otherwise generate a list of words they associate with globalization. The individual and group lists, together with the list in Exhibit 1.2 and the experts' definitions in Exhibit 1.1 (or parts thereof), can provide useful instruction materials and a framework for deeper and more informed understanding of globalization, both in a general sense and specifically to the trainees and their local context. It is on the basis of this locally grounded understanding of globalization that trainees, discussion groups, planners, or individual citizens can develop practical and realistic understanding and strategies for managing globalization to their advantage.

Exhibit 1.3 provides a description of globalization and instructional materials for those who would like to use the analogy to deepen their individual and collective understanding and management of globalization. Many people, especially those in developing countries, relate to and sympathize with this analogy of globalization.

Exhibit 1.3
Globalization as a Moving Train

As we have seen, globalization means different things to different people and different things to the same people across time and space. I like to think of globalization as a train, and I call it the G-Train. "G" stands for globalization. The G-train is a special kind of train: It has three coaches each offering first-, second-, and third-class facilities and services.

The first-class coach is the most comfortable and best equipped and has the best services. The occupants are rich, technically advanced, and interconnected among themselves and with the rest of the world, with telephones, satellites, and the Internet. They are highly competitive and produce goods and services the rest of the world is prepared to buy at high prices. They have strong and well-established organizations and institutions for governance and economic management. They are militarily strong and exert strong influence on the entire train. They eat good food, dress well, and drink clean water, but they have polluted the air, soil, and waterways. The train shakes and sends out tremors and negotiates different terrains—slopes, valleys, plains, plateaus—but those in the first-class coach are best equipped to withstand these tremors and their effects.

The second-class coach is less endowed than the first. It is less equipped and less serviced, but the occupants are working hard to catch up and move up to the first-class coach. Some of the occupants have made tremendous progress over a relatively short period of time—they used to be in the third-class coach.

The third-class coach is obviously the least comfortable with the occupants living on one simple meal a day and with limited communication facilities. The economic and political systems are fragile and they suffer from tension, conflict, and, often, open warfare and even genocide. The members would like to move to the second-class coach, but it is hard and quite competitive. This is the most crowded part of the train. Most of the people live on less than a dollar a day.

Membership in any of the three coaches is not guaranteed. It is possible and indeed likely to move up from a lower coach to a higher coach, and vice versa. Even within each coach, the relative standing of individual members changes over time depending on absolute and relative performances, productivity, and innovation. At the moment, there is one, or two, very dominant members not only in the first-class coach but on the whole train.

There are also many people standing on the platform who are trying to board the train, but they are being kept out by forces beyond their control. Elsewhere in the railway station, there are others protesting and throwing stones at the G-train, wishing to derail it. Further away from the railway station, there are millions of people who have never heard of the G-train, and although it may affect their lives and the lives of their children and grandchildren, they go about living their lives in total ignorance of the train's existence and its pervasive effects.

Everyone wants to get on the train and move up to first class. There are those who believe that there is room for everyone on the train because the train is able to expand and provide a decent livelihood for everyone, providing they all play by the rules. There are others who do not believe the train can accommodate everyone, and therefore, they seek to destroy the train and replace it with a more "humanitarian vehicle" for the human journey.

Then there is the staff: the engineers, the conductor, and other service providers. These people, working closely with members of the first class, decide on the direction, speed, and overall rules of the G-train. Many others feel left out. They also feel that the rules favor first class and are unfair to lower-class members and latecomers. They want the rules changed but in a competitive atmosphere in which every member seeks to maximize his or her own interests, which is hard to do.

Then, there is the question of ownership: Who owns the train and all the equipment and services on it, the tracks, and the land? Members of the first-class coach claim ownership to most of these assets and the revenue they generate. Other members of the train and those not yet on the train would like to see a more equitable distribution of the G-train's assets, services, opportunities, income, and so on.

Can the train survive? Despite its shortcomings, it is generally believed that the G-train is here to stay and that it offers the best opportunities for advancement for those on different coaches, and for those yet to get on the train. Alternatives are worse. The challenge is not to build another train, or to change the tracks; rather it is to build strong and enforceable rules and institutions for more equitable and inclusive economic participation and good governance. Is this the promised train to the promised land?

Note: Readers are invited to locate themselves, their family members, and their community on the train in terms of place, time, ambition, and ideology.

OPPOSITION TO GLOBALIZATION

Many people are openly opposed to globalization: the concept, its practice, and its consequences. This is in spite of its actual and potential benefits to both rich and poor countries. This opposition, if left unchecked, threatens to push the world back to the dark days of protectionism and closed societies reminiscent of the Cold War. This danger became evident immediately following the September 11, 2001, terrorist attacks in the United States. Reasons for opposition are varied and include: ideological (capitalism versus communism or socialism), historical (the rich countries driving globalization are former colonial masters), cultural (American, Christian values versus French, Islamic traditions), political, economic (for example, due to the crash in Southeast Asia), personal (for workers who lost their jobs or the middle class that lost its savings), and populist (for example, for idealistic youths). Most of the numerous books and articles on globalization, especially those from the developing countries and left-leaning academics, range from mildly supportive to violently opposed.

Many world leaders have, at one time or another, expressed doubt, apprehension, qualified support, or outright opposition to globalization and have questioned its moral justification. The list includes the Pope, Prince Charles, Nelson Mandela, Mikhail Gorbachev, Olusegun Obasanjo, and Bill Clinton.[8] The public stand taken by these world leaders gives moral support to the demonstrations and protests against globalization and the international institutions promoting it. For example, the president of the United States gave moral and political support to the violent protests in Seattle, Washington, and Prince Charles has given indirect support to environmental groups opposed to globalization.

Others opposed to globalization include trade unions, the middle class, and unskilled workers. Trade union leaders in industrialized countries are opposed to globalization because they fear that their members will lose jobs to emerging economies with cheap surplus labor. They also argue that wages within these countries will be depressed as a result of workers coming in as immigrants and competing for a declining number of jobs. They also accuse global corporations of using global competition as an excuse to put pressure on unions and their members to accept rollbacks in wages and benefits. Under globalization, the union leaders of the industrialized countries see their challenge as keeping the jobs at home and protecting the hard-won benefits and working conditions of their numbers.

In the industrialized countries, the middle class—the most politically powerful group of voters in most democratic countries—is split between those who are benefiting from the transformations and those who are being left out. Naturally, the losers are using their individual and collective leverage to oppose or slow it down. In all the emerging economies—from Argentina to Russia—members of the middle class have seen their incomes, investments, and other assets depreciate in value as a result of inflation and falling exchange rates. As well, their privileges and free government services have either been eliminated or significantly reduced as their governments divest themselves and thus are unable to finance elaborate subsidies or programs.

Unskilled workers and farmers are opposed to globalization because they see themselves as losers, at least in the short run. In the industrialized countries, there is little demand for unskilled labor because technology and automation have raised the qualifications for the entry points of most industrial jobs. In the emerging economies, unskilled workers tend to benefit during boom times, especially in construction and manufacturing. During a downturn, however, these are the workers most affected by layoffs. For example, in South Korea and other East Asian countries during the 1997–1998 economic crisis, most of the layoffs were in construction and manufacturing involving unskilled and low-skilled workers. The same was true of Mexico in 1995 and Argentina and Turkey in 2001.

Farmers in industrialized countries are opposed to globalization because of competition from low-cost emerging economies or developing countries. European, American, and Japanese farmers, historically, are among the most subsidized in the world. WTO rules require that such subsidies be reduced or eliminated and that imports of agricultural foods be allowed in. Opposition to these rules is often heard from American beef and grain farmers, Japanese rice farmers, and European farmers and winegrowers. The World Bank estimates that industrialized countries spend $1 billion a day on agricultural subsidies, which is six times the amount spent on foreign aid. These subsidies contribute to poverty in developing countries and transition economies. Yet, politicians on both sides of the Atlantic are very reluctant to touch these subsidies and to allow free flow of agricultural imports.

There is opposition to globalization from most of Africa and other poor, vulnerable and closed parts of the world as well. The fear is that these countries lack the necessary capacity—infrastructure, capital, knowledge, skills, and institutional arrangements—for meaningful and beneficial participation in globalization. A combination of weak and unstable governments, small and vulnerable economies, warlike conditions, and widespread poverty creates unattractive conditions for the major drivers of globalization, especially the global corporations and other private sector investors. Apart from mining and other natural resources extractive industries, these countries are not players in the global economy. Moreover, lack of good governance often means that the proceeds from these economic activities benefit only a select group of elites, giving rise to private armies and guerrilla movements. Critics point to examples in Afghanistan, Angola, Colombia, the Democratic Republic of the Congo, Liberia, Somalia, Sierra Leone, Myanmar, and Russia.

Even among corporate managers, there are those who are opposed to globalization. Managing globalization is very difficult because it means, among other things, that managers now face a bigger, more complex, and unknown world over which they have virtually no control and little understanding. Even for businesses producing and selling locally, producers from far away places can drive them out of business if they produce better products or services at a lower price. Technology, which connects people in different parts of the world, also keeps them connected to the best-priced goods and services. Accordingly, managers fear for their businesses, their jobs, and the jobs of their employees as well as the viability of their communities. As the rules of doing business are changed by globalization, innovation, and technology, long-term planning becomes even more difficult, and managers become prone to panicking and becoming reactive.

It is now clear why globalization is a hard sell. Many politically and economically powerful interest groups see themselves as losers, potential losers, or victims of globalization, and they let their political representatives know of their fears and anxieties. Many world leaders give credibility and moral support to the widely publicized opposition and protests. The protest movements, lead by rich nongovernmental organizations and organized labor, are well organized, savvy, and competent. Some of these nongovernmental organizations are opposed to globalization because that is their raison d'être. Even the September 11, 2001, attacks on civilian (World Trade Center) and military (the Pentagon) interests were blamed on globalization instead of seeing them as the hideous crimes they were. Even the United Nations has placed on its Web site information discussing the relationship between globalization and terrorism, and the suggestion that the "evils" of globalization contributed to the events of September 11. There are no consistent and strong voices in support of globalization from public or private sector leaders in industrialized, emerging, or developing countries. Many of the beneficiaries of globalization are too busy amassing wealth to be concerned about the negative consequences to others in far away places.[9]

Perhaps the most significant advantage for those opposed to globalization is the difference in the way benefits and losses are expressed. Advocates of globalization tend to be macroeconomists. Therefore, they tend to express the benefits of globalization in macroeconomic and, thus, impersonal terms. Globalizing countries enjoy increased trade, attract more foreign direct investment, promote democratic development, and promote overall general openness. On the other hand, the losses or potential disadvantages attributed to globalization are often expressed in local, micro community–level, personal terms: Individuals lose their jobs or value of their assets, neighborhood businesses close down, rivers get polluted, communities get destroyed, family life is disrupted, and local cultures are threatened.[10] Is it possible that globalization may be doing a lot of good to the world as a whole and damage to the parts thereof? Most people are conditioned to act locally and, maybe, think globally. Therefore, advocates of globalization need to find powerful and meaningful expressions of benefits that individuals, their families, and their communities can relate to.

Recognizing the dangers of systematic and organized opposition to globalization, a number of individuals and organizations are beginning to fight back in support of the ideals, practices, and benefits of globalization. One of the leading supporters of globalization is George Soros, whose support has been expressed in several different forms: First, his critical analysis and writings about the imperfections of the current global system have focused attention on the need for reform. Second, he has worked closely with several emerging and globalizing countries, advising them on how to manage the inevitable ups and downs of globalization and its multiple transformations. He has been particularly active in Russia, Ukraine, and other Eastern European countries, as well as Indonesia, Malaysia, Brazil, and South Africa. Third, working closely with the IMF, the World Bank and the U.S. Treasury, he has proposed specific measures to help globalizing countries in crisis and to reform the global financial system. Finally, through his Open Society Foundation, he has allocated some of his fortune to support initiatives aimed at promoting global openness, democratization, and economic transformations.[11]

The international media has joined forces in support of globalization. International journalists with the tacit support of their employers have written on a variety of personal and community incidents showing the benefits and some of the losses due to globalization. Business leaders have written to the international press asking others to speak up for globalization. Periodically, *The Economist* boldly carries cover stories making the case for globalization. Some television networks have started broadcasting town hall–type programs, which debate the local pros and cons of globalization. The United Nations has supported several expert meetings and publications on globalization.[12]

Yet, so far, governments have been most reluctant to support globalization consistently and openly. *The Economist* expressed this sense of frustration when it wrote: "These outbreaks of anti-capitalist sentiments are meeting next to no intellectual resistance from official quarters. Governments are apologizing for globalization and promising to civilize it. Instead, if they had any regard for the plight of the poor, they would be accelerating it, celebrating it, exulting in it—and if all that were too much for the public they would at least be trying to explain it" (*The Economist*, September 23, 2000, p. 19).[13]

This book is primarily concerned with the strategies for managing globalization in developing and transitioning countries. Therefore, the issue of the role of governments in these countries to promote, or at least explain, globalization to the citizens is very important. For any given developing country, it is important to determine whether the challenges of promoting globalization are a matter of will or capacity. Some governments are not willing to promote globalization openly for fear of backlash. While boom times are easier to explain or even celebrate as export revenues and increased levels of employment fill government coffers, hard times provoke unanticipated reactions. For example, in Malaysia, when the economy started its downward spiral, Prime Minister Dato'Seri Dr. Mahathir bin Mohamad, and his government closed markets, started a political crack down, and used the national media to point the blame at greedy Western capitalists and a Zionist conspiracy. In Indonesia and Mexico, the population responded to hard times by overthrowing the governing regimes and replacing them with the opposition. In Turkey, senior cabinet ministers resigned in 2001; and in 2002, Argentina went through several regime changes.

In addition to developing early warning systems, governments need strategies and tools for managing the boom and busts so intrinsically associated with globalization. A simple strategy of how to explain globalization to the citizens would be a good first step. Pusilanimous leaders, government officials, politicians, or business executives cannot advance the course of globalization. Due to its complexity and multidimensionality, globalization requires intelligent leaders who can hold at least two contrary ideas at the same time and still retain the capacity to function effectively.

REALITY CHECK:
WHAT DOES IT MEAN TO DEVELOPING COUNTRIES?

What does all this mean for governments, businesses, communities, institutions, families, and individuals in developing countries? Following are some of the key aspects of globalization that public officials, private sector managers, community leaders, and ordinary citizens should understand.

1. Globalization is multidimensional and, therefore, means different things to different people across time and space. Globalization is about transformational change with intended and unintended adverse effects. Since its dynamics and consequences are not fully predictable, some of its aspects may be emphasized or deemphasized at different times for dif-

If the periphery refers to the emerging economies as Soros seems to suggest, what about the rest of the world, especially developing countries? This is a question of both classification and inclusiveness. For the center periphery model to be useful for globalization, it must be comprehensive and inclusive. Specifically, it must account for all the countries of the world, including those countries currently almost closed to the global economy. To address this problem, the periphery is further subdivided between periphery one (P1) and periphery two (P2). P1 corresponds to the emerging economies, and P2 represents all other developing countries of the world.

What criteria do we use to differentiate between P1 and P2 countries? The literature is full of global indicators used to classify countries. These include economic indicators such as gross domestic product (GDP), per capita income, foreign direct investment (FDI), the proportion of external trade to the total economy, and debt as percentage of GDP; socio-economic indicators such as the annual UNDP human development index; and governance indicators such as Transparency International's corruption index, the economic freedom index, and democratic development. Each of these indicators provides a measure of internal development and external openness.

More recently, Professor Jeffrey Sachs of the Center for International Development of Harvard University has divided the world into three distinct parts, not by ideology but according to their own technological advancement. The first part, which corresponds to the triad, is made up of about 15 percent of the world population and provides nearly all of the world's technology innovation. He calls this "technological innovators." The second part—"technological adapters"—involves about half of the world population and is able to adopt new technologies in production and consumption. The remaining part, covering about one-third of the world population, is technologically disconnected. To be technologically disconnected is equivalent to being globally disconnected, especially since globalization is driven by technology.

These three technological groupings are very similar to the classifications of the center: P1 and P2. The technological innovators include the United States, Canada, Western Europe, Japan, Australia, Israel, Singapore, Taiwan, and South Korea. These are countries with ten patents or more per million population. They roughly correspond to the center, especially if defined in terms of actors rather than fixed nation–states. The technological adapters include Mexico, Costa Rica, Panama, Peru, Chile, Brazil, Argentina, South Africa, Portugal, Tunisia, Jordan, Turkey, most of Eastern Europe, India, most of Southeast Asia, New Zealand, and Papua New Guinea. These are countries with high-tech exports of at least 2 percent of GDP. They roughly correspond to the P1 grouping. The rest of the world, the technologically excluded, corresponds to P2.[19] This classification of countries explains and predicts chances of success or failure of globalization for given countries. The center, or technological innovators, have the highest chance of being successful with globalization. The technological adapters, or P1 countries, have the potential to make it and even advance to the center. The P2, or the technologically excluded countries, has the lowest chance of being successful at globalization. It should be noted that technological exclusions do not correspond to national borders. For example, while most of China is shown as technologically excluded, the east coast is shown as a technological adapter, the same is true of parts of South India.

For the leadership of the developing countries, the first task is one of self-assessment to determine which of these classifications best describes the prevailing conditions of the country or parts thereof. Most of the large developing countries such as Brazil, India, South Africa, and Mexico will most likely have pockets of technological adapters and extensive areas of the technologically excluded. This information is useful in the development of a management strategy and plan of action for globalization. Pockets of technological adapters—usually in urban or coastal areas—should be given priority in the development of the capital, physical, and institutional infrastructure, as well as good governance, for managing globalization. The technologically excluded areas should also be given attention for eventual development and upgrading to the level of technological adapters. These areas may have something special such as a deep-sea port, raw materials, or human capital, which they can use for global exchange. Such developments are likely to be slow, but in the long run, they are likely to pay off.

Costa Rica, a small agricultural country in Central America, provides a good example of the difference good government policy can make. In the 1990s, the government adopted policies to promote telecommunications services and the development of a high-tech culture including the Internet. As a result, the country won a regional competition for an Intel chip fabrication plant. In the first full year of operation, the plant produced an estimated $700 million in export revenue, which is more than either bananas or coffee, the country's two largest agricultural export crops.[20]

History provides lots of examples showing the relationship between technology (innovation, adaptation, imitation, commercialization) socioeconomic development, competitiveness, openness, and wealth creation. This was indeed the case for Great Britain and then Europe, the United States, and Japan during and after the Industrial Revolution. It also helps to explain why the United States leads the world in innovation and competitiveness because it accounts for more than 40 percent of the world's science spending and produces one-third of the world's high-tech products and almost one-half of all major new drugs. It spends more on research and development than all the other members of the G8 countries combined: Germany, Japan, France, Britain, Canada, Italy, and Russia. As well, the second half of the twentieth century has witnessed countries such as South Korea, Singapore, Taiwan (POC), Brazil, and Malaysia taking advantage of development-friendly policies and moving up the technological scale from being disconnected to becoming adapters and even innovators. On the other hand, other periphery countries (especially the P2 categories) whose governments have not successfully implemented technology-friendly policies and whose populations have not become technologically connected are, therefore, unable to compete in the global world.

Therefore, a key aspect of the strategy for managing competitiveness for globalization must include the development of the local technological capacity (LTC) and the necessary physical, institutional, and human capital to support and sustain it. Of course, the specific strategies would differ for P1 and P2 countries or parts thereof. For P1 countries, the emphasis should be on building the LTC, which advances technological innovation, and commercializations for producing globally competitive goods and services. For P2 situations, however, the emphasis would be on improvements in strategic and operational aspects of technology including acquisition, maintenance, repair and servicing, technical support, learning, and adaptation. The prime objective here is to develop the LTC, which enables the actors to get connected and stay connected. In both cases, P1 and P2 would need active partnership, understanding, and support from the technological innovators. It is critically important for periphery actors to develop the necessary LTC in support of electronic connectedness with the rest of the world because world trade and all other aspects of globalization are increasingly being done digitally.[21] For this to happen, America must play a significant proactive and supportive role.

CAPITAL ENDOWMENT FOR GLOBALIZATION

Globalization requires effective utilization of a wide range of capital resources. At least twelve different types of capital have been linked to successful globalization: physical, digital, financial, human, intellectual, entrepreneurial, managerial, political, institutional, social, cultural, and spiritual. As would be expected, the center is most endowed with these capital assets and combines and uses them most effectively for advancing its own competitive advantage. For example, while the center competes with a world-class physical infrastructure and a high-speed digital nervous system, P1 is struggling to maintain functioning Internet connections, and P2 is just beginning to celebrate the arrival of a working telephone.[22]

The center controls most of the world's financial, intellectual, and entrepreneurial capital resources needed for innovation and management. While P1 actors are making progress in building up these capital resources, those under P2 conditions are still very far behind. Likewise, political and institutional resource endowment favors the center and gets progressively worse for P1 and P2. This poses a serious problem for the periphery because the state, in particular, and public institutions, in general, play a very important role in the development of the enabling environment for globalization. When the country's overall governance is poor and public institutions are weak or corrupt, the chances for effective management of globalization are remote. The most serious abuses for globalization are found in weak states with powerful corrupt actors both in the private and public sectors. America need not be reminded of Somalia, the Sudan, Yemen, or Afghanistan. Reported cases of illegal diamond trading in Angola, Sierra Leone, and the Democratic Republic of the Congo, drugs in Colombia, and nuclear materials in Russia may well be the tip of a growing and moving iceberg.[23] Most P1 and P2 countries produce the largest number of immigrants and refugees. When human and intellectual capital does not feel safe or appreciated, it moves out. It is not by accident that Africa, Russia, the Balkans, and the Middle East suffer from the brain drain in favor of Western Europe, the United States, Canada, and Australia who benefit from the brain gain.[24]

Culture and spirituality are important considerations for globalization. For example, monocultural societies founded on the ideals of history, self-glorification, and hatred of outer groups may find it difficult to participate fully and freely in globalization. The Balkans come to mind, as do parts of Western Europe, the Middle East, and Japan.[25] On the other hand, multiculturalism is good for globalization. It facilitates and enriches cross-cultural exchanges, widens people's perspectives and worldview, and makes for a vibrant and dynamic community. Multiculturism allows communities of different or competing logics to coexist harmoniously and productively. However, this is only true if the country, organization, or community has well-established mechanisms or traditions of valuing diversity with opportunities for diverse populations to work and live together. If this is not the case, multiculturalism can tear the community apart.

The United States, Canada, and Australia seem to be leading the world in developing and taking advantage of multiculturalism and diversity. Western Europe is also learning, if only because it faces increasing labor shortages for its growing economy. Singapore is working very hard to attract, retain, and integrate immigrants from other parts of Asia, especially the Indian subcontinent. Japan is still a monocultural society and is likely to remain so for a long time. South Africa is trying; Zimbabwe and Fiji seem to be failing. You could look at how a country, community, or organization effectively deals with foreigners or outsiders and tell if it is ready for globalization.

Sociocultural values have always been considered important for economic development, competitiveness, and, more recently, globalization. Since Max Weber, students of European history have used Calvinism and the Protestant work ethic to explain differences in industrialization and economic performance. The East Asian "miracle" has often been attributed in part to the excellent work ethics of the people based on the religious principles of Buddhism and Confucianism (Japan, Taiwan, Hong Kong, Singapore, China, and Thailand.) The Asian model produced dramatic increases in the people's living standards faster than anywhere else in the world. Leading Asian leaders, such as Lee Kuan Yew of Singapore, Suharto of Indonesia, and Dr. Mahathir of Malaysia, declared Asian values superior to Western values. In Singapore, Lee Kuan Yew considers Western societies decadent, Mahathir resents the Western traditions of colonialism, and Suharto extolls the virtues of collectivism and nepotism. Even when the Asian model proved fallible during the 1997–1998 Asian crisis, the recovery and continuing economic growth are often associated with societal and religious values and practices.[26]

On the other side of the argument, lack of economic development, industrialization, and effective participation in the global society have been attributed to lack of developmental work ethics and values. Culprits include India's caste system, Africa's tribal and feudal values, Islam's fatalism, and Catholicism's overemphasis on "life here after" as opposed to Protestantism's focus on earthly gratification. Of course, there are as many advocates of these arguments as there are opponents. For example, Mamadou Dia of the World Bank has argued that African culture, in general, and social transfers, in particular, contribute positively to economic development because they contribute to the accumulation of social capital. However, other empirical studies have shown that such tribal practices are detrimental to the development of productive entrepreneurship.[27]

Regardless of one's point of view about the specific cases, the inescapable conclusion is that social culture and values are important for a globalizing society. Second, it is also the case that some cultural values and practices create a more enabling environment for openness, competitiveness, innovation, and other factors important for globalization. Third, societal culture and values are not static; instead, they are subject to change over time and circumstances. Therefore, for any globalizing society, national and community leaders, as well as corporate managers, can play a very important role by fostering a culture and ethical values supporting globalization. For example, trust is important because a lot of transactions are based on trust among parties who may be operating from different continents and perhaps have never met face to face. If members of a country, community, or organization send signals to outsiders, which create the impression of hostility or corrupt or unethical conduct, no trust will be established. In an open global society, opportunities and capital will flow only among mutually trusting parties. No trust—no globalization.

Globalization requires sustained high standards. In addition to honesty and hard work, it requires discipline. Discipline is required for consistency, speed, accuracy, dependability, and overall efficiency. Organizations in the center with advanced precision technology and machinelike work organization and habits are better endowed to enforce discipline and meet the required standards. They use a wide range of management techniques including continuous improvement, total quality management, quality control circles, and, more recently, enterprise resource planning. Emphasizing the importance of discipline for successful visionary organizations, James Collins and Jerry Porras wrote: "Discipline is the greatest thing in the world. Where there is no discipline, there is no character. And without character, there is no progress."[28] To this I would add that where there is no discipline, there can be no globalization.

In the periphery, it is much more difficult to maintain this level of discipline because organizations lack the necessary capital resources, as well as sociocultural supportive work values and habits. This is particularly the case for P2 actors who continue to depend on outside assistance to meet the standards of the external world. For P2 actors, continuous improvement is hard to sustain.

The future of globalization may well depend on whether the center and the periphery can forge a mutually beneficial partnership to ensure sufficient and effective utilization and capital endowments to all actors. These are some of the key challenges facing international organizations such as the G8, G20, G77, WTO, IMF, World Bank, United Nations, global corporations, international nongovernmental organizations, and civil society in general. More equitable distribution of capital resources will provide the basis for seriously addressing the causes of unintended adverse consequences of globalization such as inequality, polarization, exclusion, marginalizing, or fear of cultural domination.[29] Global actors in the periphery need to bolster their institutional capacities and human competencies to become truly competitive in an increasingly globalizing world.

NOTES

1. George Soros, *The Crisis of Global Capitalism* (New York: Public Affairs, 1998).

2. Asma Abdullah, *Going Glocal: Cultural Dimensions of Malaysian Management* (Kuala Lumpur: Malaysian Institute of Management, 1996).

3. Soros, *The Crisis of Global Capitalism*, xxix.

4. See, for example, Peter F. Drucker, *Management Challenges of the 21st Century* (New York: Harper Business, 1999); Bill Gates, *Business @ the Speed of Thought* (New York: Time Warner, 1999); Gary Hamel and C. K. Prahalad, *Competing for the Future* (Boston: Harvard Business School Press, 1994); Avinash K. Dixit and Barry J. Nalebuff, *Thinking Strategically: The Competitive Edge in Business, Politics, and Everyday Life* (New York: Norton, 1991); and Andrew S. Grove, *Only the Paranoid Survive* (New York: Doubleday, 1996).

5. UNDP, *Human Development Report* (New York: UNDP and Oxford University Press, 1999), 3–12. Also see, David Reynolds, "Globalization and Its Discontents," *One World Divisible: A Global History since 1945* (New York: Norton, 2000), 650–656.

6. Abdullah, *Going Glocal*, 200.

7. Ibid., 211.

8. See, for example, Hans D'Orville, *The Search for Global Order: The Problems of Survival*. The Tenth Session of the Interaction Council, May 28–31, 1992, Queretaro, Mexico.

9. For detailed accounts of the beneficiaries of globalization, see Thomas L. Friedman, *The Lexus and the Olive Tree: Understanding Globalization* (New York: Anchor Books, 2000), especially 145–326; and David A. Kaplan, *The Silicon Boys and Their Valley of Dreams* (New York: HarperCollins, 1999), especially chaps. 6 and 7. For the United Nations Web site, visit www.unpan.org. Also see Tina Rosenberg, "The Free-Trade Fix: A Way to Make Globalization Work for Everybody Else," *New York Times Magazine*, 18 August 2002, sec. 6, pp. 28–33, 50, 74–75.

10. The difference of how the advantages and disadvantages of globalization are expressed was vividly illustrated at the International Monetary Fund (IMF)–World Bank joint meeting in Prague (September 2000). The protesters, led by the antipoverty group Jubilee 2000, held a mock funeral march and proclaimed that globalization is promoted by the IMF and the World Bank and kills 19,000 children every day. In response, an IMF spokesman, David Hawley, was quoted as saying, "The claim that the Fund kills babies is nonsense. I speak for the Fund, but the Fund and the Bank are both dedicated to reducing poverty." As an economist, he was right, but he lost the public relations war, and the protestors won the hearts and perhaps minds of the public because they were direct and graphic. See the *Ottawa Citizen*, September 25, 2000, p. A7.

11. A detailed discussion of Soros' work on globalization can be found in his book *The Crisis of Global Capitalism*. Nadia Rybarova, "IMF Protesters Stage Mock Funeral," *Ottawa Citizen*, September 25, 2000, p. A7.

12. For detailed discussions of globalization and its effects worldwide, see Friedman, *The Lexus and the Olive Tree*; John Micklethwait and Adrian Wooldridge, *A Future Perfect: The Challenge and Hidden Promise of Globalization* (New York: Random House, 2000). For business leaders and academics calling on others to support globalization, see David De Pury and Jean-Pierre Lechmann "Speaking Up for Globalization," *International Herald Tribune*, June 14, 2000, p. 7. For the United Nations, see *Globalization and Economic Governance, Report of the Fifteenth Session*, May 8–12, 2000, ST/SG/AC-6/2000/L.4.

13. It is beyond the scope and intent of this book to review all the theoretical approaches to globalization. For a discussion of a theory of globalization, see Farhang Rajaee, "The Theory of Globalization," *Globalization on Trial: The Human Condition and the Information Civilization* (Ottawa: International Development Research Centre, 2000), 19–61. For defense of globalization after the September 2001 attack on the United States, see "The Case for Globalization: Globalization and its Critics: A Survey," *The Economist*, September 29, 2001, p. 52ff.

14. Rajaee, "The Theory of Globalization," 19–61.

15. The IMF's recent discussion of Africa and globalization provides an excellent example of the purely macroeconomic approach. See Laura Wallace, ed., *Africa: Adjusting to the Challenges of Globalization* (Washington, DC: IMF, 1999). Also see IMF, "The Shape of Global Integration," *Finance and Administration* (Washington, DC: IMF, March 2002), 29, 1, 4–43.

16. David S. Landes, *The Wealth and Poverty of Nations: Why Some Are So Rich and Some So Poor* (New York: Norton, 1998).

17. Soros, *The Crisis of Global Capitalism*, 102.

18. For a more detailed discussion of the cosmocrats, see Micklethwait and Wooldridge, *A Future Perfect*, chap. 12. Friedman (*The Lexus and the Olive Tree*) uses the Lexus and Olive Tree metaphor to distinguish between global cosmopolitan (Lexus) and local traditional values and culture. For the concept

of "organization man," see William F. Whyte, *The Organization Man* (New York: Simon and Schuster, 1956). Also see Peter F. Drucker, "The New Society," *The Economist*, November 3, 2001, after p. 54 (special insert).

19. This discussion is based on Jeffrey Sachs, "Sachs on Globalization: A New Map of the World," *The Economist*, June 24, 2000, pp. 81–83.

20. Discussed in Gates, *Business @ the Speed of Thought*, 411.

21. Local technological capacity is defined as "innovation that enhances the technological capacity of one or more organizations, and enables it to perform its critical operating and strategic management tasks with greater efficiency, economy and effectiveness on a sustained basis, and to satisfy the salient and legitimate needs of its internal and external stakeholders." See Moses N. Kiggundu, *Managing Organizations in Developing Countries: An Operational and Strategic Approach* (West Hartford, CT: Kumerian, 1989), 190.

22. Bill Gates defines the digital nervous system as "digital processes that enable a company to perceive and react to its environment, to sense competitive challenges and customer needs, and to organize timely responses. A digital nervous system is distinguished from a mere network of computers by the accuracy, immediacy, and richness of the information it brings to knowledge workers and the insight and collaboration made possible by the information. No company has an ideal digital nervous system; rather, it's an ideal use of technology in support of business" (*Business @ the Speed of Thought*, 493). As an ideal concept, it can be used at different levels of analysis and intervention in both the public and the private sectors.

23. There is growing literature on the relationship between globalization and criminal behavior. See, for example, Anna Alvazzi del Frate and Giovanni Pasqua, eds., *Responding to the Challenge of Corruption: Action of the International Conference*, Milan, November 19–20, 1999; and United Nations Interregional Crime and Justice Research Institute (UNICRI) and International Scientific and Professional Advisory Council of the United Nations Crime Prevention and Criminal Justice Programme, Publication No. 63.

24. The most refugee-producing countries, and those whose knowledge workers emigrate in large numbers (brain drain), do not attract other types of capital necessary for globalization. They are ill-prepared for the challenges of globalization.

25. For a discussion of the historical ethnic conflicts in the Balkans, see Robert D. Kaplan, *Balkan Ghosts: A Journey through History* (New York: Vintage Books, 1993). In October 2000, Greece and Turkey could not complete scheduled NATO joint military exercises because the promise of globalization could not overcome the history of hate and suspicions between these two neighbors.

26. See World Bank, *The East Asian Miracle: Economic Growth and Public Policy* (Washington, DC: World Bank, 1993); Landes, *The Wealth and Poverty of Nations*; and Geert Hofstede, *Culture's Consequences: International Differences in Work Related Values* (Beverly Hills, CA: Sage, 1980). Also see Lee Kuan Yew, *From Third to First: The Singapore Story, 1965–2000* (New York: HarperCollins, 2000). For a discussion of Islam and development, see Philip Bowring, "Look Again: Islam and Economic Development Go Together," *International Herald Tribune*, October 2, 2001, p. 6.

27. For a defender of African culture, see Mamadou Dia, *Africa's Management in the 1990s and Beyond: Reconciling Indigenous and Transplanted Institutions* (Washington, DC: World Bank, 1996), pt. 4. For a more balanced review, see Moses N. Kiggundu, "Entrepreneurs and Entrepreneurship in Africa: What Is Known and What Needs to Be Done," *Journal of Development Entrepreneurship,* in press.

28. See James C. Collins and Jerry I. Porras, *Built to Last: Successful Habits of Visionary Companies* (New York: Harper Business, 1994), 186.

29. For a detailed discussion of the evolving role of these international organizations, see Michael R. Hodges, John J. Kirton, and Joseph P. Daniels, eds., *The G8's Role in the New Millennium* (Aldershot, UK: Ashgate, 1999).

CHAPTER 2

Governance and Globalization

Like globalization, *governance* is a term used by different people to mean different things across time and space. Like globalization, it has gained prominence in descriptive and prescriptive discussions of societal transformations from the Cold War era to the "new economic order." Again, like globalization, the concept of governance is controversial and hard to explain and translate to non-English-speaking audiences.[1]

In one of its publications, the UNDP defines governance as

> The set of values, policies and institutions by which a society manages economic, political and social processes at all levels through interaction among the government, civil society and the private sector. It is the way in which a society achieves mutual understanding, agreement and action . . . compromises the mechanisms and processes through which citizens and groups articulate their interests, mediate their differences and exercise their legal rights and obligations. It is . . . the framework of rules, institutions and practices that set limits and provides incentives for individuals, organizations and businesses.[2]

This definition is useful for a number of reasons. First, it differentiates governance from government and frames the former as a broader societal responsibility with the government providing the leadership. Second, it emphasizes the importance of dialogue and interactions among different segments and levels of society. Governance is not a one-way street from the government to the governed, but a continuous process of mutual adjustments. Third, it underscores the importance, and by implication, the need to build institutional capacities and human competencies for good governance. Fourth, it does not limit its scope to only economics or politics but includes sociocultural development similar to the capital resources discussed in the previous chapter. Finally, and perhaps most important, it emphasizes the significance of shared values, mature understanding, and agreement for societal good governance.

Shared values and strong sense of vision and community help to bind together the different segments and levels of society. This, in turn, helps to develop the foundation and enabling environment for good governance. Globalization needs good governance. Only the state can provide the necessary leadership for good governance. Therefore, globalization, good governance, and the state are inextricably connected.

It has been said that globalization undermines the role of the state and advances that of the private sector. It also has been suggested that deregulation's logical conclusion is the privatization of public administration, or at best the preservation of a minimal state. This argument is now widely discredited as politically naive and lacking empirical support. Globalization or no globalization, the nation–state shall not die. In fact, the state, individually and in partnership with other actors, remains the single most important institution for shaping the future direction of globalization. After September 11, 2001, Americans, more than ever before, clearly understood the critical importance of the state, both at home and internationally.

Despite the rich and empowering interactions with other parts of the world, people are not prepared to give up their intrinsic sources of identity—language, religion, culture, and land—in exchange for a Lexus or a cell phone. History has plenty of examples to show that when people are fearful or uncertain about the future they seek protection from native institutions or what Thomas Friedman would call the "Olive Tree." I saw this in Ghana in the early 1980s when the government of Ghana was not only unable to provide public services to its citizens but also was systematically violating their human rights and perpetuating a state of terror. Many Ghanaians left the urban areas and went back to their home villages seeking protection, solace, and solidarity with the traditional chiefs. During colonial times, the same thing happened. The more the colonial authorities suppressed local traditions and institutions, the more the local population supported them. One sees evidence of this with the French and Belgians in Africa; white settlers in the Americas; Australia and South Africa, regarding native Indian and African populations, respectively; and the United States in the Philippines. During and after the struggle for independence, African new states tried to suppress traditional rulers, and the population in countries such as Ghana, Uganda, Nigeria, and Zambia responded by giving traditional institutions more support than they would otherwise deserve. Likewise, those global corporations, which tried to suppress local cultures in favor of a universal corporate culture, have not succeeded. Therefore, the lesson for us is clear; The more globalization is perceived as a threat or potential threat to the state, traditional institutions, or peoples' ways of life, the more people are likely to resist it and to support their own. A strong and smart state is good for globalization.

It is also the case that nationalism, tribalism, or ethnicity is not governed by rationality. Borders and nation–states are more than a matter of administrative logic, and while nation–states still retain the sole right to use force—even against their own citizens—the reasons often have more to do with ideology than rationality. Peter Drucker put it all in historical perspective when he observed, "Whenever in the last 200 years political passions and nation–state politics have collided with economic rationality, political rationality and the nation–state have won."[3]

It also should be mentioned in passing that globalization could be a positive force in the process of nation building. In addition to forcing societies to reexamine and reconfirm their core values and collective vision, globalization can help eliminate or reduce dysfunctional narrow nationalism, tribalism, isolationism, racism, religious fanaticism, extremism, sexism, homophobia, classism, and ageism. Therefore, it is not surprising that even recursive states such as Libya, Cuba, North Korea, Myanmar (Burma), Swaziland, Mongolia, and Bhutan are beginning to open up. Others such as South Africa, Peru, Iran,

Russia, Yugoslavia, and Fiji are making serious efforts to transform and improve their national governance systems and practices.

This chapter discusses the relationships between governance and globalization. It starts with a discussion of the need for a globalizing country to first develop or reaffirm its fundamental values—a shared vision and collective sense of purpose. Globalization involves fundamental societal changes and calls on governments, groups, and individuals to reexamine their priorities and trade-offs. It is a collective effort, and therefore, it is best done with a collective sense of purpose—in short, the essence of the state. Opposition to globalization is easier to manage if the citizens or those asked to participate understand how it fits into the broader societal values, goals, and personal lives, and if they have participated in their articulation and internalization. Governments, communities, and organizations risk invoking resistance to globalization if they do not provide the necessary leadership and involve the citizens or employees in developing a shared understanding and commitment to a global open society.

This chapter also discusses the need to reorganize government in order to manage globalization more effectively. Since globalization involves changes in priorities and the demands of the external environment, the structuring and organization of government and its relationships with the rest of society also must change. Most globalizing societies face challenges of managing multiple transitions with little or no prior experience and limited resources. These challenges and how to address them will be discussed in this chapter. Also discussed here is the need to build institutional capacity and human competencies to manage globalization and public service reform and its relevancy for globalization, technology, and E-government, civil society, and the private sector and the changing role of the military in a globalizing country. The chapter ends with a brief reflection of the need, especially for transition economies and developing countries (P1 and P2), for leadership development in a changing world.

GLOBALIZATION AND THE ESSENCE OF THE STATE

Globalization is at a crossroads. The decisions and actions of its champions and opponents for the next ten years will determine whether it will go down in history as another passing fad in international relations or if it will be an important springboard for transforming global society for much needed improvements in governance and human development in developing countries and transition economies (P1 and P2), where the human condition for the majority of their citizens still leaves much to be desired. On the basis of the lessons of experience to date, it is obvious that we need to rethink, reconceptualize, and restrategize all aspects of globalization. We need to do this collaboratively and consultatively, taking past and current lessons of experience to heart. Globalization is too important to be left to the experts: corporate leaders, politicians, economists, international bureaucrats, senior civil servants, consultants, and donors. The citizens must take center stage.

We need to understand globalization not as a series of cross-border transactions but as a fundamental societal transformational change. Transformation, as opposed to transaction, is strategic, systemwide, long-term, interactive, and process and results oriented and aims to bring about fundamental changes in values, beliefs, attitudes, systems, structures, behavior, incentives, and performance for the whole society of which government is the key player.

Figure 2.1 identifies five interrelated component parts of transformational globalization:

1. Stabilization;
2. National consensus on the essence of the state;
3. Development of civil society and indigenous institutions;
4. Good governance and democratic development;
5. Capacity development for globalization.

FIGURE 2.1
Framework for Rethinking Globalization

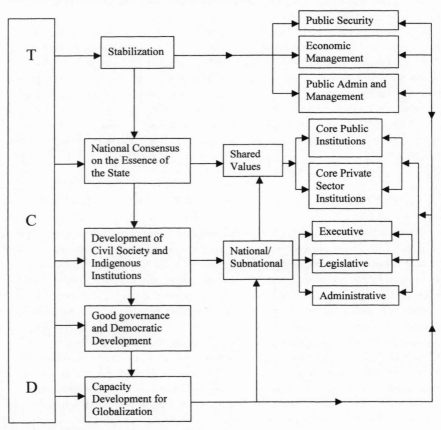

Note: TCD = transformational change and development.

Stabilization covers three areas: public security, economic management, and public administration and management. The concept of stabilization has been used for structural adjustment programs (SAPs).[4] It is being extended here to include public security—especially for countries in transition from war to peace—and public administration to management. Stabilization is not limited only to economic management; it also includes security and public sector reform, especially for transition economies, countries emerging out of war or conflict, those with a history of prolonged institutional decay and human rights abuses, and most developing countries with weak governance systems.

The second component in Figure 2.1 calls for a national dialogue to develop consensus, or a shared understanding of the essence of the state.[5] Out of this consensus should emerge a set of national shared values, which in turn help define the country's core institutions and core functions. Strategies for managing globalization and protecting citizens against its adverse consequences should be part of this broad-based and participative dialogue and consensus building. There is no point in reforming or strengthening institutions or investing in human and other forms of capital if there is no consensus on their relevance for good governance and globalization. In the twenty-first century, countries will be held together not by military force but by shared values and common vision and purpose. Those countries which fail to be bound together by virtue of strongly shared values may not hold together, and globalization would then become academic. When national governments from Afghanistan to Zimbabwe are either collapsing or being taken over by bandits, the need for reaffirmation of the essence of the state and the core values that hold society together becomes even more compelling.

The third component is the development of civil society and indigenous institutions. One of the distinguishing characteristics between the center and periphery societies is the extent to which the former has well-educated and well-organized civil society with strong national-, local-, and community-based organizations. This is what is generally called the "third sector." Predicting a growing role for the third sector during the post–market era, Jeremy Rifkin observed: "Only by building strong, self-sustaining local communities will people in every country be able to withstand the forces of technological displacement and market globalization that are threatening the livelihoods and survival of much of human family."[6]

In response to adverse consequences of globalization, real or perceived, people all over the world are organizing and forming alliances and collaborative networks like never before. Anti-globalization campaigns in Seattle, Washington; Prague; and the Czech Republic—as well as other locations—clearly show how various interest groups in the West have come together and effectively demonized globalization. For example, the demonstrations in Prague included a variety of American and European nationalities—including Czech, Italian, German, British, Dutch, French, Swedish, Portuguese, and Turks—representing a variety of organizations. Some of the organizations represented at the Prague demonstrations included Bankwatch (a nongovernmental organization [NGO] that monitors the actions of international banks), Initiatives Against Economic Globalization (a radical organization advocating for the abolishment of the IMF and the World Bank), and Jubilee 2000 (which advocates debt forgiveness for developing countries and transition economies). Well-organized, coordinated by use of modern technology, and highly motivated, these "fringe" organizations were able to mobilize more than two thousand demonstrations to do battle with the police and forced the IMF–World Bank meetings in Prague to end a day earlier and for the organizers to cancel the cultural program at the Opera House.

Unfortunately, civil society in the periphery countries is not as well organized, and indigenous institutions do not receive much government encouragement. Governments in these countries look at civil society organizations and indigenous institutions with suspicion and fear. Attempts by the international community to support the emergence and development of local NGOs have produced some positive results, but a lot more needs to be done, especially in the more closed, oppressive countries. Support for indigenous institutions should not be limited to political or social causes but also should include small- and medium-size businesses and entrepreneurial firms.

The fourth component in Figure 2.1 is good governance and democratic development at both the national and subnational levels. It focuses on the executive (political), legislative, and administrative (technical) branches and their interrelationships. The international community has put a lot of emphasis and resources in helping transition the economies of Eastern Europe and the former Soviet Union, the emerging economies of East Asia and South America, and the developing countries in Africa and South Asia to improve governance and democratization as a prerequisite for globalization. This emphasis is based on a widely held belief that clean government and democratization are preconditions to effective participation in the global society. A senior World Bank official put it quite bluntly when he said that "the causes of financial crises and poverty are one and the same . . . if [countries] do not have good governance, if they do not confront the issue of corruption, if they do not have a complete legal system which protects human rights, property rights and contracts . . . their development is fundamentally flawed and will not last."[7]

Despite all the attention given to good governance and democratic development, the results for most societies in the periphery are mixed at best. Corruption and poor institutional performance remain serious problems, and in most cases, the international community is almost powerless to stop it. Some actors from the center benefit from the corruption and institutional weaknesses in the periphery. Even where countries are making serious efforts to improve governance and democratization, such initiatives are complex, protracted, and take a long time to become institutionalized. Besides, democracy is not cheap. For example, it was estimated that the 2000 Mexican presidential election cost U.S.$8 billion (BBC, July 2, 2000).

Competitive, participatory democracy has been one of the most challenging transformations to take hold. Post–Cold War leaders from Slobodan Milosevic of Yugoslavia to Robert Mugabe of Zimbabwe, Alberto Fujimori of Peru to Alyaksandr Lukashenka of Belarus, who honed their political skills under relatively closed and ideologically driven global conditions, are having a hard time becoming democrats. Despite the various electoral activities in many of the countries of the world, true democracy is yet to come to billions of citizens of the world. Instead, what we now have is what *The Economist* calls "Phony Democracy."[8]

The fifth and final component shown in Figure 2.1 is capacity development for globalization. This points to the fact that when a country, community, or organization opens its doors for globalization it unleashes a set of complex opportunities and challenges that call for a different mix of institutional capacities and human competencies. These capacities will differ depending on the level of development and capital endowment already in place. For example, while P2 actors require institutional resources and human competencies to extend available telephone lines and to keep them working, P1 actors need to be able to keep connected to the Internet. In any case, it is important to make a complete and accurate assessment of the capacity and competency gaps relevant for globalization and to develop a collective strategy for overcoming them. This should be part of the national dialogue on the essence of the state.

Exhibits 2.1 and 2.2 illustrate how two developing countries—Botswana and Malaysia, respectively—have defined the essence of the state by developing statements of long-term national vision. Unlike the five-year development plans that characterize central planning, the vision statement is not a detailed plan of work; instead, it is a shared destination of long-term national agenda for action, which unites the citizens in a common purpose and serves as a manifesto, or road map, for the entire nation. These two countries provide excellent case studies because at the time of their independence—1965 for Botswana and 1957 for Malaysia—both countries were among the poorest in their respective regions. Over the years, both countries have raised the standards of living of their people, created credible civic institutions, and gained respect in their respective regions and international community. Malaysia is spending more than U.S. $5 billion developing the Multimedia Super Corridor, Asia's version of the U.S. Silicon Valley.

EXHIBIT 2.1
Botswana's "Vision 2016": Defining the Essence of the State

After thirty years of independence, Botswana wanted to create a national vision for the future. The vision would mobilize national resources, unite the people, and prepare the country for the challenges of technological advances and global competition to achieve economic prosperity rivaling that of the tiger economies. The vision was to be guided by the four national principles: democracy, development, self-reliance, and unity.

Process: The vision was the product of THERISANYO, a nationwide consultative process. A presidential task group provided the drive and leadership, but the thirty-one members of the group were nominated by each of the key national institutions. The process was designed to ensure that the national vision is owned by all, regardless of political, ethnic, religious, or any sectarian interests. Accordingly, the vision so produced was expected to clearly and honestly reflect the views and aspirations of a broad spectrum of the Botswana society.

Smart Partnership: The vision calls for the development of smart partnerships involving the private sector, civil service, labor, and political leaders to work together to bring about fundamental transformation of social and political institutions to achieve high levels of productivity and to create an atmosphere of continuous improvement. Partners would work together to bring about a change in attitude or mind-set and improve work ethics and habits. Smart partnership is not presented as an alternative to the free-market system but as a complementary and balanced approach between co-operation and competition, which achieves short-term gains and sustainable outcomes in which everyone participates and benefits. It is a mechanism by which the government listens to the people and incorporates their needs and desires into the ongoing process of development. It is a pragmatic process by which the people are involved in defining the problems and solutions within a long-term framework.

"Vision 2016": This sets out the broad aspirations of the kind of country the people want by the year 2016, the fiftieth anniversary of the country's independence. Botswana wants to become (1) educated and informed; (2) prosperous, productive, and innovative; (3) compassionate, just, and caring; (4) safe and secure; (5) open, democratic, and accountable; (6) moral and tolerant; and (7) united and proud.[9]

EXHIBIT 2.2
Malaysia's "Vision 2020": Values and the Essence of the State

Nine Visionary Challenges	*Guiding Values*
1. Establishing a united Malaysian nation with a sense of common and shared destiny.	Unity, loyalty, nationalism, sense of belonging.
2. Creating a psychologically liberated, secure, and developed society with faith, confidence, pride in its achievements, and a robustness to face all manner of adversity.	Confidence, resilience, psychologically liberated.
3. Fostering and developing a mature democratic society and a community-based consensual democracy applicable to other developing countries.	Democracy, pride, sharing.

4. Establishing a fully moral and ethical society, strong in religious and spiritual values and highest ethical standards.	Religious, spiritual, ethical.
5. Establishing a mature, liberal, tolerant, multicultural society within the Malaysian nation.	Tolerance, diversity, respect for others, sense of belonging, openness.
6. Establishing a scientific, progressive, innovative, forward-looking, and productive society.	Scientific, innovative, progressive, futuristic competitiveness.
7. Establishing a caring society and caring culture; the welfare of the people will revolve around a strong and resilient family system (not state or individual).	Collectivism, family orientation, philanthropy, resilience.
8. Creating an economically just society, fair and equitable distribution of wealth, partnership in economic progress.	Fairness, equity.
9. Establishing a prosperous society with a competitive, dynamic, robust, and resilient economy.[10]	Competitiveness, advancement, prosperity.

The two vision statements have several features in common. They both use the realities on the ground as the starting point and draw on the local, social, cultural, and political institutional arrangements. Malaysia recognizes its multicultural (Malay, Chinese) and multireligious (Buddhist, Hindu, Christian, Confucianist) character, while acknowledging its dominant Muslim majority. Second, they both aim to achieve balance between the technical and economic imperatives of a capitalist economy and the social, cultural, and political aspirations of their people. Third, they both emphasize the need for the development of a moral and ethical society with internationally accepted standards of ethical conduct. This is particularly important because both countries are in regions—Africa and Asia—

where corruption has eaten at the very foundation of both society and the economy. The fourth common aspect of the vision statements is that they both emphasize the need to create a learning, progressive, and competitive society. They both understand that in the twenty-first century knowledge will be the most important resource and that management of knowledge will be the key to success. Indeed, through the visionary exercise, both countries are preparing their people for the challenges of globalization.

The process by which the vision statement is developed and proclaimed is as important as the statement itself. In Botswana's case (Exhibit 2.1), this was done through a nationwide consultative and participative process to ensure broad-based understanding, ownership, and commitment to the vision. It also involved the creation of strategic alliances or "smart partnerships" among the major sectors of society—government, business, labor, civil society—with the politicians providing guidance and leadership. Partnership is important not only because it draws people and institutions together but also because it is the way of the future. In a complex and challenging world, neither government nor business nor any other sector of society can go it alone. The successful ones will be those which develop and sustain smart partnerships. Citizen engagement is the wave of the future for visionary and globalizing countries.

In developing "Vision 2016" and "Vision 2020," neither Botswana nor Malaysia did it specifically for globalization. Yet, it is clear that the values, challenges, and guiding principles of these visions provide a framework for the development of an open, globalizing society. At the same time, both countries have ongoing challenges characteristic of an emerging and democratizing developing country. Malaysia had its share of financial and economic problems in 1997–1998, as well as ongoing political and ethnic challenges. Botswana, despite its record of high persistent growth, still faces problems of poverty, a rapid increase in the prevalence of HIV/AIDS, youth unemployment, land reform, and a large and growing public sector in need of reform. Yet, these two countries show that a national visionary exercise can provide the framework and first opportunity for a modernizing society to gather strength and develop strategies for managing globalization. Other developing countries and transition economies should consider it.[11]

Indeed, several other countries such as Ghana and The Gambia have developed visions of their own. In the private sector, corporations have been doing this for years and the popular management literature is full of how-to books and other materials for corporate visioning and strategizing for globalization. In terms of its potential benefits and adverse effects, globalization is mostly local. Therefore, visioning for globalization should be encouraged at the subnational level with local governments, municipal authorities, communities, sectors, and institutions each doing their own visioning and strategizing rather than depending on national governments or big corporations. Opportunities and strategies for globalization can then be developed through a variety of collaborative mechanisms. These may include partnerships or coalition formation based on new developments of business, product or service clusters, value chain systems, or enterprise resource planning. In small developing communities, this may require complex alliances among cities, rural producers, environmental organizations, local colleges or universities, citizens in the diaspora, regional development banks, and transnational corporations. It is expected that globalization will require more of these novel arrangements, and without visioning, actors would be walking in the dark, unable to identify or protect their interests. This may be the most practical way of developing sustainable grassroots organizations for globalization.[12]

For more than a half century, social scientists and practicing managers the world over have known that the organization of work and structuring of organization matters. Changes in the structure can bring about corresponding changes in individual and collective behavior, performance, effectiveness, morale, and overall satisfaction of the employees as well as other stakeholders (for example, citizens, clients, customers). Structure can be defined as the total sum of all the ways by which the activities of an organization or other entity are divided into distinct units or subsystems and then coordinated to form a synergetic entity. It involves both division of labor, specialization, differentiation, and coordination or integration. By organization, I include here the government ministries, departments or agencies, municipal and local administrations, communities, business enterprises, NGOs, and informal or underground organizations. In all these cases, decisions about structural arrangements affect performance and goal achievement.[13]

With the advent of globalization, questions must be raised as to whether governments and other public institutions are properly structured and well organized to meet the resulting changes and to take advantage of emerging opportunities. Already, the private sector is reinventing itself in order to participate more effectively in the growing and rapidly changing competitive global society. As well, many international organizations, including the United Nations and its specialized agencies, are seeking alternative structural arrangements designed to enhance their institutional capacities and human competencies for a rapidly changing world.[14]

Table 2.1 provides a list of suggestions for reorganizing government for globalization. They are listed in an increasing order of commitment, ranging from appointment of an adviser on globalization to government to the creation of a department or ministry in charge of globalization. Of course, each country and its leaders can choose where to start and how fast to proceed. The irony of it all is that those developing countries and transition economies currently facing serious challenges of globablization (P2 countries) are the ones unable or unwilling to take the necessary bold steps to move fast. It is also prudent to move at a pace consistent with societal norms and sentiments. This is necessary to avoid creating institutional disconnects between those driving globalization and the rest of the country's governance system. Yet, when the rest of the world is changing so fast, time becomes of the essence.

The suggestions in Table 2.1 have several important considerations of note: First, it is important to ensure high-level political understanding, ownership, and commitment. Civil servants alone cannot drive globalization. Yet, experience from public sector reforms points to the difficulties of sustaining political support for public policy initiatives, which politicians consider unpopular or not well understood by the citizens. One possible suggestion is to require all political parties at all levels to articulate their policy positions on globalization. Globalization is not politically neutral, but partisan politics may be detrimental to the public good.

Second, the proposed reorganization measures should ensure active involvement and linkages with the private sector, including the business community, as well as the various institutions within the country's civil society. Important interest groups include manufacturers,

TABLE 2.1
Suggestions for Reorganizing Government for Globalization

1. Appoint senior policy adviser to government on globalization.
2. Make conceptual, policy, and operational linkages between globalization and national priorities (the essence of the state).
3. Create an interdepartmental committee of heads of departments.
4. Create a unit on globalization in the prime minister's/president's office.
5. Create an independent agency for globalization and competitiveness.
6. Restructure and refocus select ministries for globalization.
7. Contract for long-term consulting services on globalization.
8. Develop a program of public education on globalization.
9. Make globalization a central theme in the country's governance framework.
10. Support indigenous municipal and local government organizations focusing on globalization.
11. Create a department or ministry of globalization.
12. Mandate the publication of an annual report on globalization and the state.

exporters, trade unions, the media, education institutions, NGOs, youth and women's organizations, local government authorities, and religious and traditional leaders. Likewise, there should be strong linkages with the relevant actors outside the country such as donors, funding agencies, the United Nations, global corporations, professional and trade associations, and individual citizens.

Third, it is suggested that an independent agency be created on globalization and competitiveness. In addition to providing a professional institutional base for promoting globalization and competitiveness consistent with national policies and priorities, it would create a healthy distance from the ongoing political pressures. Many developing countries need to translate the two concepts of globalization and competitiveness in a language and operational terms that make sense locally and to which the population can relate. I am told that in many African languages there is no direct translation for either globalization or competitiveness. Therefore, before developing action plans for the development of an enabling environment for globalization and competitiveness, it is important to make sure people understand what these words mean and how they affect their and their children's livelihood.

Fourth, it is suggested that serious restructuring and refocusing of key ministries and departments be undertaken in response to emerging opportunities and challenges owing to globalization. Many developing countries maintain the same government structures inherited during the colonial administration with little or no regard for changes both within the country and the rest of the world. Globalization provides an excellent opportunity for governments to rethink the organization of public administration, especially since its effects are both domestic and international. The five key areas that need immediate restructuring for globalization are economic management (for example, finance, labor, trade, agriculture, telecommunications, transport, higher education), international relations (for example, foreign affairs, finance, trade), security and the administration of justice (for example, police and prison services, justice, immigration, intelligence, the military), social services (for example, health, basic education, youth and community development), and the environment. One of the consequences of the terrorist attacks on the United States is the increasing focus on the agencies responsible for public security and security of the person and their close working relationship with their domestic (civilian and military) and international counterparts.

Looked at from the point of view of globalization and its challenges, the functional organization of government along traditional-line ministries exhibits several weaknesses, omissions, and overlaps. Take the ministry of foreign affairs. For most developing countries, this is one of the most expensive ministries, with offices in most of the key capitals of the world. Traditionally, these offices are staffed by career diplomats and political appointees. The diplomats are usually trained in politics and international relations. While these are useful skills, globalization demands more than diplomacy: It requires intimate knowledge and understanding of international economics especially finance, banking, and business; international trade; law; security; migration; environmental movements; and international changes in social policy. The challenge for most of the countries with limited resources is how to reorganize ministries, such as foreign affairs, in such a way as to provide timely and useful services to the globalizing citizens at the lowest possible cost. In general, the externally oriented ministries, such as foreign affairs, have to establish effective coordinating mechanisms with internally oriented ministries, such as agriculture, as well as the rest of the country outside government. Likewise, internally oriented ministries, such as local government or internal security, have to work in harmony with those ministries or agencies with established relationships with the outside world. The U.S. government faces similar interagency coordination problems.

Another portfolio that needs rethinking, restructuring, and reorganizing for globalization is education. Traditionally, education is considered a social service and is grouped together with, for example, health and community development in the service sector. Policy makers regard education as a consumption public good, and therefore, resource allocation tends to fluctuate according to annual budgeting pressures. As a result, for most developing countries, especially the P2 countries, the overall quality of education remains poor and unevenly accessible.

Yet, in the new economy, education is not only a social service but also a competitive advantage, distinguishing winners from losers. This is especially true of higher education, which should be seen as an individual and societal investment. This mind-set has a number of structural and policy implications. First, higher education should be separated from basic (primary) education. Where institutional capacities and economies of scale allow, basic education should be decentralized to subnational local levels. Second, higher education should be taken out of the social sector policy framework or budgetary envelope and placed in the economic management sector. Third, priority areas for higher education should be determined in terms of the ability to compete in the global economy—this will vary by country or region. While most educators put emphasis on science and technology, for some small developing countries, their comparative advantage may be in languages (for example, English, Spanish, Arabic, Chinese, computer languages), assembling, or personal care. The challenge is to find a realistic niche and avoid copying what others are doing.

It is also important to deregulate higher education and to invite private sector partners at home and abroad to participate both as owners and educators. The days of public monopoly in higher education are over, and those societies which forge successful private–public partnerships will develop globally competitive education systems. Key players from the private sector include overseas universities and colleges, business corporations, research labs, high-tech firms, and NGOs involved in higher education. Countries such as India have already demonstrated the benefits of developing long-term partnerships with overseas universities and other actors. It makes sense for a small country to reorganize its higher education, not only for the domestic labor market but also for the growing global labor market. Therefore, whatever structural arrangements a government may choose for its higher education, it must ensure very close coordination with the structures chosen for globalization (see Table 2.1).

A fifth implication resulting from the suggestions listed in Table 2.1 is the need to provide public education about globalization to all segments of society. Many developing countries have relatively young populations, most of whom do not have a postsecondary education. It is unrealistic to expect these people to find the means to educate themselves about globalization and all of its consequences. Journalists, politicians, the community, labor and religious leaders, youth, women, elders, and teachers should be educated to be able to make informed decisions about globalization. For countries fairly advanced in globalization, consideration should be given to including aspects of globalization in the school curriculum.

Finally, it is proposed that globalization should be included as a central theme in the national governance framework. Following national visioning exercises, a number of countries have developed elaborate national governance frameworks setting out national development goals and priorities, identifying areas of institutional development and reinforcement, and developing strategies for overcoming national impediments to development—such as corruption, organized crime, political instability, and poverty alleviation—and regional conflicts.[15] Governments use these governance frameworks for mobilizing internal political support and external resources from donors. Including globalization as a central theme would also attract private sector support both internally in terms of business confidence and domestic investments and externally in terms of short-term capital inflows as well as foreign direct investments (FDI). A credible annual report on the state of globalization (progress, opportunities, challenges) would provide the kind of information necessary for confidence building both at home and globally.

MANAGING MULTIPLE TRANSITIONS

The problem with most developing countries and transition economies is that they are always faced with many changes all going on at the same time. Globalization then becomes one among many transformational changes all requiring attention and resources while at the same time causing systemwide disruptions. At the same time, these countries are prone to crises, emergencies, and natural disasters. As a result, priorities get displaced or mixed up, and resources are diverted to non-priority or unforeseen emergencies. They find themselves ill-equipped to sustain focused efforts for managing multiple transitions. Governments are not structured for agility and, therefore, are not capable of managing the transitions associated with globalization. This is another reason why they must form coalitions, networks, and partnerships with domestic and international actors both from the public and the private sectors.

Unable to manage multiple transitions, governments in Eastern and Central Europe have called for slowing down the pace of change. A recent U.N. report observes that while political transformation to a competitive multiparty system seems to have gained wide popular support and institutional reform, in Eastern Europe economic transformations have been particularly painful. As a result, unemployment and poverty have increased and the state social safety net has proved either inadequate or nonexistent. Instead of the "big bang" approaches to change, there are calls for selective and strategic return to active state intervention. Under conditions of multiple transitions, a strong state is still needed to cushion the impact of the market and globalization. Political rights must be balanced with economic security as well as sociocultural self-expressions. In countries lacking the necessary institutional capacity and intellectual capital to manage multiple transitions, globalization may have to be phased in at a pace consistent with the development of the necessary capacity and competencies to manage multiple transformations for globalization.

Exhibit 2.3 provides an illustration of a young independent African country—Zimbabwe—grappling with the challenges of managing complex multiple transitions and their interrelated adverse consequences. The transitions are pervasive, straddling across politics, economics, public administration, culture, national security, and social and community development, as well as international relations. With the advantage of hindsight, it now becomes obvious that even way back in the 1980s, Zimbabwe did not have the resources, institutional capacity, human and social capital, nor a social safety net to manage all of these transitions and their wider implications. Even an industrialized, rich, and well-established country would find it very challenging to stay on top of similar complex transitions. Witness the problems rich and well-established Western European countries are experiencing managing the changing structures and dynamics of their populations.

Exhibit 2.3
The Challenge of Managing Multiple Transitions:
The Case of Zimbabwe

As an independent country, Zimbabwe is very young, dating back only to 1980. Since then, Zimbabweans have had to deal with complex multiple transitions in politics, economics, public administration, national security, regional and international relations, and social and community development. The country was not even ten years old when the Iron Curtain fell and a new era of globalization began.

Politically, Zimbabwe has been on a roller coaster. The country transitioned from a race-based white minority government of Rhodesia under a unilateral declaration of independence (UDI) pariah state, subject to international sanctions and facing revolutionary guerilla warfare from black freedom fighters, to a multiparty, black majority, democratically elected government and a respectable state with membership in the United Nations, the Organization of African Unity, and the Southern African Development Cooperation. The country experienced a period of relative political calm under the political alliance of the Zimbabwe African National Union/Patriotic Front (ZANU/PF) but without organized parliamentary opposition. This was followed by growing political discontent, demand for a new constitution, formation of a coalition opposition umbrella under the Movement for Democratic Change, and, by 2000, a strong, organized, and well-funded parliamentary opposition. In 2000, ZANU/PF was on the verge of popular defeat.

Economically, change in Zimbabwe has been equally dramatic: from a strong but closed economy under UDI with close ties with other pariah states of the day (for example, South Africa) to a more open, fast-growing regional leader, diversified with a strong currency and functioning infrastructure. By the mid-1990s, Zimbabwe was experiencing negative economic indicators, mounting public debt, high inflation, a falling dollar, rising unemployment, increased poverty, and social discord. There were also ongoing fights with the IMF, donors, and the international community.

Public administration changed almost overnight: from serving the interests of the white minority of Rhodesia to addressing the growing expectations of the independent black majority. With growth in the size of public administration, dramatic changes in staffing, and improved social services to the black population, the increasing costs of the public sector begins to hurt.

National security is always important for a post-conflict state. The war with Rhodesia ended just before independence, followed by a period of relative calm and peace. With peace coming to South Africa, Zimbabwe started to demobilize its armed forces and enjoyed a peace dividend: fewer soldiers and a reduced budget for defense. Then the quagmire started with Zimbabwe's involvement in a costly regional conflict in the Congo; body bags were arriving.

Social and community services have always been better in Zimbabwe than in many African countries. With a growing population, stress on public finance, a weakening social and physical infrastructure, a declining economy, and large rural–urban movements, quality and accessibility of social services started to suffer. A serious HIV/AIDS epidemic affects everything and everybody, especially widows and orphans. Youth unemployment, urban crime, landlessness, housing shortages, racial and ethnic discord, and homophobia are fodder for the political opposition and foreign press—social capital on the decline.

International relations are difficult for Zimbabwe. No longer a pariah state under UDI, Zimbabwe enjoyed international respectability in the 1980s, but by 2000, the leadership was demonized both at home and in the international press. Is Zimbabwe on the brink again?

Zimbabwe's problems are compounded by the existence of a growing national generation gap separating the men and women who fought the war of independence and the majority of young Zimbabweans who were too young to remember the war and all of its consequences. When I visited Zimbabwe in the summer of 2000, this divide was very evident because the young people were more interested in the same things other young people in the world aspire to—jobs, family, housing, and so on—rather than whipping up revolutionary valor.

Addressing the nation at the National Heroes Acre in Harare on August 10, 2000, President Mugabe asked his fellow citizens if they still shared with him the same revolutionary values and dreams and if they were still willing to fight for them. It is obvious that the country is badly divided between those who do and those who do not or are not sure, which is a growing majority. The president also should have asked if he and his fellow war veterans have changed in light of the significant changes that have taken place both within the country and in the rest of the world. What the people of Zimbabwe really need is to undertake a comprehensive nationwide visioning exercise, one that transcends partisan politics and redefines the essence of the state for the twenty-first century. It would redefine and reassess Zimbabwe's new role in the changing global society. Hopefully, it is not too much to expect revolutionary fighters to become sincere liberal democrats and the young generation to appreciate the historical imperatives of their country, while at the same time preparing for a globalizing and changing world.[16]

Like Zimbabwe, nation–states arising out of the ashes of the former Soviet Union—such as Belarus, Georgia, and Ukraine—are also experiencing difficulties managing multiple transformations required for establishing globally open, competitive economies and democratic societies. A senior government official from the former Soviet Union—involved in public sector reform—likened his country's modernization and transformation efforts to letting free in the wild an animal born and raised in a zoo: It would be lost, would hardly know what to do, and would not survive unless it was able to quickly reassess its new situation and adapt to the demands and challenges of the wild (personal communication, June 2002).

PUBLIC SECTOR REFORM FOR GLOBALIZATION

The last quarter of the twentieth century has been characterized by a variety of administrative reforms in both industrialized and developing countries. Started in the West (the United Kingdom, the United States, New Zealand), the reform initiatives quickly spread to developing and transitional countries. Administrative reforms cover a wide range of topics, goals, and interventions including public sector reform, privatization, decentralization, capacity development, governance, economic management, civil service reform, citizen engagement, institutional and human resource development, poverty alleviation, and sectorwide approaches. The results of these reforms are quite telling. While gains and successes have been widely reported for Western industrialized countries, the results for developing countries and transitional economies have been mixed at best. These results are consistent across regions, countries, and sectors. For example, a recent U.N. study of administrative reforms in five Asian countries[17] found, among other things:

- duplication of functions and overlapping jurisdiction;
- loopholes in administrative procedures, leading to difficulties in maintaining objectivity, accountability, and transparency in decision making;
- poor coordination, policy making, and policy implementation;
- absence of corporate orientation in large central ministries, which results in blurring the distinction between policy making and policy implementation;
- generalized lack of institutional capacity and competencies to initiate and sustain reforms.

The study also found that these and similar bureau-pathological symptoms prohibit strategic thinking as well as problem-solving capacity, and that the resulting weaknesses provide avenues for ethical irresponsibility and corrupt practices. Lack of norms of bureaucratic behavior, both within these public institutions and the wider society in general, contributes to these pathologies.

A similar study done by the World Bank for the Czech Republic in preparation for its application to join the European Union[18] found similar pathologies and recommended the following bureaucratic remedies:

- drafting and enacting civil service laws;
- revising public sector remuneration structure, policies, and practices;
- strengthening mechanisms for holding administrative units accountable for policy formulation and implementation;
- strengthening mechanisms for nurturing public sector human capital by fostering career development and good strategic human resource management;
- revising current cabinet structures including creation of a single professional unit for policy making in the prime minister's office.

These recommendations are similar to those made for many developing and transition countries. They speak to the need to build institutions with strong links both to the local society and the outside world.

Most developing countries have been faced with three-phased types of reforms: economic restructuring, administrative reforms, and globalization. In general, public sector reform has not worked well in most developing countries. Attempts to develop organizations and reform institutions have had limited success. This is particularly so for those organizations, such as the public service, which are rooted in the local traditional society. Those organizations whose intellectual and material resources are from the outside and those which manage to buffer themselves from the local traditional forces tend to have better experiences with reform initiatives. Several reasons have been given for this: First, developing countries started late and suffer from a common debilitating colonial legacy. Second, too much emphasis is placed on the importance of government and the public sector, thus creating a greater burden of expectation than available resources or institutional capacity. Third, there is a disconnect between bureaucratic principles and the logic of traditional society and its institutions. Fourth, most developing countries lack the institutional antecedents as were present in Europe where the various public administrative systems were developed and gained world prominence. Historically, these countries have shown little diminution of primordial ties, which preceded or accompanied Western bureaucratization. Organizations in traditional societies cannot undertake successful reforms unless the institutional context in which they operate is also changing in support of norms of bureaucratic behavior à la Max Weber.

Public sector reform is neither a curse nor a panacea. Rather, it is a set of institutional arrangements and human resource development initiatives, which function well at a certain stage of societal and institutional development. Attempts by traditional societies and former Communist countries to ignore or discredit these reforms do more harm than good. What is needed is a case-by-case approach whereby the initial stages involve comprehensive understanding and diagnosis of the local situation to determine the level of required development, prevailing capacity gaps, and the appropriate modalities for the effective implementation of the resulting prescribed reform initiatives. For example, traditional societies with weak institutions should approach public sector reform differently than societies with mature, functioning institutions. Post-conflict societies whose institutions have been destroyed may have to start modestly by first restoring public confidence and concentrating on areas in which there is broad support, consensus, and local capacity. Countries emerging out of Communist, apartheid, conflict, or extremist, genocidal regimes need to start by developing consensus about the essence of the new state and its strategic direction and institutions. Modernizing countries, with fast-growing economies but still having traditional societies in their midst, can target their reform initiatives at different institutional levels and use different indicators to assess institutional performance and overall reform effectiveness. In all these cases, the reforms must be in line with society's capacity to learn and change.

What does all this mean for globalization? First, public sector reform should focus on helping countries, governments, societies, institutions, organizations, and individuals to take advantage of the opportunities offered by globalization and to protect themselves against the vagaries of adverse effects. This means that public sector reform initiatives should emphasize openness and competitiveness for the global society. Emphasizing this aspect, the government of Thailand states that the ultimate aims of its public sector reform is to achieve a better quality of life for its citizens: to ensure social stability and national integrity and respect and to be competitive in the global arena.[19]

It makes sense to begin by promoting openness locally and domestically. This would involve opening up government and other public institutions, opening channels of communication and enhancing understanding across local divides—race, ethnicity, age, religion, gender, and so forth. This should be followed by developing and institutionalizing norms of competitiveness not only in economic performance but also in other areas of importance to society such as sports, politics, public administration, and other sociocultural activities. The rationale for this strategy is simple: The more internally open and competitive a society is, the more likely it is to benefit from openness and competitiveness with the outside world.

The second general implication is the importance of focusing on developing institutional capacities and human resources for globalization. A recent U.N. review of public sector reform in all regions of the world underscores the importance of capacity development and reinforcement both for developing countries and transition economies. The report concludes with the observation:

Looking ahead into the 21st century, the lessons from the past strongly suggest the need to *rethink the overall strategy for public service reform*. There is need to develop consensus by focusing attention on core strategic themes enjoying a broad measure of acceptance. There is also need to mobilize resources and build effective partnerships, which broaden domestic support and transcend traditional boundaries. Creating new institutions may prove as necessary as the task of reinforcing and reforming those that exist already. Important as they are, capacity reinforcement means more than technical training and modernization of equipment. Developing core competencies, which is required, entails enhancing skills, but also cultivating new attitudes, values, beliefs and habits. Institution-building should focus on governance, leadership, strategic management, operational efficiency and rapid response to the stimuli of a complex and dynamic external environment.[20]

TECHNOLOGY AND E-GOVERNMENT

What Is E-Government?

Globalization is driven in part by advances in information technology and E-commerce (electronic commerce). Therefore, to understand E-government (electronic government), it is important to understand E-commerce first because virtually all the technologies and software that will make E-government possible are already working for E-commerce. Governments lag behind the private sector in the use of information and computer technology, including the Internet. Therefore, E-government is an attempt by the public sector to catch up and begin to enjoy the benefits of the new technology.

E-commerce refers to commercial activities that take place by digital processes over a network. Likewise, E-government refers to government or public sector activities that take place by digital processes within government and between government and the public, including private citizens. E-commerce can be business to business or E-business, between business and customers, between customers, with nonbusiness not-for-profit parties, or within the same business organization (Intranet). Likewise, E-government can be government to government, between government and citizens, with business organizations, or within the same government institution (Intranet).

E-commerce can be conceptualized in four different ways: First, it can be seen as a communications tool for the delivery of information, product/services, or payments over telephone lines, a computer network, or other digital means. Second, it can be seen in terms of business processes, in which case the emphasis is on the use of technology to automate office transactions and workflow. Third, it can be seen as a service provider whereby the new technology is used to cut service costs and improve the service and quality of service delivery to meet changing customer or citizen expectations. Finally, E-commerce can be conceptualized as an online facility providing customers and citizens opportunities to use the Internet, either to buy and sell products or to transact public services. To receive maximum benefits from E-commerce or E-government, it is important for management to be clear about the relative importance of each of these four perspectives for a particular agency at a particular point in time.[21]

E-commerce can take many different forms depending on the degree of digitization of the product or service sold or provided, the process(es) used, and the delivery agent(s) used. A product can be physical (for example, fertilizer) or digital (for example, software) and the delivering agent can be physical (for example, DHL) or digital such as E-mail. Likewise, the process can be digital or physical. In traditional commerce or government, all three dimensions are physical, and in pure E-commerce or E-government, all dimensions are digital. While an increasing number of business-to-business transactions are pure digital, most E-government transactions are mixed. An example of a mixed E-government transaction would be if a government purchasing agency bought medical supplies by using competitive bidding on the Internet (digital), and the supplies were flown in by cargo plane (physical). A pure E-government transaction would be, for example, a government chief information officer ordering software via the Internet that is paid for and downloaded via the Internet.

Why E-Government?

Every government—national or local, in rich or poor countries—must give serious consideration to the use of technology and the introduction of E-government. The pressures are many and varied, but the technology is so widely used by the private sector that governments have no choice but to introduce these technologies into public administration. One of the driving forces for E-government is its promise for a better economy and efficiency and effectiveness in public administration. It is expected that E-government saves time and money; reduces waste, duplication, and paperwork; and cuts costs. For example, E-government used for procurement advances competitiveness, saves the government money by paying competitive prices, and reduces waste and corruption. E-government also forces public agencies to change their orientation from focusing on their own internal organizational needs and narrow mandates to becoming genuinely interested in understanding the needs of the public they serve and putting systems in place to meet their needs. E-government gives real meaning to the idea of public service and gives citizens a voice regarding the quality of service from their public agencies.

While the drive for improved service delivery is associated with new public management focusing on economic efficiency, E-government is also credited with improving governance and democratization. It allows citizens to participate in the democratic process by communicating electronically with their elected representatives, and it allows government agencies to collect information about the citizens so as to understand them better and to use the information to design programs and delivery services most appropriate to their individual needs.

In the end, the ultimate drive for E-government may be fear. Governments, especially in developing countries and transition economies, may fear that if they do not get connected they will be left behind and thus will be unable to relate to and do business with their own citizens and with the outside world. They may fear that without E-government they have no chance of catching up and keeping up and may be further marginalized. Public agencies may fear that if they do not use E-government to meet changing public expectations and consult the public about their own governance the services may be outsourced or privatized. There is always the fear that public sector jobs could disappear or change significantly. There may also be the fear that without E-government, the image of public administration will suffer. Politicians may fear that without giving them what they want technocrats may vote them out of office. Within a few years, E-government will become the universal benchmark by which governments, public servants, politicians, citizens, and private corporations judge the quality of their public administration and the degree of openness and competitiveness with the rest of the world. Particularly in countries where government plays a dominant role, E-government can make a significant contribution to building an information economy, which in turn helps to open up the economy and society, establish a more inclusive and participative governance system, and improve the living conditions of the majority of the citizens.

Getting Started

Because most developing countries do not have full-service E-government systems, it is important to review the processes by which such a system may be introduced. There are basically four stages of developing E-government services. The first and simplest is the establishment of a one-way Web site whereby individual departments or agencies post information about themselves for the benefit of citizens, businesses, and other public agencies. These are basically one-way channels of communication from the government to the citizens, although in most cases an E-mail address is provided to send comments and suggestions to the Webmaster. The second is a two-way communication E-government system whereby citizens, businesses, or other visitors to the Web site, in addition to getting information about a department or agency, can provide information about themselves. For example, residents of a local municipality can visit its Web site and electronically indicate changes in their address or telephone number when they move.

The third stage of E-government is value exchange because it has the capacity to process value-adding services. Here, citizens can renew licenses, pay fines, enroll in education courses, renew library books, book seats and recreational services, and file tax returns. Most of these are local or municipal services, so they tend to be found on Web sites for local authorities. Indeed, as Bill Gates points out, much of the innovation in E-government is currently happening in smaller governments—smaller nations (for example, Singapore), municipalities, counties, and provinces.[22] Therefore, there are many unexploited opportunities for E-government innovations among most of the world's small and island states, many of which are in the early stages of globalization.

The fourth, and so far most advanced, stage for E-government is the establishment of portal services. A portal is a Web site that serves as a user's primary starting point for access to the Internet. AOL, MSN, and Yahoo are examples of portal sites. With E-government, a portal provides the user a single gateway to government. A single logon and password allows the user to get in touch with any part of government and access a combined range of government services. Examples include Singapore's eCitizen Centre—MAXI—operated by the state of Victoria, Australia, and UK Online.

Table 2.2 provides a list of guidelines for introducing E-government services, especially for countries or local authorities just starting out. To begin with, it is very important to have a modern functioning telecommunications infrastructure and the capacity to operate, upgrade, and maintain it. In most parts of the world, this has been made possible by deregulating the telecommunications and private sector investment in technology, capital, and management.[23] Without a modern functioning telecommunications system, it is not possible to have reliable and quality E-government services. In some cases, developing countries can make investments in telecommunications infrastracture at modest cost without having to deal with cumbersome paper methods, especially if they are providing new services that were never provided before. For example, a government starting a student loan program for the first time can run it as a paperless E-government service.

Second, it is important to build a digital culture both within government and in the general population through demonstration, incentives, training, and education. Introducing E-government is a major systemwide policy change initiative, and therefore, it is useful to apply change management strategies and tools. For example, it is important to ensure interagency cooperation and coordination since the most effective E-government services cut across agency boundaries or mandates.

Who Is Using E-Government?

As one would expect, the heaviest users of E-government are also the leaders in globalization. These are predominantly the rich, connected countries with a highly efficient, low-cost advanced telecommunications infrastructure. Examples include the United Kingdom, the United States, Western Europe, Japan, New Zealand, Australia, and Singapore. Basically, this is the center, or connected triad, as discussed in the previous chapter. For example, in the United Kingdom in the year 2000, the number of people using the Internet doubled over the previous year. The government has set 2005 as the latest date for achieving 100 percent E-government services. All schools are now linked to the information superhighway, and a new portal is being constructed for full E-government services.[24]

At the other extreme, there are countries and communities without E-government services; they are generally poor and disconnected, with poor telecommunications services usually run by state monopolies. They are the periphery (P2) countries and societies having a difficult time finding their niche in the global economy and global society. Most of these countries are in sub-Saharan Africa, parts of Asia, and isolated parts of large countries such as Brazil's northeast, China's north, and Indonesia's remote islands. Africa is particularly disadvantaged because it suffers from knowledge gaps, information problems, and a thin telecommunications infrastructure with poor service and inadequate technical support. For example, New York City, with a population of about 10 million people, has more telephone lines and a world-class telecommunications infrastructure than the whole of Africa with over 850 million people. This is one aspect of the global digital divide.[25]

TABLE 2.2
Guidelines for Introducing E-Government

1. Deregulate telecommunications and encourage major investments in the telecommunication infrastructure.
2. Attract investment by technology companies and encourage electronic commerce, either with financial incentives or cooperative projects. Create a framework for electronic authentication of business and citizens.
3. Review all the transactions that require citizens to stand in line or fill out forms; bring all the agencies involved together to develop a single system for handling all the transactions.
4. Develop and install a PC infrastructure in government offices, use E-mail to promote interagency cooperation, and make sure public officials learn to be responsive.
5. Put government employees on E-mail and eliminate paper filing. Move toward full digitization so that all information being shared inside the government is digital. Develop a nationwide functioning technical support services organization.
6. Put government services online with an interface designed for the user. Publish everything on the Internet.
7. Develop and retain in-house E-government institutional capacity and human capital. Use vendors and consultants strategically. Raise the skills of citizens by using technology as part of education and training
8. Establish policies to use digital information flow in place of paper. Make E-government an integral part of public sector reform. Review and amend relevant legislation (for example, privacy, access to government information, hacking).
9. Use Web technology to provide a single point of contact for the public, a single online "face" to structure information according to identified needs of the public.
10. Provide access for citizens without their own PCs by providing electronic kiosks in public places.
11. Deal with issues of security, privacy, ethics, fraud, and access. Review current practices, lessons of experience, and available technology for encryption and authentication.
12. Use the technology for high profile public administration functions such as delivery of services, law and order, and the administration of justice. Research available software solutions for the legislative, judicial, and executive branches of government and assess suitability for own E-government needs.
13. Start small, move fast, and deliver value. Small, subnational governments (state, local, municipal) can take bold innovative E-government solutions. Large, complex governments should take small pilot projects, develop expertise, draw lessons of experience, and evaluate citizen response. Take an experimental approach and keep it simple.
14. Be sure to provide ongoing political, administrative, and technical leadership.

Source: Gates, *Business @ the Speed of Thought,* chap. 20; and "A Survey of Government and Internet: The Next Revolution," *The Economist* (June 24, 2000): 4–34.

In between, there are a number of emerging E-government countries and local government authorities—the ones that are working hard to find their place in the global economy and global society, and they are having some success. Examples include Central and Eastern Europe; the Balkans, especially Turkey; South America (for example, Chile); the Caribbean; China; India; Bangladesh; and the Southeast Asian tigers. These are the P1 countries discussed in Chapter 1; they have deregulated telecommunications and invited international partners to build, operate, modernize, and manage the infrastructure and improve services. Within the next ten years or so, they will become among the heavy users of E-government.

It should be noted that the digital divide is not only between countries or continents; it also exists within countries and communities. Available evidence suggests that Internet users tend to be white, richer, more educated, urban, employed, and young, with stable family or social arrangements, and are located in such countries as the United States and the United Kingdom. The rural, poor, less-schooled, unemployed, homeless, and older citizens risk being left out of the digital E-government service train. Likewise, small businesses unable to invest in the necessary digital infrastructure may lose their competitiveness. Small local NGOs serving local communities may be equally vulnerable. Therefore, E-government must be seen as part of a wider public policy initiative designed to improve governance and to remove impediments to social, political, and economic opportunities. E-government can empower citizens and serve as an effective societal equalizer.

Exhibit 2.4 provides four examples of select E-government providers outside North America and Western Europe. Its purpose is to show current E-government practices in an environment similar to many developing countries. These examples are from Turkey, Guyana, East and South Africa, and Singapore.

EXHIBIT 2.4
Selected Providers of E-government Services

1. Guyana's National Information and Communication Network

   Aim: To promote access to development-related information via the Internet, build Web sites, and undertake training and capacity development.

   Actors: Government ministries and agencies, NGOs, schools, and international funding agencies (for example, UNDP).

   Benefits: Use E-mail to improve communication, promote interagency cooperation, and improve access to information via the Internet. Cut costs and provide gateway to international actors and sources of information.

   Lessons and Challenges: Need to develop institutional capacity and human capital to support ongoing E-government services. Need to plan for sustainable funding. Attitudes of senior management toward a digital culture and work environment. Government unwillingness to share information. Inadequate telephone lines and telecommunications infrastructure.

   Source: European Centre for Development Policy Management 7 (October 2000), 4–5.

2. Turkey's Government Social Security Organization (Emelki-Sandigi)

Aim: To link all pharmacies together with other medical service providers by Internet and Intranet to improve medical services to more than 2 million pensioners and their dependents.

Actors: IBM (vendor), pharmacies (17,000), pensioners, doctors, hospitals, government of Turkey.

Benefits: Reduce costs: Initial investment of U.S.$8 million recovered within one year of operation. Faster services and payments to pharmacies. Established electronic communication network linking pharmacies, hospitals, and doctors. Pensioners can use any pharmacy anywhere in the country. Better information for medical services planners and providers.

Source: The Economist (June 24, 2000): www.economist.com.

3. Regional Information Center on Local Government: Southern Africa

Aim: To build an electronic network to enhance communication, to share information, to provide mutual learning, to support capacity development, and to reform the local and municipal governments of East and South Africa.

Actors: Local government authorities, African Union of Local Government Authorities, Commonwealth Local Government Forum, European Union, national governments.

Benefits: Improved collaboration and information sharing among local governments in the region. One stop only for information, lessons of experience. Providing links to other Web sites within the region and internationally. Reduced costs, improved services.

Lessons and Challenges: Not all countries are at the same level of development or capacity to use E-government services. Technical problems owing to inadequate telecommunications infrastructure. Need to build local capacity and develop human capital for an electronic environment. Need for long-term commitment from an externally funded project to become part of ongoing E-government services.

Source: http://www.mdpesa.co.zw; www.capacity.org (October 2000).

4. Singapore's Learning Village

Aim: To use the Internet to make schools more outward looking, competitive, and collaborative. The Web-based platform combines a set of Internet applications to allow two-way communication and collaboration within and among schools as well as internationally.

Actors: School principals, teachers, students, parents, and members of the local community. Global society.

Benefits: Online communication among actors. Parents log on to get information about school activities, track their children's progress, attend E-meetings, arrange for private E-conferences on matters relating to their children, and provide feedback and suggestions to the schools. Students collaborate on studying and projects with others within the school, other schools, and elsewhere in the world. "Teachers' Lounge" provides electronic facilities for teachers to share ideas about lessons and to discuss effectiveness of various teaching methods. Available twenty-four hours a day, seven days a week. Saves time and travel. Builds a digital culture in schools and community.

Lessons and Challenges: Teachers, parents, and students increase involvement and commitment to education. More transparent education system. Parents may need special training to learn how to use the E-government system. Starting costs may be prohibitive. Poor schools may need special attention to ensure equity. Access to Internet reduces school dropout rates. Students may continue education on the Internet.

Source: www.economist.com (June 24, 2000).

As can be seen in Exhibit 2.4, there are noteworthy differences within this group. For example, the poorer regions or countries in Africa and Guyana have their E-government services provided by international donor organizations such as the UNDP and the Commonwealth Secretariat. This signals the fact that the individual governments in these countries are unable to provide E-government services on their own.

The other examples clearly show that the government agency is in a position to design its E-government services and engage the services of an international telecommunications vendor such as IBM (see Turkey). This distinction is important because in the former case E-government is seen as a project with a terminal end, while for both Turkey and Singapore, this is part of an ongoing government program of governance. Questions of ownership, commitment, and continuing funding for E-government development are much more critical for the donor-funded initiatives than they are for government-driven undertakings.

Singapore's "Learning Village" (see Exhibit 2.4) provides an excellent example of an E-government initiative aimed at all levels of society, as well as one that links domestic users with the international society. Its users include school administrators, teachers, parents, students, dropouts, and members of the local community. It provides links to other sites within Singapore, in the region, and internationally. It targets the young people, their parents or grandparents, and non-parents and teaches them how to log on and become skilled users. It targets schools in poor neighborhoods for assistance to become connected and avoid being left behind. It makes excellent conceptual and practical connections between E-government and globalization.

The Future of E-Government

E-government, like the digital technology that drives it and the disciples who adore it, is here to stay. For the next ten to twenty years, the world will see a rapid increase in the number of governments deepening their involvement with E-government services via the Internet and Intranet networks. E-government is intimately connected to globalization. Any government opening up to the global society and global economy and wishing to prepare itself, its people, and its institutions for global challenges must take a strategic approach to E-government. Governments that remain electronically disconnected within themselves and with the citizens, businesses, and civil society, in general, will be unable to govern effectively and take advantage of the changing global opportunities.

Like globalization, E-government is a two-edged sword. It can be used as an effective tool to bring people, institutions, and society together. Or it can be used to divide them and to keep them separate, isolated, and alienated from one another. Public policy and public choice can make a difference: When it comes to E-government, public policy must be informed by the twin challenges of the need to capitalize on the advantages of technology for the common good and the need to seriously address the social and administrative adverse effects, especially for the weak and most vulnerable members of society.

For the poor countries to get on and stay connected on the Internet, they will need a large amount of capital investment. Funding can best be achieved through strategic alliances or partnerships with international partners who have the technology, financing, and management know-how. In addition, they need to worry about two other things: maintaining reliable and high-quality technical support services and protecting the electronic system from fraud and sabotage. In a private conversation, a British international development consultant with many years of field experience in Africa and Asia, brought home the critical importance of technical support services when he said, "[P]lease do not use that expression 'I am just a click away.' First, you need a computer that works, a telephone line that works, a service provider that is actually providing a service, a line that is not always engaged . . . then when all that is in place you might get through and then you might not" (personal communication, September 2000).

For developing countries, security problems go beyond the normal problems of teenage hackers breaking into corporate Internet Web sites, sometimes just for the fun of it. For developing countries, it is also important to provide tight electronic security against fraud, corruption, and sabotage. Many of these countries have weak national integrity systems with weak institutions and weak enforcement mechanisms. How does E-government and a digital working environment affect public corruption? As well, many of these countries have internal or regional conflicts and frequent outbursts of civil war. Governments are constantly on the alert for possible attacks, sabotage, or outright hostile takeover by opposition groups. The question they would ask is whether E-government makes them more vulnerable for hostile attacks and takeovers. There is also the concern of both hardware and software vendors being foreigners who, during times of tension, conflict, or war, might take sides and hold the country's digital nervous system hostage. Important though these and similar concerns may be, they will not stop the expected phenomenal growth in E-government. Naturally, each government, each country, and each community will develop its own homegrown approach, and those who succeed in building effective E-government Internet service providers will reap the benefits of globalization. Those who fail will stay behind.

CIVIL SOCIETY AND THE PRIVATE SECTOR

The interplay of global and domestic forces causing changes in governments is also responsible for the significant changes going on in the structure and role of civil society and the private sector. In many developing countries and transition economies, the relationships among these three sectors of society are undergoing profound changes. If managed wisely, the changing relationships can be a beacon of hope for good governance, peace, and prosperity; mismanaged, they could lead to the total collapse of the nation–state. The key is to establish collaborative public administration and build effective partnerships for good governance, and government has a key role to play in bringing about mutually beneficial mechanisms for participation and citizen engagement.

The characteristics of the emerging civil society are very different than in the past. An increasing number of citizens are educated, informed, and increasingly aware of their constitutional, political, and human rights. They are also aware of the responsibilities of government, and they are prepared to press for their rights and hold government accountable for its actions. With the help of outside support, they are increasingly better organized, electronically connected with the outside world, and widely traveled. Quite often, they are more cosmopolitan than some of the government officials, especially at the subnational level. Although some of them are ideologically opposed to globalization, they are among the small percentage of people enjoying the fruits of global openness. These people have often been criticized by their own governments for being servants of foreign interests because they receive financial and technical support from the United Nations and other international/foreign organizations and because they have more in common with outsiders—values, attitudes, tastes, mind-sets, ideals—than with their own fellow citizens.

Likewise, the business private sector is undergoing significant transformations. Public sector reforms, deregulation, and privatization have created opportunities for more citizens to join the commercial sector, either as employees, managers, or entrepreneurs. As a result, most reforming developing countries and transition economies have seen significant increases in the number of small- and medium-size businesses being created and locally owned. At the same time, many global corporations have established subsidiaries in these countries to take advantage of new opportunities in markets, capital, natural resources, and labor. New institutions have also sprung up in sectors ranging from education, environment, spirituality, and public health. As a result, the governance table today is much more crowded and much more diverse than in the past. Government is neither able to nor allowed to govern alone. Managing diversity is increasingly becoming a public sector core competency.

These changes create challenges and opportunities for government and society as a whole. Government needs to draw on the experiences of other governments around the world and the experiences of the private sector, while also responding to the rising and changing public expectations about how services should be delivered and how to develop a governing ethos appropriate to both the changing domestic society and the international community. Government needs to encourage the development of grassroots, community-based organizations because ultimately these will be the champions of grassroots globalization or "glocalization." Likewise, government must actively encourage the development of local business and an indigenous entrepreneurial class. These will be the ambassadors and disciples of globalization and the linchpins with the global corporate sector. Government must promote collaboration, coalition formation, and partnerships with other sectors of society because "[t]here are no institutions strong enough to do everything. The winners will be those that successfully network and make partnerships work."[26]

In short, government must develop a new mind-set and new institutional capacities and human competencies. These include working in partnership with the private and voluntary sector, sharing responsibility and devolving power, acting responsively and flexibly in anticipation of new challenges and opportunities, and answering to a much more informed and demanding public.

GLOBALIZATION AND NATIONAL SECURITY

No discussion of globalization and governance is complete without discussing the role of national security. This is especially so in developing countries and transition economies where, historically, security forces have played a critical role in determining the political and economic development of these countries. Security forces include the army, the air force, the navy (where one exists), the police, prison services, intelligence services, presidential guards, and any other paramilitary organizations in a particular country. Although the number of dictatorial regimes is on the decline, these organizations still exert a lot of political and economic power and influence in terms of how the national government is run. Even in apparently democratically elected governments, such as Peru, Indonesia, Fiji, Nigeria, Israel, and Central and Eastern Europe, the security forces still dominate the national governance system. Therefore, they must be fully engaged in discussions about the essence of the state, visioning and making choices about national strategic directions. Efforts to exclude them, especially in post-conflict countries and countries with internal or regional conflicts, simply exacerbate the conflicts. Yet, most security organizations in developing countries lack the institutional capacity and human intellectual capital for meaningful participation in the civilian part of national governance and public administration.

The key functions of the security organizations are national defense, internal security, assistance to civilian authorities, and ceremonial duties. As well, they may have direct or indirect effects in areas such as human capital formation (for example, training), infrastructure development, and industrial development. In terms of cost–benefit analysis, the two key questions are, How much do they cost? and To what extent do they contribute or detract from the national efforts toward openness, competitiveness, democratization, collaborative partnership, and, ultimately, globalization?

To address these questions, two financial indicators and two social indicators are used. The two financial measures are military expenditure as a percentage of gross national product (ME/GNP), and military expenditure as a percentage of central government expenditure (ME/CGE). Both of these are input measures, and while they provide a good indicator of how much national security priorities crowd out other social and economic priorities, they do not provide a direct measure of the quality of the security received or the benefits the citizens receive as a result of those expenditures.

The two social indicators are the Spartan Index and the Praetorian Index. The Spartan Index is total security personnel as a percentage of total population. While there is no magic formula for determining optimal Spartan percentages, comparative data over time—and with other countries in the region or level of development and security needs—can give good indications of the country's priorities and its readiness for globalization. In a recent comparative study of military spending in developing countries, it was observed, "Where the combined number of military internal security personnel together with paramilitary personnel is high, we can question whether their real purpose is the legitimate protection of the national authority, or rather the repression of dissent through the illegitimate use of armed forces against their own population."[27]

The same study suggests that the Spartan Index can be used to determine if at any given time, the security situation of a country or parts thereof can be described as a police state. If the Spartan Index is too high compared to the past or to other countries in the region with similar security needs, it is a good indication that the national security system is degenerating toward a police army rather than a national defense army. This is not good for political or economic openness, and it is not good for globalization.

The Praetorian Index is more complex. It indicates the extent to which security forces become financially privileged members of their society through their ability to take advantage of their monopoly on the use of force and their ability to make and unmake governments, thus gaining an economic edge in the form of salary scales and benefits significantly in excess of those available to the general public. It is a direct measure of the extent to which the security forces misuse their power and influence for personal gain. It is a corruption measure for this segment of society.

Table 2.3 provides comparative data for the four financial and social indicators for thirty-three countries in six regions of the Middle East and Africa. These regions were chosen because of their high level of internal and regional conflict at the turn of the century and because they are among the most challenged regions of the world for establishing and sustaining openness, democratic development, competitiveness, collaborative partnership, and true globalization. They were also chosen because they are a potential threat to globalization elsewhere in the world. The purpose is to test whether the four indices of militarism are a good indicator of a country's readiness for openness and globalization. Regions and countries not represented in the table can construct their own profile of militarism and undertake similar comparative analysis.

The data in Table 2.3 can be used for making comparisons across regions (Middle East versus East Africa), within region, and for a single country across the four measures of

TABLE 2.3
Militarization Levels for the Middle East and Africa

Regional/Country	Financial: Economy ME/GNP%	Financial: Government ME/CGE %	Spartan Index:	Praetorian Index
Middle East				
Iraq	69.2	N.A.	36.1	20.5
Saudi Arabia	21.6	58.0	9.1	17.6
Syria	15.0	59.3	32.5	4.8
Israel	10.9	24.1	43.7	2.7
Jordan	9.3	25.6	28.1	3.0
Egypt	4.2	9.7	14.3	2.0
Iran	3.9	17.0	12.2	3.5
Means[1]	17.18	59.73	22.03	10.78
North Africa				
Algeria	2.3	6.8	6.9	4.2
Libya	8.1	16.1	18.6	3.8
Mauritania	4.0	N.A.	9.2	6.1
Morocco	5.3	15.3	12.4	6.8
Tunisia	3.0	9.3	6.5	7.2
Means	4.54	12.3	10.72	5.62
West Africa				
Senegal	2.4	8.3	1.4	17.8
Mali	1.9	14.6	1.8	25.8
Côte d'Ivoire	1.5	N.A.	1.2	27.9
Nigeria	0.9	4.2	1.0	8.9
Ghana	0.8	4.7	0.8	16.0
Means	2.38	10.42	2.32	17.09
Central Africa				
Congo	5.3	13.0	7.2	11.8

(*continued*)

TABLE 2.3 (*cont.*)

Regional/Country	Financial: Economy ME/GNP%	Financial: Government ME/CGE %	Spartan Index:	Praetorian Index
Zaire (DRC)	3.0	18.5	1.5	40.1
Gabon	3.2	9.8	8.7	7.2
Cameroon	1.7	8.2	1.1	23.1
C A R	2.4	N.A.	2.1	19.8
Means	3.27	12.4	4.45	16.89
East Africa				
Sudan	12.4	26.8	3.7	39.1
Ethiopia	8.8	37.4	2.2	7.2
Tanzania	4.8	12.9	2.2	22.9
Kenya	3.1	10.4	1.1	29.5
Uganda	2.3	12.4	3.4	6.4
Rwanda	7.2	28.9	0.8	95.8
Means	6.01	55.47	2.16	32.01
Southern Africa				
Mozambique	13.8	49.9	2.8	35.8
Botswana	5.6	10.7	5.4	10.8
Zimbabwe	4.9	12.6	7.0	8.5
Zambia	2.0	6.9	2.7	6.9
South Africa	3.0	10.0	5.2	14.7
Means	5.28	15.97	5.74	13.52

[1]The means are for all countries in the region. The table shows only a select sample from each region. For more details, see the original source.

N.A. = data not available; C A R = Central African Republic; DRC = Democratic Republic of the Congo, formerly Zaire; ME = military expenditure; CGE = central government expenditure; GNP = gross national product.

Source: Compiled from Brian S. MacDonald, *Military Spending in Developing Countries: How Much is Too Much?* (Ottawa: Carleton University Press, 1997), 28, 44, 65, 78, 109, 146.

militarism. As one would expect, the data shows that the Middle East is the most militaristic region in both economic and social terms. Imagine the financial and human resources that could be freed up for peaceful development if the region cut militarism by half. Rather surprisingly, West Africa is the least militaristic according to the data in Table 2.3. This is rather surprising because of the general impression of the prevalence of military regimes in the 1990s for several West African countries including Nigeria, Liberia, Sierra Leone, The Gambia, and Niger.

In terms of financial militarism, some countries stand out as big spenders. These include Iraq, Syria, Libya, Morocco, Zaire (now DRC), Sudan, and Rwanda. During the 1990s, and even today, these countries were characterized by internal discord, by regional conflicts, and wars. Likewise, they are countries characterized by a lack of openness, phony democracy, xenophobia, ethnic conflicts, and social–political upheavals. They are countries least attractive to the global economy and global society. They hardly attract foreign capital, technology, or management know-how, and when they do, they pay a premium for them. They are among the most refugee-producing countries of the world, and they suffer from perpetual brain drains, as their knowledge citizens (cosmocrats) seek openness and opportunities elsewhere in the world. In short, they are characterized by poor governance. The data in Table 2.3 suggests rather strongly that, at least for the developing countries in the Middle East and Africa, militarism and globalization are negatively correlated.

The data showing the Praetorian Index in Table 2.3 provide additional information about the character and fate of these countries. Recall that this index is a measure of the extent to which the security forces abuse their power for personal gain and suppress legitimate voices of dissent. Regional comparisons show that East Africa scores highest on average, while North Africa and the Middle East score the lowest. Individually, the countries that score the highest on the Praetorian Index are Rwanda, Zaire, Sudan, Mozambique, and Kenya. These data show the extent to which there is official corruption in these countries as practiced by the security forces taking advantage of their privileged monopoly position to exact an economic edge. Once again, these data show that financial and social militarism go hand in hand and that a combination of both is very detrimental to the creation of conditions and an enabling environment for openness, individual and economic freedom, competitiveness, clean government, and ultimately globalization.

It is not enough simply to advise these countries to cut back on militarism by reducing financial or human resources commitments. Current mobilization and peacekeeping efforts are necessary but not sufficient. What the data in Table 2.3 show are symptoms of deeper historical, political, economic, social, and cultural underlying causes rooted in these societies. It will take time and concerted effort to bring about the necessary transformational changes. Most of these countries cannot do it on their own because they lack the collective vision, mind-set, political leadership, institutional capacity, and human capital for the necessary perseverance. Many of these countries desperately need understanding, long-term assistance, and collaborative partnerships with key actors in the global society and global economy. However, in the present climate of international relations characterized by global competitiveness, dwindling and self-interested overseas development assistance commitments from the rich countries, global corporations preoccupied with the more profitable open markets, a divided international NGO community, and a U.N. system busy reinventing itself, it is hard to see how these countries and their societies can get the quality of assistance and partnership they need to overcome militarism in all its forms and to prepare their people to participate fully and equitably in the dynamic global economy and global society. Yet, their fate is our fate.

NOTES

1. There is a lot of literature on governance, especially for emerging economies and developing countries. See, for example, UNPD, "Reconceptualizing Governance," Discussion Paper 2 (New York: UNDP, January 1997); World Bank, *The State in a Changing World* (Washington, DC: World Bank and Oxford University Press, 1997). For a more academic discussion, see Aseem Prakash and Jeffery A. Hart, eds., *Globalization and Governance* (London, Routledge, 1999). For a critical but more balanced discussion of globalization, see Paul Hirst and Grahame Thompson, *Questioning Globalization: The International Economy and the Possibilities of Governance* (Cambridge: Polity, 1999). Also visit Web sites for USAID (gov.org), United Kingdom government, the European Centre for Development Policy Management (ecdpm.org), or any of the major international development agencies. On globalization and the state, see World Bank, *Entering the 21st Century, World Development Report* (Washington, DC: World Bank, 1999/2000). For Africa, in particular, see United Nations, *Governance in Africa: Consolidating the Institutional Foundations* (New York: United Nations Department of Economic and Social Affairs, 1999). Also see the Web site www.unpan.org. Recently, the World Bank has established the Web-Interactive Access to Governance Indicators, which contains updated composite governance research indicators for 175 countries. Each country is measured on six governance dimensions: voice and accountability, political stability, government effectiveness, regulatory quality, rule of law, and control of corruption. For more information see the Web site www.worldbank.org/wbi/governance.

2. G. Shabbir Cheema, "Good Governance: A Path to Poverty Eradication," *Choices: The Human Development Magazine* 9, no 1 (March 2000):6–7.

3. Peter F. Drucker, "The Global Economy and the Nation State," *Foreign Affairs* 76, no. 5 (September/October 1997):159–171.

4. For an example of a detailed discussion of structural adjustment, see World Bank, *Adjustment in Africa: Reforms, Results, and the Road Ahead* (Washington, DC: World Bank, 1994).

5. This discussion is based on two earlier papers on public sector reform. See Moses N. Kiggundu, "Civil Service Reform: Limping into the 21st Century," in *Beyond the New Public Management: Changing Ideas and Practices in Governance*, ed. Martin Minogue, Charles Polidano, and David Hulme (Cheltenham, UK: Edward Elgar, 1999), 155–171; and Moses N. Kiggundu "Bureaucracy and Administrative Reform in Developing Countries," in *Handbook on Development Policy and Management*, ed. Colin Kirkpatrick, Ron Clarke, and Charles Polidano (Cheltenham, UK: Edward Elgar, 2002), 291–302.

6. Jeremy Rifkin, *The End of Work* (New York: G. P. Putman, 1995), 250.

7. Address to the Board of Governors, September 28, 1999, by James D. Wolfensohn, president of the World Bank Group; see World Bank, *Reforming Public Institutions and Strengthening Governance: A World Bank Strategy* Vol. 1, *Overall Strategy* (Washington, DC: World Bank, 1999), i.

8. For a discussion of phony democracies and democracies of convenience see *The Economist*, June 24, 2000, p. 20.

9. Government of Botswana, "Long-Term Vision for Botswana: Towards Prosperity for All" (Gaborone: Presidential Task Group, September 1997).

10. Malaysia's "Vision 2020" is discussed in detail in Asma Abdullah, *Going Glocal: Cultural Dimensions in Malaysian Management* (Kuala Lumpur: Malaysian Institute of Management, 1996), 176, 182.

Exhibit 2.2 is based on information from this source. Also see Barbara Watson Andaya and Lenard Y. Andaya, *A History of Malaysia*, 2nd ed. (Honolulu: University of Hawaii Press, 2001), 318.

11. For a recent discussion of Botswana, see James Sackey, "Botswanaian Example of Prudent Economic Policy and Growth," Economic Management and Social Policy Paper 161 (Washington, DC: World Bank, June 2000). For Malaysia, see Asma Abdullah, *Going Glocal*, 176, 182.

12. For a detailed discussion of globalization from subnational perspectives, see Shahid Yusuf, Wieping Wu, and Simon Evenett, eds., *Local Dynamics in an Era of Globalization* (Washington, DC: World Bank, 2000). For the advantages of collaboration, see Yves L. Doz and Gary Hamel, *Alliance Advantage: The Art of Creating Value through Partnering* (Boston: Harvard Business School Press, 1998). Value chain systems and enterprise resource planning (ERP) are management concepts that bring together producers or service providers across corporate or institutional boundaries. For ERP, see Bill Gates, *Business @ the Speed of Thought* (New York: Time Warner, 1999), 168–170.

13. For classical management works on the structuring of organizations, see Max Weber, *The Theory of Social and Economic Organization*, trans. A. M. Henderson and T. Parsons (New York: Oxford University Press, 1947); and F. W. Taylor, *The Principles of Scientific Management* (New York: Harper, 1911).

14. For the private sector, see Jay Galbraith, *Organization Design* (Reading, MA: Addison-Wesley, 1977); and Robert T. Moran, Philip R. Harris, and William G. Stripp, *Developing the Global Organization: Strategies for Human Resource Professionals* (Houston: Gulf Publishing, 1993). For the United Nations, see Kofi A. Annan, *The Role of the United Nations in the 21st Century* (New York: United Nations, 2000).

15. World Bank, *World Development Report 2000/2001: Attacking Poverty* (Washington, DC: World Bank, 1999), chap. 6.

16. On the issue of values and dreams, see *The Herald* (Harare, Zimbabwe), August 14, 2000, p. 6. The organization Southern Africa International Dialogue organized a conference entitled "Smart Partnership 2000—Global Trends and Emerging Economics"—SAID 2000 in Maputo, Mozambique, on August 19–20, 2000. In attendance were six presidents and three deputy presidents representing a total of eight countries from southern Africa. Lower-level officials represented other participating countries. Also present was the prime minister of Malaysia, Dr. Mahathir bin Mohamad, a critic of globalization. The purpose of this high-level regional conference was to examine ways by which member states could deal with the negative impact of globalization on developing countries. See "Conference Aims to Tackle Negative Impact of Globalization," *The Herald* (Harare, Zimbabwe), August 21, 2000, p. 1. It should be noted that a conference of this type does not constitute a visioning exercise because it is not inclusive and because participation is limited to senior government officials.

17. United Nations (DESA), *Administrative Reforms: Country Profiles of Five Asian Countries: Japan, Korea, the Philippines, Thailand* (New York: DESA, 1997).

18. World Bank, *Czech Republic: Toward European Union Accession: Main Report* (Washington, DC: World Bank, 1999).

19. Government of Thailand, *Public Sector Management Plan* (Bangkok: Public Service Commission, 1999), 30.

20. United Nations, "Globalization and the State at the Threshold of the Twenty-first Century," Report of the Group of Experts on the United Nations Program in Public Administration and Finance (New York: United Nations, March 2000), 21.

21. This discussion draws on Efraim Turban, Jae Lee, David King, and H. Michael Chung, *Electronic Commerce: A Managerial Perspective* (Upper Saddle River, NJ: Prentice-Hall, 2000), chap. 1. Also see Douglas Holmes, *E-Gov. E-Business Strategy for Government* (London: Nicholas Bradley, 2001); "The Use of the Internet in Business," *The Economist*, June 26, 1999, p. 62; and Gudrun Trauner, *E-government: Information and Communication Technologies in Public Administration* (Brussels: Linz University and the International Institute of Administrative Sciences, 2002).

22. Gates, *Business @ the Speed of Thought*, 397–413. Also see "A Survey of Government and the Internet: The Next Revolution," *The Economist*, June 24, 2000, after pg. 62 (special insert). pp. 1–14.

23. For a discussion of the need to develop the capacity to deregulate and manage a national telecommunications corporation in a globalizing country, see Moses N. Kiggundu, "Capacity Development for Managing Telecommunications Reform and Restructuring: A Corporate Approach from Indonesia," *Journal of Asian Business* 13, no. 2 (1997):19–57.

24. For information on E-government applications in rich countries, see Al Gore, *The Gore Report on Reinventing Government: From Red Tape to Results* (New York: Random House, 1993); and World Bank, *Development Report: Knowledge for Development* (Washington, DC: World Bank, 1998/1999). Also visit the British government portal: www.number.10.gov.uk.

25. Several Web sites provide information, advice, and two-way discussions on technology and the Internet, especially for governments in developing countries. Try the following sites: www.undp.org; www.oneworld.org/ecdpm; www.commonwealthknowledge.int.uk; www.idrc.ca; www.unpan.org; and www.capacity.org.

26. See Moses N. Kiggundu, *Building Effective Partnerships: A Framework and Plan of Action for CAAP* (Ottawa: Department of Indian Affairs and Northern Development, Government of Canada, April 1998), 3.

27. Following the fall of Communism, the international community began many initiatives aimed at demobilization, demilitarization, and conversion of military resources to civilian social and economic applications. One of the most active organizations is the Bonn International Center for Conversion (BICC), which was established in April 1994 with funding from the German state government of North-Rhine Westphalia, in cooperation with the Investitions-Bank, other German organizations, and the United Nations. The purpose of this independent nonprofit organization is to support and promote the processes by which people, skills, technology, equipment, and financial and economic resources are shifted from the military or defense sector toward alternative, civilian purposes. After almost ten years of active work in Africa and Europe, they have now conceded that demobilization is necessary but not sufficient. In a recent publication, it was concluded that "demobilization is not a 'magic bullet,' which automatically and simultaneously takes care of a large set of development and security challenge . . . reintegration efforts in isolation are not likely to help. Politics has to come first, only then, on the basis of a real political solution of the conflict, will demobilization, resettlement and reintegration support be natural—and often inevitable—components of postwar rehabilitation and development." See Kees Kingma, ed., *Demobilization in Sub-Saharan Africa: The Development and Security Impacts* (New York: St. Martin's and BICC, 2000), 241–242 (http://www.bicc.uni-bonn.de). Also see GTZ, *Security-Sector Reform in Developing Countries* (Eschborn, Germany: GTZ, Division 403, 2000), 19–28.

PART II
Globalization and the Economy

CHAPTER 3

Globalization and Economic Management

In the previous chapter, I discussed the relationship between governance and globalization and emphasized the central role of the state in championing the necessary transformations and the need to forge effective private–public partnerships. I emphasized the central role of the state at all levels of government, in partnership with others, in influencing the country's direction, pace, and overall quality of participation in the global economy and society. An important lesson of experience from Chapter 2 is that the strong markets created by globalization need strong states. Both markets and states need not only competitiveness, but, perhaps more important for the long-term survival of the system, they also need collaborative partnerships. These partnerships are most effective with the active involvement of outsiders. This is a theme repeated throughout this book. In this chapter, the focus turns to national economic management and globalization. The emphasis here is on the productive sectors of the economy and how they are organized and managed to take advantage of, and protect themselves from, the adverse effects of globalization.

All countries in the world—those in support of or opposed to globalization—support the concept of economic growth and development. Growth means the opportunity for wealth creation and income generation. Support for economic globalization is based on the realization that it enables nations, governments, societies, enterprises, and individuals to create more wealth and generate more income through more efficient modes of production, consumption, and exchange. Increases in wealth and income give rise to higher standards of living and improved quality of life. Without a growing productive sector of the economy, it is not possible to sustain higher levels of wealth creation or income generation. Questions of inequality are related to how wealth and income are distributed among and within countries; these will be discussed in Chapter 11. Here, the emphasis is on how to create the necessary macroeconomic enablers and on the organization and management of the country's productive sector for more wealth creation and income generation through globalization.

MACROECONOMIC ENABLERS

Supporters of globalization also advocate for an open, free-enterprise capitalist economy. For most developing countries and economies in transition with a history of socialist government central planning and control and ownership of productive enterprises, this requires significant changes in defining the role of the state in the management of the economy. It does not mean total abdication of the state in economic ownership and management. Rather, it requires evolutionary changes in the dominant ideology, mind-set, institutional capacities, and private–public partnership arrangements. The key challenge is to create and sustain an enabling environment for the development and competitive performance of the productive sector.

Figure 3.1 provides key components of a macroeconomic enabling framework for a globalizing economy. It starts with a national governance system, as discussed in Chapter 2, and is based on the need for the establishment of effective, functioning, and productive private–public partnerships. The central driving force for the macroeconomic enabling framework is the productive enterprises sector, which actually creates wealth and generates income. The productive enterprises sector is supported by a credible national integrity and regulatory system; a functioning infrastructure; a competitive environment; a system of professional, trade, and business associations; and ongoing institutional sociocultural change, development, and innovation.

Private–Public Partnerships

Throughout history, one of capitalism's greatest assets has been its ability to establish beneficial partnerships between or among family members, private sector entrepreneurs, or with individuals or institutions in the public sector. Corporate law recognized this at the very beginning and established standard rules and procedures for conducting business under sole proprietorships, partnerships, private corporations, and public corporations. These forms of business organizations are on a progressive scale of partnering designed to account for the increasing complexity of the relationships and to protect the interests of all parties under law. Indeed, from the early days of the Industrial Revolution through to the period of European explorations, private companies joined kings, churches, and other wealthy civic organizations to launch expeditions in search of fortunes in far away places. From the days of Christopher Columbus in the New World through to the British and Dutch East India Companies and even King Leopold's brutal adventures in the Congo, all these enterprises were made possible by complex partnership arrangements within and across the private–public sector divide.[1]

During the Cold War, industrialized countries used combinations of imperialism, diplomacy, militarism, religion, and superior access to capital and technology to facilitate formation of partnership arrangements, which helped their private sectors to win markets in their areas of influence. Japan's Ministry of International Trade and Industry is a good example of a private–public partnership; it helped Japanese businesses to dominate world markets in a relatively short period of time. A close look at the deregulation and privatization of industry in developing countries and transition economies reveals how Western businesses use the partnership model to win contracts and buy foreign assets. Deregulation and privatization of industries—ranging from telecommunications (for example, in Indonesia, Brazil, and Thailand) to oil and gas (for example, in Nigeria and Mexico) to banking (for example, in Indonesia and Argentina)—show that Western companies worked very closely with their respective governments to win contracts.

FIGURE 3.1
Macroeconomic Enabling Framework for Globalization

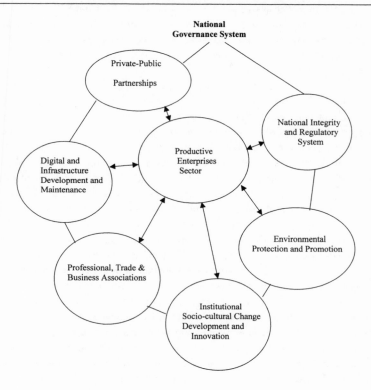

More recently, high-technology firms have benefited from private–public sector partnerships championed by competing governments. Ireland is a good example. Until recently, Ireland has been regarded as one of the poorest countries in Western Europe. Heavily dependent on natural resources, with a population of only 3.7 million, the country suffered from high unemployment of 17 percent and a mass emigration of young people, resulting in serious brain drain. It had a national debt of about 123 percent of GDP. With new leadership and a redefinition of the essence of the state, Ireland has been able to transform itself through a series of three-year agreements with trade unions and big business. These institutional arrangements, similar to Southeast Asian deliberation councils (see Exhibit 3.1 on page 73), focused on setting new strategic directions for national economic recovery and development. By putting in place very practical macroeconomic enablers and incentives such as tax cuts, investments in education, and the digital infrastructure, Ireland has been able to attract leading high-technology firms including Microsoft. By the year 2000, Ireland had emerged as the world's largest exporter of computer software, producing about two-thirds of all personal computers sold in Europe and one-half of the Pentium chips sold in the world. Because of the partnership nature of the transformation, Ireland took a balanced approach, creating a society that is both competitive and compassionate. Accordingly, spending on health care was increased by 50 percent, and university education was heavily subsidized. Mindful of the power of intellectual capital, Ireland hopes to produce as many information technology graduates as Germany, which has a population of 80 million. If Ireland can do it, so can many other countries that have been too long in the doldrums. The key is the leadership and vision and the development of effective private–public partnerships that create incentives and socioeconomic enablers.

Let's review some of the advantages of private–public partnerships. First, they provide an institutionalized arrangement for bringing together leaders from different sectors of society (for example, political, business, civil service, civil society, academic, unions) to get to know one another and develop common understanding, shared values, mutual respect, and trust. The development of a shared mind-set provides the foundation for joint decision making and collaborative partnership. Second, they provide opportunities for joint deliberations of public policy analysis that result in broad-based government policies acceptable to the wider society, thus making them easier to implement or modify as the need arises. Third, they facilitate joint action planning and joint resource mobilization. By working together a government can assist the private sector in obtaining capital through loans, grants, concessions, contracts, taxes, and other forms of guarantees and subsidies. Fourth, the partnership can provide practical solutions for eliminating impediments to competitiveness (for example, by eliminating red tape), supporting productivity improvements (for example, through training and development, research, development and commercialization, innovation, improved labor–management relations), and promoting international trade (for example, through joint negotiations, Internet technology). Partnerships also help to improve the country's national integrity and regulatory systems by making sure that the right laws, rules, and regulations are enacted fairly and are consistently enforced. This helps reduce corruption and protect the environment. Finally, these partnerships can be extremely valuable in times of national crises or emergencies. They can be used as an early warning system to prepare the country for foreseen crises, and they can be used as a vehicle for mobilizing domestic and international support and resources in the preparation and management of crises or emergencies. Unfortunately, some newly globalizing countries do not have a critical mass of credible private sector organizations for effective partnerships.

There are additional advantages for globalizing developing countries to establish and sustain effective private–public partnerships. In times of uncertainty and change, the partnership arrangements provide leaders with mutual support and common understanding, unity of purpose, and sharing experiences and learning new roles and rules, as well as reinforcing the values and principles of globalization. Gathering strength for globalization becomes less onerous in partnership.

On a global scale, most of the actors in developing countries, in both the private and the public sector, are small: Governments have smaller budgets, businesses have smaller operations, and civil society organizations have fewer members, volunteers, and donors. Partnership provides them with the opportunity to scale up and to enjoy synergy, economies of scale, and clout. This is particularly important when dealing with foreign firms that are used to handling large-scale transactions or doing business with large organizations.

In terms of policy analysis, formulation, and implementation, partnerships can be particularly important for developing countries and countries in transition. These countries need growth-oriented policies as part of the overall strategy for the development of macro-economic enablers and incentives for domestic and foreign investment. They need joint policies and strategies for rapid accumulation, including capital formation, high rates of saving, investment, and rapid growth; trade and investment, including creating an export push; productivity improvement, including technology and innovation; and public sector reform, including democratization, civil service reform, private sector development, and poverty alleviation. For most developing countries and countries in transition, the most difficult challenge is effective implementation of macroeconomic policies. By working together through private–public sector partnerships, these countries increase their chances of effective policy implementation through improved ownership, commitment, shared learning, and joint mobilization of resources.

Private–public partnerships are so important that they have become an important acid test for readiness, openness, competitiveness, and globalization. Countries, societies, institutions, businesses, and individuals who cannot sustain or be part of effective private–public sector partnerships are not ready for globalization.

Exhibit 3.1 provides a brief description of deliberation councils as an example of private–public partnership arrangements that proved useful to Asian economies at a certain level of their political and socioeconomic development. In addition, the exhibit describes what these councils do, how they work, their composition, and where they have been particularly effective in putting in place macroeconomic enablers and incentives for economic development and globalization. This is not to suggest that other countries should necessarily emulate the experiences of Southeast Asia and start their own deliberation councils. Rather, the purpose is to provide models by which other countries can extract general principles and lessons of experience relevant to their own situations. They can then draw on these experiences to establish and sustain private–public partnership arrangements most appropriate to the prevailing realities on the ground.

EXHIBIT 3.1
Deliberation Councils: Private–Public Partnerships for Effective Economic Management Policy Making

What Are Deliberation Councils? Voluntary collaborative institutional arrangements linking government, business, and civil society to discuss and develop action plans on issues of national importance such as globalization.

What Do They Do?

1. Serve as a forum to bring together the country's top corporate leaders, top political leaders, and senior public servants to exchange views on economic and business policies.

2. Provide opportunities for politicians and public servants to solicit feedback and reactions from the private sector regarding important/sensitive policy directions such as globalization.

3. Provide an organized mechanism and a process for meaning-ful consultations and frank dialogue among the leaders of the private and public sectors.

4. Contribute to a more open, transparent, and accountable gov-ernment and facilitate the development of close private–pub-lic, mutually supportive cooperation, consistent with national development priorities and indigenous processes.

5. Allow the leaders from the various sectors of society to get to know one another and develop common and shared under-standing and values, trust, and mutual respect.

How Do They Work? Funded by contributions from the public and private sector. Headed by head of government or deputy, maintain a small secretariat for administration and coordination. Closed but frank, critical, and transparent meetings. Meet several times a year with set agenda.

Composition. Comprehensive mix of ethnic, political, sectoral, geo-graphical, and political representatives. All parties are invited to join in-cluding key ministries, businesses, NGOs, academics, and trade unions. Public servants represent respective ministries or agencies, whereas pri-vate sector members attend as individuals. Appointments are for two fixed terms on a rotating basis. Each member also belongs to one or more working committees that investigate in greater depth assigned strategic issue(s) and develop a plan of action.

Examples. Various forms are found in all parts of the world. More re-cently highlighted as important institutional arrangements contributing to the high performing Asian economies. Examples include the Malaysian Business Council, the Singapore National Wages Council, and Hong Kong's Anti-Corruption Agency.

Source: Compiled from Jose Edgardo L. Campos and Joaquin L. Gonzalez III, "Deliberation Councils and Effective Policy Making: Experiences from Malaysia, Singapore, and Canada," in *Building Government–Citizen–Business Partnerships,* ed. Suzanne Taschereau and Jose Edgardo L. Campos (Ottawa: Institute on Gov-ernance, 1997), 7–26.

Although private–public partnerships are necessary for creating a positive macroeco-nomic enabling environment for development and globalization, they are not without draw-backs and unintended negative consequences. Exhibit 3.2 lists some of these shortcomings. For countries lacking democratic institutions and openness and those suffering from inter-nal discord and intractable conflicts, these partnerships can lead to cronyism, nepotism, corruption, elitism, exclusion, and just plain bad public policy. In Southeast Asia where deliberation councils (see Exhibit 3.1) were used as part of the Asian model of economic development, there were several deficiencies that became obvious during the 1997–1998 economic crisis. These included structural weaknesses in the banking system; poor corporate governance and ownership of enterprises; incestuous relationships among business, politics, and the military; lack of public accountability and transparency; and a general absence of political freedom. Although these deficiencies do not apply equally to all countries, the region as a whole continues to experience difficulties in its attempts to implement effective post-crises institutional reforms.

Exhibit 3.2
Unintended Negative Consequences of Private–Public Partnerships

1. The government (politicians and civil servants) choosing private sector winners and losers rather than allowing competitive market forces.

2. Government officials using bank credit as a key instrument of industrial policy, forcing banks to extend easy credit especially to friends and family.

3. Lack or inability to develop and sustain consensus-building democratic traditions leading to secrecy, open conflict, sectarian cliques, opportunism, vanity, and nepotism.

4. Encouraging family-owned and family-dominated businesses (for example, Chaebol in Korea) financed by bank credit rather than issuing equity.

5. Violation of minority shareholders' rights and interests, allowing major shareholders to cross-guarantee the loans of other members, thus contributing to a financial sector that is neither sound nor transparent and a corporate sector that is characterized by a high-debt-to-equity ratio and is most vulnerable to external shocks over time.

6. Both political and economic power gets concentrated in fewer powerful hands leading to interlocking directorships; weak corporate governance; in-breeding; corruption; cronyism; and lack of accountability, transparency, and openness.

7. Taking advantage of special partnership relationships to stifle competition, creating and sustaining illegal or unethical monopolistic or predatory business practices.

In industrialized countries, some of the private–public partnerships can be improper, unethical, or illegal. By choosing winners and losers, a government can stifle competition and innovation through public policy instruments such as awarding contracts, loans, grants, concessions, tax cuts, and protectionist subsidies to select businesses. Examples of this include European and U.S. subsidies to farmers and protective tariffs to their domestic textile and steel firms, thus keeping away producers from developing countries and transition economies. Recently, Canada and Brazil accused each other of unfair and illegal trade practices as a result of government subsidies to their respective aircraft industries. Japan has often used private–public partnership arrangements to keep foreign competition out.

In the competitive world of globalization, there are no angels. That is why it is very important to have an independent, an impartial, a credible, and a competent system of dispute resolution, both domestically and internationally. In developing countries, this should be an integral part of the country's national integrity and regulatory system. One of the key functions of the WTO is to resolve disputes between or among nations arising from government business practices, which are forbidden according to international law and trade rules and procedures.

National Integrity and Regulatory System

Corruption transcends history and geography. All countries and all societies have experienced (and continue to experience) some form of corrupt, unethical conduct by their political, business, and civic leaders as well as ordinary citizens. Differences occur in how different societies tolerate corruption or how much they are prepared to punish the perpetrators. As a result of globalization, there is a growing universal intolerance of high-level corruption among public officials. In any case, our interest here is not to moralize across cultures but, rather, to discuss the relationships between corruption, openness, competitiveness, economic management, and globalization. Studies show, and practical experience confirms, the widely held view that corruption impedes the development of a positive sustainable macroeconomic enabling environment for globalization. Evidence from the United States seems to suggest that corporate corruption is related to the business cycle. Boom times, associated with inflated wealth creation, provide corporate executives with opportunities for greed and fraudulent conduct. Regulatory systems are lax and unable to keep up with the growing volume of business transactions. Yet, the misconduct of large U.S. corporations, such as Anderson, Enron, Global Crossing, and Worldcom, hurts more than just their employees, customers, and shareholders—they hurt globalization.

To understand the concept of a national integrity and regulatory system (NIRS), it is important to understand corruption first. According to Transparency International, corruption can be defined as the "misuse of power for private profit . . . behavior on the part of officials in the public sector, whether politicians or civil servants, in which they improperly and unlawfully enrich themselves, or those close to them, by the misuse of the public power entrusted to them."[2] To this must be added actors in the private sector because corruption is a transaction between giver and taker, and therefore, confining it either to the public or private sector alone misses the transactional nature of the disease.

Consider the analogy of disease. The chairman of the Chinese Communist Party called corruption a disease; Dr. Mahathir, the prime minister of Malaysia, called it a cancer with all its pervasive implications. The NIRS is the country's institutional and societal response to fighting the cancerous disease. Like the global fight against cancer of the body, the NIRS is aimed at:

1. protecting society against corruption (the disease),
2. treating those already inflicted with the disease,
3. removing from the environment cosogenic agents that cause the disease,
4. preventing outsiders from catching the disease, or bringing in foreign strains,
5. ultimately finding a cure or vaccine for the disease.

The disease spreads faster and new strains come in when the borders are porous. This is particularly the case as countries begin to deregulate and open their economy to the outside world. Experience shows that the first wave of foreigners who come to do business with previously closed economies includes many with questionable business ethics. For example, Nigerians have always complained that foreign business representatives are largely to blame for the country's corrupt image because of their willingness to offer irresistibly big bribes to public officials. A recent World Bank report on corruption in Uganda found that in 1987 "more than 1,200 birds were smuggled out of the country, more than 280 tons of ivory were illegally exported, and 550 crocodile skins were sent overseas, mainly to *Italy* and *France*."[3] Therefore, it is very likely that public officials and private businesses, both in Italy and France, participated in illegal activities and corrupt practices together with Ugandans. Under globalization, an NIRS must develop the institutional capacities and human competencies for dealing effectively with the international dimensions of unethical behavior and corrupt practices in both the public and the private sectors.[4]

Table 3.1 provides a list of typical institutions that globalizing countries use to build up their NIRS to fight corruption. These include institutions at the highest level of government (Executive and Legislative branches), judiciary and law enforcement (for example, courts, policing, legislation), anticorruption agencies (for example, the inspector general of government), central agencies and regulatory boards (for example, the central bank, competition bureau, office of the auditor general), operating line ministries, departments, and agencies (for example, education, health, defense), local authorities, public enterprises, and private sector organizations.

The role of the private sector as an integral part of the NIRS is extremely important. Government alone cannot fight the disease. The two sectors must work together, share experiences, and build a system of institutions, societal values, and promote collective professional conduct designed to uphold the law and the highest level of ethical conduct by those in positions of power and influence in both the public and the private sectors. In this regard, the business sector is particularly critical because they have the resources, and are strategically positioned, to leverage their resources: either to perpetuate or eradicate corruption.

Reporting from Kekku, Myanmar, Blaine Harden wrote about a conversation he had with a local business executive in November 2000 who said that corruption in Myanmar is so bad

TABLE 3.1
National Integrity and Regulatory System: Examples of Specific Institutions

1. Executive and Legislative branches	• Cabinet office/secretariat • President/Prime Minister's office • Parliamentary Committees : Public Accounts, Appointments, Finance and Banking, etc • Political parties
2. Judiciary and Law enforcement	• Ministry of justice, public prosecution office • The court system • Attorney general's office • Police, Intelligence, and Prison services • Laws, rules, regulations: Financial Administration Act, criminal code, public service employment regulations, Corporation Act, access to information, rights and freedoms, Income Tax Act, etc. • Law society, legal aid, legal education • Investment code. General Standing Orders.
3. Anti-corruption special agencies	• Anti-corruption code/Act • Inspector general of government, ombudsman • Anti-corruption agency • Public/private sector codes of conduct
4. Central and regulatory boards, agencies	• Department of finance • Central bank • Auditor general • Public service commission • Elections commission • Competition bureau • Public works/government services/procurements/contracts • Customs and revenue agency • Registrar of companies • Inspector of financial services • Sectoral regulatory agencies (e.g. utilities, telecommunications, environment, transportation, banking, etc.) • Immigration services
5. Operating agencies/ departments	• Line ministries /local authorities • Operating agencies • Alternative service delivery • Public enterprises
6. Private sector organizations	• Indigenous businesses • Foreign-owned businesses • NGOS: Indigenous; foreign • Business/Trade/Professional associations • Consumer/Environment/Human rights/Democratic Protection associations • Corporate codes of conduct • The Press: Indigenous; Foreign • Religious organizations • Academics, artists, writers, social critics, etc.

that citizens are not free to travel abroad without paying bribes for passports, cannot import cars without paying bribes for import licenses, nor can they run businesses without the generals extorting profits (*The Globe and Mail*, November 22, 2000). Most transnational corporations provide extensive managerial training in ethics and have developed codes of conduct for their employees and business associates both at home and abroad. An increasing number of businesses are posting copies of their codes of conduct on their Web sites. General Electric and Nortel both have elaborate codes of ethics. Business, trade, and professional associations can also be instrumental in the fight against corruption by working directly with their members and the clients with whom they do business. Professional associations for auditing, accounting, purchasing, and engineering could refuse to certify work or bid on contracts if laws or rules of conduct have been broken. Some of the big NGOs are also concerned about corruption and have taken steps to play their role in protecting their employees, volunteers, donors, and aid recipients. For example, the Red Cross has established rules of conduct for employees and volunteers going overseas.

The international community is particularly active in containing corruption because of its pervasive global costs. James Wolfensohn, president of the World Bank, has been particularly active in the campaign against corruption by persuading others, including the European Union, to join in the fight. In a recent publication on corruption, he had this to say:

> Corruption is a problem that all countries have to confront. Solutions however, can only be home-grown. National leaders need to take a stand. Civil society plays a key role as well. . . . [W]e will support international efforts to fight corruption and to establish voluntary standards of behavior for corporations and investors in the industrialized world. . . . [T]he Bank Group will not tolerate corruption in the programs that we support, and we are taking steps to ensure that our activities continue to meet the highest standards of probity.[5]

This statement is particularly important because it recognizes that the bank, as well as many international organizations with lots of money, is part of the problem when it comes to corruption of senior government officials. They are indeed the supply side of the equation. A few years ago, an international consultant who is also a U.S. citizen told me that he had to stop working on a World Bank road construction project in a South American country. Mindful of the U.S. Foreign Corrupt Practices Act, he was afraid that he could be liable to criminal prosecution because of the way the World Bank task manager and the local contractor were conducting business. Other international organizations, bilateral donors, and foreign governments belatedly are taking steps to confront problems of corruption within their own ranks. Donors are pushing hard to achieve levels of accountability acceptable to their domestic constituencies. Still, it can be argued that due to the multiple roles these organizations play as lenders, donors, consultants, and clients, they often find themselves in compromising conflict-of-interest situations with governments, corporations, and even NGOs, which render them biased and ineffective in dealing with ethical questions and problems of corruption.

All available evidence points to the inevitable conclusion that corruption is bad for globalization. Exhibit 3.3 lists some of the specific areas in which corruption directly or indirectly negatively affects globalization by contributing to bad governance or poor economic management.

Exhibit 3.3
The Cost of Corruption for Globalization

1. Discriminates against foreign business and foreign capital. Discourages foreign direct investment, stimulates capital flight and brain drain, and attracts short-term speculative "hot money."

2. Impedes the growth of openness and competitiveness both domestically and with the rest of the world.

3. Encourages excessive government intervention in economic activities and discretionary regulations, leading to unfair practices and red tape. Executives are forced to spend too much time with government bureaucrats.

4. Contributes to market imperfections, distortions, and monopolistic practices. Government assets sold below market value; liabilities settled above cost.

5. Worsens misuse and misallocation of resources, away from socially desirable objectives to large "white elephant" capital projects most likely to attract large bribes and kickbacks. Inequitable and poor public services.

6. Discourages growth of small- and medium-size enterprises (SMEs), which are most critical for employment creation, innovation, competitiveness, and entrepreneurship.

7. Undermines the integrity of the banking and financial system by encouraging inside lending and unsecured loans.

8. Contributes to low levels of domestic saving and investment, low growth and productivity, reduced government revenue, and high consumption; acts as additional tax; and increases the cost and risk of doing business.

9. Puts politicians, senior civil servants, and private sector leaders in perpetual crosscutting conflict of interest situations, thus compromising professional judgment and managerial decision making.

10. Gives the country, society, institution, or business a bad name, poor reputation, and a lasting negative image both at home and internationally. Destroys reputation.

11. Contributes to poor quality of infrastructure, low operating and maintenance expenditures, and environmental degradation.

12. Is responsible for "privatization by cartel": public assets are sold to a few close family/political friends, regardless of their entrepreneurial abilities or lack thereof.

13. Contributes to poverty, inequality, exclusion, alienation, discord, disconnect, narrow nationalism, disharmony, and overall loss of social cohesion/capital necessary for transformational change.

14. Encourages popular support for military interventions or overthrow of elected government to be replaced by military dictatorship. Breeds political instability.

15. Undermines the state and public administration: disrespect and disregard for the institution of government and all that it represents

---

In general, corruption is bad for globalization because it weakens the state, undermines the market, demoralizes society, and alienates the outside world. It weakens the state through poor governance, reduced government revenue, lack of public respect, lost integrity of public officials, and overall institutional decay. As was shown in the previous chapter, a weak state is not good for globalization.

Corruption undermines the market by creating and perpetuating artificial market imperfections and preventing the normal functioning of competitive market forces. For example, a recent study of privatization in one of the Commonwealth of Independent States (CIS) found that formerly state-owned construction firms were sold to politicians, civil servants, and close associates who run the construction sector as a cartel rather than a competitive business. Worse still, corruption undermines the market by discouraging the growth of SMEs and the indigenous private sector. This is very harmful to the economy because these firms are best known for job creation, innovation, risk taking, and promoting overall competitiveness and entrepreneurship. SMEs cannot compete with big business when it comes to doing business by bribes.

Corruption demoralizes society in many different ways. It denies the people the opportunity to be the best they can be. It undermines their self-esteem and confidence in public institutions and private enterprise. It impoverishes and disempowers them. It forces them to live a life of dishonesty and lies. It alienates them from one another and creates social discord. It tears society apart. A disconnected society with so much pain does not have the necessary collective capacity for competitiveness, innovation, and equitable globalization. It is unrealistic to expect citizens to respect law and order when they are being brutalized by their own government.

Finally, corruption keeps foreign capital away. International capital goes where it is needed, but stays only where it feels welcome. Corruption discriminates against foreign business interests because local businesses are much closer to the politicians and civil servants. In another CIS example, public officials worked closely with local hotel owners to prevent foreigners from opening hotels in the country. By labeling certain industries as "strategic"—meaning that they are of national strategic importance—many developing countries in Africa and elsewhere have kept foreign capital out, deprived the economy of badly needed foreign investment, stifled innovation, and retarded growth and competitiveness. Corruption adds to the cost and risk of doing business and makes the corrupt country less competitive for foreign investment. The CIS study showed that in one country, foreign investors estimated that up to 40 percent of the cost of doing business in the first year of operation was spent on corruption. This explains why foreign investors ask for such high rates of return when they invest in chronically corrupt countries.[6] This message is very clear. Any country, society, institution, local government, business (small or large), and individual, if you are seriously interested in active and lasting participation in the global economy and global society, eradicate corruption first.

INDUSTRIAL POLICY IN A GLOBAL ECONOMY

In a globalizing economy, industrial policy formulation and implementation is key to wealth creation and income generation for society as a whole. Yet, this remains one of the most difficult public policy challenges for government and the private sector. There are a few reasons for these challenges: First, as the role of the state changes in economic management, corresponding market-friendly changes are required in the values, attitudes, and behavior of politicians, public servants, and civic leaders. In many cases, these changes have been slow to take root, and senior officials have not been consistent in their support for market-friendly industrial policies. Second, there has often been confusion and misunderstanding about the exact nature of the new role of government in an open globalizing economy.

The idea is not for government to abdicate its responsibility for providing leadership and strategic direction as would be suggested under pure laissez-faire conditions. Indeed, no country in the world practices pure laissez-faire economics. Therefore, the new role requires government officials to work as facilitators and champions of the overall strategic directions of the country's industrial policy and development. The role of the government is to remove the impediments to industrial policy development and implementation and to work closely with the private sector and the international community to ensure a positive sustaining enabling environment.[7]

A third area of challenge has been the absence of a capable and credible private sector to work with. Countries emerging out of Communism, socialism, colonialism, or conflicts do not have a viable private sector. In some cases, the emerging private sector is a reincarnation of the old regime in support of the old ideology and is connected to reactionary military, traditional, or criminal parts of society. When this happens, governments become both unable and unwilling to open up the economy for fear of being overthrown or taken over by reactionary or criminal forces.

Table 3.2 provides a list of key policy directions both before and in support of globalization. This list is a useful guide for both government and the private sector to assess the current industrial policy for the economy, to set specific goals and objectives for each of the strategic directions, and to develop a practical and realistic plan of action. For example, if the objective is to change the industrial policy from import substitution to export growth, specific objectives can be set and monitored through trade and export performance of the economy. Second, changing the direction from central planning and government ownership and control to a private sector—led economy can be achieved through privatization and private sector development. If the goal is to invite and encourage foreign

TABLE 3.2
Industrial Policy: Required Changes for Globalization

Before Globalization	*In Support of Globalization*
1. Import substitution	Export growth
2. Government ownership and control	Private sector lead, government facilitation
3. Restricted foreign ownership	Invited foreign ownership
4. Domestic savings	FDI, foreign capital
5. Natural resources, commodities	Value-added goods, services; wider mix
6. Cheap local labor	Technologists and knowledge workers
7. Limited infrastructure and utilities	World-class infrastructure and utilities
8. Few key trading partners	Regional free-trading arrangements, global markets; worldwide trading system
9. Limited demand for capital and technology	Growing demand for capital, technology, and innovation
10. Multinational corporations (MNCs) and state-owned enterprises (SOEs)	Indigenous SMEs and MNCs
11. Pollution allowed, tolerated	Green industries, environmental protection
12. Relative stability	Rapid change, holistic approach

ownership and participation in the economy, this can be assessed by looking at the legal and administrative systems in place, the extent to which it welcomes or discourages foreign investment, and the actual participation of foreign capital, technology, and management in the economy.

Before globalization, most developing economies depended on a few commodities for exports and domestic cash economy: in Ghana, it was cocoa; Brazil, coffee; Malaysia, rubber; and Australia and New Zealand, wool and mutton. With globalization, the economy needs to be diversified by using modern technology to create high-value-added goods and services sold to the global market. Indeed, successful globalizing economies are those which diversify their export portfolios and lessen their dependence on natural resources or commodities as the key exports. This does not mean neglecting traditional agricultural exports as Nigeria did with groundnuts; it means using the traditional exports as the basis for diversification. Malaysia provides a good example. At the time of independence in 1956, the country depended almost exclusively on commodities for exports. Today, its export portfolio includes electronic equipment, petroleum products, and textiles. For Nigeria, apart from petroleum products, it has no high-value-added goods or services in its export portfolio nor is it diversified.

Equally important is the diversification of trading partners from a few trading partners to increasing participation in the worldwide trading system. Many developing countries have historical ties to one or a few major trading partners resulting from former colonial ties. As the world trading system opens up and becomes more global, these countries need to diversify their trading partnerships and move closer to the global system. In some cases, this may start with one or several regional trading arrangements. Indeed, the world is now divided into regional trading blocks: in North America (NAFTA), Europe (EU), Asia (ASEAN), Pacific Rim

(APAC), Africa (COMESA, ECOWAS, TPA), South America (MERCOSUR), and South Asia (SAARC). These regional groupings have generally been positive in promoting openness, competitiveness, and trade, although some have been more successful than others. Yet, they should be seen as an interim arrangement toward a more worldwide trading system under the WTO. While developing countries benefit from and must be encouraged, and where necessary supported, to join a regional trading block, ultimately the objective should be to become active participants in the worldwide trading system.

Table 3.2 lists several other changes in key policy directions, which should be noted. Globalization requires significant policy changes in labor and employment. While the traditional approach is to draw on large pools of unskilled cheap labor and to support labor-intensive industries, with globalization, and given the need to produce high-end value-added goods and services, the emphasis changes to skilled technologists and knowledge workers. Technologists are those workers who combine both technical knowledge and manual skills. They are usually trained in community colleges or specialized technical schools, rather than academic universities. Examples include different types of technicians, automobile mechanics, health-care workers, and computer programmers. They are highly skilled and provide industry with a competitive comparative advantage. Developing countries unable to produce enough technologies are at a disadvantage because they do not have the human resources needed for producing nontraditional high-value-added goods and services. In fact, it has been argued that industrialized countries will continue to maintain a significant competitive edge over and above emerging economies as long as they educate and produce more technologists than the competition.[8]

Table 3.2 also suggests that with globalization there is a change in the mix of the major players in the industrial sector of the economy. Before globalization, the tendency is for the economy to be dominated by SOEs and selected invited MNCs. With globalization, the state gets out of direct productive and operational aspects of business, thus reducing the role and significance of SOEs. These are replaced by the emergence of indigenous SMEs run by independent entrepreneurs. As well, by opening up the economy, more foreign firms, big and small, become active participants, reducing the monopoly previously enjoyed by the select few multinationals. These changes encourage openness, competitiveness, and entrepreneurship—all of which are good for globalization.

Globalization brings greater pressures on industry to become socially responsible and to protect the environment. It is no longer acceptable for industry to pollute the air, water, and/or soil or otherwise harm the environment for industrial development and job creation. Government must make sure that it has the appropriate legal framework to protect the environment, the institutional capacity and human capital to enforce the rules, and the political will to punish the offenders. An increasing number of global businesses are beginning to take environmental concerns seriously and are taking practical steps to ensure that their operations are environmentally sound. Environmental audits have become an important part of corporate governance and reporting. Businesses that pollute the environment in the name of global competitiveness do more harm to globalization than the anarchists who demonstrate openly in opposition to globalization. Civil society—the press, NGOs—has a role to play in keeping government and business accountable and transparent in dealing with matters of environmental awareness and protection.

Finally, globalization changes the industrial policy environment from relatively stable and predictable to rapidly changing, complex, and uncertain. Therefore, managing change and transformations becomes an important capacity for all the players in bringing about the changes identified in Table 3.2. All these changes are interconnected and bring about both intended and unintended positive and adverse effects on different segments of society. In some countries, previously isolated villages have responded to openness by selling their produce to the outside market. While this has significantly increased their cash earnings, it has also made them more vulnerable to food shortages because nobody advised them of the need to keep some food in reserve instead of selling it all for cash. A government, in cooperation with the private sector, needs to develop sophisticated management systems and practices in order to anticipate and effectively manage both the expected and the unexpected changes and transformations resulting from changes in industrial policy for globalization. Risk assessment and management is a necessary critical competence for globalizing economies.

Overcoming Impediments to Industrial Development

In many cases, developing countries fail to pursue pro-globalization policies for industrial development, not for lack of good ideas but because of systemic impediments to policy implementation. Table 3.3 lists some of these impediments and suggested strategies to overcome them. One of the most serious impediments has to do with societal values and institutions. In many developing countries, societal values do not support the underlying values and principles of competitiveness, privatization, capitalism, individualism, and an economy largely driven by the private sector. In South Africa, Vietnam, Cambodia, and some of the Arab and Muslim countries, privatization and other related strategies of economic reform are slow and tentative because governments fear that these policies do not enjoy popular societal support. In the case of South Africa, the ruling African National Congress (ANC) has a long history of socialist ideology, has members of the Communist Party in its cabinet, and is strongly supported by the trade union movement COSATU which, like most unions the world over, is anti-globalization. As well, historically, the South African black population always associated capitalism with apartheid. Local industry is also dependent on cheap unskilled labor, especially in the mining and agricultural sectors. Accordingly, resistance to industrial transformation comes from all sides of the South African society.

Therefore, it is imperative that government provides leadership that will bring about changes in societal values. This is not easy and cannot be done overnight. Values can and do change through carefully designed programs such as public awareness, education, demonstration and pilot projects, various incentives, opportunities for influential community leaders and decision makers to travel abroad, and exposing society to different frames of reference. Participation is a very powerful instrument for bringing about sustaining changes in personal and societal values, attitudes, and behavior. As the old saying goes, "Tell me and I might forget, show me and I might remember, but involve me, and I will understand." Involving various segments of society in those aspects of industrial development for globalization which affects them most will help transform values, belief systems, attitudes, and behavior. In southern Africa where there is increasing pressure on the land, local communi-

TABLE 3.3
**Overcoming Impediments to Effective Industrial Development
and Implementation for Globalization**

Impediments	Strategies to overcome
1. Societal values and institutions	• Changes in societal values through : - Awareness - Education - demonstration/pilot projects - participation - travel abroad - incentives - changes in frame of reference
2. Political instability/lack of political will, leadership	• peace making/keeping • leadership development • change in leadership • policy development and implementation
3. Weak indigenous private sector	• supportive government policy • private sector development • privatization • entrepreneurship development
4. Lack of management know-how	• management consulting contracts • management training and development • staff interchange • overseas executive services
5. Lack of capital/resources/capacity	• mobilize domestic savings • encourage donors to give more targeted aid • foreign borrowing, equity, capital markets • FDI • Improve export earnings • Improve tax collection, government revenue • Build private-public institutional capacities • Recapitalize the financial and banking system
6. Exogenous variables	• Modeling • Risk assessment and management • Environmental scanning • Planning, monitoring, evaluation • Emergency management systems • Diversification : industry, sector, region • International collaboration

ties are often in conflict with wildlife conservation because there is not enough land for both human settlement and wildlife. In response, several countries have started to experiment with involving the local community in wildlife conservation and management. The communities are asked to share the land with wildlife, and in return, they participate in making wildlife management decisions and share in the resulting economic benefits. As a result, wildlife resources become community resources, and the community becomes the best frontline agent for conservation and fighting poaching.

For the weaker nation–states, especially those categorized as P2 in Chapter 1, a key impediment to effective implementation is political instability, lack of political will, and poor or misguided leadership. Here, any efforts at overcoming these impediments must start with peacemaking and peacekeeping initiatives. These initiatives are usually supported by an international or U.N. force. The last quarter of the twentieth century witnessed many nation–states either totally collapsed (for example, Somalia) or on the verge of collapsing (for example, Afghanistan, Sierra Leone, Cambodia, Haiti, Liberia, Congo, Rwanda). These countries are in no position to participate meaningfully in the global economy. Unfortunately, they are also in no position to stop the illegal globalization of their economies. This is done through the illegal exportation of minerals (such as diamonds), wildlife, drugs, human beings, and arms as well as other illegal trade. Under the Taliban regime, Afghanistan contributed 90 percent of the heroin sold on the streets of London. There are no short-term solutions or quick fixes for such weak states. Here, the international community must intervene and help build national institutions, develop new leadership, encourage change in leadership, and introduce new policies in support of rehabilitation and eventual development toward legitimate globalization. After the war, Vietnam's wounds were deep, industries weak, technology backward, infrastructure deplorable, and the country was unable to manage globalization to its advantage. For such countries, it may be advisable to close them off from the global economy until they have reestablished a strong state with credible governance systems.

The third impediment identified in Table 3.3 is the existence of a weak indigenous private sector. Before globalization, many developing countries were hostile to their own indigenous private sector, and many years of official harassment and unsupportive public policy have left the local private sector small, unorganized, poorly resourced and managed, and lacking in public esteem and respect. Globalization is not possible without a vibrant local/indigenous private sector. Steps can be taken to support the development of the sector; the most important of which is there must be a significant change in government policy and public support for the private sector. It is not enough for government to retreat from active participation in the economy; it must also make sure that it is replaced by a private sector with the capacity to perform and deliver results and the reputation, credibility, and support from the citizens it serves. Therefore, it may be necessary for government to undertake confidence-building measures between the private sector and the general public.

The fourth impediment is lack of management know-how in either the private or the public sector. The simplest way to address this is through management consulting contracts. There are many global management-consulting firms providing a wide range of expertise. Some developing countries have developed their own local consulting firms and may not need to buy the services on the open market. Some other countries prefer a combination of local and foreign consulting firms working together and reinforcing each other's areas of strength. No matter what mode of application a country chooses at different stages of development, it must understand the challenges and limitations of using management consultants.[9]

Other strategies for overcoming lack of management expertise include management training and development, staff interchange, and use of volunteer executive services from other countries. With many schools offering MBAs at various locations and on the Internet, the opportunities for management training and development have never been greater and are becoming less expensive. For most developing countries interested in managing globalization, there is room for more creative use of executive interchange both domestically—within a country but across sectors, industries, or regions—and internationally.

In addition to lack of management expertise, many developing countries experience generalized lack of capital, resources, and capacity for policy development and implementation. The strategies for overcoming these impediments are listed in Table 3.3 and include better mobilization and utilization of resources both at home and abroad, increased government revenues through a more efficient tax collection system, economic growth, wealth creation, and income generation. They also include building institutional capacities for policy analysis and implementation and attracting foreign capital and FDI (capital, technology, management).

Even after a country has taken steps to overcome these impediments, it may still find itself unable to effectively implement its industrial development policies or enjoy the benefits of globalization. This may be due to a group of impediments collectively referred to as "exogenous variables" in Table 3.3. These are "external" factors over which the country has no direct and effective control. The sources of exogenous variables are many and varied. As I have discussed, for weak states they may be associated with internal discord and the inability of the government to hold the country together let alone implement industrial development policies. They may be caused by acts of God, as often happens with small island and coastal states that periodically suffer from massive floods (for example, Bangladesh, India, Mozambique), hurricanes and typhoons (for example, the Caribbean), earthquakes (for example, Turkey), droughts (for example, Ethiopia), land slides (for example, Venezuela), or diseases such as HIV/AIDS or Ebola.

Exogenous variables also include changes going on elsewhere in the world that have profound effects on the fortunes or misfortunes of other countries. These may be technological, economic, political, or sociocultural changes. For example, changes in technology that make it possible for the world to produce cheaper and almost equally attractive synthetic products have profound negative effects on producers of natural products. Recent examples include wool (for example, Australia), leather (for example, the Middle East), ivory (for example, Africa), hardwood (for example, Ghana, Brazil, Indonesia), cotton (for example, Egypt), and rugs (for example, Iran). When this happens, the affected country needs to make immediate and fundamental changes to its industrial development policies and strategies. Technologically advanced countries with strong economies and institutional capacities can make these changes in a relatively short period of time with minimal adverse effects to the majority of the citizens. This is what happened, for example, when Switzerland lost world leadership in the production and marketing of watches to the Japanese when they invented digital and more functional watches. But the Swiss economy did not collapse. The affected watch-making firms and communities either adjusted to the new technological changes by producing and marketing watches that would compete with the Japanese or simply exited from the industry and invested in other sectors of the economy. Unfortunately, firms and communities in developing countries have very limited resources and capacities to make the necessary adjustments to technological change.

Changes in the world economy can also cause several exogenous variables, making it difficult for developing countries to effectively implement industrial development policies in support of globalization. These changes could cause the value of the U.S. dollar to go up significantly relative to the local currency, interest rates to rise, world oil prices to skyrocket in response to political changes in the Middle East, or commodity prices to rise or fall as a result of unexpected weather conditions in key producer countries. Any of these factors or combinations thereof can directly affect the country's capacity to pursue industrial development policies in support of globalization. Economic downturns in the United States and other industralized countries cause economic hardships to many developing and transition economies.

What strategies can a country use to protect itself against these exogenous variables? There are no easy solutions or quick fixes, especially for the weaker developing countries. Perhaps, the first and most important strategy is to create public awareness about the realities and possible advance consequences of exogenous variables. Economic crises are most painful and destructive when they are least expected. This is what happened to the Southeast Asian economies because before 1997–1998 they were considered "miracles" and therefore not subject to the normal economic cycle. On the other hand, when the government and its institutions, businesses, civil society, and the public in general are made aware of the likelihood of unanticipated events and their possible negative consequences, they can take individual and collective measures to protect their interests. The evidence from China supports this: Scientists have been able to predict earthquakes with increasing accuracy, thus allowing citizens to take defensive measures and reducing loss of life and property.

Other possible strategies against exogenous variables include modeling, risk management, strengthening planning systems at all levels of society, environmental scanning, and developing a national emergency management system. Modeling is commonly used in management and economics. In macroeconomics, it can be used to predict the effects on the national economy or parts thereof of changes in the value of the U.S. dollar, interest rates, oil prices, or terms of trade. For example, if a country has a large percentage of its external debt in U.S. dollars, modeling external debt management at different levels of exchange rates can reveal to the debtor the net effects on their cash flow and the levels at which it becomes impossible for them to keep up with debt payments.

Risk and Emergency Management

Risk management provides tools and techniques for controlling the effect of exogenous variables. It involves risk assessment—determining the level of risk associated with a given event or activity—and risk management, which involves taking steps to protect individuals or collective interests in line with the level of assessed risk. Everything we do in life involves a certain level of risk, but in most cases, we consider the risk involved so low that we hardly think about it. In other cases, the risks involved are considered high enough to necessitate taking practical steps to manage such risks. For example, crossing a residential street is considered a very low risk event, and for most people, no special steps are taken to manage the risk. On the other hand, driving a car and taking a plane trip are events associated with high enough levels of risk to require special risk management undertaking. In both cases, we buy insurance policies for protection, and for driving we are required to take training, driving tests, and certification for additional protection. Likewise, globalizing government institutions, societies, businesses, and individuals should assess the risks associated with various activities and take the necessary risk management measures as protection. Businesses buy insurance against operational losses, farmers buy insurance against crop failures due to a range of natural or human-made causes, and most individuals buy life insurance as protection against premature death. It makes sense for anybody in the public or private sector actively involved in globalization to take risk management steps, such as buying insurance, as protection against predictable and unintended adverse effects of globalization. To do otherwise is to expose oneself to dangerous and unacceptable levels of risk.

It is also possible to control the effects of exogenous variables by strengthening planning, monitoring, and evaluation systems. This can be done at both macro and micro levels involving the national government and its institutions, subnational governments, business firms, NGOs, or individual citizens. Planning is one of the most effective management tools business organizations use to mobilize resources and to achieve unity of purpose. Management sets strategic directions, develops business plans and operational targets, determines objectives, and establishes individual performance goals. Regular ongoing reporting is used to monitor performance, compare achievements vis-à-vis planned targets, and take corrective measures. Management is always looking for opportunities for continuous improvements. The public sector can learn and draw lessons from business organizations and use planning, monitoring, and evaluation tools to control the effects of exogenous variables on various aspects of globalization. While most public agencies do a fair amount of strategic and operational planning, they tend to be less rigorous when it comes to monitoring, evaluation, and taking corrective measures for continuous improvement. They tend to assume that plans are deterministic rather than probabilistic. Planning is not an exact science, and all the facts and important factors cannot be known at the time of planning. So every plan is associated with a probability that it may not be accomplished either in its entirely or parts thereof. This is why monitoring and evaluation are so important—as a basis for drawing out lessons of experience, which should inform subsequent planning and operations. One of the reasons why public agencies shy away from continuous monitoring and evaluation is because the results are often used for finger pointing rather than problem solving. Public servants feel threatened because feedback is used to punish employees rather than to encourage creativity.

Therefore, it is necessary for government agencies to create conditions for the development of learning communities/organizations as part of the management of globalization. A learning community refers to having the capacity to adapt to changes in the environment and to respond to lessons of experience by making changes to the way the community functions and people behave.[10]

Table 3.3 suggests that developing emergency management systems would help developing countries in dealing with the effects of exogenous variables. Most developing countries are susceptible to emergencies and crises. While some of these are due to natural causes, many are due to weaknesses in the systems and structures that exist in these countries. For example, the physical infrastructure is often weak, overworked, and underserviced with minimal and infrequent repairs and maintenance. The technology used is often old, and new technology may be pirated. There is often a shortage of experienced technologists, and management is also in short supply. Opportunities for skills training and upgrading are limited. Budgetary limitations make it difficult to upgrade equipment and to undertake necessary repairs and maintenance, especially if these require foreign currency expenditures.

Therefore, as part of their industrial policy for globalization, developing countries need to develop multilevel emergency management systems in preparation for emergencies or crises. These systems should be able to deal with disasters, epidemics, industrial accidents, food and gasoline shortages, rationing, factory closures, massive layoffs, liquidity problems, political unrest, and economic crises. Once again, government needs to work in partnership with the private sector, other levels of government, civil society, and the international community to ensure that effective practical arrangements are in place and that all sectors of society are actively involved in the design and implementation of the country's emergency management systems. If developing countries cannot rule out the likelihood of emergencies and crises arising from activities associated with globalization, the least they can do is put in place effective emergency and crises management systems. These measures would not prevent crises from taking place but would help to mitigate their negative consequences.

Diversification

Another exogenous variable is diversification. Diversification as part of industrial policy is not new, but with globalization, it becomes much more significant. Diversification as part of a country's industrial development strategy means that a country develops capacities, competencies, and competitive advantages for producing a wider range of marketable goods and services. Its advantages include distribution of risks and rewards and providing a broader industrial knowledge base and competitive advantage, broader export base, more trading partners, and more opportunities for spin-offs and entrepreneurial development in different sectors and regions of the economy.

Diversification strategies can be developed by industry, sector, or region. Within industry, it is common to think in terms of the new (high-tech) economy, and the old economy. While developing countries can pursue opportunities in the new economy such as international call centers and data processing in India and electronic assembling in the Philippines and Costa Rica, they should not forget opportunities in the old economy. The old economy such as textiles, food-processing services, and light manufacturing is still important and continues to offer these countries greater competitive advantages and niche opportunities. Indeed, it appears that the more successful globalizing developing countries are pursuing this strategy. For example, while pursuing industrial opportunities in the new economy, Thailand continues to export high-value agricultural products such as seafood and rice and provides attractive world-class tourist services. Likewise, Chile's economic recovery and growth is largely based on the old economy of mining, especially copper that makes up almost 40 percent of exports by value, and high-value-added agricultural products including wine, fruits, and high-quality wood products. At the other end of the spectrum, the challenge for globalizing countries, such as Ghana, is to diversify the economy, especially the export base. Ghana continues to depend on exports of mining (gold, bauxite) and agriculture (cocoa) with a rather small and underdeveloped tourist industry. What the country now needs is to develop niche specialization, which will allow it to produce high-value products or services marketable to the global market.

The third area of diversification is by region. Many developing countries have large territories or landmasses with a variety of natural and human resources. These provide opportunities for regional diversification of industrial development for globalization. Coastal areas rich in marine life and tourist attractions, interior forests teeming with plant and animal life, dry desertlike lands with rolling sand dunes, and mountain ranges capped with snow all year round all provide fertile grounds for the development of regional economic specialization.

One of the subsectors that offers developing countries greater but as yet unexploited opportunities is agri food for the global market. These countries have interesting variations in topography, soil types, and climatic conditions and an abundant supply of freshwater. They have a large supply of inexpensive labor: young, eager to work, and easy to train. On the demand side, there are a number of factors that also work in their favor. The world population is growing, and almost all of this growth is in developing countries. More people are moving into urban areas where they are increasingly dependent on commerce for food supplies. Many of the world's hungry and those who do not get adequate nutrients in their diets are in developing countries. As income rises, tastes and eating habits change, and people seek high-value, specialty food for enjoyment. With globalization also comes multiculturalism, which means that foods previously found in one part of the world are now successfully marketed globally. Examples include Mexican food, Italian pasta, Chinese and Thai food, and Indian curry.

Looking for niche markets in the agri-food business, developing countries can draw on and take advantage of various technological advances and management know-how in areas such as biotechnology, genetic engineering, marine science, farm management, international marketing, and transportation including canning, packaging, and shipping. Recent experiences seem to suggest that the agri-food business is relatively easy for developing and emerging economies. Witness how fast Eastern Europe has been able to revive its wine industry in a relatively short period of time. Competitive wines are now available on the world market from Bulgaria, Hungary, Croatia, and Romania. South African exports include wine and other agri-food products. Countries such as Brazil, Argentina, Sudan, South Africa, Iran, Indonesia, Syria, and Ukraine have a lot of potential for producing specialized high-value regional goods and services for the global economy. What developing countries need is diversification that cuts across industrial, sectoral, and regional dimensions and brings together private–public partnerships drawn from both the indigenous private sector and international business.

PRIVATIZATION AND PRIVATE SECTOR DEVELOPMENT

A lot has been written on privatization and private sector development by academics, journalists, governments, and international organizations. Most of the literature is not neutral; rather, it speaks either for or against privatization. The keen interest and intensity is quite understandable. Privatization is at the core of political and socioeconomic reforms for all globalizing countries. It is controversial in terms of ideology, objectives, processes, and results. It significantly changes the role of the state from owner and manager of productive assets to partner, facilitator, or enabler of economic development. Like globalization, it produces winners as well as losers. Needless to say, the ideological debate is not about to be settled anytime soon.

Our interest here is not to review the literature on privatization and private sector development or to weigh in on the ideological debate. Rather, the purpose is to discuss briefly the relationship between privatization and private sector development and globalization. The question of interest here is whether developing countries and transition economies enhance their capacities for meaningful participation in the global economy through privatization and private sector development. We are also interested in drawing out lessons of experience from privatizing countries for the benefit of others. It should be pointed out at the outset that privatization is not an issue only for developing countries. Rich, industrialized countries also face challenges of privatization, although the net impact may be greater for the poor countries.

The three common forms of privatization are:

1. Partial or complete sale of SOEs to new private sector owners,
2. Private provision of public services,
3. Alternative service delivery arrangements.

Most of the discussions on privatization focus on the sale of public enterprise (SOEs) to the private sector. For most developing countries, this form of privatization is the most practical manifestation of public commitment to reform and, ultimately, to globalization. During the period 1980–1991, a total of 2,162 SOEs were privatized in developing countries representing all regions of the world—Latin America and the Caribbean (37 percent) and Eastern Europe (37 percent) had the largest percentage and sub-Saharan Africa (17 percent), Asia (6 percent), and the Middle East and North Africa (3 percent) had the smallest percentage. With all its economic, management, legal, technical, and social problems, privatization—sale of SOEs—on the whole has benefited the countries and their citizens.[11]

Private provision of public goods and services is an extension to the privatization of SOEs. Here, instead of the government selling public assets, it invites the private sector, through a process of competitive bidding, to provide a defined set of public services for profit. These may be social services such as health care and welfare administration; utilities such as water, roads, and electricity; or security services such as prisons, or in the case of weak states, private military service. These services are usually provided under contract, which, among other things, specifies the expected level of performance, the cost of providing the services, and the duration of the contract. The government retains responsibility for the management of the contract and the supervision, monitoring, and evaluation of the services. The contract can be suspended or cancelled if the private contractor does not meet performance specifications, and contract renewal is subject to review and competition. The private sector contractors may be drawn from the local business community, NGOs, academic institutions, foreign companies or institutions, or combinations thereof. Sometimes, government agencies can also bid to get their jobs back through a competitive process. They can do this individually or in partnership with private sector organizations.[12]

Alternative service delivery (ASD) is derived from the idea that there is no one simple best way of managing and providing services to the public. As part of the new public management paradigm, ASD is a creative attempt to find solutions to the government challenge of meeting the growing and changing demands and expectations of the citizens, within the context of increasing citizen awareness of service delivery options and value for money. ASD can be defined as a creative and dynamic process of public sector management and restructuring that aims to improve the delivery of services to citizens or clients by sharing governance and operational functions with individuals, community groups, business organizations, and other government agencies. Some of the common delivery options include co-location, single-window service centers, common-service providers, special operating agencies, and other forms of government-owned but commercially operated organizations such as airports. Although they may have different operating rules, all these arrangements share one common characteristic: They are still managed and directed from inside government. Therefore, ASD mechanisms combine some of the aspects of privatization (private operators) and the private provision of public service (government ownership). They are also different in that they deliberately treat the citizens as an informed and active participant and decision maker in the design and delivery of important public services.

ASD is a form of private–public partnership arrangement. It facilitates the pooling together of resources, capacities, skills, and experiences from all sectors of society instead of depending only on government agencies. The tools associated with ASD mechanisms allow governments to tailor various options to meet prevailing needs on the ground, challenge traditional hierarchical structures, and allow public servants in partnership with others the flexibility to adapt to the changing environment of public administration and economic management.[13]

Having defined the parameters of privatization, let's now address the question of how all this relates to globalization. First, all three types of privatization—sale of SOEs, private provision of public service, and ASD—reduce the burden of administration to the state. SOEs traditionally lose money and are a constant drain on the national treasury. Selling them reduces the financial burden of the state, including foreign debts and contingent liabilities. The other two types of privatization also reduce the burden of management for the state as private sector operators take over some of the functions and responsibilities previously handled by the state alone. Contracting out public services usually contributes to a smaller and more streamlined public service. The social burdens arising from privatization can also be shared with the private sector, which can provide creative solutions or social safety nets for those who are left behind. The more these burdens are removed from the state, the more politicians and senior civil servants are freed up to concentrate their efforts on good governance and creating an enabling environment for globalization.

Privatization contributes to enterprise efficiency, creativity, transparency, and accountability. There are many examples in which money-losing SOEs have been privatized and turned into profitable ongoing enterprises. Privatized enterprises provide better services, operate more efficiently, introduce more new products and services, and have a better and regular reporting relationship with their stockholders. This commercial approach to enterprise management contributes to the development of a local business-like climate and a culture of entrepreneurship. These developments help to prepare the local population for globalization and make the country attractive to outside investment.

Privatization also generates revenue for the treasury. Sales of SOEs generate millions of dollars, whereas the other two types save governments money by providing services at reduced costs. The additional revenue allows the government to spend more on social services and to build up the national infrastructure. Both of these are necessary preconditions for effective globalization.

Privatization also encourages and prepares the ground for the development of a local indigenous private sector. Some countries, such as Indonesia, insist on local participation in the privatization of SOEs, government contracting, and ASD. Foreigners with capital, technology, and management expertise are required to form alliances with local businesses in order to qualify to bid on large government contracts or sales. Although this can lead to abuse by the government choosing winners, if done openly and competitively, it has the potential of providing local businesses with the boost they need to grow and to become globally competitive. It also provides foreign businesses the opportunity to work in partnership with those who are intimately knowledgeable about and experienced with the local political economy, culture, and business practices. The partners give each other a window into the unknown: Foreigners learn about the local society, and the local partners learn about international business and the global economy. These personal relationships can be instrumental in subsequent development of outside contacts for globalization.

Privatization also has the added advantage of bringing together various sectors of society to learn to work collaboratively in partnership. The private provision of public services and ASD are particularly good in advancing private–public collaboration because they both seek organizational arrangements that facilitate participation from across institutions, sectors, and regions. This gives rise to the development of institutional capacities and human competencies such as corporate governance, negotiations, conflict management, dispute resolution, organizational restructuring, change management, and cross-cultural decision making, information sharing, and joint problem solving. All these capacities and competencies are necessary for managing globalization.

Exhibit 3.4 illustrates some of the lessons of experience of deregulating, corporatizing, and privatizing of telecommunications services in Indonesia. The first lesson speaks to the need for planning. The reform followed a long process of technical, economic, social, political, and managerial planning by Indonesians with the help of outside experts. This process allowed the government to evaluate different reform and privatization options before deciding on a course of action. For example, the use of a joint operations scheme (JOS; see Exhibit 3.4) and division of the country into separate telecommunications market areas was aimed at ensuring development of telecommunications services in rural, remote, and isolated areas. It was also aimed at responding to local pressures for indigenous participation by insisting on local leadership for each bidding consortium. The JOS also ensured international competition because each of the five consortia would include a foreign telecommunications firm with the necessary capital, technology, and management expertise. This was important because directly and indirectly, through donors and financing agencies such as the World Bank, Indonesia was getting pressure from powerful and influential countries such as Japan, the United States, Australia, the Netherlands, and Germany for their national telecommunications firms to get a piece of the action in the Indonesian growing market.

Exhibit 3.4
Indonesia: Telcom Privatization and Globalization

Background: By the mid-1980s, Indonesian planners had concluded that the country needed a more modern, functioning, nationwide telecommunications network to meet the growing demand of a "miracle" economy. In 1988, the government launched a U.S.$4.5 billion expansion program, introduced the integrated service digital network and more than doubled the number of telephone lines from 0.75 million in 1982 to 2.2 million in 1992. In 1991, the country's domestic telecommunications provider, PT. Telkom (PTO) was inaugurated as a state-owned limited liability company from a state corporation (PERUMTEL). This legal-administrative reform initiative was designed to give PTO the corporate authority and responsibility to play the lead role in fulfilling the country's telecommunications development plans.

The Plan: PTO responded to the challenge by developing a very ambitious five-year (1994–1998) corporate plan, which among other things included:

1. Target network expansion from 3 million to 8 million new line units;

2. Line unit subscriber growth from 1.8 million to 6 million;

3. Improvements in service completion ratio from 45 percent to 65percent local, and from 36 percent to 45 percent long distance;

4. Target financial performance in the range of 16–18 percent rate of return on investment;

5. Complete change of PTO as an organization from a bureaucratic state monopoly driven by technology to a more organic, competitive, market-driven, flexible organization responsive to the needs of its multiple clients and stakeholders at home and abroad.

The president-director of PTO described the corporate plan as the fastest infrastructure expansion ever attempted anywhere in the world. The strategy for achieving the plan targets was multifaceted, involving the resources of nearly a dozen countries and specific areas of expertise from more than five countries. Yet, control of PTO was to remain in Indonesian hands for reasons of "national security."

Challenge: Despite all the reform measures, the physical expansion and service improvement were not keeping up with the rapidly growing and changing telecommunications demand for the Indonesian economy and society. Performance measures such as call completion rates, telephone failure rates, and teledensity were all below ASEAN averages. A more serious challenge was the realization in 1994 that there was serious underutilization of new telecommunications infrastructure, suggesting that PTO did not have the necessary institutional capacity and human competencies to meet the targets of its corporate goals. (*Note:* The term *call completion* is used in telecommunications to refer to the rate at which calls are successfully completed on first attempt.)

Joint Operations Scheme: In response to PTO's challenges, the supervising ministry established a JOS whose purpose was to provide an institutional framework to screen and select domestic and international private sector partners with whom PTO would have to work to achieve its corporate goals. JOS made the following arrangements:

- The country was divided into twelve telecommunications service areas (WITELS) each with separate targets, but these were later collapsed into five large markets in order to attract foreign investors.

- Excluding Jakarta and Surabaya, a total of 2 million new line units were to be added at an estimated total cost of U.S.$2.4 billion.

- JOS participants were to come from national private sector companies, national or provincial SOEs, cooperatives, NGOs, or MNCs.

- Interested partners were to organize themselves into consortiums, each with a maximum of five corporate entities.

- Indonesian companies were required to lead the consortium.

- A consortium that included a cooperative or a local small- or medium-size company would receive special consideration from the government.

- Each consortium had to include a reputable telecommunications company with the necessary capital, technology, and management expertise.

- Each consortium was to perform the following functions: planning, engineering, construction, operations, human resource development, and technology transfer. Operations included marketing, maintenance, and related operational management functions.

- Each consortium would share revenue with PTO in the ratio of 70:30.

Source: Based on the results of a field research project in 1994, partly published by Moses N. Kiggundu, "Capacity Development for Managing Telecommunications Reform and Restructuring: A Corporate Approach from Indonesia," *Journal of Asian Business* 13, no. 12 (1997):19–57.

Another important lesson from the Indonesian experience is the importance of having the right legal framework for deregulation and privatization. Indonesia reformed the PTO's legal framework by upgrading it from a government department to a corporate entity. Corporatization gave it the autonomy and responsibility to conduct business with local and foreign firms and to pursue its own corporate mission and business objectives, separate from the supervising ministry. It sent out the message to the outside investors that government was serious about reform and privatization. Yet, PTO still remained as a state monopoly. Private investors could not operate in the country independently—they needed to be licensed through PTO. The supervising ministry still controlled PTO, its operations, and investments. The government took out as much as 50 percent of PTO's profits for general purposes, leaving the corporation with a shortage of investment capital. Therefore, while the reform of the legal framework was moving in the right direction, there were serious impediments to corporatization and privatization that needed to be addressed.[14]

The Indonesian experience also teaches us the importance of time and the need to learn from reform experiences. Things did not happen as fast as the planners had hoped. PTO did not have the institutional capacity or the human capital for the effective implementation of the five-year corporate plan. For example, a March 1994 report by Japan's Overseas Economic Cooperation Fund concluded that:

> [p]roblems or difficulties . . . remain unresolved . . . in asynchronization among subsystem expansion programs, poor quality of services and low productivity. . . . [D]iscrepancy of numbers between installed switching capacity and newly installed subscribers is considerable due to unsatisfactory coordination and synchronization among subsystem expansion programs and inaccuracy of demand forecast. One of the major causes for unsatisfactory

coordination among subsystem constructions comes from separately planned programs. . . . OSP (outside plant) and transmission were planned separately with separate funds.[15]

The president-director of PTO seemed to agree with this assessment when he admitted to a local telecommunications gathering, "My minister asks me, 'Are you ready for competition?' I say yes, but my 43,000 employees are not yet ready." A detailed study of capacity assessment identified many operational and managerial gaps where PTO needed significant improvements. These included improvements in network management; service, repair, and maintenance; contract management; managing domestic and international alliances; and change management especially relating to strategic management of major business shifts and internal corporate changes. PTO had no sales or marketing experience because, as a monopoly, it did not have to compete for customers, but instead maintained a ten-year waiting list for residential telephone installations. PTO needed resources and time to build the necessary institutional capacity and human capital to undertake the necessary reforms and to meet its corporate goals and objectives.

One of the advantages of corporatization is that it helps to introduce competitiveness and a business-like culture, know-how, and discipline with modern management. For PTO, this included the development of a corporate and business plan for the first time and learning to focus on the market and the customers instead of focusing on technology and the bureaucracy only (internal operations). PTO started taking human resource development seriously and was measuring performance by results rather than inputs. Still, one area that needed much improvement was the management of all the private sector alliances arising out of the JOS (see Exhibit 3.4). Some thought that these were marriages of convenience, whereas others were concerned that they perpetuated cronyism rather than reform.[16]

Exhibit 3.5 provides a brief description of Mozambique's experience with reforming the cashew industry, with contrasting lessons from Indonesia.

Exhibit 3.5
Mozambique's Cashew Industry: Challenges of Globalization

Background: In 1975 when Mozambique gained independence after a bloody civil war, it was still the world's leading cashew producer, and processed cashew kernels were the country's most important export. But the war had taken its toll on the industry. By the early 1990s, production had significantly declined. The national cashew orchards had a large proportion of old and diseased trees. The state-owned processing plants badly needed new capital, technology, and management expertise. Something had to be done soon.

Reforms: The cashew industry was privatized. The state cashew company was broken up and sold off to local Mozambican companies on the assumption that the industry would continue to enjoy government protection from foreign competition. In 1995, as a condition for more than U.S.$400 million in loans, the World Bank demanded the liberalization of the cashew industry. Accordingly, the export surtax on raw nuts was reduced from a high of 26 percent to 14 percent. This would encourage the export of raw cashews but not discourage domestic processing. Domestic processing was discouraged because the plants were considered inefficient, and the reduction in export taxes was expected to benefit farmers.

Challenges: Within three years, ten out of the fifteen sizable processing plants had closed; more than 5,000 workers were laid off. Under the new arrangements, it became impossible for the industry to compete with traders selling raw nuts to places such as India. An independent study by Deloitte and Touche concluded that the reforms were benefiting the traders, not the farmers. It also found that the country would earn an extra U.S.$150 per ton by processing the cashews locally rather than exporting raw nuts. Parliament then intervened and put a ban on exporting raw cashew nuts for ten years and passed a compromise bill raising the surtax to between 18 percent and 22 percent, depending on prevailing economic conditions. The World Bank did not object to these new arrangements.

Source: Based on information in "Africa Recovery," United Nations Department of Public Information, 14, no. 3 (October 2000):15. Also available at www.un.org/ecosocdev/geninfo/afrec.

With Mozambique, there does not seem to have been adequate local planning and consultation with the various private–public interest groups. The government of Mozambique seems to have relied almost exclusively on outsiders for information, analysis, and advice— as it turned out some of the advice was wrong. The failure to bring together the cashew farmers, traders, and exporters with various government departments and agencies (for example, industry, finance, agriculture) meant that there was no local common understanding and commitment to reform. As expected, the lack of consultation on the ground bred resentment and resistance to reform. This made it difficult for the government to manage and deal with the adverse consequence of the reform.

Another lesson from the Mozambique experience is the apparent lack of direct involvement of private sector foreign investors with intimate knowledge about the cashew business in a global economy. While the major telecommunications companies of the major industrialized countries were actively lobbying for active participation in Indonesia's telecommunications reform, there were no equivalent foreign private investors seeking to participate in restructuring of the cashew industry in Mozambique. As often happens with most of the weaker developing countries (P2 countries), Mozambique depended too much on the advice of the U.N. agencies rather than drawing on the practical expertise of the relevant international private sector. Consequently, Mozambique's reform program did not make a serious attempt to modernize the industry by means of new capital, technology, and management expertise. The changes in taxation were perhaps necessary but not sufficient to bring about the needed changes in the cashew industry and to make it globally competitive.

It is also clear that both the government and the industry—farmers, traders, factory owners, exporters—did not have sufficient understanding and capacity to sustain the reforms, modernize the industry, and become globally competitive. Unlike the Indonesian case, no serious attempts were made in Mozambique to develop the local indigenous private sector.

Mozambique represents many cases, especially in weak developing countries involved in premature deregulation and privatization. When the local key players, in both the public and the private sector, are not ready for reform and if no attempts are made first to bring them together, enhance their understanding, and build capacities, moving ahead with deregulation and privatization can create opportunities for exploitable globalization. This is when smuggling, tax evasion, and other criminal activities including civil war become the inevitable consequences of premature globalization. It is important for globalizing countries to experience successes early on in the process for positive reinforcement. Unmanageable negative consequences do more harm than good, not only to the directly affected individuals and institutions but also to the entire society and its overall support for openness and globalization. International assistance and intervention, carefully conceived and implemented, can help mitigate the dangers of false start.

NOTES

1. For a detailed discussion of the Belgian king's brutal partnership dealings and their legacy on Africa's possible understanding of globalization, see Adam Hochschild, *King Leopold's Ghost: A Story of Greed, Terror, and Heroism in Colonial Africa* (New York: Houghton Mifflin, 1898). For European explorers, see David S. Landes, *The Wealth and Poverty of Nations: Why Some Are So Rich and Some So Poor* (New York: Norton, 1998), chap. 2. For an enjoyable fictional account, see Barbara Kingsolver, *The Poisonwood Bible* (New York: HarperPerennial, 1999).

2. Transparency International, *Transparency International Sourcebook* (Berlin: Transparency International, 1996), 1.

3. Emphasis added; quoted from Petter Langseth, Rick Stapenhurst, and Jeremy Pape, "National Integrity System: Country Studies," EDI Working Paper 400/144/E1978 (Washington, DC: World Bank, Regulatory Reform and Private Enterprise Division, 1997), 10.

4. There is an incredible amount of literature on corruption. Rather than providing a partial list here, the interested reader is advised to visit the Anti-corruption Knowledge Center, which is part of the World Bank (www.worldbank.org) and has an annotated bibliography. Transparency International, a nongovernment international organization, is by far the most authoritative source of information on global corruption. It brings together civil society, business, and government in a powerful coalition against corruption. Readers are encouraged to visit the organization's Web site (www.transparency.org), especially the annual sourcebooks.

5. James D. Wolfensohn, Bank–Fund annual meeting speech. Cited in Langseth, Stapenhurst, and Pape, "National Integrity System," iii. For a humorous account of official corruption of World

Bank funded projects, see Robert Klitgaard, *Tropical Gangsters: One Man's Experience with Development and Decadence in Deepest Africa* (New York: Basic Books, 1990).

6. For case studies of corruption and its effects on governance and economic management in different regions, see Vito Tanzi and Hamid Davoodi, "Roads to Nowhere: How Corruption in Public Investment Hurts Growth," Economic Issues Paper 12 (Washington, DC: IMF, 1989); and Thomas Wolf and Emine Gurgen, "Improving Governance and Fighting Corruption in the Baltic and CIS Countries: The Role of the IMF," Economic Issues Paper 21 (Washington, DC: IMF, 2000). For South Asia, see Robert Klitgaard and Heather Baser, "Working Together to Fight Corruption: State, Society, and the Private Sector in Partnership," in *Building Government–Citizen–Business Partnerships*, ed. Suzanne Taschereau and Jose Edgardo L. Campos (Ottawa: Institute on Governance, 1997), 59–81.

7. For a discussion of the changing role of government in industrial policy development for emerging economies, see Wolfgang H. Thomas, "Mixing Market Freedom and Social Planning: In Search of Appropriate Economic Policies," in *Policy Options for South Africa*, ed. Fannie Cloete, Lawrence Schlemmer, and Daan van Vuure (Pretoria: Human Sciences Research Council, 1991), 203–220; and Philip Frankel, "Business and Politics: Towards a Strategy," in *Critical Choices for South Africa: An Agenda for the 1999s*, ed. Robert Schrire (Cape Town: Oxford University Press, 1990), 393–410.

8. In his recent book, Peter Drucker makes a distinction among manual workers, technologists, and knowledge workers. See his *Management Challenges for the 21st Century* (New York: Harper Business, 1999), 145–154.

9. For a critical assessment of the role of foreign consultants for developing countries, see Moses N. Kiggundu, "Outside Consultants: Dilemma for Developing Countries," *Business Forum* (Summer 1989):23–26. For an advocate of local consultants, see Frederick J. Kaijage, ed., *Managing Consultants in Africa: Utilizing Local Expertise* (West Hartford, CT: Kumarian, 1993). Also see, "Trimming the Fat: A Survey of Management Consultancy," *The Economist*, March, 22, 1997, pp. 1–22.

10. For a discussion of the concept of the learning organization, see Anthony J. DiBella and Edwin C. Nevis, *How Organizations Learn: An Integrated Strategy for Building Learning Capability* (San Francisco: Jossey-Bass, 1998).

11. For evidence of the benefits of privatization in different parts of the world, see Sunita Kikeri, John Nellis, and Mary Shirley *Privatization: Lessons of Experience* (Washington, DC: World Bank, 1992).

12. For an early but detailed discussion of private participation in public management, see Gabriel Roth, *The Private Provision of Public Services in Developing Countries* (New York: Oxford University Press, 1987).

13. For a detailed discussion of ASD, see Robin Ford and David Zussman, *Alternative Service Delivery: Transcending Boundaries* (Toronto: KPMG Center for Government Foundation and the Institute of Public Administration of Canada, 1997).

14. For a discussion of the legal implications of privatization, see Pierre Guislain, "Divestiture of State Enterprises: An Overview of the Legal Framework," Technical Paper 186 (Washington, DC: World Bank, 1992).

15. Overseas Economic Cooperation Fund, *Final Report on Special Assistance for Project Sustainability on Telecommunications Projects in Indonesia* (Bandung, Indonesia: SAPS Team for Overseas Economic Cooperation Fund, 1994), chaps. 2 and 3.

16. Discussion of Indonesia's telecommunications reforms are based on Moses N. Kiggundu, "Capacity Development for Managing Telecommunications Reform and Restructuring: A Corporate Approach from Indonesia," *Journal of Asian Business* 13, no. 2 (1997):19–57. Also see Overseas Economic Cooperation Fund, *Final Report*.

CHAPTER 4

Globalization and Entrepreneurship

Globalization needs entrepreneurs. No country in the world has made it as a significant, active, and meaningful player in the global economy and global society without a critical mass of entrepreneurs operating in a supportive but competitive environment. The level and quality of entrepreneurship is a good indicator of overall development of society and readiness for globalization. Historically, countries with successful entrepreneurs operating in different societal endeavors have achieved faster rates of economic growth, enjoyed more broad-based improvements in peoples' standards of living and quality of life, and participated more competitively in the global economy and global society. The lesson from history is clear: Any developing country or economy in transition wishing to gainfully participate in globalization must have in its midst a dynamic critical mass of active entrepreneurs operating in all sectors of society. The state must actively support and help create a positive environment for the development and renewal of this kind of entrepreneurship.

WHAT IS ENTREPRENEURSHIP?

Although there are many different definitions of entrepreneurship, most of which are related to business activities motivated by financial gain, here I take a more generic approach to include other forms of entrepreneurship. Following Joseph Schumpeter, I define entrepreneurship simply as a process of "creative destruction"—the continuing cycle of destroying the old and less-efficient or appropriate system, process, procedure, product, or service and replacing it with more efficient or relevant ones. This process of creative destruction is not only limited to business activities, it is equally relevant in public administration, politics, the military, the arts, the voluntary sectors, and society in general. The more widespread entrepreneurship is across levels and sectors of society, the better the chances of progress and advancement for the majority of the people of that society. [1]

There are four characteristics associated with entrepreneurial activities: the capacity to conceive or identify an opportunity for creative destruction, the ability and willingness (motivation) to act on the perceived opportunity, the mobilization and organization of resources to persevere in the pursuit of the opportunity to its logical conclusion, and the need for ongoing support and reinforcement from the relevant environment. The environment plays such an important role in the promotion of entrepreneurship that many observers have blamed it for the lack of dynamic entrepreneurship in many developing countries, Communist and Socialist countries of Eastern Europe, and elsewhere. Likewise, many have argued that, as it was with Britain two hundred years ago, American superpower status and economic might are driven and sustained by a formidable entrepreneurial class competitively supported and positively reinforced by all institutions of the state, the market, and society as a whole. In a globalizing society, entrepreneurship is everybody's business.

WHY ARE SOME SOCIETIES MORE ENTREPRENEURIAL THAN OTHERS?

It is important to state at the very beginning that there is no consensus as to why some societies are more entrepreneurial than others. There is also no consensus as to whether a more entrepreneurial spirit is a good thing for society as a whole. There are those who argue that entrepreneurship, individualism, and competitiveness are Western values that should not be encouraged in the cultures of other societies. These are, indeed, very interesting and challenging arguments especially in a world not only globalizing but also glocalizing. Unfortunately, a full treatment of the whole debate is beyond the scope of this book. Instead, I shall proceed to examine the factors that promote or impede the development of entrepreneurship and leave it to individuals—countries, societies, institutions, businesses—to decide on the merits or otherwise of promoting entrepreneurship for their own growth and development.

Economic Conditions

Five economic conditions seem to be associated with the development of entrepreneurship. The first has to do with productivity. This is the ability to operate, manage, and build the systems or instruments of production and to create, adapt, and master new methods or techniques using the most advanced technology possible. This is where the process of creative destruction is put into practice. It involves three stages: First is the realization that the old method(s) of doing business is unsatisfactory, inefficient, costly, dated, uncompetitive, and needs to be destroyed. The second stage is the creation of a better, modern, more competitive method to replace the old. The third stage is using the new method and realizing the anticipated benefits. The skills and competencies required for these three stages are varied, including creativity, engineering, adaptation, operations, and an overall change in management. It is unlikely that all these skills and competencies will be found within a single individual. This explains why in most cases entrepreneurship is a collaborative effort involving close partnerships between or among individuals with complementary attributes. It also explains why in some societies entrepreneurship fails: because the people are not used to working together collaboratively.

The second economic condition has to do with learning. This is the ability to impart knowledge and know-how to the younger generation either through formal education or apprenticeship training. Intergenerational learning for economic performance and continuing competitiveness differs from learning for the preservation of social traditions, culture, and religious beliefs and practices. With the former, it is important to decide what aspect of the knowledge and know-how to pass on, which one to discard, and how much new knowledge and know-how to introduce. These decisions affect the economic performance and competitiveness of subsequent generations as they grow up and take over the management of the economy. The most effective way of making these learning decisions is through entrepreneurial activities so that individual entrepreneurs are allowed to destroy and create and let the market choose the winners or losers within the context of the state and society.

In Western civilization, this learning is both formal—conducted in schools, colleges, universities, and places of work—and informal—passed on within families, villages, communities, industries, sectors, and regions. As society becomes more multicultural and urban and as the technological changes require more new knowledge and know-how, more and more of the learning is done formally through training institutions. Still, the old industries continue to pass on practical knowledge informally through long periods of apprenticeships. For example, in the Netherlands, they still make pottery in the same old way, and the best way to learn is not to go to school but to work with the village people whose families have been in the pottery business for generations. Likewise, stone and wood carving knowledge and know-how in East Africa are passed down from generation to generation.

Many developing countries and economies in transition, in response to the demand for learning for economic performance and competitiveness, continue to support a variety of training programs both at home and abroad, often with funding from international donors. The results have been mixed. The countries benefiting the most from such training activities are the ones where corresponding supportive activities are also going on in the economy and society in general. Mid-career managers and public servants going abroad to study for a two-year M.B.A. will come back home and find ready applications for their newly acquired knowledge and know-how if the domestic economy is open and working competitively and if the public sector is sufficiently reformed. On the other hand, students who return home to find their economies still operating in a closed, monopolistic environment or a bureaucratic public sector impervious to reform will find it almost impossible to find opportunities to apply their newly acquired knowledge. They will become frustrated, leave, or simply forget the training as just an aberration. Training does not work in isolation. It must be connected to changes going on in the economy and the wider society.

The third economic condition in support of entrepreneurship is competence. Entrepreneurial competence refers to the total sum of the entrepreneur's requisite attributes, attitudes, values, knowledge, skills, abilities, wisdom, expertise (social, technical, managerial), and behavioral tendencies needed for successful entrepreneurship. Education, training, work experience, apprenticeships, overseas study visits, and other forms of human capital development initiatives are relevant for entrepreneurial success or failure to the extent that they contribute to the development of entrepreneurial competences.

In theory, most people subscribe to the merit principle. Yet, politically, it may not be popular to advance it. In many countries with past injustices, corrective measures such as employment equity are more popular than merit. Today, South Africa provides one of the most challenging examples. After decades of white oppression of the black majority, the country gained majority rule in 1994 after a violent struggle for independence, which left many black freedom fighters without the necessary skills to compete with whites for employment. Mindful of its obligation to help its black population, the African National Congress government introduced a system whereby black contractors would bid on government contracts in competition with whites. After several competitive rounds, it became obvious that the black contractors could not compete successfully against the white establishments. Should the government lower contracting requirements to accommodate black contractors? This would be condemned by the white contractors and by the few successful black contractors as lowering performance standards. At the same time, the majority of black contractors were losing interest in bidding because they felt that they had no realistic chance to win any of the contracts.

When I discussed this with a South African economist and industrialist, the proposed short-term solution was for the government to request the services of an industry association to provide training and technical support to African contractors before submitting bids to government. In addition, successful African contractors would continue to receive support from the association to ensure that contract performance was up to standard. This would encourage African entrepreneurs to participate on a more level playing field with their white competitors.

The fourth economic condition for entrepreneurship is enterprise. This is the extent to which entrepreneurs are afforded the opportunity and freedom to individually or collectively engage in enterprising activities, take initiative and risks, compete, and emulate. It is the freedom to create, innovate, experiment, learn, adapt, and improve the way things are done. The fifth condition is the extent to which entrepreneurs have the freedom to enjoy and employ the fruits of their labor and enterprise. Both of these conditions are related, and they speak to the freedom and openness in the economy and society in general.

Just by looking at the five economic conditions, it is possible to differentiate between those countries, societies, institutions, or businesses where entrepreneurship is bound to thrive, and those where it is more likely to be suppressed. If a government of a globalizing country wishes to promote entrepreneurship, it can begin by looking at the prevailing conditions of its economy in the areas of productivity, learning, competence, enterprise, and private enjoyment of entrepreneurial benefits.

Political and Social Conditions

Entrepreneurship requires good governance and a supportive social system. In Chapter 2, the requirements for good governance were discussed in detail, and will not be repeated here. The need for an effective national integrity and regulatory system (NIRS), discussed in Chapter 2, should be emphasized here specifically for advancing the interests of entrepreneurship and reducing corruption, greed, and the abuse of power. Other requirements include secure rights of private property, rights of personal liberty, enforcement of contracts, an efficient and predictable public administration, and mobility of factors of production.

Society plays an important role in the evolution and development of entrepreneurship. Social values and how they relate to risk taking, individual achievement, respect for the new against the old, youth against experience, local against foreign, rich against poor, fast against slow, big against small, and rewards against punishment combine to influence the level, type, and quality of entrepreneurship. Social mobility is important because, like education, entrepreneurship facilitates social mobility. It is also important for society to support a more even distribution of income, wealth, and opportunities. Entrepreneurship, if successful, generates a lot of income and wealth and accentuates inequalities. Some of this inequality is due to the risks entrepreneurs take, but some is simply a result of market imperfections and political opportunism. For the long-term success of entrepreneurship, it is important for society to support or at least tolerate some inequalities and not demand equal distribution of resources. It helps to have a sizable middle class with a critical mass of educated, informed, and active citizens who, as producers and consumers, also understand how the economy works and are more likely to support entrepreneurship than other segments of society.

Compared with all regions of the world, sub-Saharan Africa lags behind in the development of entrepreneurship. Yet, at a very microeconomic or informal level, one finds many entrepreneurial activities carried out by traders, West African market women, and informal financing systems exemplified by Tontines and Susu groups. Why then does sub-Saharan Africa lag behind other regions? Most African writers increasingly put the blame on the prevailing governance, social, and economic management systems. In short, they blame the government for not creating an entrepreneurial supportive environment, while also acknowledging impediments due to societal values and practices. Complaining about lack of progress of entrepreneurial development in his native country of Ghana, one writer put it this way:

> The obvious thing is that the Ghanaian socio-economic environment is rather characterized by collective social orientation, collective achievement, collective financial security, functional diffusion, dysfunctional and prismatic bureaucratic structures and *affective* transaction, limited institutional environment . . . . [B]oth during the colonial period and since independence, governments have tended to act in ways that obstruct rather than encourage local entrepreneurial activities.[2]

Characteristics of the Entrepreneur

There is a large and growing body of literature, mainly from social and personality psychology, which supports the view that the individual attributes and characteristics of the entrepreneur are the best predictor of entrepreneurship in any given economy or society. Some of this literature goes back to people such as Max Weber using the concept of the Protestant work ethic to explain industrialism and industrial development in Europe, to the more recent discussions of Silicon Valley high-tech entrepreneuring with highly dysfunctional and antisocial behavioral tendencies.[3]

In the mainstream literature, the main characteristics of the entrepreneur are discussed under five main categories: demographics, traits, race/ethnicity, behavior, and managerial expertise. Each of these is discussed here briefly in terms of its relationship to entrepreneurship with emphasis on developing countries.

Demographics

The most commonly studied demographic variables are age, gender, education, and marital status. Studies from developing countries show that the majority of entrepreneurs are male, older, more educated than the community average, married (often more than once) and have large families. The entrepreneurs also tend to be the heads of their families and play important leadership roles in their respective communities. They also enjoy a high level of respect and status in the community. It is not clear, however, whether social status is acquired as a result of being a successful entrepreneur or whether people become successful entrepreneurs because they already enjoy high social status and use their social standing to promote personal economic interests. However, this relationship is important because it shows that entrepreneurship can be a useful training ground for societal leadership. Openness and globalization require an active society with capable individuals exercising leadership roles at different levels of the economy and society. The more developed entrepreneurship is, the more likely it is for the economy and society to have a pool of capable and experienced people to occupy the emerging leadership roles.

Perhaps the most important demographic variable for predicting entrepreneurial success in developing countries is education and experience. Successful entrepreneurs tend to be more educated with more relevant industry experience than less successful ones. This is not surprising because as Schumpeter observed, in the process of creative destruction and innovation, entrepreneurs put together new combinations of materials and resources for economic or socially desirable benefits. Therefore, they are expected to comprehend the environment around them much better than non-entrepreneurs. Education and experience give them the knowledge and skills they need to understand and manipulate the environment to advantage. It is also reasonable to expect entrepreneurs to have higher-than-average intelligence, which allows them to use tacit knowledge to competitive advantage.[4]

It has been said that globalizing developing countries need a critical mass of "global technopreneurs": young men and women who use technology to develop innovative, profitable businesses and socially desirable services not only for the home market but also regionally, continent-wide, and globally. This, however, is not going to be easy. The problem starts with a conformist education system that rewards rote learning and paper chase rather than independent thought, innovation, and creativity. To the experienced observer, the link between rote learning and authoritarian society and governance is obvious. As a start, developing countries and their public institutions must embrace and reward independent thought and action. This may require fundamental changes in these countries' education systems: the underlying philosophy, the way educational services are organized and delivered, how pupils and students study and learn, and the relationships between learning, work, and life. Even Asian countries such as Singapore, Korea, Taiwan, Hong Kong, and Japan, whose students score top marks on the International Mathematics and Science Study, need to reform their education system to emphasize independence and problem solving as core values and skills for the next generation. As part of their education reform, all globalizing developing countries should have an important component on education for entrepreneurship.

There is another twist to the relationship between educational attainment and entrepreneurship especially for family-owned firms. Chinese and Indians operating in Asia and Africa complain that when they send their children abroad for education they inevitably develop career interests outside the family business and are reluctant to return to the family. This is true of the Chinese in Southeast Asia, the Indians in Fiji and South Africa, the Ismael in East Africa, the Palestinians in the Middle East, and the Lebanese in West Africa. Since most of these are patriarchal societies, they are particularly concerned about their sons not coming back to manage the business and lead the family. They also worry about the daughters marrying outside the family-business network or "importing strangers" into the network.

For most of these family businesses, it is a real Catch-22. While the parents recognize the importance of education and the need for their children to study abroad and network, they are also aware of the risks involved in losing them to other career choices. These decisions are not easy for the young adults either. In my role as professor of business, I meet a number of them who are seeking advice as to what choices to make, trying to balance the interests of their parents and their own personal interests. Since our educational programs emphasize individualism, independence, and problem solving, most of these students decide to pursue their individual interests.

Traits

According to research evidence compiled by Wayne Stewart,[5] more than twenty traits have been studied showing relationships to entrepreneurial success. Traits are relatively stable personal attributes or personality types that distinguish people in many different ways. They have been used widely for selection and training of workers and managers in a variety of work organizations.

Table 4.1 summarizes some of the personality traits commonly associated with entrepreneurial success and how they manifest themselves in a business situation. The top four—need for achievement, internal locus of control, tolerance for ambiguity, and self-confidence/self-esteem—are widely and commonly associated with entrepreneurial success across cultures. Need for achievement (nAch) was popularized particularly by the late Harvard Professor David C. McClelland with his well-designed field experimental studies of Indian entrepreneurs in the late 1950s. McClelland defines nAch as the desire to do well because of inner feelings of personal accomplishment. He argued that as the general environment improves in support of entrepreneurship, individuals with a high nAch would do better in taking advantage of emerging entrepreneurial opportunities than those who score low. He also believed that nAch is a malleable trait that can be developed in people through various clinical and social processes such as training. Thus, he set out to train groups of Indian entrepreneurs in separate groups according to their nAch scores. Over time, he was able to demonstrate that the entrepreneurs in the experimental groups who were high on nAch or were trained to improve their scores performed better on various measures of entrepreneurial and financial performance than the control groups. McClelland studied two other traits: need for power similar to internal locus of control and need for affiliation. Need for affiliation was not considered important for entrepreneurial success.[6]

McClelland's work has been replicated in various settings in developing countries with surprisingly consistent empirical support. In 1996, Robert Alan LeVine tested the evidence of nAch among the Ibo, Yoruba, and Housa of Nigeria.[7] The purpose of the study was to explain the relatively higher levels of entrepreneurial success among the Ibo as compared with

TABLE 4.1
Personality Traits Commonly Associated with Entrepreneurship

Trait	_Manifestation_
1. Need for achievement	Driven by individual actions directly toward achievement of moderately challenging goals
2. Internal locus of control	Strong belief that he/she controls own destiny
3. Tolerance for ambiguity	Able to tolerate situations with high degree of uncertainty
4. Self-confidence/self-esteem	Feelings of competence, strong belief in self, willingness to make decisions and live with the consequences
5. High-level of energy	Perseverance, hard working, willingness to exert extra effort to achieve desired goals
6. Action-oriented	Desire to get things done, practical, not procrastinating, values time, results oriented

Source: Based on Wayne H. Stewart Jr., _Psychological Correlates of Entrepreneurship_ (New York: Garland, 1996); and Charles R. Kuehl and Peggy A. Lambing, _Small Business: Planning and Mangement_, 2nd ed. (Chicago: Dryden, 1990), 39.

the Yoruba and the Housa. Consistent with the relative entrepreneurial success of these three groups, the results showed a direct correlation between nAch scores and status mobility. As expected, the scores were highest for the Ibo, lowest for the Housa, and the Yoruba took the intermediate position.

Burton Benedict, in a 1979 study of African (Creole), Chinese, and East Indian entrepreneurs in Seychelles, concluded that successful entrepreneurs were characterized by high physical energy, confidence to act on opportunities, adaptability to altered conditions, and ability to inspire others.[8] More recently, a group of European researchers, led by Professor Michael Frese of the University of Giessen (Germany), undertook an international research program investigating the efficacy of achievement-oriented traits such as need for achievement for entrepreneurial and managerial success. Empirical findings from India, southern Africa, and Europe, collectively, provide strong evidence in support of the trait theory of entrepreneurial success. One of the European studies is particularly interesting. It compares small-scale entrepreneurship in a post-socialist environment in the former East Germany. Almost ten years after the collapse of Communism in East Germany, the study investigated the differences between entrepreneurs and managers in order to learn more about the personal attributes that account for who becomes a small-scale entrepreneur in a post-socialist environment. The five traits studied were achievement orientation (nAch), autonomy, innovativeness, proactiveness, and competitive aggressiveness.

The authors found that, as predicted, the entrepreneurs scored higher in a measure of achievement motivation, self-efficacy, innovation at work, readiness to change, and Machiavellianism than a comparison group of East German managers. Autonomy and innovation showed up as powerful predictors of the desire to become an entrepreneur.[9]

This study has significant implications for globalizing developing countries and their quest for entrepreneurial development. During the Cold War, many of these countries adopted Communist or Socialist policies that discouraged entrepreneurial development. The East Germany study seems to suggest that even after half a century of Communist/Socialist rule, there are still people with the necessary attributes to become successful entrepreneurs. The study also shows that the people who aspire to become entrepreneurs are significantly different in their personality traits than managers of established large corporations. These results support the view that countries ranging from Albania to Zimbabwe, despite their ideological past history, have the potential to develop a critical mass of entrepreneurs for globalization provided they develop and sustain a supportive and positively reinforcing environment. There is hope not only for the former Soviet Union and Eastern Europe but also for Vietnam, Cambodia, Cuba, Syria, and South Africa.

Despite the strong empirical evidence in support of the trait approach to entrepreneurial development, there is a small but vocal group of researchers, especially the natives of developing countries, who strongly oppose this approach. The arguments against the trait approach include inadequate theorizing, measurement problems of traits, temporary effects of clinical treatments such as training for enhancing nAch which wash out over time, cultural imperialism, and the fact that the trait approach ignores the importance of environmental factors. Representing this school of thought, one Ghanaian writer put it this way: "Traditional literature in the field of entrepreneurship has laid great emphasis on the psychological attribute of the individual as the underlying factor for engaging in entrepreneurial activities. . . . This study intends to argue and show that such individual characteristics, in themselves are not enough in influencing the development, nature and organizing of entrepreneurial activities."[10]

Race / Ethnicity

Wherever society is differentiated along racial/ethnic lines, race and ethnicity have been used to predict entrepreneurial success or failure. Successful racial groups include ethnic Chinese, East Indians, overseas Lebanese, and various East and South Asian groups operating in Europe and North America. Among the often-mentioned less-successful groups are the blacks in Africa, African Americans, native Canadians, native Malays, Afrikaners in South Africa, and the Russians or Soviets. Table 4.2 lists some of the common entrepreneurial winners and losers by race. However, differences in race and ethnicity may be symptoms of deeper societal characteristics, which relate to opportunities or lack thereof for entrepreneurial successes.

In Southeast Asia, the Asian miracle is often referred to as a Chinese success story. For example, in Indonesia, the Chinese make up only 4 percent of the population, but in the early 1990s, they controlled seventeen of the twenty-five largest business groups. In Thailand, they make up 10 percent of the population, but account for 90 percent of the richest families and own 90 percent of manufacturing firms and 90 percent of all commercial assets. In Malaysia, the Chinese dominate the economy, ethnic differences are sharp, and open resentment is just below the surface. The ruling party governs by a careful balancing act in support of business interests and special favors to the ethnic Malay majority. For these countries, the challenges of managing multiculturism owing to globalization start at home.

Within the African society, the literature has also attempted to identify more- and less-successful entrepreneurial ethnic groups. The often-cited successful groups include the Ibo of Nigeria, the Ashanti of Ghana, the Kikuyu of Kenya, and the Temme/Limba and Fulani/

TABLE 4.2
Entrepreneurship, Race, and Ethnicity: Winners and Losers

Successful Racial/Ethnic Groups	*Less-Successful Racial/Ethnic Groups*
• East Indians	• Native Malays
• Ethnic (overseas) Chinese	• Afrikaners (South Africa)
• Koreans	• Russians/Soviets
• Indians (Bengal)	• Native Canadians
• Lebanese (overseas)	• African Americans
• Asians in North America	• Africans in Africa
• White Americans	• Creole (Seychelles)
• Europeans	• Native Fijians
• Ibo (Nigeria)	• Mende/Sherbro (Sierra Leone)
• Kikuyu (Kenya)	• Housa (Nigeria)
• Ashanti (Ghana)	
• Baganda (Uganda)	
• Temme/Limba/Fulani/Mendingo/Susu (Sierra Leone)	

Mendingo/Susu of Sierra Leone. The less-successful groups include the Creole of the Seychelles and the Housa of Nigeria.[11]

Behavior

The Industrial Revolution gave rise to the discipline of organizational behavior (OB). Drawing on the behavioral and social sciences as well as industrial engineering, OB focuses on the systematic study of behavior in work organizations. It attempts to identify what people do or do not do (behavior), the decisions and choices they make or avoid, the conditions or contingencies for or against certain behaviors, and the reasons for them. The practical aspects of OB seek not only to explain but to predict and control behavior at work. The goal is to help organizations eliminate or reduce incidences of dysfunctional behavior and to promote the quality and consistency of economically beneficial and socially desirable behavior.

Although most of the OB research has focused on ordinary employees and managers in large organizations, some has been directed to the study of entrepreneurial behavior. There are several reasons for studying the behavior of entrepreneurs: First, it is useful to know if entrepreneurs behave differently than non-entrepreneurs and if there are certain behavioral patterns that consistently and accurately differentiate successful from less-successful entrepreneurs. This information can be quite useful in selecting, training, developing, and providing assistance to entrepreneurs and would-be entrepreneurs. It can also be used to predict future behavior and performance of different entrepreneurs under different conditions or contingencies.

The literature indicates that successful entrepreneurs display a pattern of behavior different than that found for non-entrepreneurs. This should not be surprising given that entrepreneurs differ on important demographic and trait variables from non-entrepreneurs. Identifying behaviors characteristic of successful entrepreneurs is particularly appealing to those who believe that entrepreneurship can be taught and learned. After all, the North American training and development industry is based on behavioral science theories of social learning theory.

African entrepreneurs have reported that hard work and the ability to perform multiple roles are important behaviors. For example, in her South African study, Gillian Patricia Hart found that more than 50 percent of the entrepreneurs interviewed reported hard work and commitment to the business as the most important requirements for success. They also reported honesty and discipline as important determinants of success. One of the interviewees summarized his behavioral pattern as follows: "I am a strict disciplinarian. I have never had a chum because this would lead to night life and drinking parties. Fellows who are interested in an easy life will never make much success. . . . Also starting early in the morning is essential. I always get up at 5 A.M. and start work straight away. . . . I must always be an individualist and devote everything I have to the business."[12]

In a review of almost one hundred studies of administrative theory and practice in developing countries, Jan Jørgensen and his business coworkers captured these multiple extraorganizational roles when they wrote:

> The entrepreneur may be simultaneously president of the firm, chairman of the local branch of the political party, head of the parents' association, officer in the local credit union or trade association, officer in the local chamber of commerce or Rotary Club, and head of the local branch of the ethnic, religious or caste welfare association. This pattern, also found among family-owned firms in small towns in industrialized countries, represents the functional equivalent of overlapping corporate directorships.[13]

The relentless work of the entrepreneur parallels that of the corporate manager as described by Henry Mintzberg's nature of managerial work.[14]

Managerial Expertise

Successful entrepreneurs are associated with effective managerial performance. In fact, one of the reasons often given as an obstacle to entrepreneurial development in many developing countries is lack of managerial expertise. The required areas of expertise include business planning and strategic management, financial control and management, capital budgeting, assessing and taking moderate business risks, marketing, and building and sustaining a wide cobweb of business clusters and social networks. The successful entrepreneur practices at least the basic elements of planning, staffing, directing, coordinating, reporting, and budgeting.

One of Hart's entrepreneurs illustrated the importance of business planning when he said: "I always set a target for sales. If the target is not realized, I have a big inquiry to find out the reasons."[15] Hart also found in her study that the apparent problem of capital shortage was a result rather than a cause of capital shortage.

Kelfala M. Kallon came to a similar conclusion when he observed that an entrepreneur's perception of opportunities, while important, is by far less crucial to the development of local enterprises than the ability to manage ongoing enterprise. Specifically, he found that bringing in a certified external auditor to periodically examine a firm's books contributed to its successful expansion. On the other hand, an entrepreneur's inability or unwillingness to delegate responsibilities to his/her subordinates limited his/her managerial capacity and thus the firm's opportunity to grow.[16]

International development organizations are particularly strong on the virtues of entrepreneurial management training and development. Mamadou Dia, drawing from his vast World Bank experience, suggests that entrepreneurs could be assisted through a twinning program of training and capacity building similar to the training and visit approach in agriculture, bringing larger and experienced firms together with the smaller and newer firms. He gives Kenya's Management Assistance Program as an example of such a collaborative approach designed to transfer technology and management know-how from the experienced to the less-experienced players.[17] Kenneth Loucks, writing for the International Labour Organization and advocating for direct training interventions put it more bluntly: "The single most indispensable element of a successful entrepreneurship development programme, . . . is an intensive, comprehensive business planning activity wherein prospective entrepreneurs are subjected to the discipline of collecting, analyzing, presenting, defending and promoting all aspects of what is necessary to start and operate their business."[18]

Field studies suggest that initiating, building, and sustaining business, social, community, and political networks is the most critical managerial function facing entrepreneurs in globalizing developing countries. Evidence suggests that the East Indians—ethnic (domestic)—and overseas Chinese do better as entrepreneurs because they are better at networking. For example, in South Africa, the East Indian entrepreneurs operate through a cobweb of organic, extensive networks that are rich, varied, and crossing oceans and generations. One of the East Indian entrepreneurs in South Africa illustrated it nicely when he said: "[T]he small factory owner who was my dad's closest friend for forty years and whose son is to marry my niece."[19]

In summary, research and experience support the view that certain personal attributes such as demographic variables, traits, social status, race/ethnicity, behavior, and managerial expertise distinguish entrepreneurs from non-entrepreneurs and the successful from the less-successful entrepreneurs. Therefore, entrepreneurs are different in significant ways from the average person of the community to which they belong. As people driven by the desire for creative destruction, they can be regarded as society's change masters. Professor Rosabeth Moss Kanter of Harvard University defines change masters as "those people and organizations adept at the art of anticipating the need for, and of leading productive change . . . the right people, the right places, the right times."[20]

Entrepreneurs play a special role in society. They thrive on destroying the status quo and creating a new order in their own image. Accordingly, they are not always popular or easy to deal with, especially in traditional societies. Public officials, custodians of tradition, and champions of stability find it difficult to deal with entrepreneurs and their constant drive for innovation and change. Yet, globalization needs them. Therefore, as a government and society, globalizing developing countries should learn not only to tolerate entrepreneurs but also to encourage, promote, reward, and celebrate them and their achievements. This may be hard for totalitarian regimes and young democracies in which nonconformist behavior is not normative. Managing differences and drawing the best from diversity are a couple of the key lessons traditional societies and conservative governments need to learn to put into practice in preparation for innovation, openness, and globalization.

The Entrepreneurial Firm

Car racing is one of the most competitive human endeavors. Yet, with all the excitement and anticipation, to say nothing of the inherent danger, only three factors separate the winners from the losers: the race track, the driver, and the car. Likewise, in entrepreneurship, the winners and losers are separated by three factors: the overall condition of the economy and society, the entrepreneur, and the entrepreneurial firm. I have already discussed the economic, political, and social conditions, as well as the personal attributes of the entrepreneur, that help explain the probability of success or failure. Here, I turn to the entrepreneurial firm, which is the vehicle by which entrepreneurship is organized and driven. Like the racing car, the entrepreneurial firm is the machine through which entrepreneurship is created, nurtured, developed, and sustained for competitive advantage.

The entrepreneurial firm is discussed under the headings: the organization form, the octopus, capital resources, and corporate governance. The discussion will end with an outline of how entrepreneurial firms operating in small markets can find ways to grow and enjoy competitive economies of scale.

The Organization Form

Organization form refers to the various aspects relating to the design, structuring, and management of the entrepreneurial firm. Commonly discussed variables include descriptive ones such as the firm's age, size, location, and sector and the structural ones such as ownership, governance, and the way it is structured.

The chronological age of the entrepreneurial firm is an important predictor of success because infant mortality is very high among such firms not only in developing countries and transition economies but the world over. It is estimated that more than 50 percent of entrepreneurial start-ups do not live to see their fifth birthday. When bank credit managers and other financiers ask the question "How long have you been in business?" they are collecting important information that helps them assess the risks of whether the business will still be around five years down the road to pay the loan back. As is clearly shown in population studies, with high mortality rates, the best way for the survival of the species is to encourage correspondingly high birth rates. Developing countries with high entrepreneurial firm mortality rates need to generate lots of entrepreneurial start-ups in the hope that at least some of them will succeed. Since there are no foolproof methods of determining who and what will fail or succeed, the best way of encouraging large numbers of entrepreneurial firms is through openness and competitiveness by making it easy for people to start and to get out if they fail. Some entrepreneurs decide to reduce their business risks by joining franchises such as McDonald's. In fact, franchises, especially from the West, are very popular with new entrepreneurs in developing countries and former Communist countries because they have better survival rates and because they bring with them capital, technology, and managerial expertise. They also provide excellent training opportunities for young local employees who aspire to become entrepreneurs.

Size, location, and the sector in which the firm belongs are some of the descriptive variables known to predict an entrepreneurial firm's success or failure. Size is important because many entrepreneurial firms in developing countries are too small to enjoy competitive economies of scale, especially if they are competing with large multinational corporations. Yet, size is a double-edge sword. Large, established (old) firms may become too rigid and lose the agility and flexibility needed for innovation and entrepreneurship. Indeed, the history of corporate America is about how small, young innovative companies take on the giants and beat them at their own game. A classic example is how Microsoft, when it was a relatively small and unknown corporation, beat out IBM, then the undisputed industry giant in the computer business. The lesson for entrepreneurs in developing countries is that while small can be vulnerable it can also be not only beautiful but competitive as well. With the advances in technology and increasing global opportunities, small entrepreneurial firms have a much better chance of making it in the global economy, no matter where they may be located.

Still, location plays an important role in determining the success or failure of entrepreneurial firms in developing countries. Leaving out the mining, agricultural, and natural resources industries whose location is pretty well predetermined by nature, the key factor determining successful location of entrepreneurial firms in developing countries is the quality and reliability of the physical, digital, and social infrastructure. Firms located in areas enjoying excellent physical, digital, and social infrastructure services—such as housing, water, electricity, transportation, telecommunication, and social and recreational services—are more likely to succeed because of the obvious competitive advantages they enjoy at relatively low cost. Since most of these facilities are much better in urban areas, this explains why most of the entrepreneurial firms in developing countries seek urban locations. Yet, urban locations are often associated with both direct and indirect business costs such as high operating costs, urban congestion, pollution, crime, and a hectic lifestyle not particularly conducive to creativity and innovation.

There is a lesson here for globalizing developing countries to rethink the relevancy of local dynamics in an era of globalization. For example, in the past, most developing countries have depended on one or a few large unmanageable megapolitan cities. These have tended to grow and consume resources at the expense of other regions of the country. They have also created physical and social problems that are very costly to resolve. By rethinking their urban development strategies and drawing on the new telecommunications technology and global openness, these countries can adopt an alternative model of urban planning. This would require the development of carefully selected, relatively small regional urban clusters. With the necessary infrastructure, these clusters would become the new location of choice for the entrepreneurial firms. They would also have the added advantage of providing opportunities for more regionally balanced growth in the country, which would promote more regional equity and development, especially because many developing countries suffer from regional imbalances which cause political and social tension and conflict.

There has been an increasing tendency for developing countries to attract industrial development, in general, and entrepreneurial firms, in particular, in coastal areas. Examples include China's eastern coastal provinces, Brazil's Sao Paulo–Rio de Janeiro corridor, India's Mumbai (Bombay) area, and the Abu Dhabi–Dubayy northeastern coast of the United Arab Emirates. Some of these areas have been specifically designed to attract foreign investment through tax incentives or by providing world-class infrastructural services at significantly reduced costs. Mexico (maquiladoras), the Philippines, and Kenya are some of the developing countries setting up tax-free export development zones and industrial development ports to attract entrepreneurial firms both domestically and internationally. These areas provide opportunities for local entrepreneurial firms to develop close operational and management linkages among themselves and with international business.

One of the challenges facing developing countries is the need to promote meaningful industrial decentralization so that entrepreneurial activities take place between the urban and rural areas, coastal areas and hinterlands, farm and nonfarm sectors, and majority and minority areas. Japan's history of rural-based industrialization during the Meiji period (1868–1912) and Taiwan's rural–urban balanced growth after World War II may provide useful lessons of experience for today's globalizing developing countries. Globalization can promote industrial decentralization because it gives entrepreneurs in formerly isolated areas—hinterlands, rural locations—access to national and international markets for products, services, technology, and capital. The effective use of these linkages and trade networks to fully exploit business opportunities created by technology and globalization rests on the active participation of entrepreneurs in the otherwise isolated regions.[21] With increasing globalization, entrepreneurial location will have less to do with geography and everything to do with interconnectedness.

Supposing we took a representative sample of entrepreneurs from different parts of the developing world and made a certain amount of money available to them (say, U.S.$100,000) for investment, where (sector) would they invest? When entrepreneurs from different traditions and backgrounds have their first opportunity to invest, which sectors do they choose? This question is important for entrepreneurship because different investment portfolios provide different rates of return and opportunities for further growth. For example, those who invest in the same business areas as their competitors (emulators) seeking to satisfy local demand are limited by the size of the domestic market.

Although there are no worldwide studies on this question of entrepreneurial sectoral preferences in different parts of the world, certain impressions have started to emerge. For example, we know that entrepreneurs and would-be entrepreneurs from traditional societies tend to make their maiden investments in fixed assets associated with land and related natural resources. They tend to invest in real estate, farming, forestry, fishing, and ranching. For these societies, wealth is associated with land, and the more of these visible fixed assets one has, the more social status and standing one receives from the community. Accordingly, for most modernizing and globalizing developing countries, the first boom and bust cycle takes place in urban real estate investment. For example, a recent World Bank study shows an increasing oversupply of housing in Bangkok for the entire 1992–1998 period.[22] While the local entrepreneurs were putting so much money in real estate, other sectors of the economy such as telecommunications were receiving less attention. This bias has been noted in other globalizing developing countries in Asia, South America, and Africa. Government and other development agencies can be useful here by advising and broadening the scope of new entrepreneurs and would-be entrepreneurs to avoid copycat investments and seek opportunities in nontraditional business areas. Societal values also need to change so that entrepreneurs without extensive real estate holdings are also accorded the same social status and respect.

An example of the extension of the land-based, fixed-asset entrepreneurship is the popular investment in flowers and fresh vegetables for export in many globalizing developing countries. A number of economic considerations make these investments quite attractive. Land is cheap, and inexpensive unskilled labor is abundant. The products—cut flowers and fresh vegetables—are light in weight and are of a relatively high value to make air transport economically viable. As planes move from north to south, they carry cargo made up of mainly manufactured goods, and on moving back to the north, the empty space can be used to transport horticultural products, making them available to European and American markets within twenty-four hours. The seasonal variations between north and south proved an added advantage so that northern consumers can buy fresh vegetables and cut flowers at relatively affordable prices in the middle of winter. Entry (and exit) in this line of business is relatively easy. Therefore, for the past forty years, there has been a steady growth of this export business to Europe and North America from Asia, South America, and Africa.

The African case is particularly interesting with useful lessons of experience. Most of the entrepreneurs in this line of business have been supported by the African Project Development Facility (APDF). APDF is a donor-funded facility within the World Bank's International Finance Corporation. It provides advisory services to African entrepreneurs with the objective of promoting viable small- and medium-size enterprises (SMEs) and new business establishments. APDF does not provide direct funding but helps entrepreneurs prepare the necessary market, technical, and other feasibility studies to obtain financing from development or commercial banks, venture capitalists, or investors. It also works with local consultants to help build local capacities for project preparation and feasibility studies. It has been operational since 1986.

A recent review of the performance of APDF drew attention to the dominant presence of the cut flower, hotel, and fishing projects for the 1986–1995 period, and observed that projects for the export of cut flowers have continued to grow in importance during the same period. The report also warned that the European market for flowers appears to have reached the saturation point and increased competition. African producers were at risk of becoming bankrupt because prices had declined by 60 percent between 1992 and 1998. The report questioned the wisdom of APDF management and the business acumen of the African entrepreneurs of concentrating on a single subsector exposed to overcapacity and declining profitability.[23]

The APDF provides at least three lessons of experience for entrepreneurs in developing countries. The first is the realization that entrepreneurship is more than capital investment. The inexperienced "fixed-asset" African entrepreneurs thought that the best way to make money was to invest in the same line of business as the competition. Instead of earning a higher rate of return, this created overcapacity, declining profitability, and possibilities for bankruptcies. The second lesson of experience is that entrepreneurs must broaden their perspectives and look for investment opportunities beyond the tunnel vision of traditional society. You do not have to invest in land and other traditional assets in order to be a successful entrepreneur. Entrepreneurship means innovation, not "status quo" emulation.

The third lesson of experience has to do with the role and usefulness of APDF as an agency for promoting entrepreneurship and entrepreneurial development. Like other donor-funded agencies, APDF is limited in its ability to help entrepreneurs because it is not directly involved in any business and, therefore, has no firsthand business knowledge, experience, or competitive competencies. Rather, it is more of a consulting and lobbying organization, and while these services are necessary especially for new entrepreneurs, they are no substitute for the need to establish direct contacts with business organizations directly involved in the relevant line of business. Perhaps the best APDF can do for emerging entrepreneurs is to assist them in making direct contacts and building viable, ongoing networking arrangements with the people and business organizations directly involved in the particular line of business. APDF and other U.N. agencies may have a role to play, but they cannot be expected to provide relevant and timely investment advice in a globally complex and dynamic business environment.

It is also the case that foreigners or minority groups unsure of their long-term status in the marketplace tend to make their maiden investments in movable or liquid assets. They are particularly attracted to commerce, retail, import–export, tour operations, and similar businesses. This is true of the Lebanese in West Africa and the Asian entrepreneurs in East and South Africa. When they get into the fixed assets such as manufacturing, the businesses tend to be highly leveraged so that they are always operating with a large overdraft loan from a local bank or financial institution. This is a sign of lack of confidence in the local economy and the ease with which this kind of speculative capital can leave the country. The traditional government policy response of instituting capital controls does not always work because the insecure entrepreneurs, often working in collusion with local officials, find loopholes to get their capital out. A better strategic policy response is to build long-term business confidence, but this takes time and requires political leadership and commitment not easily found in divided societies.

Then there is the young generation of entrepreneurs who grew up in urban areas playing with Nintendo games and other electronic gadgets. When they make their maiden investments, these people are likely to invest in digital assets in areas such as computers, telecommunications, biotechnology, space science, and the Internet. They are more likely to open an Internet café in their hometown than to buy heifers and start an animal farm. These people have a different sense of business and a more sophisticated understanding of the relationship between wealth, value creation, and income flows than their traditional fellow countrymen/women still investing in fixed assets. Globalizing developing countries need more entrepreneurs in this category. They are the true change masters, or agents of change, as they help diversify the economy from traditional areas of business to include sectors of the "new economy." They are more likely to be globally connected to others in the world from whom they get new business ideas and opportunities.

Like the insecure minority groups discussed previously, the young digital investors tend to be quite mobile. They are much more willing to move in and out of business sectors within and across countries or continents. They are not committed to a single country or business sector. They only stay if they feel welcome and if the business opportunities are attractive. They are not like the traditional investors who tend to be more "permanent" and "fixed" to the land. Therefore, attracting and retaining these young digital entrepreneurs requires active government and societal understanding and support.

Most globalizing developing countries have combinations of these three types of entrepreneurs: the traditional investors in fixed assets, the insecure investors in movable assets, and the new economy investors in digital assets. Government support for entrepreneurship must include understanding each of these types—their needs, fears, and expectations—so that government policy and programming can respect them accordingly.

The Octopus: A Costly Strategy for Managing Entrepreneurial Risks

One of the most common and interesting structural forms of entrepreneurial firms in developing countries is the octopus. This structural form was first identified by a group of researchers at McGill University's Faculty of Management when they were developing a market imperfections theory of organizational structuring in developing countries. They found that the typical entrepreneurial family-owned firm in a newly globalizing country is structured like an octopus: with a central core and many tentacles.

The octopus is believed to be the entrepreneur's strategic response to environmental market imperfections and risk management by engaging in several, often unrelated, businesses at once. The McGill researchers describe the octopus and its relationships to environmental market imperfections as follows: "The firm becomes a cluster of disparate enterprises linked by the entrepreneur and other family members. Because limited opportunities to liquidate assets raise the barriers to exist, unsuccessful ventures are shelved rather than liquidated. They can be reactivated if market conditions change. Such risk minimization impairs efficiency and may over-extend the managerial capacity of the entrepreneur."[24]

Figure 4.1 provides an illustration of the structural arrangements of an octopus. It is made up of the core and the tentacles. The core is made up of the entrepreneur's holding company or corporate officers and a group of businesses directly managed from the central offices. The tentacles are the associated businesses that are indirectly linked with one of the core businesses. Both the core and the tentacles and their associated businesses belong to different lines of business or subsectors. The principal entrepreneur may be the sole owner or he/she may own them in partnership with family members or other associates. In any case, the principal entrepreneur seeks to exercise total control over both the core and the tentacles.

Figure 4.1, a real example constructed from field data, provides some interesting illustrations. Of the six core businesses directly linked to the corporate office, at least three are land-based investments in real estate, hotel and tourism, and horticultural exports (cut flowers and fresh vegetables). The financial services businesses (banking, insurance, foreign exchange bureau, and so on) provide an in-house source of investment capital to finance the

FIGURE **4.1**
The Entrepreneurial Octopus: An Illustration

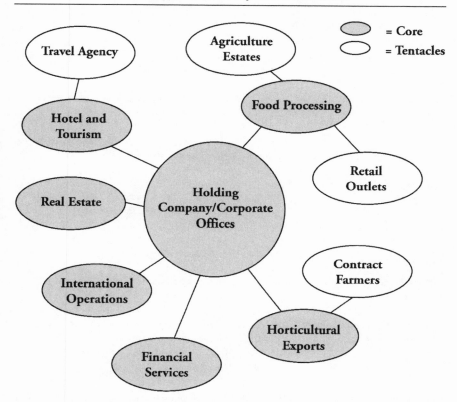

Inspired by information from Jørgensen, Hafsi, and Kiggundu, "Towards a Market Imperfections Theory"; Kiggundu, "Management in Uganda"; Kennedy, *African Capitalism*; and Dia, *Africa's Management in the 1990s and Beyond*.

octopus and its operations. The international operations are the same lines of business as some of the core lines of business. The business rationale to open outside (international) operations is not so much for growth and advantages of scale but to diversify business risks to different economic, security, and political environments.

The octopus structural arrangement is associated with several negative business consequences, and several of these are listed in Table 4.3 together with their corresponding consequences. In general, business resources are spread too thin and utilized inefficiently, with little or no synergy or economies of scale from the whole enterprise structure. Since business decisions are made on the basis of avoiding risk rather than return on investment, both working and investment capital is invested and left in unprofitable lines of business. Rather

TABLE 4.3
The Octopus and Its Business Consequences

Key Market Imperfections	Business Consequences
1. Thin capital market, creating financing problems	Operations are stopped or projects delayed due to lack of finance or inputs
2. Thin capital market, causing barriers to exit	Unsuccessful/unprofitable lines of business are stalled or scaled down rather than liquidated
3. Social transfer demands put pressure on working capital and long-term investments	High inventory levels to hedge supply and fend off extra business demands for cash
4. Intergenerational succession problems	Expansion/diversification of business, spin-offs, decentralization, and so on to keep offsprings attracted to work for the octopus
	Dividing up the firm among children before father figure retires or dies; closure of business
5. Later in life cycle, shortage of managerial talent	Employment of same family members across business lines
6. Political interference/patronage/red tape/crony capitalism	Efforts of chief executive officer spread too thin; inability to protect the core of the firm: diversification to "hide" capital, avoid "nationalization," reduce taxes

Inspired by information from Jørgensen, Hafsi, and Kiggundu, "Towards a Market Imperfections Theory," table 1, p. 429; and Kiggundu, "Management in Uganda."

than looking for the most profitable business opportunities, the principal entrepreneur is busy diversifying or "hiding" the capital from social and political vultures, protecting the business from formal or informal "nationalization," and reducing the exposure of the business' income to a wide range of levies, licenses, and taxes.

Perhaps one of the biggest disadvantages of the octopus structure is its poor use of executive and managerial human resources. The principal entrepreneur is spread too thin, providing strategic leadership in a wide range of unrelated businesses. It is not possible for one person to have the necessary experience or competencies to direct competitive businesses ranging from banking to contract farming (see Figure 4.1). In one field research trip, I saw one such entrepreneur having to make strategic investment and operational decisions of unrelated businesses within a period of a few hours on a single morning. First thing in the morning, he had to deal with complicated matters of capitalization of the financial institution in accordance with government regulatory requirements. Immediately following that meeting, he met with engineers and equipment manufacturers to decide on appropriate investments in the food-processing plant. Immediately after a short coffee break, he met with local farmers to develop a common response to the government's land tenure bill designed to significantly change the traditional relationships between landowners and the peasant contract farmers. He was doing all this without the help of a single executive assistant. Under these conditions, the quality of management suffers, and yet, as a structural instrument of central control, the octopus does not facilitate decentralization or delegation of business authority.

The octopus impedes business growth. All the businesses under the structural arrangements of the octopus are forced to remain small and inefficient. They lack the economies of scale and the operational efficiency to compete in an open, globalizing environment. The principal entrepreneur's motive is to keep each of the individual businesses small enough to be controlled by a single entrepreneur and to hide from government and other potential competitors or vultures. Consequently, these businesses have no opportunity to scale up— to become big enough or efficient enough to be able to compete on a global scale. Therefore, the octopus structural arrangement is not good for entrepreneurial and competitive development, and thus, it is not good for globalization.

The octopus has been particularly detrimental to the development of entrepreneurs and competitive entrepreneurial firms, especially in the weaker and less developed part of the developing countries (P2 countries). Professor Malcolm Harper, founding editor of *Small Enterprise Development*, a quarterly journal begun in the early 1990s, has been studying entrepreneurship and SMEs since the early 1970s. Reflecting on these problems, especially as they relate to Africa, Dr. Harper observed:

> There is a lively tradition of enterprise, African market women for instance are admired world-wide for their entrepreneurship, and there are well established traditional informed financial systems . . . such as Tontines and Susu groups. There are also many examples of successful formal enterprise development and micro-finance institutions, ACEP in Senegal, K-REP in Kenya, lots coming up in Uganda. . . . But, none have really grown to reach hundreds of thousands, never mind millions, of people, none has made a major contribution to poverty alleviation or to their countries' economies or societies, and . . . in no African country has there evolved, or does there appear likely to evolve, that entrepreneurial middle class, the German mittelstand, the French petit bourgeoisie, on which a sound civic and political society can be founded. Nowhere have small and medium enterprises developed the export marketing success on which the growth of many other economies has been built.
>
> There is no shortage of talented people, some countries . . . have a long tradition of good education, many have been free of the total mindless violence that has destroyed some others, natural resources (maybe a curse, see Congo vs. Hong Kong) are in abundance, land is not scarce, why doesn't it work? Is it the neo-colonialism of aid, is it the greed of the multi-nationals, is it the kleptocracy of politicians, is it all these and much more?[25]

Every globalizing developing country must find valid explanations and practical solutions to the questions and issues raised by Professor Harper. Without a viable critical mass of entrepreneurs, and competitive entrepreneurial firms, no country is ready for gainful participation in the global economy.

Capital Resources

Every entrepreneur is concerned about capital for the entrepreneurial firm. Obviously, capital is important for the survival and growth of any business. Many would-be entrepreneurs use lack of capital as the primary excuse for not getting started, or for having failed in their previous attempts. Many donors work on the assumption that lack of capital is the most important impediment to the development of entrepreneurship. Some economists define poverty in terms of lack of capital. Accordingly, researchers have investigated the extent to which the nature and availability of various forms of capital resources predict the start, survival, growth, and profitability of entrepreneurial firms in developing and transition economies. Most of the investigations focus on various types of capital including:

1. Investment and working capital;
2. Human and intellectual capital;
3. Social capital, social transfers, and networks;
4. Technology, innovation, research, development, and commercialization;
5. Organizational capital.

Contrary to popular belief, most researchers have found that capital by itself is not a major obstacle to the growth of the entrepreneurial firm in most globalizing developing countries. These findings have been supported even in Africa, which remains the least attractive continent for private investment capital. Several studies have found that lack of access to external sources of investment capital, such as development banks, commercial banks, or government loans or grants, did not have any adverse effects on the profitability of the entrepreneurial firms. In one of these studies, the author concluded: "The stock of capital with which the firm was initiated . . . is negatively, and significantly related to the rate of growth of the firm's real assets . . . access to commercial credit . . . does not contribute to entrepreneurial success to any significant degree, and even if it did, the relationship would be negative."[26]

According to these findings, in the absence of managerial, technical, and entrepreneurial expertise, any investment or working capital that the entrepreneur or would-be entrepreneur might acquire would be wasted. This may explain why so many development and commercial banks as well as other financial institutions in most of the developing world are loaded with so many nonperforming, dead commercial loans. The people and firms who have access to official sources of capital are not necessarily the most successful entrepreneurs. George Soros has provided a detailed discussion of the role of nonperforming loans in Southeast Asia, Japan, China, Eastern and Central Europe, and South America and the global financial crisis. For Asia, he observed that estimates of expected nonperforming loans (that is, loans that cannot be paid back) amount to almost U.S. $2 trillion.[27] This mismatch between the supply and effective demand for capital is detrimental to the development of entrepreneurship and, ultimately, to globalization.

A distinction must be made between access to capital at the time of starting the business and later on when the firm is a viable ongoing concern. In general, problems of access to capital resources are more serious at the start of business than later. This is particularly important because the most important source of start-up capital for most small entrepreneurial firms is personal and family savings. In the initial period, there is no money coming in, thus putting pressure on the family budget. In traditional societies, social transfers make it difficult for profits to be plowed back into the business. In other situations, market imperfections such as unpredictable supply of raw materials make for inefficient use of working capital (for instance, overstocking). However, even here evidence suggests that the apparent problems of capital shortage are a result rather than a cause of managerial shortcomings. Therefore, it is misleading to isolate the question of capital from the complex constellation of forces that determine entrepreneurial firm performance.

The entrepreneurial challenges of human/intellectual capital are different. Most entrepreneurial firms have very limited access to experienced managerial and technical knowledge workers beyond immediate family, friends, and coworkers. Sometimes, they are forced to give friends and relatives employment preferences rather than getting the best person for the job from the open market. Family firms are particularly culpable because of the need to preserve managerial positions for the children to ensure succession. True entrepreneurs tend to be more interested in creative destruction and innovation rather than in enterprise management. Therefore, as the firm begins to grow and business expands, it becomes critically important for the entrepreneur to partner with and bring in individuals with solid technical (for example, manufacturing) and management (for example, finance, marketing) background and expertise. It is the quality of the management of the dynamic business relationships between the innovating entrepreneur(s) and the "nuts-and-bolts" general and functional managers that determines the long-term success of the entrepreneurial firm as it goes through various initial stages of growth and development.

Corporate Governance

Every successful innovation requires a corporate entity to take it to market and turn it into an ongoing profitable business enterprise. Without corporations, entrepreneurs would be limited in their ability to mobilize resources, organize the business, and compete in the marketplace with other established corporations. Indeed, as an economy opens up and allows the private sector to play an increasingly dominant role in economic management, more and more private corporations spring up, and their roles and responsibilities become important issues of public concern. Every globalizing country needs a system of good corporate governance because it provides the framework, or "rules of the game," within which private enterprise operates. Governance practices of private corporations are the subject of increasing critical examination and scrutiny by public and private regulators in both industrialized and developing countries. Civil society is also increasingly interested in corporate governance because of the concern that private corporations, as major players, should be held accountable for the consequences of globalization.

What is corporate governance? This refers to the processes, structures, laws, bylaws, rules, conventions, and procedures used to direct and manage a corporation's affairs: operations and activities. It defines the powers, roles, and responsibilities and establishes mechanisms to achieve accountability among the board of directors, management, minority and majority shareholders, employees, and other stakeholders. As corporate citizens, corporations are governed by the laws and regulations of the country, state, or province of their incorporation. In addition, they are governed by their individual articles of incorporation, bylaws, and approved procedures for conducting business. A good corporate governance system is effective, accountable, and transparent.

There is a difference between management and the board of directors. Management is made up of senior employees hired by the board to run day-to-day affairs of the corporation and report to the board. The board of directors plays the central and most important role in corporate governance: It bears the ultimate responsibility for the stewardship of the corporation. Board members are not employees of the corporation; they do not work for the corporation on a day-to-day basis, they do not draw a salary, although they may earn directors' fees and allowances, and they may maintain an independent relationship with management. Like management and employees, they may or may not own shares in the corporation, although it is quite common for most of the corporate directors of the board to be minority or majority shareholders.

The corporate board of directors can be described in terms of roles, responsibilities, and mandate; structure, size, composition, and organization; processes, decisions, and information; performance assessment, reporting, and accountability; and corporate culture, values, and philosophy. In terms of its stewardship role, the corporate board of directors performs five key roles: corporate strategic planning, risk identification and management, managing corporate effectiveness and succession, communicating with shareholders and other stakeholders, and exercising internal controls and the management information system.

Very few studies of entrepreneurship concern themselves with corporate governance. This is particularly so in developing and transition economies where by far the majority of entrepreneurial firms are very small and young and operate in the informal sector. Since the 1980s, these countries have undertaken political and economic reforms such as liberalization, privatization, and democratization. These have given rise to a new breed of entrepreneurs—either taking over privatized state enterprises or establishing sizable firms operating in the formal sector—and they are in need of good corporate governance. Available limited evidence suggests that these nouveaux riche, like the directors of state-owned enterprises (SOEs) before them, still need to understand the basic principles of corporate governance. They need to understand the differences in the respective roles and responsibilities of the corporate board of directors and senior management and the need for the separation of power and responsibilities between the two. Some board members often interfere with the day-to-day running of the corporation, and because of this, senior managers will keep sensitive information away from board members because they fear that it will be sold to the highest bidder. Few firms have functioning corporate boards; of those that do, fewer still function strategically. Questions of corporate strategic management, accountability, transparency, responsibility to minority shareholders, and compliance with incorporation regulations, such as disclosure rules, remain problematic among the emerging entrepreneurial class. The World Bank has recognized the need and, among other things, has established a Web site (www.worldbank.org/wbi/corpgov) dedicated to improving corporate governance by fostering entrepreneurial accountability, transparency, responsibility, and fairness. In October 2001, the World Bank Group approved U.S. $2.8 billion for SMEs. The money is to be used in direct and indirect financing, training, and support for improved business environment and corporate governance (*World Bank Press Review*, October 22, 2001).

The corporate board of directors—its role and responsibilities, structure, and decision-making processes and mechanisms—is important for entrepreneurial development and globalization for several reasons. First, the quality of the overall corporate governance, of which the board plays a central role, is a key factor in determining the overall attractiveness of the investment climate of any newly globalizing country. Second, due to a number of historical and sociological reasons, corporate governance is not well developed or properly practiced in most of the emerging economies. Third, poor corporate governance impedes the development of entrepreneurship, openness, and capitalism. Fourth, potential shareholders, investors, and other business associates need reassurance about the safety of their investment. One way of doing so is by ensuring good corporate governance, characterized by independent, objective, and professionally organized corporate boards of directors. Globalizing countries that are unable to establish and maintain an effective corporate governance regime should seek assistance from the international community, especially from private sector regulators such as the U.S. Securities and Exchange Commission.

ENTREPRENEURSHIP IN TRANSITION: LESSONS FROM CENTRAL AND EASTERN EUROPE

I conclude the discussion of the relationship between globalization and entrepreneurial firms by looking briefly at the recent developments and lessons of experience from Central and Eastern Europe (CEE), which are relevant to other globalizing countries for several reasons. First, like many of these countries, the countries of the CEE region are working hard to transform their economies from Communist or Socialist systems dominated by SOEs to free-market systems dominated by private enterprise. Second, with varying degrees of success, the CEE countries have made significant progress in transforming their economies by promoting entrepreneurship and private sector development. Third, it is generally believed that because of its historical and strategic importance as a bridge or wall between the West and the East, the CEE region must succeed in its political and economic reforms and become part of the West by joining NATO and the EU. With so much at stake, the countries of Western Europe, especially Germany, France, and Britain, are doing everything possible to ensure successful and sustaining transitions to democratic and free-market systems for each of the countries of the CEE region. Yet, despite all the efforts, resources, and goodwill, the CEE region continues to experience challenges in transforming the economy and building an effective entrepreneurial sector.

Therefore, the lessons of experience from these countries should be instructive for others in similar situations.

Exhibit 4.1 summarizes information about entrepreneurs and entrepreneurial firms in several CEE countries in the mid-1990s. The information—which includes corporate structure, profiles of successful entrepreneurs, major obstacles to entrepreneurial development, and methods used to establish global contacts—was obtained from a series of entrepreneurial studies for Bulgaria, the Czech Republic, Hungary, Poland, Romania, and the Slovak Republic.[28]

Exhibit 4.1
Entrepreneurship in Transition:
Summary Evidence from Central and Eastern Europe

1. Corporate Structure

   - Predominantly individual/family ownership.

   - Independent, not subsidiaries; started as new after 1989.

   - Little or no foreign ownership.

   - Small in size: 50 percent employ at least twenty people; 80 percent at least fifty.

   - Balanced location between urban and local communities.

   - Key sectors: clothing, knitting, plastic, metalworking, machinery.

2. Profile of Entrepreneurs

   - Majority are middle-age males.

   - Well educated: technical and commercial, university and college.

   - Motivated by personal achievement, independence, and economic necessity.

   - Previously worked for, managed, or owned similar business.

   - Innovative, risk takers, technocrats, business acumen.

   - Ability to analyze foreign markets and negotiate foreign contracts.

   - Limited experience in business risk assessment and management.

   - Close ties with the outside world.

3. Major Obstacles

- Excessive taxes.

- Delinquent payments by SOEs.

- High interest rates.

- Limited access to credit.

- Inability of local suppliers to deliver the order.

- Poor services from banks.

- Clientelism and bribery to local officials.

- Unstable, unpredictable business conditions.

- Weak domestic demand.

- Vague government regulations/laws/policies.

- Lack of information about changing government regulations.

- Unhelpful, uncaring government officials.

- Red-tape fees.

- Negative societal attitudes toward private enterprise.

- Limited export opportunities.

4. Global Contacts

- Travel, study, work abroad.

- Seek ideas, technology, expertise from the West.

- Form joint partnerships with foreign businesses.

- Develop export markets for inputs and products.

- Attend, exhibit at international trade shows.

- Joint research, development, commercialization, or new product development with foreign businesses.

- Obtain and maintain ISO (International Standard Series) 9000 certification.

Source: Based on studies of entrepreneurship in Central and Eastern Europe (Bulgaria, the Czech Republic, Hungary, Poland, Romania, and Slovakia) by Galen Spencer Hull, *Small Business Trickling Up in Central and Eastern Europe* (New York: Garland, 1999).

In terms of corporate structure, the studies found that for most of the CEE countries, the private sector firms are predominantly owned by individuals or families. They are independent, not subsidiaries of larger or foreign corporations, and most of them were started after 1989 in response to the political and economic reforms. Most of these are small firms employing twenty to fifty people. They were well balanced in terms of location between urban and rural areas. For example, in Hungary, 50 percent of the firms were located in Budapest; the other half was located in small communities in the country. The firms were found in five key sectors: clothing, knitting, plastic, metalworking, and machinery.

These structural properties of the entrepreneurial firms in the CEE region provide some useful observations. First, the emphasis is on the development of an indigenous entrepreneurial infrastructure made up of many small-to-medium-size, individually or locally owned firms diversified by sector and location. This is a much better and more sustainable approach to entrepreneurial development than using either a few large monopolistic "chaebols"-type corporations, as seems to be the case in Russia, or using "greenfield" enterprise zones isolated from the local economy and community. Second, since most of the firms are new, this supports the view that the citizens are responding positively to the business opportunities and challenges offered by the reforms. Private sector development requires local support and must be homegrown. Third, the balanced location of the entrepreneurial firms between urban and local communities is consistent with expert thinking on sustainable private sector–driven industrial policy and the need to build urban–rural linkages for globalization.[29]

Exhibit 4.1 also summarizes profiles of successful entrepreneurs in the CEE countries. As would be expected, the majority is well educated, with technical or commercial education from universities or colleges. They have had previous industrial work experience either as employees, managers, or owners of similar businesses. They are innovative, technologically apt, ready to take risks, and have good business sense. When asked why they became entrepreneurs, the typical response was that they are motivated by the drive for personal achievement, independence, and economic necessity. Here, we see clear evidence of the entrepreneurs' high need for achievement and autonomy combined in a very practical way with intuition and the capacity to read, understand, and gainfully respond to the changing political and economic environment. It is a strategic combination of intrinsic motivation and practical realism producing a can-do mind-set characteristic of successful entrepreneurs the world over. The studies also show that the successful entrepreneurs were able to analyze foreign markets, negotiate foreign contracts, and develop close business relationships with the outside world. This is good for globalization.

The profile, however, does show two areas of weakness: First, most of the entrepreneurs had limited experience in assessing and managing business risks. This finding is not surprising since most of the firms were quite new and the entrepreneurs and their managers had limited time to develop the necessary managerial experiences, including risk management. This is an area in which government agencies, private sector development agencies, industry associations, academic institutions, consulting firms, and the international community can help.[30]

The second weakness in the profile of the entrepreneurs is the observation that the majority are middle-age males. In one of the Hungarian studies, it was reported that the profile of the typical owner/manager was a forty-five-year-old male. The two weaknesses have to do with gender and age. While it is not surprising that most of the entrepreneurs are male, it draws attention to the fact that half the population is underrepresented or excluded from participating in the exciting and important national endeavor of entrepreneurship and private sector development. Indeed, this is a worldwide problem, perhaps made worse in the CEE region because of its Communist past and prevailing social values and attitudes. Needless to say, there is an urgent need to increase the number of women entrepreneurs in each of the CEE countries. This is important not only because of the need for internal equity, fairness, and inclusion but also because women bring different perspectives to entrepreneurship and private sector development. In the interests of globalization, it is particularly important to have a critical mass of women entrepreneurs because opponents of globalization often cite women as one of the excluded, marginalized, and victimized groups. Globalizing developing countries need more women as active participants, beneficiaries, and advocates of globalization.

The second weakness of the profile of successful entrepreneurs in CEE countries has to do with age. There is a global trend for more and more young entrepreneurs, especially in the new digital economy. Everyday, one reads about young entrepreneurs in their twenties, and increasingly in their teens, churning out successful innovations—new products and services—that draw on the new digital—Internet—technology, and exploiting the opportunities of a global economy. Therefore, CEE countries, like other newly globalizing countries, need to find strategies for getting more young people, especially those with entrepreneurial and technological potential, involved in private sector development. This may require carefully designed interventions in the homes, communities, and schools during early childhood development and education.

Exhibit 4.1 also provides an interesting list of the main obstacles to entrepreneurial development as reported by the CEE entrepreneurs. The three top obstacles reported were excessive taxes, delinquent payments by SOEs, and high interest rates. Other obstacles included problems with the banking sector, the inability of local suppliers to deliver on demand, corruption from local government officials, unhelpful and uncaring government agencies, and negative societal attitudes toward entrepreneurship and private enterprise.

As expected, businesses are heavily taxed. In the CEE region, as part of the economic reforms, a wide range of taxes and licensing fees were introduced that proved burdensome, especially to the small, honest entrepreneurs. Among the most hated were the payroll taxes, turnover taxes, taxes on profits, and red-tape fees. In the Slovak Republic, for example, payroll taxes (labor taxes) accounted for more than half of the wage bill. Turnover taxes were required when firms produced goods or services but before sales were made. This caused hardships to small firms, especially in terms of managing cash flow. Government agencies compounded the problem by charging interest on outstanding balances in an environment of high interest rates, limited access to credit and other banking financial services, weak domestic demand, and slow supply management and distribution infrastructure. Red tape was so bad that firms had to hire professionals and pay them red-tape fees before they could open for business.

The other frequently mentioned obstacle to entrepreneurship relates to the role of the SOEs in entrepreneurship and private sector development. As noted, most of the entrepreneurial firms in the CEE region were new and individually owned. They were not spun off from the SOEs; yet, the SOEs remained as important customers for the small entrepreneurial firms. They were attractive customers because they often placed larger orders than the local private sector customers. Yet, most entrepreneurial firms suffered from delinquent payments by SOEs. In the study of Czech entrepreneurs, delinquent payments, mostly by SOEs, accounted for 70 percent of sales in 1991 for some of the firms surveyed.[31] In fact, the general conclusion is that in the CEE region, SOEs have not been a positive force in the development of entrepreneurship and a competitive private sector.

An obstacle to entrepreneurial development reported in the CEE region, which many other developing countries and transition economies can relate to, is widespread negative social attitudes toward entrepreneurs and private sector development (see Exhibit 4.1). In the Czech Republic, entrepreneurs regularly had to confront social prejudice against profit making, which had been illegal under the Communist regime. In the Slovak Republic, entrepreneurs were struggling to overcome negative images within society where profit-seeking business entrepreneurs were considered greedy, selfish, uncaring, and detrimental to the community. This was compounded by negative or unsupportive attitudes and behavior of government officials who had to administer complex, ambiguous, and often contradictory laws, policies, and regulations. Local officials made matters worse by continuing the old rent-seeking practice of clientelism and bribery. In one case, entrepreneurs complained that government environmental impact assessment regulations and procedures were vague, and workplace health and safety inspections were arbitrary.

The obstacles listed in Exhibit 4.1 provide a useful checklist or benchmark for other newly globalizing countries. They also provide a basis for analysis and policy development aimed at helping entrepreneurs to overcome these obstacles. Here, the government has a lead role to play, but as I have argued already, the best long-term strategy must be a partnership involving various government departments and agencies, the business community, civil society, and the international community, including foreign business organizations.

Finally, Exhibit 4.1 lists some of the key strategies used by the successful entrepreneurs from the CEE countries to initiate, establish, and sustain gainful global contacts. Most of them had visited businesses in neighboring countries in Western Europe such as Germany, Austria, Switzerland, and Italy; a few had gone as far as the United States. During their travels, they collected ideas and updated their technological knowledge and skills, and perhaps more important, they developed the inspiration to become entrepreneurs. David Landes reminds us of the importance of personal visits in spreading the Industrial Revolution first between Britain and mainland Europe, then Europe and the United States, and then Europe, the United States, and Japan.[32] Newly industrializing and globalizing countries need to encourage and support these private sector–driven foreign study tours among their citizens.

Successful entrepreneurs also sought export markets, joint partnerships, and joint research, development, commercialization, and new product development with foreign counterparts. Contrary to popular belief, the evidence from the CEE suggests that the successful entrepreneurs were not necessarily seeking business partnerships with large multinational corporations; rather, they were looking for business or investment partnerships from individuals or SMEs operating within the same or similar line of business.

Perhaps one of the most important findings for the benefit of other newly globalizing developing countries is the use of ISO 9000 certification as a mechanism for making and sustaining global contacts. ISO 9000 provides written certification that a given firm has the technology, the expertise, the processes (including quality control and quality assurance), the training, and the organization to produce goods and services that conform to internationally accepted standards. This is an important global statement about the production integrity of the firm and the confidence in the quality and consistency of its products and services. It has become a requirement for doing international business because most of the leading corporations will not outsource or accept bids or proposals from firms or businesses that are not ISO 9000 certified.[33]

One of the companies studied provides evidence of the importance of ISO 9000 certification. Process Control Systems is a Slovakian power, engineering firm formed in 1992. In 1994, it started developing export markets in Western Europe, the United States, Asia, and South Africa. Since most of its revenue was coming from exports, the company needed to assure its overseas customers of the high quality of its products. It became the first Slovak company to receive the ISO 9001 certification. In 1996, the company was approved by Lloyd's Register of Quality Assurance, which specifies quality management system standards.[34]

It must be emphasized that ISO 9000 certification is not easy to earn, especially for small firms with limited resources. It costs money, takes time, and requires a certain high level of technical and managerial expertise and absolute and sustaining commitment from the owner/manager. For a small firm, the direct costs can be upwards of U.S.$100,000, and certification can take at least two years. There must be sound training and human resource development systems that are continuously monitored and updated. Once the certification is achieved, which requires extensive and detailed documentation, the firm is subject to periodic reviews and assessments to ensure continuing compliance with the certification requirements. Most of the emerging private sector firms in the newly globalizing developing countries do not have the resources to seek, obtain, and retain ISO 9000 certification. Yet, it is becoming a basic requirement for doing business in the global marketplace. Once again, government policy is key here. By working in partnership with the private sector, donors, and investors (both at home and abroad), government can provide assistance for the most promising entrepreneurial firms in key strategic sectors to receive and retain ISO 9000 or similar certification.

The results of the studies of entrepreneurship and private sector development from the CEE region led to a number of observations and policy recommendations instructive not only to the countries of Central and Eastern Europe but also to other reforming and globalizing countries, such as the former Soviet Union, as well as the traditional developing countries. Exhibit 4.2 summarizes the key recommendations and lessons of experience particularly relevant for globalization.

Exhibit 4.2
Entrepreneurship in Transition:
CEE Lessons of Experience for Globalization

1. After more than ten years of reform, the CEE region continues to be in transition mode from a Communist command economy to a free-market globalized economy.

2. Contrary to expectations, the privatization of SOEs has not been the key to successful transition to a free-market economy.

3. The main impetus for economic growth in the CEE region is coming from the SMEs driven by small private entrepreneurs.

4. To join NATO and the EU, CEE countries need to attain certain standards, including a healthy entrepreneurial private sector. Institutions and policies that promote entrepreneurship and the SME sector are beginning to contribute to economic development and social development.

5. The growth of SMEs reflects a global trend: the bigger the world economy, the more powerful its smallest players become.

6. As part of the reform process, ancient pent-up sentiments and values have been unleashed, including nationalism and individualism. These countries are going to have to strike a balance between narrow nationalism (appealing to traditional sentiments) and modern requirements for globalization (for example, Europeanism, Westernism).

7. While individualism is making a reappearance and the CEE countries are opening doors to individual initiative and entrepreneurship, old attitudes die hard. The regulatory environment and social attitudes are generally hostile to entrepreneurship and private enterprise. This is bad for globalization.

8. Many entrepreneurs do not see government officials as helpful or caring; rather, they see them as the enemy and seek to minimize their dealings with government agencies.

9. After examining various models of industrial growth and development, most CEE countries have concluded that the wise policy is one that places emphasis on promoting an entrepreneurial culture: recognizing the entrepreneurial firm as the dynamic engine of growth that creates wealth, income, employment, and competitiveness and provides outlets for individual initiatives and creativity.

10. A related aspect of the industrial development policy is the realization that the small and micro-enterprise segment is of great importance because it is the cradle of entrepreneurship, especially in areas of high poverty, high unemployment, and a depressed economy (for example, military base closures).

11. The private sector must operate within a clear and predictable legal framework, taxes must be paid, regulations must be enforced fairly, and society must respect private enterprise. There must be allowance for failure.

12. The promotion of entrepreneurship through the establishment of SMEs is crucial for transformation to a market economy, the democratization of society, and overall globalization.

Source: Adapted from Hull, *Small Business,* chaps. 8 and 10, and 233–271.

An important observation from Exhibit 4.2 is the fact that after more than ten years of reform, the CEE countries are still in a transition mode. While they are making significant progress toward an open, competitive, entrepreneurially driven market economy, they still have a long way to go. The obvious lesson is that reforms take time. Extended to other parts of the world, this lesson of experience suggests that traditional societies that might have had small entrepreneurs but little or no experience of well-structured entrepreneurial firms would need even more time to reform their economies. This seems to be the case with, for example, the Malay business community in Malaysia, the black population of northeast Brazil, and the majority of African societies.[35]

The second lesson of experience relates to the roles, relationships, and relative importance of the SOEs and the entrepreneurial firms in fostering private sector development and globalization. Contrary to expectations, the privatization of SOEs has not been the key to successful transition to a free-market economy. These enterprises appear to have been more of an obstacle to the development of the entrepreneurial firm. They have provided unfair competition, crowded out the more efficient entrepreneurial firms, refused or delayed payments to the legitimate entrepreneurial businesses, and colluded with government officials to perpetuate corruption and distort the market.

As the SOEs lose their instrumentality for entrepreneurship and private sector development, attention must be paid to the positive role the entrepreneurial firms can play. In most reforming and globalizing countries, very little attention has been paid to the entrepreneurial firm as the driver and linchpin between the individual entrepreneur and the macroeconomy. Available evidence seems to suggest that those economies with a critical mass of small-to-medium-size competitive entrepreneurial firms are more successful at economic reform and achieve it more quickly than those who do not have this business institutional infrastructure. This may explain the difference in experience with economic reforms between the CEE countries and the countries of the former Soviet Union (FSU) in the mid-1990s, which provide some interesting results.

In a series of studies supported by the World Bank, the FSU was represented by Russia, Estonia, and the Kirgiz Republic, and the sample for the CEE region was drawn from Bulgaria, Hungary, and Poland. They measured each country's Cumulative Liberation Index (CLI), which measures the degree of overall cumulative progress in three areas of economic reform: privatization, liberation of internal markets such as prices and trading, and liberation of foreign trade and investment. The CLI is a measure of actual behavioral changes resulting from the overall policy reforms. The studies also compared the scope and depth of poverty in the CEE and FSU countries.

The results show a positive correlation between reform and poverty alleviation. Those countries with a high CLI had lower incidences of poverty than those with a lower CLI. For example, both Poland and Hungary scored high on CLI and reported lower poverty incidences, whereas both Russia and the Kirgiz Republic scored lower on CLI and reported higher incidences and deeper rates of poverty. Russia had the worst poverty results: a poverty incidence of almost 40 percent and an average poverty gap of 30 percent. Hungary and Poland showed the most favorable results: respective poverty rates of 21 percent and 23 percent.[36]

In addition, the CEE region has been more successful in attracting foreign direct investment than the FSU. For example, according to World Bank reports, during the five-year period 1996–2000, Poland, Hungary, and the Czech Republic—the three most successful transition economies with an active and competitive entrepreneurial private sector—attracted foreign direct investment of approximately U.S.$22 billion, U.S.$13 billion, and U.S.$15 billion, respectively. This compares with only just more than U.S.$4 billion Russia received during the five-year period 1990–1995. As well, the CEE countries have been able to dramatically increase their trade with the rest of the world, especially the EU and OECD countries.[37]

By pulling together the results of the studies of entrepreneurship—the degree of success with economic reform and liberation as measured by CLI, determinants of poverty in the CEE and FSU countries, and the ability to attract foreign direct investment—a clear picture begins to emerge. The countries of the CEE region most successful in developing a viable entrepreneurial business sector are more successful at economic reform and have higher household incomes. On the other hand, countries such as Russia with a rather ineffective entrepreneurial business sector are less successful at economic reform and report higher incidences of household poverty. These results point to the importance of the entrepreneurial business sector as the critical moderating variable between economic reform and improvements in household incomes. Accordingly, these results have significant implications for economic reforms and globalization. They speak to a more significant role of the entrepreneurial business sector in advancing economic liberation and raising household incomes than has so far been acknowledged. In practical terms, globalizing countries cannot expect to make quick and sustaining progress in reforming their economies and raising standards of living of the majority of their citizens without a viable entrepreneurial class linked to the macroeconomy by a critical mass of an effective and competitive entrepreneurial business institutional infrastructure. Just as political reforms and personal freedoms are impossible without democratic institutions, economic reforms and improvements in personal income are impossible to sustain without corresponding entrepreneurial institutions. This is a lesson for all reforming and globalizing countries.

In concluding this discussion of entrepreneurship and private sector development in the CEE region, I note with profound regret that the studies of the entrepreneurial firms did not include discussions of corporate governance. This is an unfortunate omission and a lost opportunity because, as I have discussed, the quality of corporate governance is directly related to opportunities for entrepreneurship, private sector development, competitiveness, and globalization. Newspaper reports and journalistic accounts seem to suggest that those countries experiencing difficulties in carrying out effective economic reforms (low CLI), lacking a competitive entrepreneurial business institutional infrastructure, and reporting low household incomes (high incidences of poverty) are also experiencing poor corporate governance. This is because reforms are multidimensional and longitudinal. Therefore, together with entrepreneurship and private sector development, reforms for globalization are needed in areas such as landownership, property rights, pensions, monopolies, the court system, social assistance, and corporate governance. The need for outside assistance has never been greater.

NOTES

1. Joseph A. Schumpeter, *Change and the Entrepreneur* (Cambridge: Harvard University Press, 1949).

2. Emphasis in original; Samuel Kwasi Baume, *Entrepreneurship:A Contextual Perspective* (Lund, Sweden: Lund University Press, 1996), 23–24. Also see D. C. Mead, and C. Liedholm, "The Dynamics of Micro and Small Enterprises in Developing Countries," *World Development* 26, no. 1 (1998):61–74.

3. For personal accounts of dysfunctional and antisocial behavioral tendencies among Silicon Valley entrepreneurs, see Andrew S. Grove, *Only the Paranoid Survive* (New York: Doubleday, 1996); and Tim Jackson, *Inside Intel* (New York: Penguin, 1998).

4. See Vijaya Ramachandran and Manjou Kedia Shah, "Minority Entrepreneurs and Private Sector Growth in Sub-Saharan Africa," Discussion Paper 086. Regional Program on Enterprise Development (Washington, DC: World Bank, July 1999).

5. Wayne H. Stewart Jr., *Psychological Correlates of Entrepreneurship* (New York: Garland, 1996).

6. For the original study of Indian entrepreneurs, see David C. McClelland, *The Achieving Society* (Princeton, NJ: Van Nostrand, 1961). Also see David C. McClelland and D. G. Winter, *Motivating Economic Achievement* (New York: Free Press, 1969).

7. Robert Alan LeVine, *Dreams and Deeds: Achievement Motivation in Nigeria* (Chicago: University of Chicago Press, 1966).

8. Burton Benedict, "Family Firms and Firm Families: A Comparison of Indian, Chinese, and Creole Firms in Seychelles," in *Entrepreneurs in Cultural Context*, ed. Sidney M. Greenfield, Arnold Strickon, and Robert T. Aubey (Albuquerque: University of New Mexico Press, 1979), 305–326.

9. Professor Michael Frese and his coworkers have published a stream of research papers dealing with various aspects of trait theory and entrepreneurship. For example, see Andreas Ulsch, Andreas Rouch, Rainer Rothfuss, and Michael Frese, "Who Becomes a Small Entrepreneur in a Post-Socialist Environment: On the Differences between Entrepreneurs and Managers in East Germany," *Journal of Small Business Management* 37, no. 3 (July 1999):31–42. Also see, Michael Frese, ed., *Success and Failure of Microbusiness Owners in Africa* (Westport, CT: Quorum, 2000).

10. See Buame, *Entrepreneurship*, pg. 17.

11. For a review and summary of the various studies on race/ethnicity and entrepreneurship, see Moses N. Kiggundu, "Entrepreneurs and Entrepreneurship in Africa: What We Know and What We Need to Know," *Journal of Developmental Entrepreneurship* (in press).

12. Gillian Patricia Hart, "Some Socio-Economic Aspects of African Entrepreneurship," Occasional Paper 16 (Grahamstown: Rhodes University, 1972), 194

13. Jan J. Jørgensen, Taieb Hafsi, and Moses N. Kiggundu, "Towards a Market Imperfections Theory of Organizational Structure in Developing Countries," *Journal of Management Studies* 23, no. 4 (July 1986):417–442.

14. Henry Mintzberg, *The Nature of Management Work* (New York: Harper and Row, 1973).

15. Hart, "Some Socio-Economic Aspects," 194.

16. Kelfala M. Kallon, *The Economics of Sierra Leonean Entrepreneurship* (Lanham, MD: University Press of America, 1990).

17. Mamadou Dia, *Africa's Management in the 1990s and Beyond: Reconciling Indigenous and Transplanted Institutions* (Washington, DC: World Bank, 1996), 170–174.

18. Kenneth Loucks, *Training Entrepreneurs for Small Business Creation: Lessons from Experience*. Management Development Series A26 (Geneva: International Labour Organization, 1998), 87.

19. See Gillian Godsell, "Entrepreneurs Embattled: Barriers to Entrepreneurship in South Africa," in *The Culture of Entrepreneurship*, ed. Brigette Berger (San Francisco: ICS Press, 1991), 85–97.

20. Rosebeth Moss Kanter, *The Change Masters: Innovation and Entrepreneurship in the American Corporation* (New York: Simon and Schuster, 1983), 306.

21. A recent World Bank publication discusses various aspects of industrial decentralization drawing on and linking various local entrepreneurs. See Yusiro Hayami, "Toward a New Model of Rural–Urban Linkages under Globalization," in *Local Dynamics in an Era of Globalization*, ed. Shahid Yusaf, Weiping Wu, and Simon Evenett (Washington, DC: World Bank, 2000), 74–83.

22. Utis Kaothien and Douglas Webster, "Globalization and Urbanization: The Case of Thailand," in *Local Dynamics in an Era of Globalization*, ed. Shahid Yusaf, Weiping Wu, and Simon Evenett (Washington, DC: World Bank, 2000), 140–147.

23. For a review of the APDF, see Swedish Development Advisors, *The African Development Project Facility Development Impact Study, 242 Projects Completed in 1986–1995* (Golhenburg: Swedish Development Advisors, April 1999). Also see David J. Smith, *The African Development Project Development Facility Impact Study 1996–1998 Update Review* (February 2000). Background materials are available from the recent annual reports of the APDF, 2121 Pennsylvania Avenue, NW, IFC/World Bank, Room F3P-114, Washington, DC. Also available at www.ifc.org.

24. This section is based on several studies. See Jørgensen, Hafsi, and Kiggundu, "Towards a Market Imperfections Theory," 417–422; Moses N. Kiggundu, "Management in Uganda," *Regional Encyclopedia to Business and Management: Management in the Emerging Countries* (London: Thompson Learning Business Press, 2000), 228–236; Paul Kennedy, *African Capitalism: The Struggle for Ascendancy* (Cambridge: Cambridge University Press, 1998); Dia, *Africa's Management in the 1990s and Beyond*.

25. From Malcolm Harper, "Enterprise in Africa," personal communication, June 20, 2000. Professor Harper can be reached at malcolm.harper@btinternet.com.

26. Cited in Kiggundu, "Management in Uganda," 233.

27. George Soros, *The Crisis of Global Capitalism* (New York: Public Affairs, 1998), table 7.1, p. 144.

28. This section is based on a synthesis of various studies on entrepreneurship and private sector development in Central and Eastern Europe. See, for example, Galen Spencer Hull, *Small Business Trickling Up in Central and Eastern Europe* (New York: Garland, 1999). For each country, the study sampled more than one hundred firms, and because of the details involved, readers are advised to see the original study.

29. See for example, Venon Henderson, "On the Move: Industrial Deconcentration in Today's Developing Countries," and Allen J. Scott, "Global City—Regions in the New World System," in *Local Dynamics in an Era of Globalization*, ed. Shahid Yusuf, Wieping Wu, and Simon Evenett (Washington, DC: World Bank, 2000), chap. 7 and chap. 10, respectively.

30. For a discussion of the role of technical assistance in entrepreneurship and private sector development, see Hull, *Small Business*; also see Bernt Schiller, M. Donald Hancock, and John Logue, "The International Context of Economic and Political Transitions," and John Logue and M. Donald Hancock, "Domestic Reform and Transnational Support," in *Transition to Capitalism and Democracy in Russia and Central Europe: Achievements, Problems, Prospects*, ed. M Donald Hancock and John Logue (Westport, CT: Praeger, 2000), chap. 14 and postscript, respectively.

31. Hull, *Small Business*, 78. Also see Leila Webster and Dan Swanson, "The Emergence of Private Sector Manufacturing in the Former Czech and Slovak Federal Republic: A Survey of Firms," Technical Paper 230 (Washington, DC: World Bank, 1993).

32. David Landes, *The Wealth and Poverty of Nations: Why Some Are So Rich and Some So Poor* (New York: Norton, 1999).

33. Detailed information about ISO 9000 certification can be obtained from the Internet: www.iso-9000.co.uk or www.isoseek.com.

34. See Hull, *Small Business*, 225.

35. For detailed discussions of reforms and private sector development for a country in transition, see Laszlo Andor, *Hungary on the Road to the European Union: Transition in Blue* (Westport, CT: Praeger, 2000), especially chap. 4. For journalistic but informative accounts of New Zealand, see "New Zealand's Economy: Can the Kiwi Economy Fly," *The Economist*, December 2, 2000, pp. 69–71, and the readers' letters "New Zealand's Reforms," *The Economist*, December 16, 2000, p. 8.

36. Based on detailed discussions by Jeanine Braithwaite, Christiaan Grootaert, and Branko Milanovic, *Poverty and Social Assistance in Transition Countries* (New York: St. Martin's, 1999), 33.

37. Ibid.

CHAPTER 5

Trade and Investment

Trade and investment are at the heart of globalization. The countries most active and benefiting most from globalization are the same ones with the largest share of global trade and foreign investment. Countries lacking the institutional capacity for global trade and investment cannot gainfully participate in economic globalization. Newly globalizing countries must be able and willing to open up their foreign markets in goods, services, and investments. Trade remains the principal key for creating and distributing wealth among and within nations. Since World War II, world merchandise trade has grown by almost fifteen times, whereas total world output has grown by only five times. Countries are much richer today than they were fifty years ago because of trade, and many more would have been richer if the world enjoyed free trade and investment during the second half of the twentieth century. World trade volumes were expected to increase by 12.5 percent in 2000, the highest rate of growth since before the first oil shock of the 1970s.

Although most of the world trade takes place among the developed countries within the Organization for Economic Cooperation and Development (OECD), the European Union (EU), and the North American Free Trade Agreement (NAFTA), developing countries are increasingly becoming significant players both as exporters and as potential markets for the developed countries. In the 1990s, ten years after the end of the Cold War and the opening up of various economies of the world for developing countries, the average ratio of exports of goods and services to GDP grew to over 21 percent. For most of these countries, trade and investments provide the best and most sustaining opportunity to alleviate poverty among their citizens and to catch up to the developed countries in terms of wealth creation, income generation, and rising standards of living. According to the World Bank, abolition of all trade barriers would boost global income by U.S.$2.8 trillion and lift 320 million people out of proverty by 2015.[1] This is more people out of poverty than foreign aid, in general, and U.S. Agency for International Development (USAID), in particular, has been able to lift since the end of World War II. Indeed, the future of globalization may well depend on the world community's ability and willingness to manage global trade and investment for the benefit of all nations and all their citizens.

TRADE THEORY: COMPARATIVE ADVANTAGE, PROTECTIONISM, AND EXPORT SUBSIDIES

Trade theory originates from the work of the English economist David Ricardo (1772–1823) who coined the term *comparative advantage*. Comparative advantage refers to the sustaining capacity of a place, sector, or industry to produce goods or services more cheaply, efficiently, and profitably than the competition. It helps to explain the spatial division of labor, as well as industrial specialization. According to the theory of comparative advantage, the market rewards efficient producers and punishes the less-efficient ones. Countries, industries, and firms continue to produce goods and services for which they have a comparative advantage and exit from those for which there is no practical comparative advantage.

Globally, comparative advantage explains why manufacturing is concentrated in the OECD countries; agriculture, mining, and textiles in developing countries; oil production in the Organization of Petroleum Exporting Countries (OPEC); and gold and diamonds in southern Africa. Within countries, there are also industrial clusters reflecting regional comparative advantage. For example, in the United States, New York City specializes in financial services, Los Angeles in entertainment, the Silicon Valley in computers and information technology, and Florida in fruits and tourism. However, comparative advantage is not a static concept; rather, it is a complex and dynamic concept that shifts across time and space. For example, Liverpool, England, used to be world famous for textiles and shipbuilding— no more. Switzerland used to be the leading world producer of watches, but that was before the Japanese entered the market with digital watches. France used to have a virtual monopoly on fine wines. Today, liquor stores are full of fine wines from all continents of the world.

Comparative advantage as a dynamic concept is what gives developing countries and transition economies hope in globalization. They, too, can find tradable goods and services for which they have developed comparative advantage, enabling them to compete in the global market. For example, the "Green Revolution," resulting from the early scientific experiments funded by the Rockefeller Foundation and spreading to various developing countries including India, Mexico, Indonesia, and Egypt, has enabled many developing countries to produce surplus agricultural produce for export markets. Today, most of the world's rice is produced in Asia. Likewise, the garment industries in Asia and Central America have developed comparative advantage and are producing consistently at cheaper prices than American and European producers, causing plant closures and job losses in the latter markets. Indeed, Southeast Asian countries built their economies by carefully developing niche export markets while restricting nonessential imports. At the other end of the spectrum, the poorer and weaker developing countries experiencing difficulties with globalization have failed to develop a competitive, diversified export portfolio for the global market.

Unfortunately, trade has never been left free to the economic forces of comparative advantage. Historically, all countries of the world—developed and developing, weak and strong, big and small—have always practiced some form of protectionism. Protectionism is the total sum of societal mind-set and government institutional policies and instruments designed to protect domestic producers from foreign competition by limiting or blocking imports through legislation, tariffs, quotas, and other nontariff barriers. For example,

America, Europe, Japan, and Canada have a long history of subsidizing farmers and protecting agriculture from foreign competition. This allows the farmers to produce more than the market can absorb but get paid at a fair price. It also keeps agricultural goods, produced elsewhere more cheaply and efficiently, out of these countries' markets. Most developing countries used to pursue an industrial development policy of import substitution that protected local "infant" firms from foreign competition by tariff and nontariff means of protectionism. During the Cold War, protectionism was used to differentiate allies and strategic trading partners from enemies and strategic competitors.

Globalization, as it relates to trade, is aimed at reducing or eliminating protectionism in order to maintain a level playing field for all trading nations. Indeed, the WTO and the General Agreement on Tariffs and Trade (GATT), especially before the Uruguay round of negotiations, have helped to significantly reduce protectionism by reducing tariffs. Still, developing countries continue to face a wide range of nontariff administrative instruments of protectionism, which keep their exports out of the rich markets of developed countries. Protectionism by the developed countries—aimed at keeping developing countries out of the formers' markets especially in sectors such as agriculture, textiles, and light manufacturing where the latter have a decided comparative advantage—is a serious impediment to free trade and globalization and a constant source of conflict in multilateral negotiations.

As tariffs have been negotiated down over time, global trade has become more competitive. Accordingly, both developed and developing trading nations use a variety of nontariff instruments to promote exports. Export subsidies are widely used by poor and rich countries alike to enhance their presence in the global market. Export subsidies are the other side of the protectionist coin because they protect inefficient domestic producers and keep out efficient, unsubsidized producers. Governments offer subsidies to exporters in order to protect jobs at home and promote domestic growth. These subsidies are also defended on the ground that they protect infant industries, compensate for protectionism by the other "bad guys," help small entrepreneurial firms overcome capital–market problems, and contribute positively to trade and balance of payments accounts, including strengthening the national currency. Subsidies are also defended because they help maintain national culture, the countryside, and rural lifestyles. Subsidies take different forms, including ad valorem payments to exporters, tax credits, loans, insurance policies, price support, underwriting research and development, and lobbying foreign governments. Governments of globalizing trading countries take it as their responsibility to engage in a wide range of public policy undertakings aimed at subsidizing and supporting the national export sector, and the citizens expect them to. Yet, protection hurts the poor in developing countries and is an obstacle to fair trade and globalization.

Contrary to public perception, export subsidies are not an efficient public policy instrument for allocating resources. This is particularly important for developing countries with limited tax revenues competing for many deserving demands. Studies also show that export subsidies are a regressive form of taxation: Tax revenues are given to corporations, who least need them, thus depriving the poor of much-needed social support. By definition, export subsidies discriminate against domestic producers who may be equally deserving or even contributing more to growth. As well, studies seem to suggest that there is no evidence to support the claim that export subsidies help a country to boost its exports significantly as compared to countries that do not provide such subsidies. India's experience shows export subsidies to have little impact on exports. Brazil and Mexico's experience shows export subsidies to be costly instruments of export diversification. Instead of subsidies, governments should develop public policies aimed at improved productivity and economic growth.[2]

In Chapter 1, a distinction was made between the center and the periphery. The center is made up of the developed countries that control most of the economic activities of the world, including global trade and investment. The periphery was divided between the advanced developing countries (P1) and the less-advanced developing countries (P2). P1 countries are actively involved in global trade and are increasing not only their share but also the influence they exert over trade matters. Examples include the countries of Southeast Asia, Brazil, Mexico, Egypt, and South Africa. P2 countries, on the other hand, continue to experience difficulties in establishing themselves as competitive global trading economies. Their share of the overall global trade is small, and they exert little or no influence over global trade matters or negotiations.

The typical export portfolio of a P2 country is made up of one or a few agricultural commodities or minerals. This portfolio has not changed significantly for the last fifty years or so. For example, Ghana continues to export cocoa and gold as it has done for most of the twentieth century, and Jamaica continues to depend on bananas, bauxite, and tourism for export as it has always done. This makes for a very thin and high-risk export portfolio and vulnerable economy. In the long run, the terms of trade for commodity prices tend to decline in favor of manufacturing goods. Yet, most of the P2 countries have not been able to diversify their export portfolios to include high-value merchandise exports, manufactured goods, or tradable services.

Therefore, the challenge of managing trade for P2 countries is different than for P1 countries. P1 countries, such as Thailand, South Korea, and Brazil, are more interested in increasing their share of total global trade and having greater influence and decision making in matters of multinational trade at the WTO level or at the regional level with organizations such as the Association of Southeast Asian Nations (ASEAN) or NAFTA. On the other hand, P2 countries such as Kyrgyzstan, Bolivia, and Malawi still need to develop a viable, competitive, and diversified export portfolio that reflects not historical modes of production but the changing global demand and supply trends for merchandise trade and tradable services. For these countries to increase their share of global trade and to have a meaningful voice at the international or multinational trade negotiations, they must first have a credible export portfolio and establish themselves as serious competitive trading economies. This is not easy because, among other things, it necessitates major economic structural changes and requires collaborative efforts between the government and the entrepreneurial business private sector. Yet, in the future, at least in matters of global trade, countries will be able to scale up from P2 to P1 only if they successfully manage these challenges.

TRADE REFORMS AND FIRM COMPETITIVENESS

If protectionism is no longer allowed and export subsidies do not work, what can developing countries do to boost their export trade? Of course, detailed responses to this question differ across countries and time and need to take into account the particular circumstances and dynamics of each globalizing country. Still, one of the options available to most globalizing developing countries is to undertake comprehensive trade reforms. The rationale for these reforms is that by undertaking macroeconomic reforms aimed at loosening or eliminating trade restrictions and liberalizing or opening up the economy there are micro-level benefits including improved efficiency of the individual business firms. In addition to creating wealth and contributing to economic growth, improvements in business efficiency enhance competitiveness and comparative advantage for the firms or sectors involved. With improved competitiveness, firms can successfully compete for export markets. Therefore, trade reforms, if successful, can lead to growth and diversification of a country's export portfolio.

Exhibit 5.1 provides evidence of how liberalization of trade brought about operational efficiency among manufacturing business firms in Peru. Like many other developing countries, Peru's industrial development strategy was based on import substitution with a wall of tariff and nontariff protectionism. Naturally, the protected industrial firms had little or no incentive to strive for efficiency gains. They produced only for the domestic market and passed on the costs of their inefficiency to the consumers. All this changed in 1990 when Alberto Fujimori became president and introduced a national program of macroeconomic adjustments and reforms that included trade liberalization. Tariff categories were consolidated, and tariff rates were significantly reduced over a very short period. Price and wage controls were removed, the public service reformed, and a range of fiscal and monetary measures introduced.

Exhibit 5.1
Trade Reforms Bring About Business Efficiency:
Evidence from Peru

Background: Peru was one of the last Latin American countries to abandon import substitution as the core of its industrial development strategy. During the period 1960–1990, the manufacturing sector was protected by a set of tariff and nontariff barriers allowing local but high-cost production of automobiles and computers only for the domestic market. In July 1990, Alberto Fujimori was elected president and started implementation of a neoliberal package, which included a range of trade reforms.

The Reforms: A comprehensive economic reform package included:

- October 1990, consolidation of tariff categories from fifty-six to three.

- March 1991, tariff rates reduced to 5 percent, 15 percent, and 25 percent, with 82 percent of all goods subject to the 15 percent rate.

- Mean effective rate of protection fell from more than 90 percent in July 1990 to 36 percent in December 1990, then to 30 percent in March 1991. Standard deviation of the effective rate of protection fell from more than 70 percent in July 1990 to less than 20 percent in March 1991.

- Price and wage controls were removed.

- Subsidies to public services were eliminated, prices were allowed to rise, public service employment was reduced.

- Unification of a multiple exchange-rate system, liberalization of interest rates.

- Improved tax collection system; removal of interest rate ceiling on dollar—denominated deposits and loans.

- Introduction of private pension system.

- Creation of regulatory agency for private sector firms and consumer protection.

The Results: Looking at the data two years before (1988) and two years after (1992) the reforms were introduced, the study found:

- The reforms increased technical efficiency in Peru's manufacturing sector.

- A positive correlation was noted between tariff reduction and firm efficiency gains.

- Seventy-five percent of industries studied improved their unweighted efficiency scores between 1988 and 1992.

- The standard deviation (dispersion) of the unweighted efficiency scores declined in 70 percent of the industries studied.

- Relatively inefficient plants improved their performance following the trade reforms.

- Comparison of surviving and existing firms suggests that two years after the reforms were introduced, relatively inefficient firms were still in business.

- There is a time lag between the time the liberalization trade reforms are put in place and the firms' gains in efficiency.

Source: Based on a longitudinal empirical study by Ila M. Semenick Alam and Andrew R. Morrison, "Trade Reform Dynamics and Technical Efficiency: The Peruvian Experience," *World Bank Economic Review* 14, no. 2 (May 2000):309–330. Readers are advised to consult the original for technical details.

With the support of Peru's Ministry of Industry, Tourism, Integration, and International Trade Negotiations, a longitudinal study of the effects of the trade reforms on the operational efficiency of the individual business manufacturing firms was undertaken. The study compared measures of productivity two years before the reforms were introduced (1988) and two years after (1992). The results show that, as a whole, Peru's manufacturing sector became more efficient and more competitive as a result of the implementation of the trade reforms. Most of the firms studied improved their efficiency scores between 1988 and 1992. This was particularly so for the firms that were inefficient and, therefore, had a lot more room for improvement.

The results also confirm that there is a time lag between the time the reforms are introduced and implemented and the time when the individual firms begin to achieve particularly significant gains in efficiency. These results are similar to those found for the countries of Central and Eastern Europe (CEE) where the macroeconomic transition reforms to an open-market economy took time before significant positive behavioral changes could be noticed at the microeconomic and individual levels. Likewise, in Peru, one would expect a similar time lag between the time the manufacturing firms improve their efficiency and the time when they begin to develop strategies and business plans for export markets.

The Peruvian case study contains useful lessons of experience for newly globalizing countries, especially of the P2 category. The first lesson is that carefully designed and strongly implemented macroeconomic trade reforms can have significant positive effects at the microeconomic level for individual business firms and entrepreneurs. By the same token, if the macroeconomic reforms do not translate into practical changes at the microeconomic and individual levels, there can be no improvements in trade and other macroeconomic indicators. The second lesson resulting from the Peruvian study is that rather than applying protectionism and export subsidies developing countries can create wealth, generate income, and improve export performance by implementing measures of trade reform and liberalization. Third, it is important to remember that reforms take time. Full implementation of reforms often takes longer than planned, and the private sector takes even more time before they take note of the reforms, build confidence that such reforms are irreversible, and develop strategies and business plans consistent with the provisions of the reforms. Therefore, it is important for those managing reforms for globalization and the intended beneficiaries to understand the implications for time, timing, and sequencing of the reforms and the flow of the expected benefits.

Another lesson of experience, which is not obvious from the empirical evidence of the study, is the relationship between the domestic and export market performance. When trade reforms are successful, they enable entrepreneurial firms to take a bigger share of the domestic market, which they then use as a basis for developing export markets. This happens because, as I have discussed, trade reforms enhance firm operational efficiency, reduce costs, and improve competitiveness and profitability. This allows the firms to produce more, enjoy economies of scale, and become more competitive in the domestic markets. With more revenue, profits, and economies of scale, such firms can then improve their corporate governance and, thus, enhance their attractiveness to potential investors and creditors. With additional resources, the firms can begin to invest in areas that make their goods or services competitive on the global market. For example, drawing from the results of their domestic success, such firms can begin to undertake operational and management changes for quality and product improvements, including ISO 9000 training and certification. They can also begin to develop business alliances and partnerships with foreign firms for joint undertakings in areas such as market research, new product development, and commercialization and begin to develop overall business management know-how improvements.

Naturally, charity begins at home: The road to being able to export successfully starts with the success of entrepreneurial firms in the domestic market. Domestic success provides the necessary resources, capacity, and stature to build the platform for penetrating and competing in the export markets. Once again, this underscores the importance of having a critical mass of competitive and successful entrepreneurial firms not only for effective private sector development but, perhaps more important, also for trade and investment. Successful trade reform and export performance need a dynamic private sector made up of a critical mass of competitive entrepreneurial firms. Indeed, the individual entrepreneurs are the foot soldiers of the global economy, and the entrepreneurial firms are its battalions.

EXPORT DEVELOPMENT CORPORATIONS

Most developed countries have export development corporations as part of their national institutional infrastructure for managing international trade. Originating from the Cold War era, export development corporations are state-owned financial institutions devoted exclusively to providing financial services to local exporters and investors to make them globally competitive. They work with both the private and the public sectors to enhance the country's export capacity and to prepare the country to respond to international trade opportunities and challenges. The most common services provided by export development corporations are:

1. global reach,
2. support to small business and new exports,
3. insurance services,
4. financial services,
5. clearing house for international market information,
6. promoting the development of an export business culture.

Global reach means assisting local firms to reach out in search of international export markets, especially in regions, countries, industries, or sectors in which the local firms would not otherwise consider for export. This is particularly important in a rapidly changing international situation in which old markets disappear and new ones emerge almost overnight. An important aspect of global reach is the development of an international export-oriented mind-set among the country's most promising entrepreneurial firms so that they begin to see the relationships between their domestic success and export markets.

Almost 90 percent of the export development corporations' clients are small- and medium-size enterprises (SMEs) and new exporters or overseas investors. In this case, export development corporations are an important part of the country's institutional infrastructure for private sector development and the development of a viable globally competitive entrepreneurial sector. Small businesses often lack the information, resources, contacts, stature, and experience to develop export markets. Export development corporations provide the necessary resources and support for these firms to become successful exporters. For example, the Canadian Export Development Corporation (EDC) has an export development program specifically tailored for Canadian SMEs.[3] The program includes accounts receivable insurance for small business whereby up to 90 percent of the loss is covered if the export buyer does not pay. It also includes financing arrangements whereby the federal government's financial institution provides soft loans to international buyers of Canadian capital goods. This means the Canadian exporter gets the cash up front, and the EDC takes the responsibility for collecting from the foreign buyer. Also, the small exporters can get extra financing through guarantee of foreign receivables. For example, if a Canadian commercial bank refuses to accept foreign accounts receivable as security for the firm's operating line of credit, the EDC can step in and help the bank to increase the firm's operating line of credit. As well, small firms get specialized technical assistance to help them develop export expertise and capabilities.

Perhaps the most common areas of support by export development corporations are in finance and insurance services. Exporters can get insurance coverage in areas such as accounts receivable, bonding products, political risk investment, and political risk loans. By providing insurance coverage in these export and investment areas, the export development corporation is providing technical, financial, and management resources for managing the risks associated with global trade and investment. In fact, such services make it very attractive for firms to export and invest abroad because they reduce the risks significantly without affecting the potential profits and other benefits.

What are the implications of export development corporations for globalizing developing countries and transition economies? There are both positive and problematic implications. On the positive side, export development corporations make it possible for the high-risk countries to import capital goods and attract private investment from producers and investors who would otherwise shy away. Second, the services of export development corporations make it possible for small- and medium-size firms in newly globalizing countries to establish business relationships and partnerships with counterparts in the advanced countries so that together they can advance the interests of international trade, investment, and globalization. Over time, these business strategic alliances can help the newly globalizing countries to improve the volume and quality of their export trade and foreign investment. These alliances also provide excellent channels of communication for technology transfer relationship building and for the entrepreneurial firms of the newly globalizing developing countries to acquire technical, operational, and managerial know-how from the advanced countries.

On the other hand, the services of the export development corporations, provided by a government agency, must be seen as a series of subsidies to the potential exporter and overseas investor. Like all subsidies, these services distort the market and may impede competitiveness. Therefore, countries such as Canada, whose EDC supported more than five thousand customers and more than $37 billion (Canadian) worth of business volume in almost two hundred countries in 1999, provide an unfair advantage for their exporters and overseas investors. Most of the newly globalizing developing countries cannot afford that kind of support for their producers. SMEs whose governments cannot afford such elaborate and expensive subsidies are at a disadvantage in competing with similar small enterprises in advanced countries that offer these subsidies.

There is a need for all potential exporters, in both advanced and developing countries, to compete on a level playing field. Perhaps the role export development corporations play in subsidizing export trade and foreign investment needs to be rethought. At the same time, newly globalizing countries need to pull resources together to identify areas in which they can support their own entrepreneurial export firms and investors. This could be done through the emerging regional trading blocks such as COMESA (Common Market for Eastern and Southern Africa), ASEAN (Association for Southeast Asian Nations), SAARC (South Asian Association for Regional Cooperation), and MERCOSUR (Common Market of South America). As believers and promoters of fair global trade and investment, donors, other members of the international community, and the WTO, in consultation with developing countries, should address the issues associated with the services of export development corporations and provide corresponding support and financial assistance to the export sectors of the developing countries. Ultimately, the services of the export development corporations may have to be outlawed as unfair and inequitable trade practices.

TRADE, INVESTMENT, AND THE GLOBAL CORPORATION

Globalization has given rise to the emergence of the global corporation. This has been a natural evolution from the national to the international then multinational or transnational and now global corporation. A global corporation differs from other corporate forms in that it operates with a single global strategy with a worldwide system and plan for products, marketing, manufacturing, logistics, research and development, accounting, and human resource management. The global economy and society define the global corporation's competitive environment. The global corporation has no geographical boundaries but carries out its operations and management functions holistically in the context of a unified worldwide system. It balances its global obligations with local needs in order to provide excellent customer service both globally and locally. It locates its operations, including corporate headquarters, anywhere in the world, regardless of nationality. It recruits and selects the best people available as management or knowledge workers regardless of their nationality. Examples of global corporations include IBM, General Electric, Coca-Cola, McDonald's, Phillips, Time-Warner (CNN), Shell, General Motors, Siemens, Toyota, Microsoft, Alcatel, and Nortel Networks. Almost all global corporations operate in the English language.

Global corporations are the major players and drivers of global trade and investment. They dominate global trade, finance and investment, research and development, technology transfer, and commodity chains that permeate the world economy. By the end of the year 2000, global corporations employed over 65 million people worldwide, of whom about 22 million, or almost 40 percent, were in developing countries. They derive most of their revenue (about 60 percent) from outside their original home country, and trade goods and services among themselves. They operate on the basis of global strategic alliances, competing and cooperating with other corporate entities in the global economy. In all aspects, global corporations are the most important force in the control and acceleration of global trade and globalization.

For globalizing developing countries and transition economies, global corporations are a mixed bag. They are advantageous in that they facilitate economic openness and competitiveness, bring in foreign direct investment (FDI), technology, management know-how, and help create jobs for the local labor market. They also bring with them corporate goodwill because global corporations tend to go where other global corporations have decided to go. They train local staff to become knowledge workers, managers, and entrepreneurs, and they provide a private sector–driven environment for private sector development. They provide a local market for SMEs and help the development of local entrepreneurs. For example, Coca-Cola provides business opportunities for local bottlers, distributors, wholesalers, and retailers. McDonald's provides business opportunities for poultry farmers, potato growers, and other agri-food entrepreneurs. Perhaps one of the long-term advantages that global corporations bring to globalizing developing countries is the development of a global mind-set not only among the employees but the entire host society.

Global corporations are widely criticized for being responsible for the negative consequences of globalization, especially for developing countries and transition economies. They are accused of perpetuating the "corporate agenda," focusing on wealth creation and profit making with little or no concern for the environment, social justice, social responsibilities or democratic governance. (For example, IBM's global strategy has four primary goals: corporate profits, quality, efficiency, and growth with no direct reference to the host country.[4]) They are also accused of causing local disruptions in the economy, markets, and indigenous economic relations. Since most of these corporations originate in developed countries, they are accused of subjecting their host countries to foreign domination, foreign values, and foreign practices with little or no regard for indigenous values and practices. With so much power and influence, they force host governments to compromise national sovereignty, which allows companies to meddle in local politics, the economy, and public administration.

It has also been argued that the net economic benefits global corporations bring to the local economy are often exaggerated. Their operations, especially in mining and other extractive industries, have limited local multiplier effects. They place costly and excessive demands on the local infrastructure, expatriate profits out of the host country, and disregard local concerns in making corporate strategic decisions such as plant locations or closures. They cause internal labor market distortions, making it difficult for the public sector to attract and retain the best and brightest nationals. Because of these drawbacks and because the benefits global corporations bring to the local economy are not always made clear, often there is tension between the corporation's drive for profitability, openness, and competitiveness and the host country's need for national economic development, integration, and local control and ownership. As well, the relationship between the global corporation and the host government is not symmetrical, with the former wielding more power, resources, and negotiating skills than the local partners. Consequently, global corporations have very few friends or active supporters in developing countries, which makes them subject to excessive regulation, including requirements for profits to be invested locally.

Despite these negative consequences attributed to global corporations, no country, developed or developing, can sustain a viable economy without the active participation of these corporations in many different sectors and industries. Therefore, newly developing countries have no choice but to attract global corporations as key players in the local economy. They need to develop a better understanding of the essence and behavior of these corporations and how best to establish and manage mutually beneficial relationships with them. In a recent article, John Roth, the former chief executive officer of Nortel Networks, argued that national companies are going to disappear, and that in the future, there will be only SMEs and global corporations.[5] If this is true, then the leaders in both the public and the private sector of the emerging globalizing countries must develop a more comprehensive understanding of these corporations and a national capacity and practical skills for dealing with them to mutual advantage.

FOREIGN DIRECT INVESTMENT AND GLOBALIZATION

FDI is long-term capital investments made by the private sector across national borders. By far, the bulk of the world's FDI is carried out by global corporations, which move capital investments in accordance with their respective global business strategies and in response to emerging global opportunities. Because it is private and voluntary, FDI is often used as a measure of a country's overall openness, competitiveness, and globalization. Countries are generally regarded as successful at globalization if they continue to attract quality FDI and unsuccessful if they fail to sustain increasing FDI inflows. There are two types of FDI: retrofit and greenfield. Retrofit FDI is when the foreign investor buys into an existing firm and takes over its operations and management. An example of retrofit FDI is when a global corporation buys a state-owned enterprise (SOE) from a reforming developing country as part of its privatization program. This type of investment is retrofit because it takes place within the context of an already existing corporate entity. On the other hand, the greenfield FDI involves the establishment of a new production entity, or significantly modifying or expanding existing facilities beyond recognition. Examples of greenfield investments include exploitation of natural resources such as oil and gas, mineral production, and manufacturing export platforms, all of which are common in developing countries and transition economies. The most successful globalizing countries maintain a dynamic balance between retrofit and greenfield FDI.

Why is FDI important for globalization? For most countries, FDI is the oil that drives the engine of growth, competitiveness, trade, entrepreneurial private sector development, and globalization. It increases a country's capital stock, creates employment, generates domestic income and savings, increases government revenues either through the sale of SOEs or taxation, and facilitates technology transfer and management know-how. Above all, it is a private sector vote of confidence in the country's political and economic reforms and its long-term investment prospects. Therefore, FDI creates international goodwill for the receiving country. Since global corporations compete with one another, they always scan the global environment to see what the competition is doing. When a respectable global corporation decides to make significant FDI in a country, others are likely to follow. In fact, FDI tends to follow globally discernable and predictable trends.

In most of the emerging markets such as Hungary, FDI has helped increase domestic savings, brought in modern technologies and managerial skills, and contributed significantly to capacity building, especially in the manufacturing, service, and export sectors. Greenfield investments tend to create jobs immediately and create multiplier effects in the local economy. Retrofit investments, on the other hand, especially those associated with money-losing SOEs, are often associated with staff layoffs. When FDI is integrated in the local economy, it helps create a positive business environment, a growing domestic market, and the emergence of local entrepreneurs and a competitive entrepreneurial private sector. FDI boosts exports because global corporations provide the best vehicle for global trade. For example, in 1996, foreign-owned companies in Hungary accounted for more than 80 percent of all investments in manufacturing, more than one-third of employment, and more than three-quarters of export earnings.[6]

It is also the case that in the early stages of reform, FDI tends to be linked to privatization. Global corporations are attracted to newly reforming countries through carefully prepared and financially attractive sales proposals of state-owned assets or operational corporations. This happened to the transition economies of Eastern Europe where less than 50 percent of all FDI was not related to privatization. For example, in 1991–1992, Hungary's FDI inflows were mostly acquired under the country's privatization program. In the late 1990s, it also happened in Africa where countries such as Ghana, Tanzania, Uganda, and Zambia attracted more FDI by privatization of SOEs, especially in the mining sector. For example, for the period 1990–1995, Ghana and Zambia attracted 6 percent and 4.6 percent, respectively, of the total FDI to sub-Saharan Africa. These investments were for the privatized Ashanti gold mines (Ghana) and the copper mines of Zambia.[7]

Despite the vital role it plays in accelerating globalization for developing countries and transition economies, FDI is not without problems and challenges, especially for the receiving countries. First, there are the usual negative sentiments associated with any foreign ownership by nationalists of any country. They see global corporations' ownership of local or national assets as an affront on national sovereignty and pride. Accordingly, governments have responded by putting restrictions on foreign ownership, especially in sensitive or strategic areas such as culture, agriculture, financial services, utilities, transport, and communications. These restrictions limit the free flow of FDI and may deprive some countries of badly needed capital for development. Yet, in many countries, society is willing to pay for the opportunity costs resulting from loss of investment owing to perceived fear of domination by outside corporate interests.

Second, FDI can be associated with instabilities in capital flows. Global corporations are very efficient in managing liquidity and flows of goods and services, but they do so in the best interest of their global business strategy, rather than in the best interest of the host country. They also have tremendous resources that allow them to leverage their assets and borrow locally or globally in pursuit of their global strategy and to protect themselves against changing circumstances of the host country. Accordingly, host countries may find it difficult to sustain a positive environment for attracting and retaining FDI. Third, and connected to the second, FDI is not evenly distributed, and those countries that need it most, especially the P2 countries, continue to experience problems attracting and keeping adequate levels of FDI. The global distribution of FDI is so important that it is closely associated with global poverty, so that the poorest parts of the world—especially sub-Saharan Africa, South and Central Asia, and parts of Latin America and the Caribbean—are the ones that receive the least amount of FDI. When they do receive FDI, it is often of the enclave type, limited to a single firm, sector, purpose, or location. Indeed, a more even global distribution of FDI, accompanied by enhanced trade and competitiveness, would do more to alleviate world poverty than the widely advocated solutions of debt forgiveness and increased aid flows.

The fourth problem associated with FDI is that it may force countries into unhealthy competition as they compete among themselves for quality FDI in different sectors. FDI tends to play different roles at different stages of a country's reform and development. In the early stages, it is largely associated with investments in natural resources, capital infrastructure projects, and nationalized assets. This is the easiest type of FDI to attract. Even countries such as Angola, Nigeria, and Kazakhstan with minimal success at reform continue to attract this type of FDI because of their natural resources. However, as the country continues on the path for reform and globalization, it needs to attract FDI in the more complex and competitive sectors such as manufacturing, high technology (such as computer and information technology), and value-added tradable services. For this type of high-quality FDI, developing countries and transition economies have to compete with the rest of the world.

The more advanced developing countries and transition economies have responded to the challenge by providing attractive incentives for high-quality FDI. For example, in April 1998, the government of the Czech Republic announced a comprehensive six-point package aimed at attracting this type of FDI. The package covers incentives such as corporate taxation, waivers of customs duty and value-added taxes on imported equipment, the provision of low-cost land, the opportunity to create special customs zones for major investors, job training grants, and job creation benefits for investments in less-developed regions of the country.

In 2000, Hungary came up with a similar FDI incentive plan designed to compete with the neighboring Czech Republic and other emerging markets. The Hungarian plan, developed and promoted by the Hungarian Investment and Trade Development Agency, was named the "Széchenyi Plan," after the nineteenth-century innovator Count István Széchenyi. It is part of the seven-year national development strategy designed to prepare Hungary for membership in the EU and NATO. Under the plan, the country makes available to potential investors a fund of U.S.$1 billion, from which government grants cover 25–30 percent of the cost of eligible projects. The plan identifies seven priority sectors for FDI: SMEs, tourism, regional development, transport infrastructure, housing, research and development, and information technology. The overall aim of the plan is to integrate FDI and global corporations' strategies into the country's local economy across sectors and regions.[8]

These two examples from the Czech Republic and Hungary provide useful lessons of experience for other globalizing countries regarding the capacity to attract high-quality FDI. First, they both show that liberalization of FDI policy is by itself not sufficient for emerging economies to continue to attract high-quality FDI; rather, in addition, governments must come up with financial and other types of incentives. These incentives cost money—in the form of subsidies, grants, or tax holidays. Connected to this is the realization that membership in reputable international or regional organizations such as the EU and NATO helps to attract high-quality FDI. For Hungary, it is important to join the EU and NATO; for Vietnam, it is the ASEAN; and for Russia, it is the WTO. Second, the experience of the two European countries demonstrates the inherent inequalities in the global distribution of FDI. The small, poor, highly indebted developing countries (P2), currently attracting little or no FDI, have very limited capacity and resources to develop and successfully implement a competitive FDI incentive plan similar to the ones developed by these two European countries. Therefore, they have practically little or no chance of improving their opportunities for attracting quality FDI beyond natural resources. The third lesson of experience is for the international community, both public and private, to find ways of helping these poor countries so that they, too, can become attractive to high-quality FDI. This would be good for globalization.

FACTORS DETERMINING THE GLOBAL FLOW OF FOREIGN DIRECT INVESTMENT

As I will show, the bulk of FDI takes place within the industrialized world, with the United States taking the lion's share. Within the developing countries and transition economies, once again FDI is very unevenly distributed, with the big emerging economies (BEMs) and the more reform-minded countries of the CEE region receiving most of the FDI both by volume and quality. Here, I briefly discuss the factors that help to explain the flow of FDI among developing countries and transition economies.

In general terms, FDI flows are determined by a combination of economic, social, and political conditions prevailing in a country at any given time and how they interact with the relevant forces and interests in the global economy and society. National or regional economic factors in favor of FDI include the country's history, overall policy framework, specific economic conditions on the ground, governance, and the quality and competitiveness of the commercial and corporate sector and institutional infrastructure. It is important for global corporations to clearly understand the country's rules of the game regarding entry; operations; standards of treatment of foreign affiliates; competition policy; the structure and functioning of the domestic market; existence and enforcement of international agreements relating to commerce, in general, and FDI, in particular; trade policy; privatization; property rights; fair and consistent enforcement of the law; and a functioning public service including a credible national integrity and regulatory system. Specific economic factors include organization; size; growth; competitive factor endowment; the quality and cost of the physical and digital infrastructure including power, water, ports, railroads, airports, hotels, and telecommunications; and the overall efficiency with which resources are utilized. Also considered are factors relating to the local technological and innovative capacities including the capacity to absorb and utilize new technologies and the quality of social services such as education, health, policing, recreation, and the quality of urban life and work. After the terrorist attack on U.S. interests, more attention will be given to security of the person, especially in countries where American and European citizens feel particularly vulnerable.

Sociopolitical factors relevant for FDI flows relate to the quality of governance: political stability, progress in democratization and institution building, parliamentary and electoral reforms, development of an informed and active civil society with an independent and responsible media, membership in regional and international organizations, and overall openness and interactions with other parts of the world. When the leaders of global corporations are making FDI allocation decisions not only do they take into account comparative direct cost–benefit analyses relating to taxation and labor productivity but, perhaps more important, they give serious consideration to the long-term quality and quantity of available or projected physical infrastructure, human capital infrastructure such as training schools, and the overall organization and management of society. As well, a national policy framework that encourages domestic saving and investment is likely to attract and retain FDI.

Small economies that have established efficient infrastructure and a conducive and stable macroeconomic policy in support of export-oriented manufacturing such as Singapore, Taiwan, and Malaysia have been able to attract high volumes of quality FDI seeking low-cost value-added export platforms. In contrast, large strategically important countries such as Russia, India, China, Indonesia, Mexico, and Brazil attract FDI not necessarily because of the progress they have made in reforming their economies and governments but because global corporations compete for a foothold in the potential markets these countries promise when they finally reform and open up.

A close look at the factors that determine the global flow of FDI provides at least two lessons of experience for developing countries and transition economies. First, those countries that do not have the "right" mix of economic, sociopolitical, and international policies or the necessary infrastructure and human capital cannot compete successfully in attracting and retaining quality FDI. Without FDI, they are less likely to have the necessary resources and capabilities for undertaking economic investments and growth. Without FDI and the active participation of the global corporations, they are unlikely to develop an integrated, competitive local economy and an entrepreneurial private sector made up of innovative SMEs. Without FDI and a competitive domestic private sector, these countries are less likely to develop a globally competitive export sector for their economies. Without a competitive export portfolio, they cannot gainfully participate in economic globalization. The lesson for these countries is clear: no FDI, no gainful globalization.

The second lesson for these countries is that important as these economic, sociopolitical, infrastructural, and institutional factors may be they are necessary but not sufficient for attracting and retaining quality FDI. With limited success, many countries, especially in Asia, South America, and Africa, worked very hard during the 1990s to reform their economies, governments, and societies in order to create conditions for attracting FDI. This suggests that there are other factors that must be considered in order to create the necessary and sufficient conditions for attracting and retaining FDI. This is particularly true for the less-known or newly created countries in central Asia and Africa.

Following are some of the additional factors that must be considered in creating a competitive environment for FDI. First is the need to develop a national globalization strategy with a specific plan for the development of trade and investment as has been illustrated for Hungary and the Czech Republic. In addition to the monetary incentives to potential investors, it is important for the globalizing country to think in terms of building institutional capacities for the ongoing management of FDI through the country's different stages of reform and development. Newly globalizing countries need to strengthen their agencies responsible for trade and investment. The requirements for quality FDI have become so complex and the competition so keen that the responsibilities for trade and investments should not be left only to line ministries. Consideration should be given to the creation of specialized trade and investment agencies, drawing on the institutional expertise of the government, business, and the international community. It is no longer sufficient for the leaders of these countries to declare their economies "open for business"; they must also be "ready" for business.

A second consideration is for the newly globalizing countries not only to reform their current accounts but also to take measures to satisfy conditions of the international financial agencies. For example, global corporations find it useful to deal with a country that belongs to a number of international organizations and those with international credit ratings such as those provided by Standard and Poor's or Moody. In the mid-1990s, several countries in the CEE region, including Russia, Romania, Latvia, Lithuania, and Moldova, received such ratings for the first time, and these ratings have played a role in the ability of these countries to attract foreign capital. These ratings provide information that global corporations, financial institutions, and other potential investors can use to assess the level of risk associated with different investment products. Without the kind of information independent credit rating agencies provide, potential investors are kept in the dark and are faced with situations of unknown risks; thus, most investors will choose to stay away and take their money elsewhere. By subjecting itself to the international assessment and comparative framework with others, a country becomes a member of the international community and is evaluated by the same set of criteria as all others. This makes the country "ready" for globalization.

Third, in addition to the economic and political factors, a country's ability to attract FDI may also depend on regional developments and relationships with its neighbors. This is particularly so for newly globalizing countries or regions with a history of political and/or economic instability and no track record with FDI. For example, in South Africa—the second largest recipient of FDI in sub-Saharan Africa after Nigeria—fears were expressed that Zimbabwe's continued political problems of the late 1990s could have negative effects on the region's ability to attract and retain FDI. In South America, Colombia's neighbors also expressed concern that growing insurgency activities in the country could negatively affect the inflows of FDI for countries such as Venezuela, Equador, Panama, and northern Peru. Continuing political problems in Afghanistan have affected investment prospects in Pakistan and other neighboring countries. Therefore, in addition to creating and sustaining attractive domestic policies and conditions, newly globalizing countries must also worry about events, trends, and developments in their respective regions and the relationships with their neighbors. Effective regional organizations can help bring about common understanding and approaches to globalization and foreign investment among member states for the benefit of potential investors.

A fourth consideration is the quality of personal and working relationships between the country's top leaders and the top leaders of the leading global corporations. For most of the newly globalizing countries, senior political leaders and public servants have had little or no direct contact with the chief executive officers and other top decision makers representing the global corporations. In some of these countries, the relationship is characterized by bad history, ideological differences, and acrimony (for example, Cuba, Russia, Libya). Despite the formalities and apparent cold calculations surrounding corporate governance and decision making, personal relationships and experiences still play a very important role in influencing corporate decisions, including foreign investment decisions. Indeed, those who vacation, dine, or play golf with Bill Gates, Henry Ford III, or other leaders of the global corporations have a better chance of getting favorable investment decisions than those who meet them as strangers or adversaries. It is also the case that most senior officials of the newly globalizing countries have years of experience trying to influence decisions in the political capitals of the world such as Washington's Capitol Hill, London's Whitehall, and Moscow's Kremlin. They must now learn to influence decisions in the economic capitals of the world such as Wall Street (New York), Fleet Street (London), Chicago, Houston, Frankfurt, Hong Kong, Tokyo, and Los Angeles where big foreign capital flow decisions are made every day.

Finally, it must also be said that some countries or regions suffer from a perpetual negative perception regarding FDI. This is particularly so for Africa, which has historically been one of the least attractive regions for FDI. Africa's share of FDI has been declining: from 3.1 percent in 1985 to 2.2 percent in 1990 to 1.9 percent in 1997. Moreover, most of the FDI Africa receives is of the enclave type and of relatively poor quality, dominated by extractive investments in natural resources such as oil and gas and mining. Sub-Saharan Africa receives very little FDI for manufacturing or high-value tradable services outside tourism. Global corporations do not include Africa in their global strategies for manufacturing, transportation, or distribution.

Historically, a combination of factors—such as low-to-negative economic growth, fragmented and small domestic markets, perceived political instability and never-ending conflicts, limited human capital and a weak institutional infrastructure, and widespread poverty and disease—have combined to keep high-quality FDI away from Africa. Yet, according to available information, the average FDI return on investment for sub-Saharan Africa was 24–30 percent compared to an overall average of 16–18 percent for all developing countries. Therefore, if FDI decisions were made purely on the basis of the profit motive, Africa would receive a lot more FDI than other developing regions. Clearly, in the real world of corporate decision making, perceptions matter. It is clear that Africa is not likely to increase its share of quality FDI until global corporate decision makers have changed their perception of it as a safe and profitable place to invest. International public relations was never emphasized as a core competence among senior political and public officials, or domestic private sector investors. With globalization and the need to compete for FDI and other resources on a worldwide scale, this must change. At the moment, these are some of the challenges developing countries must take on with help from the outside.

FOREIGN DIRECT INVESTMENT'S GLOBAL
WINNERS AND LOSERS

Table 5.1 provides a summary of the FDI global flows at the beginning (1990) and toward the end (1998) of the 1990s. The 1990s is an appropriate period to study the global behavior of FDI because it is the ten-year period following the breakup of the Soviet Union and the beginning of a new world order. As well, the 1990s constituted a time in history when most of the developing countries implemented wide-ranging political and economic

Table 5.1
FDI Global Flows in the 1990s: Winners and Losers

Country/Region	Millions of Dollars		
	FDI		Net Private
	1990	1998	Capital Flows: 1998
World	193,382	619,258	--
USA	48,954	193,373	--
Indonesia	1,093	-356	-3,759
Top-Ten BEMs	21,127	125,699	179,033
1. China	3,487	48,751	42,676
2. Brazil	989	31,913	54,385
3. Mexico	2,634	10,238	23,188
4. Singapore	5,575	7,218	--
5. Thailand	2,444	6,941	7,825
6. Argentina	1,836	6,150	18,899
7. South Korea	788	5,415	7,644
8. Malaysia	2,333	5,000	8,295
9. Chile	590	4,638	9,255
10. Venezuela	451	4,435	6,866
By Income Levels			
Low Income	2,201	10,674	12,231
Middle Income	21,929	160,267	255,469
High Income	169,252	448,316	--
By Region: Low and Middle Income			
East Asia and Pacific	11,135	64,162	67,249
Europe and Central Asia	1,051	24,350	53,342
Latin America and Caribbean	8,188	69,323	126,854
Middle East and North Africa	2,458	5,054	9,223
South Asia	464	3,659	7,581
Sub-Saharan Africa	834	4,364	3,452
Sub-Saharan Africa: Top Ten	588	3,417	2,755
1. Nigeria	--	1,051	1,028
2. South Africa	48	550	783
3. Côte d'Ivoire	-335	435	181
4. Angola	17	360	40
5. Lesotho	9	265	281
6. Mozambique	0	213	209
7. Uganda	0	200	198
8. Tanzania	95	172	157
9. Botswana	-12	95	95
10. Zimbabwe		76	-217

Note: BEMs = Big Emerging Markets.

Source: Compiled from World Bank, *World Development Report: Attacking Poverty* (Washington, DC: World Bank, 2000/2001), table 21, p. 314. Readers are advised to consult the original source for technical details.

reforms designed to earn them greater acceptance into the international community. By the end of the decade (the beginning of the new century), many developing countries were beginning to assess the results and effects of these reforms and to develop new strategies for the new millennium.

As Table 5.1 shows, total world FDI grew from just less than U.S. $200 billion in 1990 to more than U.S. $600 billion in 1998. These amounts had never been seen before in the history of the world. By far the largest movements of FDI took place within the industrialized countries. For example, a 1997 U.N. report estimated that approximately 68 percent of world FDI flows were received by the already industrialized countries. Corporate mergers and acquisitions of the 1990s accounted for most of this.[9] These mergers and acquisitions were part of the overall restructuring of the international business in response to the pressures of globalization.

Within the industrialized world, the United States leads the way both as a recipient and a provider of FDI to the rest of the world. As shown in Table 5.1, FDI for the United States grew from just under U.S. $50 billion in 1990 to almost U.S. $200 billion in 1998. This is because many European, Japanese, and other foreign firms invested in the U.S. economy. At the same time, approximately 50 percent of U.S. FDI goes to Europe—the single largest recipient of American foreign investment. Canada, the second largest recipient of American investment, received 20 percent, and Japan, the third largest recipient, received approximately 3 percent. Developing countries and transition economies receive only small amounts of American foreign investment, although China, Southeast Asia, and the CEE region are receiving increasing attention. What Table 5.1 clearly shows is that global FDI flows are essentially a North Atlantic affair.

Why does FDI remain within the industrialized countries? First, these countries have experienced increasing globalization, characterized by integration into world markets, and these trends are likely to continue well into the 2000s. Second, these countries' economies and markets are growing increasingly similar in size, structure, organization, and overall behavior. As would be expected, FDI tends to flow into familiar terrain and territory. Third, improvements in technology, communications, and management, and growing convergence in international technological capacities such as research and development, manufacturing, and transportation have combined to make it attractive for firms to seek business opportunities in Europe and North America. Fourth, and perhaps most important, these countries have undertaken structural reforms and convergences to open up their economies and markets to the rest of the world. These reforms include reduction in trade protectionism by lowering tariff and nontariff barriers, liberalization of capital account transactions and its consequences for increasing integration of their financial markets, and increased exchange rate stability. Fifth, the same countries, despite their historical protectionist tendencies, have been strong advocates of freer trade during the 1990s. They have worked together in forming regional trade organizations such as NAFTA and the EU, building close associations with regional organizations such as ASEAN, and facilitating and regulating multilateral trade through GATT and the WTO. These countries share a common history, defense (NATO), and overall Western civilization. Sixth, it should be noted that most global corporations still have their roots and headquarters within the industrialized countries. Since these corporations are the primary movers of FDI, it is natural that they should give preference to opportunities closer to home. Finally, it is also the case that these same countries have superior and the most competitive physical and digital infrastructure, human capital, and the institutional framework to attract, retain, and effectively utilize quality FDI. Therefore, they are likely to remain the destination of choice for global FDI well into the 2000s.

After the industrialized countries, the second most attractive destination for FDI during the 1990s is the BEMs. There is no precise definition of BEMs. However, in 1993, the U.S. Department of Commerce began a process of identifying markets holding the greatest potential for dramatic increases in U.S. exports. This process led to the conclusion that the greatest commercial opportunities for the future would be found in the ten BEMs. At the time, the list included the Chinese economic area (including Hong Kong and Taiwan), India, South Korea, Argentina, Brazil, Mexico, Poland, Turkey, and South Africa. The U.S. Department of Commerce predicted that by 2010 these BEMs would have a bigger market for U.S. exports than the EU and Japan combined. In August 1995, the U.S. secretary of commerce announced that six Southeast Asian countries were being named as BEMs: Vietnam, Malaysia, Thailand, Brunei, the Philippines, and Singapore, all members of ASEAN. Indonesia, also a member of ASEAN and previously included among the ten BEMs, was dropped from the top-six Asian BEMs.[10]

Table 5.1 lists the top-ten BEMs, based on the volume of FDI they received in 1998. This list corresponds with the U.S. Department of Commerce's list with the exception of Chile and Venezuela, both of which are included here but not on the Commerce Department's list. The top ten BEMs were very successful in attracting FDI during the 1990s. In 1990, they grossed a total of more than U.S.$20 billion, but by 1998, this had grown to more than U.S.$125 billion. During the same period, they doubled their share of world FDI from just more than 10 percent to more than 20 percent. China was by far the single greatest winner increasing its share of global FDI from just more than approximately 1 percent in 1990 (U.S.$3.5 billion) to more than 7 percent (almost U.S.$50 billion). Brazil was also very successful: its share grew from less than U.S.$1 billion in 1990 to more than U.S.$31 billion, making it the second largest recipient of FDI, and it took in more than 5 percent of total world FDI in 1998. As expected, the ASEAN emerging markets—Singapore, Thailand, South Korea, and Malaysia—continued to attract high levels of FDI through the 1990s despite the 1997 economic crisis.

Apart from Brazil, the four other South American BEMs listed in Table 5.1 did not do well in attracting FDI in the 1990s. Mexico increased its volume from U.S.$2.6 billion in 1990 to more than U.S.$10 billion. However, its share of the ten top BEMs declined from 9 percent in 1990 to approximately 8 percent in 1998. Argentina also made gains both in terms of total volume and as a percentage share of total FDI from 1 percent to more than 4 percent during the same period. Chile and Venezuela both made significant gains from approximately U.S.$500 million worth of FDI in 1990 each to approximately U.S.$6.5 billion in 1998. Their individual share of FDI as a percentage of the total for the top-ten BEMs grew from about 0.25 percent to more than 5 percent.

It should be noted that during the same time the BEMs were attracting increasingly large sums of FDI, they were also transforming their economies. Specifically, the composition of their exports changed from overdependence on primary commodities to low-, medium-, and high-technology products. For example, in 1985, Malaysia's exports were 35 percent resource based and only 31 percent high-technology based. Ten years later, in 1996, the proportions had changed: 60 percent high-technology based and only 18 percent resource based. Similar transformations took place during the 1990s for Brazil, Argentina, China, and India.[11]

Why did the BEMs do so well in attracting FDI during the 1990s? These are not a homogeneous group of countries, therefore, different factors explain the phenomenon success for different countries. Some of these countries owe their success for similar reasons as the industrialized countries discussed previously. For example, some of the BEMs undertook varying degrees of political and economic reforms including trade and financial liberalization. Singapore—a city–state smaller in size than New York City—is one of the wealthiest countries per capita in the world, partly because of its world-class financial services, trade, shipping, and manufacturing. It succeeds in attracting high-quality FDI because of its highly efficient physical and digital infrastructure and because of its stable and liberal policy framework for export-oriented manufacturing, including ports services, air travel, and international telecommunications. On the other hand, China, the largest country in the world by population (1.3 billion people) has been able to attract FDI, especially during the second half of the 1990s, not because of its internal political and economic reforms but because of its large size, the promise of a large and growing domestic market, and its geopolitical strategic location in Asia. Global corporations invested heavily in China in the 1990s not because of what it was, but what they hoped it would become in the future: one of the single largest markets for global merchandise, exports, and tradable services. With this kind of success, China's leaders have little incentives to speed up reforms. On the other hand, executives of global corporations and civil rights advocates hope that over time large sums of FDI will provide the incentive for the country to generate its own internal dynamics, which will inevitably lead to fundamental economic and political reforms. China's membership in the WTO is expected to speed up reforms.

The Southeast Asian countries succeeded in attracting FDI because as miracle economies they were always the favored destination by Japanese, European, and American global corporations. Before 1997, in the eyes of the international investors, these countries could do no wrong. They continued to receive large sums of FDI despite their internal structural weaknesses, especially in the areas of banking, human capital, and domestic market competitiveness. It should be noted, however, that not all the ASEAN countries depended on FDI to finance development. For example, the Philippines has never been a big recipient of FDI. In 1990, the country received about U.S. $500 million, and by 1998, this had grown to only U.S. $1.7 billion—a very small fraction of what Singapore was getting. No comparable figures are available for Taiwan (because it is not a member of the United Nations), but it is generally understood that FDI did not play a significant role in financing the island's development and capital investment for trade and globalization.

The remaining BEMs listed in Table 5.1 are all from South America. Brazil was very successful in attracting FDI in the later part of the 1990s. This is largely because of the internal economic and financial reforms it introduced in 1994, which included currency reform and privatization. It is also because with a population of 168 million people, it is the dominant country in the region. With increased FDI, Brazil's export trade has both grown and become more diversified. Without large oil, gas, or mineral resources, most of Brazil's FDI is of high quality and is invested in manufacturing, services, and agriculture. Despite frequent regional financial and economic shocks (for example, Argentina in 2001–2002), Brazil is expected to continue to do well in terms of attracting FDI well into the 2000s.

Mexico's success is mainly due to its membership, with the United States and Canada, in NAFTA. The country also started a program of economic and political reforms, including privatization of SOEs in sectors such as oil and gas (the United States needs more oil and gas), transportation, telecommunications, and financial services. Steps are also being taken by the Fox administration to reduce official corruption, improve transparency in public administration, and enhance the country's international image. In response, the United States has been actively involved in supporting Mexico's economic and political reforms, including a massive bailout following the 1994–1995 collapse of the peso and the subsequent near collapse of the economy. By the mid 1990s, it was estimated that more than 3,500 American corporations were doing business in Mexico, and a number of them owned or operated facilities in the country's oil and gas sector as well as manufacturing plants near the U.S.–Mexico border. It should also be pointed out that both Brazil and Mexico, once the world's biggest debtors (together with Argentina), have significantly reduced their international debt obligations, and enhanced their domestic capacities for public debt management.

The remaining BEM countries—Chile and Venezuela—have been able to attract FDI largely because of their natural resources. Chile continues to depend on copper as its principle export, and for Venezuela, oil makes up almost 80 percent of its export earnings. Chile has also undertaken economic and political reforms, thus increasing its attractiveness to international investors. Chile should continue to attract increasing sums of FDI because most observers consider its political and economic reforms irreversible. Venezuela, on the other hand, needs to deepen its economic and political reforms, and if it were not for its extensive oil reserves, it would not attract significant sums of FDI.

Table 5.1 also provides data on FDI by income level and region. Low-income countries (GDP per capita of U.S. $755 or less in 1999), mostly in sub-Saharan Africa, South and Central Asia, and parts of Southeast Asia, received the lowest amount of FDI—just about the same amount as Mexico alone. Middle-income countries (GDP per capita U.S. $756–$9,265 in 1999) received more than ten times as much as the low-income countries, or just over 25.8 percent of total world FDI in 1998. Not surprising, the high-income group of countries (GDP per capita U.S. $9,266 or more in 1999) received the lion's share of FDI in both 1990 and 1998. In 1990, these countries accounted for approximately 87.5 percent of the total, but by 1998, this had declined to approximately 72.4 percent—still high given their share of world population. Since the low-income countries did not increase their share of FDI during the 1990s, the decline from the high-income group was taken up by the middle-income countries. This would be seen as promising for countries whose per capita incomes are rising. However, the data shows that not all middle-income countries shared equally in the increasing sums of FDI made available in the latter part of the 1990s. Made up of eighty countries, the middle-income group includes only two of the BEMs listed in Table 5.1. Only Singapore (high income) and China (low income) are excluded. It also includes CEE countries such as Hungary, the Czech Republic, Russia, and Slovakia, which have attracted increasing sums of FDI during the 1990s. The rest of the middle-income countries, such as Jamaica, Sri Lanka, Belarus, and Macedonia, continued to attract insignificant sums of FDI through the 1990s.

Looking at the global distribution of FDI by region, Table 5.1 shows that among the low- and middle-income groups, the biggest winners were Latin America and the Caribbean, and East Asia and the Pacific. The losers were South Asia, and sub-Saharan Africa. These results are not surprising given that the two losing regions have no BEMs (except South Africa), whereas the other two regions each share equal numbers of the top-ten BEMs. India, which is often included as one of the BEMs and is part of South Asia, does not seem to have attracted significant sums of FDI during the 1990s, receiving only about U.S. $2.6 billion in 1998.

It is a well-known fact that sub-Saharan Africa is a loser when it comes to attracting FDI during the 1990s. Still, Table 5.1 lists the top-ten African winners of FDI for 1990 and 1998. In addition to showing relatively small sums of FDI, the data on Africa is interesting in other respects. First, most of the FDI goes to resource-based investments such as oil (Nigeria, Angola) and mining (South Africa, Botswana, Zimbabwe). This type of enclave FDI is used to simply extract and export and creates little or no opportunities for developing the local entrepreneurial private sector or integrating the overall local economy with the global economy. Instead, this type of FDI, with little or no local multiplier effects, contributes to further marginalization of these economies, and where the national governance institutional infrastructure is weak or corrupt, it can lead to internal conflict and civil war or breakdown of civil order and good government. In the case of Nigeria, in addition to contributing to widespread official corruption during most of the 1990s, the oil industry led the continent in catching the "Dutch disease." The Dutch disease often happens when a country has a dominant natural resource in high demand for export, which causes the country's exchange rate to appreciate in relation to other currencies. In the case of Nigeria, during the oil boom, the nira (the country's currency) significantly appreciated in value. As a result, the demand for the country's non-oil exports fell sharply and eventually led to the destruction of the local entrepreneurial firms that were involved in the production, processing, distribution, marketing, and exporting of agricultural commodities such as nuts, palm oil, kernels, cotton, and hides and skins. This, in turn, contributed to the weakening of the local economy and the neglect of the non-oil infrastructure and increased the country's dependence and vulnerability on a single commodity for export.

Another group of sub-Saharan African countries listed in Table 5.1 made the list for different reasons. Côte d'Ivoire, Mozambique, Uganda, and Tanzania received almost no FDI in 1990. By 1998, they were among the top-ten recipients of FDI. Why? All these countries have internal economic and political reforms. More significantly, they have introduced reform programs involving the privatization of national assets and SOEs. With the help of the World Bank and other international donors, each of these countries prepared financially attractive proposals for the sale of these enterprises, often at discounted prices. Accordingly, most of the FDI showing up in Table 5.1 for these countries is accounted for through the sale of national assets. These sales have included SOEs in sectors such as agriculture, tourism, breweries, tobacco, transport, textiles, and garment and food processing.

The problem with FDI associated with the sale of state-owned assets is that it tends to be a one-off, non-repeat business. It is a "one-night stand" because after the assets have been sold off the country may not continue to attract FDI for other investments. This happened in Ghana, Zambia, and Angola when each of these countries received relatively large sums of FDI for the purchase of SOEs, but the FDI inflows did not continue in subsequent years.

Therefore, according to these experiences, unless these countries develop strategic plans to attract and retain FDI for purposes other than the sale of public assets, one would not expect countries such as Cote d'Ivoire, Mozambique, Tanzania, and Uganda to continue to make the top-ten recipients of FDI in Africa.

During the 1990s, South Africa became an important source of FDI for a number of other African countries, mainly buying into existing SOEs and forming partnerships with private sector entrepreneurs. Most of these were in investments such as airlines (for example, Alliance Airline with Uganda and Tanzania); breweries in Mozambique, Uganda and Tanzania; pharmaceuticals; and supermarkets (grocery stores). South Africa's sudden interest in investing in the rest of Africa is the direct result of the end of white minority rule (apartheid) in that country in 1994 and the expectation that the new South Africa will become an engine of growth and investment for the rest of Africa. Although South Africa continues to seek direct investment opportunities in the rest of Africa, it is expected that its role as a major source of FDI for the continent will decline in the future. This is partly because South Africa does not have a sufficient supply of FDI to satisfy Africa's needs, and partly because the white South Africans business executives have realized that doing business in Africa is more challenging than originally thought.

Among the top-ten sub-Saharan African countries listed in Table 5.1 is Lesotho, which is a small mountainous country completely surrounded by South Africa with a population of just over 2 million people. It is one of the world's poorest countries, listed as one of the least developed countries. It has no oil or minerals resources, but on a per capita basis, it attracts more FDI than Africa's giants, such as Nigeria, South Africa, or the mineral rich Democratic Republic of the Congo (DRC). Because it has no oil or mineral resources, Lesotho's FDI is of high quality and is invested in export-oriented manufacturing enterprises, which are much more integrated into the local economy. In 1998, Lesotho attracted more than U.S.$260 million of FDI, about 50 percent as much as the whole of South Africa in the same year. Most of this went into the clothing and garments industry, which is Lesotho's leading export sector. According to the World Bank, Lesotho is Africa's largest exporter of ready-made garments, producing more than twice as much as South Africa.[12] In this regard, Lesotho is Africa's shining star and the sub-Saharan Africa moral equivalent of Singapore. If a small landlocked country with no rich oil deposits can identify a successful niche for attracting high-quality FDI and develop a profitable export-oriented manufacturing sector through persistent efforts of creating and sustaining a conducive policy environment, then there must be hope that other African countries with better natural resources. Hopefully, in future, Africa will produce more success stories like Lesotho. For the 1990s, however, Lesotho stood alone in a land starved for FDI.

Looking at specific countries as losers in the competition for FDI in the 1990s, Table 5.1 lists three countries of particular interest: Indonesia, Angola, and Zimbabwe. Indonesia is listed in the table immediately below the United States because of the contrasts these two countries provide. While the United States stands out as the leading winner in attracting FDI during the 1990s, Indonesia is clearly one of the biggest losers. A big country (population more than 210 million), endowed with extensive natural resources such as oil and gas, timber, water, fisheries, and minerals, and listed as one of the Asian miracles, Indonesia was destined to become a successful BEM. Like most other BEMs, it was expected to become a magnet for FDI during the 1990s and beyond. Instead, as Table 5.1 shows, during the same period, Indonesia recorded a net loss of FDI. While in 1990 the country received only just more than U.S. $1 billion, by 1998, it received just over U.S. $350 million. In the same year, Indonesia recorded a net loss of U.S. $3.7 billion net private capital outflows. Two other countries experiencing similar loses were Zimbabwe and Angola. Zimbabwe recorded a net loss of more than U.S. $200 million net private capital outflows in 1998. These three countries have the potential to do better. All of them performed well below potential because of domestic political governance problems. Despite their extensive natural resources, the three countries scared off potential foreign investors, even forced those who had come in to pull their investments out. The lesson for other newly globalizing countries is clear: FDI will not come in an atmosphere of political instability, and if it comes in, it will not stay.

In addition to providing summary FDI information, Table 5.1 provides corresponding data on net private capital flows for 1998. This was done to provide a more complete picture of capital flows for developing countries and transition economies. For any of these countries, total capital flows are made up of official funding and private capital flows. Official funding is made up of development assistance (aid) and government borrowing. Private capital flows are made up of FDI, if any, commercial lending, and portfolio investment. Portfolio investment can be in the form of equity or bonds. Bonds can be public (issued by different levels of government) or corporate (issued by private corporations). Bonds can be short term (lasting for thirty, sixty, or ninety days) or they can be long term (lasting for five, ten, fifteen, twenty, or thirty years). As part of their economic reforms and in order to attract foreign private capital, many developing countries and transition economies have established local capital markets, which makes it possible for various investment products to be tradable on a regular basis.

The global picture of the net private capital flows in Table 5.1 is very similar to the trends for FDI. The top-ten BEMs took in approximately U.S. $200 billion in net private capital flows in 1998, and this is expected to grow in the 2000s. Likewise, the middle-income countries took in more than U.S. $250 billion in the same year. Latin America and the Caribbean took in the single largest net private capital inflows of any region: more than U.S. $126 billion. On the other hand, with only U.S. $67 billion, East Asia and the Pacific took less than would have been expected because of the 1997 Asian financial crisis, which was associated with significant amounts of capital flight. As expected, the regions and countries that did not attract significant amounts of FDI did not end up with large sums of net private capital flows. Sub-Saharan Africa ended up with less net private capital flows than FDI in 1998, suggesting that the region as a whole and the top-ten recipients of FDI both suffered net capital losses for the year. This is a more direct measure of the region's attractiveness for private foreign capital investment because what the data in Table 5.1 show is that while Africa was able to attract some modest levels of FDI more private foreign capital was withdrawn from the region as a whole.

Once again, these findings emphasize the challenges facing developing countries in managing foreign capital investments. It is not enough to attract foreign capital; a country must maintain its attractiveness for foreign capital to stay, and more of it to keep coming in. As the economy grows and diversifies, the country must attract and retain higher-quality foreign capital, which helps the economy to integrate internally across sectors and regions and globally with the rest of the world. At the same time, a country must remain politically stable with an impeccable national integrity and regulatory system. These conditions are relatively easy to maintain for the old established democracies and some of the BEMs. They are not so easy for most of the other developing countries, especially the small, poor, least-developed countries and the newer democracies emerging out of internal conflicts, civil war, or prolonged dictatorships. Therefore, the international community, both public and private, must find practical solutions and help these globally marginalized countries and their communities to become globally competitive in attracting and retaining quality foreign private capital. The international trade and investment community has a special role to play. This will serve the legitimate interests of globalization. The more countries win, the better for globalization.

NOTES

1. See World Bank, *World Bank Press Report* (Washington, DC: World Bank, November 7, 2001). Even Oxfam, a London-based international nongovernmental organization traditionally opposed to globalization, has grudgingly accepted that trade offers poor people better opportunities for poverty alleviation and sustainable development than foreign aid. The report also points out that current rules of international trade and the behavior of the developed countries work against the trade interests of developing countries and transition economies. "Nontariff barriers raise the average of EU barriers against poor countries from 5.1 percent to 9 percent." See Oxfam, *Rigged Rules and Double Standard* (London: Oxfam, April 10, 2002).

2. Arvind Panagariya, "Evaluating the Case for Export Subsidies," Trade, Development, and Research Group Working Paper 2276 (Washington, DC: World Bank, January 2000). Also see "Going Too Far in Support of Trade," *The Economist*, December 16, 2000, p. 88. In May 2002, the U.S. Senate gave final approval to a controversial farm bill, which will boost the federal government's support to agriculture by at least U.S. $82 billion over the next ten years. The bill is expected to antagonize members of the EU and NAFTA, as well as trading developing countries and transition economies. It violates WTO rules and is in conflict with the conclusions of the 2001 WTO Ministerial Conference held in Doha, Qatar. Moreover, it does not advance the cause for the global fight against poverty and terrorism. See World Bank, *World Bank Press Report* (Washington, DC: World Bank, May 9, 2002).

3. Information on the Canadian Export Corporation can be obtained from their Web site: www.edc-see.ca.

4. For perspectives on IBM as a global corporation, see Pierre Hessler, "Being Global and the Global Opportunity," in *Globalization Technology and Competition*, ed. Stephen P. Bradley, Jerry A. Hausman, and Richard L. Nolan (Boston: Harvard Business School, 1993), 243–255. For global corporations in general, see Robert T. Moran, Philip R. Harris, and William G. Stripp, *Developing the Global Organization* (Houston: Gulf Publishing, 1993).

5. John Roth, "A New World's Coming," *Globe and Mail*, December 19, 2000, p. A15.

6. Ewa Ruminska-Zimmy, "Globalization and Transition Economies: Regional and Country Perspectives," in *Globalization with a Human Face: Background Papers* Vol. 2, *Human Development Report* (New York: UNDP and Oxford University Press, 1999), 223–259. Also see the OECD's Development Assistance Committee (DAC) "Guidelines on Strengthening Trade Capacity for Development." Available: http://www.oecd.org/pdf/M0022000M0022182.pdf.

7. Nguyuru H. I. Lipumba, "Opportunities and Challenges of Globalization: Can Sub-Saharan Africa Avoid Marginalization?" in *Globalization with a Human Face: Background Papers* Vol. 2, *Human Development Report* (New York: UNDP and Oxford University Press, 1999), 157–222.

8. See "Hungarian Economic Review," *The Economist* (promotional supplement), December 23, 2000, pp. 73–76.

9. United Nations, *World Development Report 1998* (New York: United Nations, 1997), quoted in Lipumba, "Opportunities and Challenges of Globalization," 189.

10. The U.S. Department of Commerce, International Trade Administration, has created and maintains a BEMs Web page mainly for the information of American exporters. As of December 2000, the Web site (www.commerce.gov) included a BEM map listing eighteen countries: China, South Korea, Taiwan, Hong Kong, the Philippines, Vietnam, Brunei, Malaysia, Thailand, Singapore, Indonesia, India, South Africa, Argentina, Brazil, Mexico, Poland, and Turkey. Russia was not included.

11. Based on World Bank, *World Development Report 1999/2000* (Washington, DC: World Bank, 2000), fig. 2.6, p. 59.

12. World Bank, *World Development Report 1999/2000*.

CHAPTER 6

The World Trade Organization: Challenges for Developing Countries

As the 1990s came to a close and the new millennium began, the WTO became the leading international symbol for or against globalization. Yet, ten years before, nobody had ever heard of the WTO, and only academics and senior trade officials, mainly in industrial countries, paid much attention to its predecessor, GATT. Today, no serious discussion on globalization is complete without a close examination of the role of this controversial organization and its impact on the global economy, different regions and countries of the world, and ordinary citizens. This chapter begins by providing the history, mission, structure, and governance of the WTO. It then looks at the relationship between the WTO and developing countries, focusing on current issues important for developing countries. The chapter concludes with a discussion of the strategies needed for developing countries to develop the necessary human competencies and institutional capacities to deal effectively with these and future emerging issues and to enhance the quality of their participation in the WTO and related institutions.

HISTORY, MISSION, STRUCTURE, AND GOVERNANCE

Like most international organizations, the WTO owes its origins from the time immediately after World War II when the Allies were creating new institutions for a world order that would promote peace, reconstruction, and development. At the time, a suggestion was made for the creation of an international trade organization, but opposition from the U.S. Congress blocked the idea. Instead, the world had to settle for less institutional arrangements and less legal and moral force under GATT.

In 1947, GATT was a relatively small organization with only twenty-three member states. This was because most of today's nations were not yet born. The purpose of GATT was to negotiate trade rules and to negotiate down tariffs and other trade barriers. It conducted its business in sessions called "rounds." The first round, started in 1947, covered approximately 50 percent of world trade and lasted for two years. The second round, started in 1949, involved only thirteen trading nations. For the next twenty-five years, there were several rounds involving various countries. The most famous of these is the eighth round called the "Uruguay Round," which lasted for seven years, was concluded on December 15, 1993, and was signed into force in March 1994. By this time, more countries had joined GATT, so the Uruguay Round involved 117 nations, especially the developed countries and the big emerging markets (BEMs). The Uruguay Round was the most comprehensive international trade negotiations the world has ever undertaken. It involved more nations and a higher percentage of world trade. It covered not only tariffs and other trade barriers but also trade agreements in a wide range of sectors and topics including agriculture, services, manufacturing, and intellectual properties. The Uruguay Round is famous because it created the WTO. Unlike GATT, the WTO is not just a "general agreement," instead, it has legal status and powers to enforce its decisions and rulings. It was also given powers to enforce the general agreements made under GATT.[1]

GATT started out as a trade club for the rich industrial nations, and although it eventually broadened its membership to include some of the advanced developing countries, it never truly reflected the serious concerns of the poor developing countries (P2), who generally had minimal involvement in GATT's governance, negotiations, or decisions. Yet, all GATT's decisions were passed on to the WTO. Therefore, as far as developing countries are concerned, the WTO inherited the problems of GATT and passed them on to the developing countries.

As the only multilateral organization dealing with global rules of trade between and among nations, the WTO is charged with the responsibility of ensuring that trade flows as smoothly, fairly, freely, and predictably as possible. After the fourth Ministerial Conference in Doha, Qatar, in November 2001, membership in the WTO stood at 143 nations of which about 110 were developing and transition economy members. More than three-quarters of the members are developing or least-developed countries; special provisions for these members are included in all WTO agreements. Yet, while all members of the WTO may sleep in the same bed, they have different dreams. The trade, investment, and development dreams of developing countries and transition economies are significantly different both in content and context than those of the rich industrial countries or their trading blocks. Therefore, the WTO's greatest challenge is to bring to bear greater understanding of these differences and to reconcile the often widely divergent interests among member states in a way that is fair and technically and politically credible. Future prospects of the WTO depend on its ability to do so.

In terms of structure and governance, WTO's highest authority is the Ministerial Conference which is made up of one representative from each member state and meets about once every two years. The first conference took place in December 1996 in Singapore. The second was in 1998 in Geneva, and the third was the infamous meetings in Seattle, Washington, from November 30 to December 3, 1999. The fourth meeting took place in November 2001 in Doha, Qatar. The conference acts as a governing council and sets the agenda and program of work for the organization.

The administration of the organization is overseen by the General Council, which is headed by the director-general who is appointed for a six-year term. The council performs two broad administrative tasks: dispute settlement and trade policy review. Decisions are made by consensus, but when voting is required, each member has one vote. A two-thirds majority is required to amend provisions of the multilateral agreements and to admit new members.

World Trade Organization Membership

Table 6.1 lists 144 WTO member countries as of November 2001 (the end of the fourth Ministerial Conference in Doha, Qatar). It also lists thirty-seven countries that sent observers to the conference and fifteen countries—the isolates—that stayed away. The list of members is testimony to the support the world community has given to the WTO as an agent of globalization. The WTO represents mainstream countries of the world: big and small, rich and poor, from all continents, races, creeds, and cultures. Most of the nonmembers are former Communist states such as Russia, Vietnam, Cambodia, North Korea, and Yemen; Islamic states such as Saudi Arabia, Libya, Iran, Iraq, and Syria; and post-conflict states such as Bhutan, Tuvalu, Micronesia, and East Timor. Overall, these countries make up a small fraction of the total global economy and world population. Most of the observer countries listed in Table 6.1 are actively taking steps to join the WTO. For example, President Vladimir Putin of Russia has asked for American support in his bid to become a member of the WTO and other international organizations. Over the years, it is expected that many more countries will seek membership in the WTO, and those who do not will become isolated from the global economy and global society.

Exhibit 6.1 provides a list of the key benefits of the WTO to the world. As the world becomes more global and as trade becomes the driving force for growth, wealth creation, poverty alleviation, innovation, entrepreneurship, openness, and globalization, there is need for a credible multilateral system of regulation and enforcement to create, protect, and preserve a level playing field for all nations, big and small, rich and poor. The WTO is supposed to form the core of this global regulatory and enforcement system. It also provides a mechanism for settling disputes among trading nations, and if the recent experience is indicative of future challenges, dispute settlement and enforcement is becoming the most active and important work of the organization as more and more members seek to settle their trade disputes using this multilateral system. As well, the WTO is expected to promote transparency, accountability, and respect for the rule of law, thus contributing both to global economic and global democratic/political development.

EXHIBIT 6.1
Benefits of the World Trade Organization to the World

1. Making, interpreting, and enforcing rules for global trade. Supercedes regional trading blocks.

2. Settles trade disputes between trading members.

3. Helps to promote peace by providing a global forum for conflicting parties.

4. Through free trade, it promotes economic development by raising incomes and standards of living.

5. Free trade encourages innovation, contributes to competitiveness and efficiency, and cuts the cost of doing business and the cost of living.

6. Trade stimulates economic growth and contributes to global poverty alleviation.

7. Trade encourages more choice of goods and services at more competitive prices.

8. Provides mechanisms for regulating the behavior of global corporations, especially advantageous for the smaller and weaker emerging markets.

9. It provides a level playing field for big and small nations alike and harmonizes global trade, and with a broad-based membership, it can effectively bring more trade sectors under multilateral negotiations.

10. It promotes transparency, accountability, and respect for the rule of law, thus contributing to good governance, economic management, and global integration under a single multilateral regulatory system.

11. It helps with the enforcement of environmental regulations and labor standards.

12. It helps the developing countries, especially the least-developed ones, to build human capital and institutional capacity to manage trade and development.

Source: World Trade Organization and related Web sites: www.wto.org and www.unicc.org.

Supporters of the WTO argue that at least the organization is a necessary evil because the world cannot continue to enjoy the fruits of growing free trade without a global regulatory system. There is a lot at stake because while the first GATT round dealt with goods worth about U.S. $10 billion the Uruguay Round involved almost U.S. $7 trillion, and since the fall of Communism, global trade has been growing faster than the world economy. Therefore, the WTO is needed as the core for the necessary global institutional infrastructure for managing global trade.

However, as the events of Seattle and subsequent meetings clearly show, there is worldwide opposition to the WTO, as an organization, as an institution, and all that it represents. Opponents are vocal, articulate, and well funded and organized. However, they are not a

TABLE 6.1
World Trade Organization Membership

Members (142: 72.5%)

Albania	European Community	Malta
Angola	Fiji Islands, Republic of the	Mauritania
Antigua and Barbuda	Finland	Mauritius
Argentina	France	Mexico
Australia	Gabon	Moldova
Austria	Gambia, The	Mongolia
Bahrain	Georgia	Morocco
Bangladesh	Germany	Mozambique
Barbados	Ghana	Myanmar
Belgium	Greece	Namibia
Belize	Grenada	Netherlands
Benin	Guatemala	New Zealand
Bolivia	Guinea, Republic of	Nicaragua
Botswana	Guinea-Bissau	Niger
Brazil	Guyana	Nigeria
Brunei Darussalam	Haiti	Norway
Bulgaria	Honduras	Oman
Burkina Fuso	Hong Kong	Pakistan
Burundi	Hungary	Panama
Cameroon	Iceland	Papua New Guinea
Canada	India	Paraguay
Central African Republic	Indonesia	Peru
Chad	Ireland	Philippines
Chile	Israel	Poland
China	Italy	Portugal
Colombia	Jamaica	Qatar
Congo	Jordan	Romania
Costa Rica	Kenya	Rwanda
Côte d'Ivoire	Kirgiz Republic	St. Kitts and Nevis
Croatia	Korea	Saint Lucia
Cuba	Kuwait	St. Vincent and the Grenadines
Cyprus	Latvia	Senegal
Czech Republic	Lesotho	Sierra Leone
Democratic Republic of the	Liechtenstein	Singapore
Congo	Lithuania	Slovak Republic
Denmark	Luxembourg	Slovenia
Dominica	Macau, China	Solomon Islands
Dominican Republic	Madagascar	Brazil
Ecuador	Malawi	South Africa
Egypt	Malaysia	Spain
El Salvador	Maldives	Sri Lanka
Estonia	Mali	Suriname

(continued)

TABLE 6.1 (*cont.*)
World Trade Organization Membership

Members (*cont.*)

Swaziland	Togo	United States
Sweden	Trinidad and Tobago	Uruguay
Switzerland	Tunisia	Zambia
Taiwan	Uganda	Zimbabwe
Tanzania	United Arab Emirates	
Thailand	United Kingdom	

Observers (37: 18.9%)

Algeria	Ethiopia	São Tomé and Príncipe
Andorra	Holy See	Saudi Arabia
Armenia	Kazakhstan	Seychelles
Azerbaijan	Lao, People's Democratic	Sudan
Bahamas	Republic of	Tajikistan
Belarus	Lebanon	Tonga
Bhutan	Liberia	Ukraine
Bosnia and Herzegovina	Libya	Uzbekistan
Cambodia	Macedonia, Former Yugoslav	Vanuatu
Cape Verde	Republic of	Vietnam
Comoros	Russian Federation	Yemen
Equatorial Guinea	Samoa	Yugoslavia, Federal
Eritrea	San Marino	Republic of

Isolates (15: 7.6%)

Afghanistan	Marshall Islands	Palau
East Timor	Micronesia	Somalia
Iran	Monaco	Syria
Iraq	Nauru	Turalu
Kiribati	North Korea	Turkmenistan

Note: Members as of November 2001 (the end of the fourth Ministerial Conference, Doha, Qatar). Observer governments at the conferences and isolates were not represented at the conference. China and Taiwan became members at this conference. The numbers in parentheses indicate total number and percentage of total, respectively.
Source: Based on information from www.wto.org and www.countrywatch.com.

homogeneous group and have different ideological or pragmatic reasons for opposing the WTO and its work.

Exhibit 6.2 summarizes the most frequently mentioned reasons for opposition to the WTO. Some of these are similar to the reasons given for opposition to globalization (see Chapter 1), others are specifically related to the WTO's structuring and governance.

There is also concern about the relationships between the WTO and the developing countries, especially the small and weak least-developing countries, which are not currently major beneficiaries of global trade. Western trade unions are also opposed to the WTO because they see it as facilitating the export of jobs to low-cost developing countries. Others, especially on the right, do not want to see the WTO getting involved in environmental protection because of its implications for industrial operations and production. Membership in the WTO can be used as a scapegoat to explain away problems caused by internal economic weaknesses such as high unemployment, runaway inflation, business bankruptcies, and currency depreciation.

Exhibit 6.2
Opposition to the World Trade Organization

1. It is a tool for globalization for powerful nations and their global corporations.

2. It is undemocratic, secretive, unaccountable, and colonial.

3. It promotes free trade at any cost.

4. It destroys jobs and worsens poverty, especially for developing countries and transition economies.

5. It dictates its policies, especially for the small and weak developing countries that have little or no voice or representation.

6. It puts pressure on weak countries to join before they are ready. Weaker economies feel that strengthening enforcement mechanisms and opening markets rapidly hurts the infant economies.

7. It allows trade and investment interests to take priority over indigenous development.

8. It is forced by the industrial countries to deal with nontrade issues such as the environment and the social consequences of development.

9. It does not protect workers' rights, health, safety, and wages.

10. It encourages poor countries to get into debt by borrowing from the international capital markets in order to develop export commodities.

11. It perpetuates developing countries' dependence and marginalization inherited from the GATT era.

World Trade Organization Calls for Reforms

Among the avid supporters and opponents, there are reformers. Reformers accept the need for the WTO but point out that it needs fundamental changes, both as an organization and as a multilateral regulatory institution. Reforms have been proposed in various areas including structure, function, and governance; leadership and succession; litigation and negotiation; regionalism; and relationship with developing countries and transition economies.

At the governance level, it has been suggested that the WTO lacks a board of directors, steering committee, or similar structure for providing vision, strategic direction, and long-term planning. The proposed body should not have executive decision-making authority; rather, with broadly representative and rotating participation, similar to the rotating membership of the Trade Policy Review, it could provide the full membership with nonbinding, thoughtful advice and council. It would also take some of the pressure off the Ministerial Conference, which is inherently political in its composition. Drawing from corporate governance, the Ministerial Conference would become something like a biannual meeting of shareholders. It has also been suggested that the dispute settlement mechanism (DSM) should be reformed to make it simpler, more inclusive and participative, transparent, and speedier. According to the WTO's current rules, the proceedings are private, exclude third parties including NGOs, and on average last thirty-four months from start to dispute settlement. The costs are more than most developing countries can afford. Reformers have also suggested that the WTO should streamline its processing of applications for new membership. By the end of 2000, there was a long queue for new nations wishing to join, especially developing countries and transition economies. While membership has its costs, it also bestows status, voice, and respectability. It also sends a powerful message to the rest of the world that the new member is ready for globalization. In September 2001, China was admitted as a full member, but important countries, including Russia, are not yet members. Therefore, it is important for the WTO to stream its membership procedures and make them faster and affordable.

The WTO's leadership and succession problems are political and geopolitical in nature, but they need to be addressed because they affect its functioning and credibility, especially in the eyes of the developing countries. These problems are perhaps best illustrated by the organization's short history of the appointment of its director-general. The first director-general, Renato Ruggiero, an Italian, served only one four-year term to April 1999. A European could not succeed him because the position has to rotate among the major regions of the world. Each of the four world regions proposed a candidate. North America proposed a Canadian, Roy McLaren, because an American would not have had a chance. South America proposed Mexico's former President Carlos Salinas de Gortari, but scandal made his candidacy untenable. Africa proposed Morocco's Hassan Abouyoub; and Southeast Asia put forward Supachai Panitchapakdi of Thailand. Finally the Oceania region proposed New Zealand's Mike Moore. After a period of intense lobbying and failing to come up with a broad-based acceptable candidate, a compromise solution was reached. Moore was finally appointed as the WTO's director-general only on the condition that he be replaced by Panitchapakdi of Thailand halfway between the mandate. With this kind of compromise solution, the industrial countries and the developing countries each win half the battle, but the WTO loses in leadership and institutional continuity, especially at a time when it is beginning to get its feet wet and has so much to do to win the confidence of the world.

Regarding litigation and negotiation, since 1994 the WTO has functioned more like an international trade court than a forum for trade negotiation, harmonization, and development. This is because of the increasing number of disputes coming before the WTO from both industrial and developing countries. The biggest trade blocks are mired in bilateral trade disputes only the WTO can help to settle. For example, both the EU and the United States are involved in trade disputes harmful to overall global trade. They are depriving developing countries of trade opportunities, which would otherwise help their economies and citizens. Nick Stern, chief economist of the World Bank, describes protectionism as "a rip-off of the rich consumers, a rip-off of rich-country taxpayers, and intensely damaging to the poor of the world."[2] Since the end of the Uruguay Round in 1993–1994, with the exception of sector-specific and side agreements in areas such as financial services and telecommunications, no new rules have emerged from negotiations. Rather, new global trade rules from the WTO have so far resulted from dispute settlement panels. By refusing to engage in meaningful multilateral negotiations, the world leaders are depriving the world of the evolution of a sound global trading regulatory system based on a balanced consideration of technical trade matters as well as political needs and realities of the majority of the member states. The way the WTO has been operating for the first seven years of its existence is akin to a country being taken over by a dictator, closing its legislature, and governing by the law courts. The world leaders, especially those from the leading industrial countries, are abdicating their global leadership responsibilities in trade matters, and this hurts the long-term interests of developing countries and transition economies.

Reformers have also suggested that the WTO should be concerned about the growing trend toward the emergence of regional trading blocks. The debate about regionalism and global trade has not yet been settled. There are those who support the development of regional trading blocks on the grounds that they are more "home grown" and more sensitive to local, national, and regional issues. Others support them as an evolutionary stage and learning process in preparation for global trade participation. It is also argued that Europe (EU), Southeast Asia (ASEAN), and North America (NAFTA) have become avid global traders because of their respective regional trading blocks. These regional trading blocks have provided member states with the opportunity to develop institutional capacities and political support most useful in managing trade both at the regional and global levels.

Yet, WTO reformers are concerned that too many regional trading blocks undermine the authority of the WTO as the single authoritative global regulator of trade. As of 2000, there were about 172 existing regional trade agreements, with another 70 or so under negotiation or discussion. Because the third Ministerial Conference in Seattle ended in failure, there are renewed fears that most nations resort to regionalization as the only realistic option for trade negotiations and development. This would be a disservice to globalization.

Perhaps the most important area of reform for the WTO, as far as its potential effects on the majority of member states and citizens of the world, is the relationship between the WTO and the developing countries. Here, it is important to note that some of the reformers have argued that none of these reforms deal with the fundamental problems facing developing countries. For example, J. Michael Finger, lead economist for trade policy of the

World Bank, has argued that the transaction costs associated with membership in the WTO are too high for most of the least-developing countries to afford. Furthermore, the WTO, as a trade organization, does not have the mandate or the institutional capacity to promote development among the poor countries. Yet, for most of the developing countries, what they need more than anything else is development. Undoubtedly, trade and development are positively correlated, but a development agenda is not necessarily identical to a trade agenda, especially for poor countries with weak infant economies and fragile political democracies.[3]

Lessons from Seattle

Before discussing the relationship between the WTO and developing countries and the issues most important to these countries, it is important to look briefly at the impact of Seattle on the future of the WTO. First, it is important to note that the highly publicized thousands of anti-globalization demonstrators who successfully battled police and forced the city to shut down did not cause the failure of the Seattle ministerial meetings. Rather, the failure at Seattle was because the third Ministerial Conference, dominated by member states from developing countries including among the poorest countries of the world, could not agree on the agenda for the next round of negotiations. It had been expected that a new round, called the "Millennium Round," would begin in the year 2000 to coincide with the beginning of the new millennium. The Millennium Round was expected to be even more comprehensive and far more reaching in its scope to regulate different forms of merchandise trade and tradable services. The Ministerial Conference failed to approve the agenda for the Millennium Round because the developing countries voted en masse to block the proposed agenda. As a result of the substantive failure of the Ministerial Conference and in response to the highly publicized protestors' demonstration, Western leaders appeared to distance themselves from the WTO and its ambitious proposals of the Millennium Round. For example, President Bill Clinton publicly supported the demonstrators because many in the labor and environment movements are traditional supporters of the Democratic Party and 1999–2000 was a presidential election year. At the same time, the political leaders from the developing countries did not seem to have paid any political cost back home in their political constituencies. Either the long-term implications of the failure of Seattle were not fully understood in the developing countries or the general opposition to globalization provided cover for these failures. Either way, the WTO and the ideals of free trade were the immediate losers. Only seven years old, the WTO looked like an orphan with no champion, no defender, and lots of bashing. As a result of Seattle, the WTO became widely known all over the world, but it also lost credibility and remains badly wounded.

Seattle also taught us some other lessons of experience. As the WTO begins to assert its authority, it will need to find an acceptable balance between external pressures for greater openness, transparency, and accountability and the member–states' insistence on privacy and confidentiality. No organization can be completely open in all its transactions, but after Seattle, the WTO is forced to respond to the legitimate demands for greater openness. Another lesson coming out of Seattle is the new power of numbers that developing countries have acquired in the governance of the WTO. With a system of one nation–one vote, no major decisions can be made without the support of the developing countries, and Seattle confirmed this. It is not clear how this newly acquired power will be used in the future. One hopes that it will be used facilitatively and will not always lead to failure or deadlock. In any case, it is a very different global trade-negotiating environment than the one that existed during the GATT period (1947–1993) when industrial countries called the shots.

Another lesson of experience for the WTO that came out of the Seattle conference is the realization of the complex nature of global trade. Both the failure of the conference and the demonstrations outside the conference underscore the point that trade is not only a technical macroeconomic and administrative matter, it is also a social, political, geopolitical, and cultural matter. To become a competent, credible champion and institutional home for global trade, the WTO must become a center of excellence in all aspects of trade. The failure to predict the failure of the Ministerial Conference and the extent and damage of the protests and demonstrations suggests that the WTO has a lot to learn beyond the technical dimensions of global trade.

Supporters of free global trade must also learn from Seattle. For example, it became clear after Seattle that public awareness and reactions to the events in Seattle were different in industrial and developing countries. In the developing countries, there was only limited discussion and awareness of the significance and long-term consequences of the Seattle outcomes. If trade is so important for the overall development of developing countries, why didn't the public put pressure on the leaders to work for the successful conclusion of a new trade agenda for the Millennium Round? The wider implication for this is that trade negotiations do not take place only in Geneva, where the WTO has its headquarters; rather, they take place first and foremost in every constituency of every country. Most developing countries, especially the least developed, have not started or championed the process of discussing and debating the merits of global trade in their domestic constituencies. It is as if they have no mandate to negotiate on behalf of their people. This must change. There must be active and informed trade discussions and debates within each of the developing countries in order to develop the necessary domestic support for international engagement and negotiations. Once again, the international community has a role to play in helping these emerging weak countries develop a trade-positive, enabling domestic environment. Seattle has taught us all that trade is too important to be left only to the experts.

The private sectors of the developing countries must also draw instructive lessons from both the hotel conference rooms where the delegates of the failed Ministerial Conference were meeting and the city streets where the demonstrators and the uninvited representatives of the northern private sectors were promoting their respective alternative interests. By private sector I include all the different civil society groupings including NGOs, labor and trade unions, the media, environmental activists, traditional chiefs, academics, youths, professional associations, reformists, the business community, and so on. From the streets of Seattle, the private sector from the developing countries learns at least two things: One, is that they, too, have a role to play in shaping trade policy and implementation in their respective countries and regions; and two, their interests are not necessarily identical to the interests of the northern protestors. Therefore, they must develop their own strategies and responses to the WTO and global trade based on an informed assessment of the economic, political, social, and cultural realities on the ground. While northern counterparts can and should provide technical support and advice, they should never dictate the agenda for how the civil society in the developing countries responds to the WTO and global trade.

Two examples—labor and the environment—help to explain the different policy interests between northern and southern opposition to the two issues and global trade. Northern trade unions are opposed to global trade because they fear that jobs will be exported to low-cost developing countries. The natural extension of this logic is that the trade union movement in developing countries should support trade-positive public policies because of the opportunities to create well-paying jobs in the private sector. Likewise, some northern environmental activists are opposed to global trade because industry destroys the natural environment and pollutes the air, water, and soil. Yet, while southern environmental activists are also opposed to pollution, they see much more clearly the relationship between poverty and environmental degradation. Therefore, to the extent that trade and industrialization help to alleviate poverty, southern environmentalists should be supportive of trade-positive public policies. This said, northern anti-globalization groups are beginning to link up with their like-minded southern counterparts. For example, in January 2001, the first meeting of the newly formed Global Social Forum, representing more than one hundred countries, took place in Brazil's southern city of Pôrto Alegre. The timing and location were deliberately chosen by the organizers to show solidarity between northern and southern anti-globalization forces and to demonstrate against the meeting of the Global Economic Forum that was taking place in Davos, Switzerland. The demonstrations in the summer of 2001 in Quebec City against the Free Trade Area of the Americas also included many NGOs from the south.

The private sector business community in each of the developing countries must become more actively involved in promoting trade and investment in their respective countries or regions. Global trade is good for business, even for those firms that are not yet actively involved in the export–import sector. In every globalizing developing country, business leaders should take up the challenge to explain to the public, especially the rest of the business community, the relationships between the WTO and global trade and the practical implications for their respective countries. Traveling through some of the small and weaker less-developed countries, one gets the impression that many business leaders are not adequately aware or informed about matters of global trade and trade policy. This must change because in any globalizing country the business sector constitutes a very important part of the national institutional infrastructure for managing global trade.

IMPORTANT ISSUES FOR DEVELOPING COUNTRIES

Following the successful conclusion of the Uruguay Round and the establishment of the WTO, concern has been expressed that the issues and needs of developing countries and transition economies have not been given serious consideration, let alone finding practical solutions to problems. As a result, in preparation for the third Ministerial Conference that took place toward the end of 1999, various publications came out identifying trade and development issues most important for developing countries and transition economies. Some of these publications focused on single sectors such as agriculture or financial services, others looked at specific regions such as Latin America and Central and Eastern Europe, others looked at specific topics such as participation and commitment, and others talked about all developing countries in general. This section highlights the most important trade investment and development issues for developing countries.

As I have emphasized previously, developing countries are not a homogeneous group, and globalization is making them even less so as some countries seem to adjust to global competition faster and more successfully than others. In Chapter 1, a distinction was made between the center and the periphery. The periphery was divided between the advanced developing countries (P1) and the least developed countries (P2). In the discussion of foreign direct investment (FDI), a subgrouping of successful developing countries—the BEMs—was also identified. P1 and BEMs are almost identical groups, and their issues and concerns regarding the WTO, global trade, investment, and development are different than the P2 or least-developed countries. The issues and concerns I will discuss apply to all developing countries, but they are more serious, severe, and limiting for the P2 least-developed countries than for the P1 countries or the BEMs.

Table 6.2 summarizes twelve key issues that have been identified as important for developing countries. Most of these have been discussed in great technical detail by U.N. experts and World Bank staff. For example, in preparation for the Seattle conference, a group of U.N. experts met in September 1998 and identified ten of the twelve issues listed in the table. As is evident in the table, some of these issues relate to specific sectors such as agriculture and tourism; others deal with technical matters relating to the administration of trade such as tariffs, standards, antidumping, and competition. Other issues deal with specific agreements such as TRIPs (trade-related intellectual property rights) regulations, technology such as E-commerce, and special treatment and consideration for developing countries (special and differential [S&D]) treatment. There are also issues related to questions of national ownership, commitment and capacity for managing trade, and taking an integrated approach to trade, investment, and national development. The least-developed countries are particularly most challenged because they lack the necessary national human capital and institutional capacity to implement the obligations arising from GATT agreements and to make the necessary technical and political preparations for future negotiations.[4]

Agriculture is a very important economic sector for developing countries because this is traditionally the area in which these countries have enjoyed competitive trade advantages. Yet, as Table 6.2 shows, there are serious issues associated with market access, export subsidies, and domestic support, all resulting from protectionist behavior of developed countries. Agriculture also illustrates the differences among developing countries in terms of their trade policies and interests. Three groups can be identified among developing countries: exporters of tropical products, exporters of temperate products in direct competition with Europe and North America, and importers of food stuffs and grains who are also the ones least likely to have the capacity to produce for export any agricultural commodities. One of the key differences in interest among developing countries lies between those who are not importers of food grains (P2 countries) and those who are net exporters such as the BEMs. Exporters are interested in opening up more market access for their commodities and devising rules to prohibit export taxes, quotas, and other forms of trade

TABLE 6.2
Important Issues for Developing Countries

Issue	*Specific Illustrations*
Agriculture	1. Market access
	2. Export subsidy
	3. Domestic support
	4. Rules of origin
Services	1. Safeguards
	2. Movement of natural persons
	3. Economic needs tests
	4. Facilitation of movement of business visitors
	5. Construction, tourism, telecommunications, health, maritime, financial services
Electronic Commerce	1. Scope and definition
	2. Legal aspects/considerations
	3. Intellectual property aspects
	4. Business development aspects
	5. Treatment within the WTO framework
Antidumping	1. Preferred means of imposing import restrictions
	2. Changing patterns of antidumping
	3. Relation to competition policies
	4. Anti-circumvention messages
Standards	1. SPS and TBT agreements
	2. Conformity and risk assessment
	3. Equivalency and mutual recognition
	4. Participation and transparency
Industrial Tariffs	1. Tariff peaks, escalation, formulas used to cut rates
	2. Simplification and harmonization
	3. Specific and nuisance rates
	4. Approaches to future negotiations
The TRIPs Agreement	1. Difficulties with compliance
	2. Limited transfer and diffusing of technology
	3. Technical cooperation (Article 67)
	4. Future negotiations
Trade and Competition	1. Competition at the international level
	2. Competing and existing agreements
	3. Proposals for future negotiations
Trade and Investment	1. Issues of implementation of the TRIMs Agreement
	2. Increases in bilateral investment treaties (BITs), FDI, and MAI discussions
	3. FDI, trade and development
	4. Investment and competition
	5. Future negotiations

(continued)

TABLE **6.2** (*cont.*)
Important Issues for Developing Countries

Issue	*Specific Illustrations*
Special and Differential Treatment (S&D)	1. Future relevancy of S&D 2. New forms of S&D
Ownership and Commitment	1. Extent of national/local participation/involvement 2. Political commitment and ongoing support 3. Broad-based understanding/informed debate
National Capacity	1. Integration of trade and national development 2. Human and institutional capacity 3. Trade representation in Geneva (WTO) 4. Technical and administrative capacities 5. Public–private partnership and support

Note: MAI = Multilateral Agreement on Investment; SPS = Sanitary Phytosanitary System; TBT = Technical Barriers to Trade; TRIMs = Trade-Related Aspects of Investment Measures.

Source: Compiled from various sources. For example, United Nations, *Preparing for Future Multilateral Trade Negotiations: Issues and Research Needs from a Development Perspective* (New York: UN/UNCTAD, 1999); Constantine Michalopoulos, "Trade Policy and Market Access Issues for Developing Countries: Implications for the Millennium Round," Development Research Group, Trade, Policy Research Working Paper 2214 (Washington, DC: World Bank, October 1999). The reader is advised to consult the original sources for technical details.

protectionism. Therefore, they are, at least in principle, in support of the WTO and the resulting agreements and rulings. These are mainly the twenty to twenty-five countries that are mostly BEMs, middle income from Asia and Latin America, and are almost fully integrated in the multilateral trading system. They participate actively in the WTO, abide by the rules, use similar types of trade remedies, such as antidumping, as the industrial countries do, and take full advantage of the opportunities offered by the WTO's trade DSM.

Then there are the fifty to sixty least-developed countries members of the WTO who are net importers of food. They are mostly concerned with increases in the price of imported food, the negative impact on their limited foreign exchange earnings, and the net impact on their poor populations. They want to keep the option to support domestic agriculture with export subsidies in the future should they then have developed the capacity to export. Most of these countries are not yet effectively integrated in the multilateral trading system. They have only minimal participation in the WTO and little or no national capacity to implement the Uruguay Round commitments, WTO rulings, or the preparation of future negotiations. They tend to focus on the S&D aspects of trade negotiations. Although they enjoy exemptions under the aggregate measures support for agriculture as provided for the urban and rural poor and a ten-year grace period for full implementation of commitment, they still resist trade liberalization because they are not ready.[5]

In terms of agriculture, the small, poor developing countries are subjected to negotiating pressures from three powerful forces. First, there is the United States that is seeking improved market access for its wide range of agricultural products, while at the same time protecting its domestic producers of commodities such as sugar. Second, there is the EU that is seeking to maintain import restrictions, export subsidies, and domestic support in accordance with the Common Agricultural Policy. Third, there is the Cairns Group that is pressing hard for agricultural liberalization and removal of all tariff and nontariff trade restrictions. The poor developing countries with limited technical capacity and negotiating clout are hard-pressed to counter these powerful forces and to identify, articulate, and actively pursue their legitimate long-term agricultural interests.[6]

Several other issues point to the qualitative differences between the advanced developing countries such as the BEMs and the least-developed members or prospective members of the WTO. Examples of such issues include phytosanitary standards; movements of natural persons; TRIPs agreement, ownership, and commitment; and national capacity. SPS standards require that exporters of animal products such as beef build and maintain technical facilities to guarantee quality and sanitary safety of the exports. The advanced developing countries such as Argentina and Brazil are interested in discussing and sharing their experiences with other exporters under the Uruguay Round to ensure that any changes made to the regulations are aimed at improving SPS standards and not a disguised form of trade protectionism, especially by the industrial countries. On the other hand, the facilities required to meet the GATT/WTO SPS standards are well beyond the means and capacities of the least-developed countries. A World Bank official estimated that such facilities would cost about U.S.$150 million, which is more than the entire annual capital development budget for many of the small and poor countries. He also observed that almost ninety countries were in violation of the SPS, customs valuation, and TRIPs agreements and are not likely to meet their commitments any time soon.[7]

Liberalization of services is another trade issue that differentiates the interests of the BEMs from the less-developed countries. An important aspect of the service sector is the movement of natural persons so that citizens of developing countries can move freely to work in other developing or developed countries. In addition to the various professional areas, construction is one industry that is important for developing countries. Countries such as Turkey, South Korea, and China have the capacity to export construction services, providing they can bring in temporary workers. There are examples of this already happening, especially in the Middle East where oil revenues have attracted construction services from South Korea and other BEM countries. Once again, the small poor countries have not developed an exportable construction service industry and issues of access are not important to them. Instead, they are more concerned about the brain drain implications of liberalization whereby their technical and professional nationals, already limited in number, would leave and seek employment opportunities in the more competitive countries.

After the end of the Uruguay Round, several sectoral negotiations were undertaken. By the end of 2000, four such negotiations had been undertaken on market access. Maritime transport negotiations reached no agreement and were suspended. Negotiations on the movement of natural persons have not achieved much, especially for developing countries. The only two service areas in which successful negotiations have been beneficial to developing countries, especially the more advanced BEMs, are basic telecommunications and financial services. Domestic reforms of the latter two sectors are of particular advantage to globalizing developing countries and transition economies.

NATIONAL CAPACITY DEVELOPMENT FOR TRADE AND DEVELOPMENT

It is now clear that most developing countries, especially the least developed ones (P2), lack the capacity to take full advantage of the opportunities offered by a liberalized global trading system as well as their membership in the WTO. Without building the necessary national capacity, the majority of P2 countries will continue to focus on maintaining S&D treatment as their protective negotiating strategy instead of moving toward openness, liberalization, and gainful participation in trade and globalization. This would be bad for everybody. The areas particularly difficult for these countries in terms of technical capacity include TRIPs, SPS, TBT, and Customs valuation. These countries need to develop the necessary capacity and take a strategic approach to trade and development that is goal directed, focused, systemic, long term, and national in scope.

Evidence of the lack of capacity to manage trade and its negative consequences for P2 countries comes from various sources. Their participation in world trade seems to be declining as their share of total global trade is falling even in primary commodities such as agriculture, mining, and textiles—areas in which they have had a historical comparative advantage. The African, Caribbean, and Pacific group has lost or are in the process of losing market access as a result of dilution of preferences previously enjoyed in the EU countries.[8] Lack of capacity explains why these countries are unable to meet their obligations arising from the Uruguay Round and the WTO rulings within the given transition period and why they are unable to prepare for and engage in effective trade negotiations. Mindful of this problem, the 1998 Ministerial Conference expressed concern about the increasing marginalization of the P2 countries and called on WTO member states to address the issue and come up with practical solutions to reverse the trend. To that end, the WTO draft preparatory document for the 2001 Ministerial Conference clearly stated: "We recognize that the further integration of the least-developed countries (LDCs) into the trading system requires combined and inter-related action at three levels namely, market access, trade-related technical assistance and capacity-building, and LDCs' domestic reform."[9]

One area in which these countries are at a serious disadvantage is the DSM established by the WTO. According to the procedural rules, only government officials are allowed to participate in panel hearings. Yet, most P2 countries do not have enough government officials with the necessary knowledge, skills, and experience to provide effective representation and negotiation. Lacking the necessary background in areas such as international economics and legal knowledge and experience, these countries often fail to identify and defend their interests in WTO disputes. At the same time, they cannot hire foreign legal consultants because of the rules limiting participation only to government officials. Indeed, from the perspectives of these countries, DSM rules are legalistic, obstructive, and not sensitive to matters of equity.

The lack of an effective national capacity for trade and development manifests itself in many important areas: weak or no representation at the WTO, failure to develop a domestic trade-positive institutional infrastructure, inability to conceptually and operationally link trade to overall national development, maintaining a low profile and low prestige of the trade profile within the public service, and weak interdisciplinary academic, research, and training in areas relevant for managing trade and development.

Trade Representation at the World Trade Organization

One of the best indicators of a country's effective representation and participation in the global trading system is the quality and quantity of representation at the WTO, or before at GATT. Developing countries have always complained about the outcomes of the Uruguay Round because they were poorly represented. For example, when the round started in 1987, there were sixty-five developing countries belonging to GATT. Twenty of these countries did not have representation in Geneva. Fifteen of the twenty were represented by their embassy staff stationed elsewhere in Europe, and the other five were represented from their national capitals where distance and poor infrastructure make effective communication and consultation difficult.

In contrast, the industrial countries and the BEMs were much better represented in Geneva. For example, the EU had ten trade representatives plus fifty-seven from the individual member European states; Japan had fifteen, and the United States had ten. Among the BEMs, Korea and Mexico each had seven, Brazil and Indonesia had six each, and Thailand and Hong Kong had five each. By contrast, of the tweny-nine least-developed countries, which are members of the WTO, only eleven maintain permanent delegations in Geneva. Part of the reason is that it is expensive to maintain a permanent staff in Geneva, especially for P2 countries. A senior Canadian official once told me that it costs about U.S. $150,000 annually to maintain a trade officer and his/her family in Geneva. Therefore, a staff of seven would cost more than U.S. $1 million, which is more than most P2 countries can afford. Another reason for poor representation is because of the low priority that most of these countries give to matters of global trade. Since they are not fully integrated in the global trading system and since most of their foreign capital comes in by means of overseas development assistance (ODA), rather than trade and private sector investments, the public policy makers of these countries do not see the need to invest in trade and development. It took China fifteen years of hard technical, diplomatic, and political work before being admitted as a full member of the WTO. Many developing countries and some of the transition economies do not have the capacity to persevere.

Table 6.3 illustrates the problems of trade capacity by showing the number of WTO trade officials for selected P2 countries. Out of the forty WTO member states listed in the table, nineteen (or almost 50 percent) did not have any representation in Geneva; another twelve had only 1–3 trade officials, and only six had 4–5. It is interesting to note that the countries that attract the most FDI among those listed in the table—Nigeria, Egypt, and South Africa—each had six or more trade representatives in Geneva. South Africa, as a newcomer to the global trading system, and as a member of the Cairns Group, needs strong representation at the WTO.

Table 6.3 also shows the Catch-22 in which most of the P2 countries find themselves. They are the least integrated in the global trading system and have the least liberalized trad-

TABLE 6.3
Africa's World Trade Organization Capacity Problem:
Number of Trade Officials in Geneva, 1997

Number of Trade Officials	Country
6+	Egypt, Nigeria, South Africa
4–5	Mauritius, Morocco, Tanzania, Uganda, Zambia, Zimbabwe
1–3	Angola, Burundi, Cameroon, Congo, Côte d'Ivoire, Democratic Republic of the Congo, Djibouti, Gabon, Ghana, Kenya, Senegal, Tunisia
None	Benin, Botswana, Burkina Faso, Central African Republic, Chad, Gambia (The), Guinea, Lesotho, Madagascar, Malawi, Mali, Mauritania, Mozambique, Namibia, Niger, Rwanda, Sierra Leone, Swaziland, Togo

Note: WTO membership is growing with new members and applications. Readers should consult the original source for details.

Source: Compiled from World Bank, *Entering the 21st Century: World Development Report 1999/2000* (New York: Oxford University Press, 2000): fig. 2, p. 57.

ing system. They need to improve their participation and increase their share of benefits from trade and the WTO. They need to become active trading nations. Yet, they are, at best, only minimally represented in the international forum where important trade and investment decisions and rulings are made. Without effective representation and participation in these decisions and rulings, these countries cannot guarantee that their individual and collective interests will be protected and preserved. In fact, recent experiences seem to suggest that they are losing out. This is one area in which critics of the global trading system, in general, and the WTO, in particular, have a strong economic and moral justification. When these P2 countries lose out, everyone loses. Global trade is not a zero-sum game, and therefore, it is imperative that the WTO and other international organizations work in partnership with the P2 member states to build a win–win global trading system.

There is a link between representation and participation, on the one hand, and understanding, commitment, acceptance, motivation, and support, on the other hand. With minimal representation and participation, P2 governments and their publics enjoy a low level of understanding of the strategic importance of trade, and consequently, their levels of commitment, acceptance, and intrinsic motivation to support liberalization is low. This, in turn, leads to limited political will to push for trade and liberalization, which in turn results in lack of ownership or weak identification with the ideals and practical realities of the WTO and the global trading system it represents. The sentiments and lessons of experience are similar to those of the 1980s when most of the same P2 countries were required to implement political and economic reforms such as structural adjustment programs without the necessary national commitment, political will, or institutional capacity. Drawing from the lessons of the earlier experiences, it is clear that each of the P2 countries must develop a sustainable national capacity for trade and development as a prerequisite to effective globalization.

There are several efforts by the international community and several specialized UN agencies to help developing countries enhance their individual and collective capacities to become more effectively integrated into the global trading system. The WTO, and GATT before it, makes special provisions for developing countries, especially under the S&D treatment. The special provisions either involve positive action by developed countries and/or international institutions or they are exceptions to the overall rules contained in the agreements that apply to developing countries in general, or more specifically to the less-developed developing (P2) countries. In general, developed countries support S&D by extending preferential access to their markets, primarily through the voluntary provisions of the Generalized System of Preferences, implementing the agreements and rulings in ways that are beneficial or least damaging to developing countries, and providing technical and other forms of assistance. As well, developed countries have accepted the need for the developing countries, especially the P2 countries, to undertake policies that limit access to their markets or provide support to domestic producers and exporters, which would otherwise be prohibited under WTO agreements and rulings. Developed countries are also willing to give the weaker developing countries more time before they are required to fulfill their WTO obligations and commitments.

The United Nations Conference on Trade and Development (UNCTAD) is a specialized agency that provides technical support to developing countries in the areas of trade and development. Historically, most developing countries have always found UNCTAD more sympathetic to their special circumstances than the more hard-nosed GATT/WTO. According to Rubens Ricupero, UNCTAD's secretary-general, UNCTAD's new mandate is to help developing countries, and particularly the least-developed countries (P2), to better integrate into the global economy and the global trading system. To fulfill its mandate, UNCTAD must assist these countries to:

1. identify and take advantage of trading opportunities;
2. fulfill their multilateral trade obligations;
3. formulate and pursue development strategies within the framework of these obligations;
4. protect, defend, and preserve their acquired trading rights;
5. set objectives and affectively pursue them in trade negotiations.

In addition to organizing conferences, UNCTAD works collaboratively with the WTO and other international organizations—such as the World Bank, IMF, UNDP, ILO, Food and Agriculture Organization of the United Nations (FAO), and World Health Organization (WHO), as well as bilateral donors—to provide training and other forms of assistance to developing countries either individually or in groups. The World Bank's International Trade Center has been particularly active in providing traditional forms of training and development. The Swiss government provides subsidies to selected developing countries to support their trade missions in Geneva.

Still, the general conclusion is that so far these initiatives are necessary but not sufficient to overcome the problems of marginalization, alienation, and inadequate national capacity for trade and development, which characterize more developing countries. There are many reasons why the results of these initiatives have been limited thus far. They are primarily focused on the WTO and Geneva, taking a rather narrow technical approach to trade. Like the earlier efforts at capacity building, following the introduction of SAPs and other reforms, they are essentially externally donor driven with limited meaningful local participation or national ownership. They do not take a holistic approach to integrating, trade, investment, and overall national development. They tend to shy away from confronting the domestic political, administrative, social, and cultural impediments to liberalization and trade. They also tend to focus on government-to-government relationships with minimal and superficial involvement of other sectors of P2 societies such as the business community, the labor movement, the media, academic institutions, and the NGO sector. In other situations, the developing countries have not paid enough attention or given high priority to the WTO and global trade. Instead, they have been preoccupied with short-term domestic problems of survival, confrontation, or open conflict. The countries with no trade officials in Geneva, such as Sierra Leone and Rwanda, or that are not members of the WTO, such as Sudan, Liberia, Somalia, and Ethiopia, are characterized by internal conflicts or civil war.

It is also the case that developed countries have not been consistent in their support for developing countries in the area of trade and development. For example, while providing technical and other forms of assistance to developing countries, developed countries have sought to use labor and environmental standards, antidumping, and countervailing duty to target the exports of the more successful exporting developing countries. As well, in the area of SPS, developed countries have shown less flexibility in accommodating variations in systems structure and performance in developing countries.[10] While showing an increasing tendency to be cooperative in the areas of technical assistance and international development, developed countries have become uncompromisingly competitive when dealing with developing countries in the areas of trade and investment. This schizophrenic approach has not been helpful for developing countries wishing to integrate trade into their overall national development nor has it helped in the overall efforts to build a national capacity for the effective management of trade and development. Developed countries seem to have given with the left hand and taken away with the right.

This message was driven home in January 2001 when the fourteen countries of the Caribbean community (CARICOM) and Canada held a summit to discuss trade. Canada and the Caribbean have a trade agreement already in place that was signed in 1986. P. J. Patterson, the prime minister of Jamaica, explained that the agreement was not working in favor of the small island Caribbean nations because of Canada's protectionist policies. While 95 percent of Caribbean exports are supposed to enter Canada duty-free, exceptions imposed by Canada on clothing, footwear, and agriculture mean that only a tiny fraction of about 7.3 percent of all Caribbean goods in fact qualify as duty-free. It should be noted that these are the areas in which the Caribbeans, like other developing countries, have competitive advantage over Canada and other rich industrial countries. The message from Canada to the CARICOM countries seems to be that: You can bring in your exports duty-free as long as they do not compete with Canadian producers. Not surprisingly, the Caribbean nations are lukewarm about the Free Trade Area of the Americas.

This "mixed-signals" approach to international cooperation and trade on the part of industrial countries is further evidenced by the British government's recent White Paper on globalization and poverty alleviation. On the one hand, the government promised to work with others to strengthen the capacity of developing countries to participate in international negotiations and to take advantage of new trading opportunities, including through improved infrastructure and transport links. This is commendable. On the other hand, the United Kingdom, together with other members of the EU, still retains the same tariff and nontariff barriers, which keep tradable goods and services from developing countries out of these markets.

A Model for National Capacity Development

The case has been made for the need for developing countries, in general, and the least-developed ones (P2), in particular, to develop a sustaining national capacity for the effective integration and management of trade and development. In this section, a model for such capacity development is proposed with a brief discussion of its main attributes, overall goal, objectives, and expected results. This model is mainly developed in response to the special trade development needs of the least-developed P2 countries. At the same time, some aspects of the model may be of interest to the more advanced developing countries and transition economies.

The proposed model for capacity development for trade and development is strategic, national in scope, integrative, holistic, dynamic, and participative. It is strategic in the sense that it is goal directed, results oriented, and long term. It is long term because of the realization that most P2 countries do not have the capacity to initiate and sustain drastic changes. It is national in scope because of the need to ensure the understanding and active participation of various segments of society and institutions both in the public and private sectors. It is integrative because of the need to make both conceptual and practical links between trade, investment, and development. One of the problems facing countries with a history of minimal involvement in the global trading system is a general lack of understanding and appreciation of the role trade plays in attracting foreign capital and investment, poverty alleviation, and economic and overall national social development.

The proposed model is also holistic in that it looks at the whole global trading system in several ways. First, it recognizes that building the necessary capacity is not only a matter of technical training and physical infrastructure. Perhaps, more important, in the long run, corresponding trade-positive capacities must be built in the political, social, cultural, and administrative sectors of the country. Political capacity building for trade is particularly important partly because of the dominant role politics continues to play at WTO and global trade negotiations and partly because most politicians and rebel leaders of the least-developed countries do not consider trade liberalization a matter of national priority. The model is also holistic because it attempts to ensure that what happens in Geneva at the WTO is perceived as having relevancy for development back home as well as internationally. If the governments of the P2 countries do not see any practical relationship between the priorities in Geneva and those in their capital, they are much less likely to support the development of the necessary capacity for trade and liberalization. This holistic approach is intended to ensure effective coordination between the Geneva delegations and the relevant agencies in both the public and the private sectors.

Finally, the proposed model is both dynamic and participative. It is dynamic because of the changing circumstances within each of the developing countries, among groups of developing countries, within the global trading system, and within the WTO as a multilateral trade organization. One of the biggest challenges of the least-developed countries is that they lack the capacity, the resources, and the tools to keep abreast of changes in the global economy. Therefore, it becomes difficult for them to plan and take advantage of changes and developments in the global economy and its trading system. Within the individual countries, changes are also taking place. For example, as a country begins to liberalize and the economy becomes more competitive, it requires different trade policies and policy management capacities and institutional arrangements. The dynamic aspects of this model ensure that these changes are constantly monitored and the results are reflected in changes in the overall strategy and plan of action for national capacity development. Critics argue that China is not ready for globalization or membership in the WTO beyond Beijing and the eastern provinces.

The model is participative because experience has shown that governments cannot succeed in building national capacities alone. In addition to the role currently being played by the international community, it is suggested here that the private sector must play a much more active role than is presently the case in most developing countries. There are four groups of stakeholders whose participation in national capacity development for trade is crucial: members of civil society, municipal and local governments, the local private sector, and the international private sector.

Civil society should participate in sensitizing the public to the issues of trade and raising the general level of awareness, understanding, and debate about trade, national trade policy, and people's standards of living and quality of life. The institutions most likely to be active here are the trade unions; the mass media; professional associations; academic, educational, and research institutions; youth organizations; women's organizations; and other NGOs operating in areas such as the environment, poverty alleviation, and human and social services. Without their active participation, it would be almost impossible to mobilize the population and to develop national consensus on the essence of trade and development.

The participation of municipal and local governments is necessary because they are closer to the people than the central government, and they can help develop nationwide political capacity for trade. They are also interested in promoting growth and development in their areas through trade and globalization. Some day, local government authorities may play a direct role at the WTO and may be allowed to have their own trade representatives.

The third aspect of participative capacity development is the role of the local business sector. It is proposed here that the business sector should form a partnership or close working relationship with the government in the development of the national capacity for trade and investment. The business community should be involved in developing informed opinions about global trade within its ranks, working with the government in the formulation of trade policy, and developing the necessary capacity within both the business and the public sectors. The business sector may have resources, tools, and competencies necessary for capacity development that the public sector needs but does not have. Likewise, the public sector may have information or competencies that the business sector needs to build its own trade development capacities. Therefore, the partnership would be mutually beneficial and reinforcing.

One of the novel ideas proposed here as part of the capacity development model is the active, direct involvement of the international business community, especially the global corporations. These corporations have the resources and the expertise and it is in their long-term best interest for more countries to liberalize trade and become active, integrated participants in the global trading system. While the active participation and assistance of global corporations makes sense, issues relating to incentives and mechanics by which they can become meaningfully involved need to be discussed. Here, it is proposed that a multilateral organization such as the WTO, UNCTAD, UNDP, or the World Bank–IMF should develop an "Adopt a Nation Global Program." The purpose of the program would be to get global corporations directly involved in working with the least-developed countries and assist them in developing the necessary national capacities and competencies for their affective liberalization and integration into the global trading system. One or two carefully selected global corporations could be matched with one or a group of neighboring least-developed countries and their respective private sectors to work together and identify capacity gaps in which the corporation's resources and expertise could be both useful and useable. Global corporations would be required to make their training, management, facilities, and other resources available to the matched P2 countries for the development and maintenance of their national capacities for trade. Obviously, such a program would be voluntary on both sides and would have to be carefully monitored and supervised by the sponsoring multilateral organization. If, however, a number of high-profile global corporations got involved initially with highly publicized positive results, it could become popular among both the global corporations and the least-developed countries.

The model proposed here can benefit from the experiences of similar initiatives in international cooperation. For example, the fight against river blindness (onchocerciasis) in West Africa is regarded as one of the most successful programs in the history of international cooperation. Before the program started in 1974, more than 1 million people were infected with the disease, and more than 100,000 people were blind. By the time the program ends in 2002, 34 million people will be protected, 600,000 cases of blindness will have been prevented, and 5 million years of productive labor will have been saved. The program was successful because it was strategic, long term (lasting almost thirty years), and involved the active participation of local, national, regional, and international partners. The partners in the program included eleven African governments, local communities, international organizations, bilateral donors, foundations, NGOs, and corporations. Merck Corporation, a global drug company, was the lead corporate partner in the program, providing medical advice and the drug ivermectin for free. This is the kind of multipartner, strategic approach developing countries need to develop their trade sectors, human capital, and institutional capacities for global competitiveness.

As for incentives, in addition to selling the program as part of corporate global social responsibility and long-term self-interest, developed countries could demonstrate direct support to the least-developed countries by providing tax credits to the participating global corporations. As well, the reforming countries could eventually develop business opportunities of interest to the participating global corporation. The participation of the leaders of the local business community would also provide opportunities for building business relationships and eventual partnerships. This would be an important side benefit because it would promote the development of the local private sector.

The success of this program would be based on quality, not quantity. As of 2000, there were about five thousand global corporations. If 10 percent were targeted and invited to participate, that would give an estimated pool of about five hundred global corporations. In the same year, there were about twenty-nine least-developed countries listed as members of the WTO, indicating their willingness to undertake liberalization for globalization. If only 10 percent of the five hundred global corporations agreed to participate, that would mean a total of fifty corporations available to be matched with twenty-nine countries.

Exhibit 6.3 summarizes the main attributes of the capacity development model. Specifically, the exhibit provides a brief statement of the model's overall goal, purpose, and expected results. The overall goal is the development of a homemade national capacity for the country to be able to achieve effective integration and ongoing management of its global trade, investment, and development. The holistic approach proposed here differs significantly from the narrow functional approach to capacity development often associated with SAPs. The intended results go beyond the narrow technical capacity often undertaken by international organizations and include local political, social, and cultural considerations at both the national and subnational levels. Most important, it gives the private sector, especially the business sector, which is the vanguard for global trade, a direct role in the development of the national capacity for liberalization, trade, and globalization. A recent UNCTAD report concluded that a policy of cheap labor combined with currency devaluation is no longer sufficient for developing countries to achieve continued export success. Drawing on case studies in the textile, garment, and electronics industries for Korea, Taiwan, Thailand, Indonesia, and Vietnam, the report recommended that learning and developing technological capacities are critical for sustaining competitiveness for developing countries.[11]

Exhibit 6.3
Main Attributes of the Capacity Development Model

Goal
To develop and sustain an indigenous national capacity for the effective and beneficial integration and management of global trade, investment, and development.

Purpose
1. Create nationwide awareness among all sectors of society of the importance of interrelationships among liberalization, global trade, development, and globalization and facilitate a national debate and consensus.

2. Undertake a complete assessment of the country's trading system: strength, limitations, opportunities, and threats and develop a national strategy and plan of action for trade liberalization and development.

3. Identify specific capacity gaps by comparing available and required capacities for the effective implementation of the plan of action.

4. The government, in partnership with the private sector and the international community, facilitates the development of the identified capacities and competencies.

Results

1. Maintain broad-based national understanding and informed debate about the relevance of global trade for national development.

2. A critical mass of qualified and networked trade experts in both the public and the private sectors with active professional association(s).

3. Ongoing, active political understanding, commitment, and ownership.

4. Higher profile and status accorded to the trade portfolio and trade experts especially in the public sector.

5. Ongoing locally based multidisciplinary academic and professional training and development programs and activities.

6. Ongoing effective public–private partnership for trade development.

7. Steady improvements in trade liberalization and managed integration into the global trading system.

8. Improved quantity and quality of trade and investments.

9. Enhanced quality of participation in the WTO and other trade negotiations.

10. Improved openness, competitiveness, and more equitable gainful globalization.

Required Skills and Core Competencies

Although it is widely believed that most trade representatives of the least-developed countries lack the necessary qualifications to perform their duties effectively, no attempts have been made to spell out the required skills set and core competencies for these positions. This information is necessary for effective human resource management and institutional development as part of the overall capacity development. For example, this kind of information is critical for the effective recruitment, selection, placement, training and development, motivation, retention, and promotion of the trade representatives in both the public and the private sectors.

Exhibit 6.4 summarizes the results of the first attempt to identify the dimensions and elements of the job specifications of trade representatives for developing countries. Four dimensions of the required skills set and core competencies are presented: areas of specialized knowledge, practical work experience, specific job skills, and areas of general working knowledge.

Exhibit 6.4
Required Skills Set and Core Competencies for Trade Representatives

Areas of Specialized Knowledge
1. Economics, specializing in trade and development

2. Public and international finance, taxation, customs

3. International trade law

4. International relations, diplomacy, politics, geography, history

5. Public administration and change management

6. Interdisciplinary/regional/national social studies

7. Tropical agriculture, veterinary science, biotechnology

Practical Work Experience
1. Home government line ministries/agencies/private sector

2. Foreign/diplomatic service

3. Multilateral/U.N. institutions, international organizations

4. Overseas travel, work, study

5. Program/project/policy management

Specific Job Skills
1. Cross-cultural communications, language skills

2. Negotiating, lobbying, consulting skills

3. Writing, presenting ministerial briefing notes

4. Computer, Internet, office management skills

5. Networking skills within and outside one's organization

6. Extensive reading, independent study, and research skills

7. Quantitative skills

8. Skillful driver of the "Lexus" and climber of the "Olive Tree"

Areas of General Working Knowledge

1. The political economy of the major regions of the world

2. The history, economics, politics, and sociocultural institutions of home country/region

3. International NGOs

4. Information and computer technology

5. The structure and functioning of the global/private/business/ corporate sector

6. International donors and financial institutions

The specialized knowledge, which is often acquired through advanced university degrees, is quite varied: culled from various branches of economics, law, international relations, agriculture and veterinary science, and administration and management. Most of the least-developed countries would be hard-pressed to have a critical mass of educated nationals with advanced degrees in each of these disciplines, let alone those with combined specializations. It is not common for local universities to offer advanced combined academic programs such as economics and law or agriculture and international relations. In the short run, these shortcomings can be addressed best through in-service and on-the-job training, giving the trade representatives the multidisciplinary skills, competencies, and perspectives they need for effective performance of their demanding and varied duties.

The required practical experience is also varied: ranging from time spent working with various government line ministries and agencies involved with trade, finance, and economic development to working overseas in the foreign diplomatic service, multilateral institutions, and other international organizations such as NGOs and global corporations. Experience in living, working, traveling, and studying abroad is also useful because it exposes the trade representatives to foreign cultures, mind-sets, and ways of doing things. It is helpful in international negotiations to have a point of reference from one's native experiences.

Exhibit 6.4 also lists a number of specific job skills trade representatives should have. These include cross-cultural communications and languages skills (for example, English, French, Spanish, Japanese); negotiating and lobbying skills; computer, Internet, and networking skills; quantitative and research skills; and practical management skills. It is also suggested that to be effective, trade representatives for globalizing developing countries should be skillful drivers and climbers of Thomas Friedman's metaphorical "Lexus" and "Olive Tree." This means that they must be equally comfortable and skilled in dealing with the modernizing global world as well as their own traditional cultural institutions. It is their ability to find common ground from both worlds and integrate them into practical solutions to advancing their country's trade and development that makes them especially competent and qualified to represent the interests of their people in a changing and globalizing world. This is something foreign consultants would be hard-pressed to replicate.[12]

Using Sectorwide Approaches

Building effective and sustainable capacities for development remains one of the most daunting problems facing developing countries, especially the least-developed ones. Various attempts by governments, donors, and the international development community have often produced mixed results. The capacity development model I proposed for trade and development runs the risk of facing serious implementation problems. To minimize these risks, it is proposed here that the sectorwide approaches (SWAPs) be considered in the implementation of the model. This section provides a brief description of SWAPs, their current applications in development, and why they are considered particularly appropriate for capacity development, especially for P2 member states of the WTO.

SWAPs are used in international development in an attempt to move away from project-specific aid and technical assistance to focus on an entire sector. They are a mechanism by which the donors, government, and other invited stakeholders agree on sectorwide priorities, develop a sectoral national strategy and plan of action, determine the resources required and the action to be taken, outline the responsibilities for implementation, and monitor the results and the procedures by which decisions are to be made and disputes resolved. All this is usually outlined in a working document available to all parties. SWAPs have the advantage of mobilizing significant resources from the recipient government and from the donors and channeling them to a single identified priority sector or subsector. The recipient government takes the leadership role in priority setting and implementation, and the donors agree to use government procedures for program management, including budgeting, disbursements, and overall accountability.

Donors like the SWAPs because they allow them to work together toward common goals (without invoking the unpopular memories of aid coordination), reduce donor transaction costs, enhance local ownership, and help the recipient government build its own capacity in the priority sectors. Governments of developing countries like SWAPs because they make it easy for them to mobilize and channel donor support in areas of their choice. They also see it as a sign of donor support for the UNDP's approach of "national execution." It is important to note that SWAPs are basically a general approach to technical assistance, not a blueprint. Therefore, they are quite flexible.[13]

SWAPs are fairly new, having been started in the 1990s. They are almost exclusively used in highly aid-dependent poor countries with weak physical, digital, and institutional capacities for development policy formulation and implementation. These are essentially the P2 countries where, historically, donors have experienced difficulty in the successful implementation of aid programs. Likewise, these are the same countries needing a lot of help from the WTO and the international community. Therefore, the lessons and experiences gained in SWAPs should be useful for these countries as they begin the process of capacity development for trade liberalization and development.

As of 2000, there were eighty SWAPs programs in various stages of implementation. Of these, 85 percent were in sub-Saharan Africa and the rest were in Asia and Latin America.

The countries most actively involved include Bangladesh, Ethiopia, Ghana, Tanzania, Uganda, Vietnam, and Zambia. Most of the programs are in social services (health and education), but other sectors such as agriculture, the environment, energy, roads and transport, water, and urban development are also represented. Various international donors—Department of Foreign and International Development (DFID; United Kingdom), Danish International Development Agency (DANIDA), Canadian International Development Agency (CIDA), Irish Aid, Dutch Ministry of Foreign Affairs and International Development, United States Agency for International Development (USAID), and Norwegian Agency for Development (NORAD)—are working together using the SWAPs framework to provide technical and financial assistance to Uganda's educational sector, especially the Universal Primary Education national initiative launched in 1997. As of the year 2000, there were no SWAPs programs aimed at trade as a sector. This may be a reflection of the low priority that both donors and governments of P2 countries give to trade and trade development as an instrument of poverty alleviation.

Exhibit 6.5 lists a number of advantages and possible drawbacks for using SWAPs for national capacity development for trade for the least-developed countries. One of the advantages is that SWAPs are deliberative, creating a mechanism for key stakeholders to come together in a spirit of partnership to discuss various aspects of sector-specific development and to come to a consensus regarding the priorities and how to address them. This deliberative aspect is particularly important for national capacity development for trade because most of the P2 countries still need to undertake a national dialogue on trade, its priority within national development, and the strategies by which to address it. The presence of outsiders is also useful because, as proposed in the model, P2 countries will need a lot of direct participation from the international community.

EXHIBIT 6.5
SWAPs: Advantages and Disadvantages for
National Capacity Development for Trade

Advantages

1. An approach, not a blueprint

2. Deliberative

3. Local leadership, ownership, commitment

4. Based on participative partnership

5. Outsiders, foreigners as active stakeholders

6. Sensitive to practical issues of political processes

7. Focused on results, accountability, transparency

8. Explicit mechanisms for joint decision making and dispute settlement

9. Concerned with poverty alleviation and issues of equity

10. Can be linked with other capacity development approaches such as Comprehensive Development Framework, Poverty Reduction Strategy, and National Strategy for Sustainable Development

Disadvantages

1. Minimal private sector involvement, especially the business community

2. Strong donor influence: not sustainable without donor support

3. Centralized control by the national government

4. Creates extra workload and pressures for line ministries and central agencies

5. Not yet used for trade development

Other advantages SWAPs bring to the national capacity development for trade include local leadership and local political processes focusing on results, accountability, and transparency; explicit mechanisms for decision making and disputes settlement; concern for poverty alleviation and equity; and the potential for linking with other development approaches such as the Comprehensive Development Framework, the Poverty Reduction Strategy, and the National Strategies for Sustainable Development. The framework and strategies are considered priority areas for the international donor community, funding agencies, and the multilateral institutions, especially for the poor countries. Therefore, it is advantageous for the national capacity development strategy for trade to be linked with the Comprehensive Development Framework and the other two strategies. This should not be difficult because, ultimately, all of these approaches share the same goal of poverty alleviation and growth with equity for the P2 countries.

Exhibit 6.5 also lists several potential disadvantages for using SWAPs for capacity development for trade. Perhaps the greatest drawback is the rather minimal involvement of the private sector, especially the business sector. In the model I presented, the business community is given a key role in the development of the national capacity for trade. While SWAPs programs have allowed private sector participants, these have been from the NGO or nonbusiness sectors. To use the SWAPs effectively for trade as a sector, changes must be made to allow business leaders a bigger role in policy formulation and policy implementation. As well, up until now, the outside partners for SWAPs include only official donor agencies such as USAID, CIDA, and DFID. The national capacity development model I proposed explicitly invites the international business community, including global corporations, as full partners and participants. This is another area in which adjustments need to be made to current SWAPs practices. Otherwise, the basic principles on which SWAPs is formulated and practiced are consistent with the rationale and practical considerations for the national capacity development strategy for trade, especially for the least-developed WTO member states.

The Way Forward: Doha and Beyond

Unlike the third Ministerial Conference held in Seattle, the fourth Ministerial Conference held in Doha succeeded in getting WTO members to agree to launch a new round of trade talks and to keep the global economy on track toward freer trade and investment. Coming only two months after September 11, 2001, in the middle of the global fight against terrorism in Afghanistan and elsewhere and with the world economy on the verge of a recession and mindful of the catastrophic failure in Seattle two years earlier, the delegates knew that failure at Doha could be fatal for the WTO as an organization, which would be a major setback for the multilateral economic system. Accordingly, both developing and rich countries made last-minute compromises in order to reach a deal: The conference agreed to establish a Trade Negotiation Committee under the authority of the General Council and to conclude negotiations by January 2005. This is very ambitious given the many outstanding issues (see Table 6.4) and given that the Uruguay Round, with a smaller and less-diverse WTO membership, took seven years to negotiate.

Doha was good for developing countries in several ways. First, they benefited from the failure of Seattle because the WTO would not have survived two Ministerial Conference failures in a row. Therefore, Doha paid a lot more attention to the needs and concerns of the developing and least-developed countries. Second, China and Taiwan were admitted as full members of the WTO, thus strengthening the voice and representation of the developing countries in all future negotiations. China, with a population of 1.3 billion people and one of the fastest growing economies in the world, is likely to change the balance of power at the WTO negotiating table, mostly in favor of developing countries. Third, Europe, America, and Japan agreed to negotiate the opening of their markets to goods and services from developing countries. Finally, the rich countries promised to help the developing countries build their competencies and capacities for more effective membership in the WTO and gainfully participate in the multilateral trading system and global society.

Still, developing countries remain suspicious because they remember the Uruguay Round when most of the benefits went to the rich countries. They also fear that the rich countries could use environmental concerns and labor standards as nontariff barriers to trade. Concerned with the difficulties of implementing earlier commitments, developing countries need firm commitments from the international community for practical assistance to build their capacities.

Table 6.4 lists nineteen key issues arising out of the Doha conference and their relevancy for developing (P1) and least-developed (P2) countries. It was agreed that priority be given to negotiating outstanding implementation of decisions made in earlier rounds by the end of 2002. Implementation-related problems cover a wide range of issues including S&D, SPS, rules of origin, subsidies, and countervailing measures. Implementation issues are very important for developing countries because as Iddi Simba, Tanzania's trade minister, said before Doha, many developing countries would have preferred to solve the implementation issues remaining from the Uruguay Round agreement before advancing to the next round

Issues	*Implications*
1. Implementation Issues	• Priority negotiations of outstanding implementation of decisions made in earlier rounds by the end of 2002.
2. Agriculture	• Opening of European, American, and Japanese markets for developing countries.
3. Services	• Negotiation to be aimed at development of developing and least-developed countries.
4. Market Access for Nonagricultural Products	• No product exclusion of nonagricultural products. • Technical assistance and capacity development allow developing and least-developed countries effective participation and negotiation.
5. TRIPs Agreement	• Issue of declaration on the TRIPs Agreement and public health. • Cheaper drugs for developing and least-developed countries in case of public health emergencies. • Protection of traditional knowledge and folklore.
6. Relationship between Trade and Investment	• Negotiations postponed after fifth Ministerial Conference to allow time for technical assistance and capacity development in policy analysis and development. • Special needs of developing and least-developed countries to be taken into account.
7. Interaction between Trade and Competition Policy	• Negotiations postponed after fifth Ministerial Conference to allow time for technical assistance and capacity development.
8. Transparency in Government Procurement	• Working group on transparency in government. Procurement to do preparatory work. • Technical assistance and capacity development for developing and least-developed countries.
9. Trade Facilitation	• Negotiations postponed after fifth Ministerial Conference to allow time for technical assistance and capacity development.
10. WTO Rules	• Clarification and improvement of WTO disciplines on fisheries subsidies and regional trade agreement with special reference to developing and least-developed countries.

(continued)

TABLE 6.4 (*cont.*)

Issues	Implications
11. Dispute Settlement Understanding	• Negotiations on dispute settlement understanding to be concluded by May 2003.
12. Trade and Environment	• Committee on Trade and Environment to give special attention to effects of environmental measures on market access for developing and least-developed countries, TRIPs and labeling requirements for environmental purposes. • Technical assistance and capacity development for developing and least-developed countries.
13. Electronic Commerce	• No customs duties on electronic transmissions.
14. Small and Island States	• A study to recommend the integration of small and vulnerable economies into the multilateral trading system; not to treat them as separate category.
15. Trade, Debt, and Finance	• Establishment of working group to recommend durable solutions to external indebtedness of developing and least-developed countries.
16. Trade and Technology Transfer	• Working group to study relationship between trade and technology and recommend ways to increase flows of technology to developing and least-developed countries.

of multilateral negotiations. Murasoli Maran, India's minister of commerce and industry, abstained from voting for the new round on behalf of other developing countries because of the failure of the rich countries to open their markets to developing countries in areas such as agriculture, textiles, labor, and apparel where they have a comparative advantage. Table 6.4 also provides information on TRIPs, whereby the Doha conference issues a separate declaration on TRIPs and public health, allowing poor countries to access cheaper drugs in cases of public health emergencies such as HIV/AIDS, malaria, and tuberculosis.

Perhaps one of the most important decisions from Doha for the least-developed countries is the emphasis placed on the need to develop their competencies and capacities to enable them to participate most effectively as members of the WTO and to benefit from the global economy and global society. Table 6.4 provides several areas in which technical cooperation (foreign aid) will be provided for capacity development for the poor countries. This includes issues such as trade and the environment, transparency in government procurement, and adjustments to WTO rules, disciplines, obligations, and rights. In technical areas in which developing and least-developed countries were particularly weak and vulnerable, the conference agreed to postpone negotiations until after the fifth Ministerial Conference, when studies will have been done and capacities will have been developed. The

TABLE 6.4 (cont.)

Issues	Implications
17. Technical Cooperation and Capacity Development	• WTO to support mainstreaming track into national plans for economic development and poverty reduction. • Technical assistance and capacity development for developing and least-developed countries to adjust to WTO rules, disciplines, obligations, and rights. • Support for Geneva representation for developing and least-developed countries' members and observers. • Better coordination and rationalization of Integrated Framework for Trade-Related Technical Assistance to least-developed countries and the Joint Integrated Technical Assistance Program. • Report progress developing and least-developed countries have made at the fifth Ministerial Conference.
18. Least-Developed Countries	• Commitment for duty-free, quota-free market access for products originating from least-developed countries. • Periodic report on progress by December 2002 and fifth Ministerial Conference.
19. Special and Differential Treatment	• Conference reconfirmed S&D treatment provisions as an integral part of WTO agreements. • All S&D treatment provisions to be reviewed to make them precise, effective, and operational.

Source: Compiled from WTO, *Ministerial Declaration* (Geneva: WTO, November 2001). Available: www.wto.org.

conference also made provisions for periodic reporting to monitor progress made on issues important to developing countries.

Yet, Doha was no more than a promise to negotiate and assist developing countries. The real challenges are ahead for both rich and poor countries. The rich countries will need a lot of political support from their domestic constituencies in order to live up to the Doha commitments. For example, the United States will have to negotiate countervailing duties and allow a wide range of imports from developing and least-developed countries. President George W. Bush will need fast-track negotiating authority from Congress, and the administration must campaign for a new domestic consensus in support of free trade. Europe must accept fundamental reforms to the European Common Agriculture Policy, which subsidizes European farmers and keeps agricultural products from developing countries out of European markets. Japan must also open its markets to both developing and developed countries.

The challenges for developing countries are also many. They must build the momentum and aspirations from Doha and make sure that their legitimate needs and concerns continue to be heard and receive high priority from America and other members of the international community. They must take advantage of the additional funding and support promised at Doha to develop their national competencies and capacities to participate more effectively as members of the WTO and to reform their economies for more gainful participation in the global economy. They must continue to work together in groups or clusters that will advance their individual and collective interests. Finally, they must convince their domestic constituencies that globalization offers the best hope against poverty, joblessness, inequality, ignorance, and disease.

Was Doha a tactical "feel-good" retreat, especially for the rich countries whose economies were on the verge of a global recession? If so, then the ghosts of Seattle will continue to haunt members of the WTO as they begin to negotiate the new round. If, on the other hand, Doha was a strategic decision by the United States and other rich countries to show leadership and genuine support to the rest of the world, then the future of globalization looks promising. Only time will tell.

NOTES

1. Thomas C. Fischer, *The United States, the European Union, and "Globalization" of World Trade: Allies or Adversaries?* (Westport, CT: Quorum, 2000), chap. 14.

2. "Nick Stern: A Quiet, Stern Voice," *The Economist*, January 20, 2001, pp. 18, 69.

3. J. Michael Finger has written extensively often in sympathy with the problems facing developing countries. For example, see "The WTO's Special Burden on Less Developed Countries," *Cato Journal* 19, no. 3 (Winter 2000):425–437, and "Developing Countries in the Next WTO Round: Is that Enough?" in *The Fifty Years of the GATT/WTO: Past Performance and Future Challenges*, ed. Il Sakong and Kwang Suk Kim (Seoul: Institute for Global Economics, 1999), 99–131. In defense of the WTO, see World Trade Organization, "Seven Common Misunderstandings about the WTO," in *Globalization: A Reader*, ed. Frank J. Lechner and John Boli (Malden, MA: Blackwell, 2000), 236–239, and visit the organization's Web site: www.wto.org. In January 2001, Europe suspended its plans to liberalize trade with the world's poorest countries from 2004 to 2006. Following complaints from farm lobbies, Pascal Lamy, Europe's trade commissioner, pushed back the proposed transition period for opening up everything except arms. The Ministerial Conference in Doha, Qatar, taking place only two months after the terrorist attacks on U.S. interests and Western desire to build an international consensus against terrorism, may well open a new window for more trade liberalization.

4. See Anne O. Krueger, "Developing Countries and the Next Multilateral Trade Negotiations," Development Research Group Trade Research Policy Working Paper 2118 (Washington, DC: World Bank, May 1999); and J. Michael Finger and L. Alan Winters, "What Can the WTO Do for Developing Countries?" in *The WTO as an International Organization*, ed. Anne O. Krueger (Chicago: University of Chicago Press, 1998), 365–392. For the challenges of small island states, see Roman Grynberg, "The Pacific Island States and the WTO: Towards a Post-Seattle Agenda for Small Vulnerable States," in *Small States in the Global Economy*, ed. David Peretz, Rumman Faruqi, and Eliawony J. Kisanga (London: Commonwealth Secretariat and World Bank, 2001), 329–342.

5. See Constantine Michalopoulos, "The Role of Special and Differential Treatment for Developing Countries in GATT and the World Trade Organization," Development Research Group Policy

Research Working Paper 2388 (Washington, DC: World Bank, July 2000). Also see various chapters of Bernard Hoekman, Aaditya Mattoo, and Philip English, eds., *Development, Trade, and WTO: A Handbook* (Washington, DC: World Bank, 2002).

6. The Cairns Group, who coordinates the WTO's agricultural negotiating strategies for its members, is made up of thirteen developed and developing agricultural exporting countries: Argentina, Australia, Brazil, Canada, Chile, Colombia, Malaysia, New Zealand, Paraguay, the Philippines, South Africa, Thailand, and Uruguay. For a detailed discussion of the WTO, agriculture, and developing countries, see Bernard Hoekman and Kym Anderson, "Developing Country Agriculture and the New Trade Agenda," Development Research Group Policy Research Paper 2125 (Washington, DC: World Bank, May 1999).

7. Finger, "The WTO's Special Burden," 435.

8. See Antonique Koning, "Challenges to ACP Trade with Europe after the Uruguay Round." Policy Management Brief 1 (Maastricht, Netherlands: European Centre for Development Policy Management and Overseas Development Institute, July 1994). Also see "Eliminating World Poverty: Making Globalization Work for the Poor," United Kingdom Government White Paper on International Development (December 2000). Available: www.globalization.gov.uk.

9. World Trade Organization, "Draft Ministerial Declaration" (Geneva: WTO, September 2001). Posted on New Zealand's government Web site in October, 2001: http://www.mft.govt.nz/foreign/tndtead/wto/4thsession.html.

10. For a discussion of trade and the environment, see Shahin Magda, *Trade and the Environment in WTO: A Review of Its Initial Work and Future Prospects* (Penang, Malaysia: Third World Network, 1997). For a survey of the achievements of developing countries in the Uruguay Round, see T. N. Srivasan, *Developing Countries and the Multilateral Trade System* (Boulder, CO: Westview, 1998).

11. For a discussion of capacity development in financial reform, see Saleh M. Nsouli, "Capacity Building in Africa: The Role of International Financial Institutions," *Finance and Development* 37, no. 4 (December 2000): 34–37. For a more detailed discussion of capacity development for trade liberalization, see Finger, "Developing Countries." According to Finger, capacity development for making trade an effective vehicle for development and globalization covers five dimensions: developing the private sector, infrastructure, improved policy and policy management, using the WTO more effectively, and openness. Also see Dieter Ernst, Tom Ganiatsos, and Lynn Mytelka, *Technological Capabilities and Export Success in Asia* (London: UNCTAD and Routledge, 1998); and Raymond Saner, "Globalization and Its Impact on Leadership Qualifications in Public Administration," *International Review of Administrative Sciences* 67, no. 4 (December 2001): 649–661. Also visit www.capacity.org.

12. Thomas L. Friedman, *The Lexus and the Olive Tree: Understanding Globalization* (New York: Anchor Books, 2000).

13. See Mick Foster, "New Approaches to Development Cooperation: What Can We Learn from Experience with Implementing Sector-Wide Approaches?" Working Paper 140 (London: Overseas Development Institute, October 2000). Also see Mick Foster, Adrienne Brown, Andy Norton, and Felix Naschold, *The Status of Sector-Wide Approaches* (London: Overseas Development Institute, 2000). Available: www.globalization.gov.uk.

CHAPTER 7

Managing Banking and Financial Crises

THE BANKING SYSTEM AND GLOBALIZATION

Globalization has transformed the nature, roles, and operations of banking and financial institutions. In the past, banks and other financial institutions operated in relatively stable, highly regulated, and predictable environments. They focused mainly on the local or domestic economy and were regarded as national institutions of a strategic industry rather than business enterprises operating according to commercial bases. These changes have come about mainly because of deregulation, technology, and the increasing volume of internal and external transactions in response to the growing global economy and global trade.

Deregulation of the banking and financial services industry has changed the rules of the game, injected competition, and stimulated innovation. It has allowed banks to operate more globally and restructure themselves through domestic and international mergers and acquisitions. It has allowed them to gain deeper levels of integration, thus allowing them to provide services and products such as insurance, which they were forbidden to sell before deregulation. Although most countries, both industrial and developing, still retain control over the industry, especially regarding foreign ownership, changes in the regulatory environment have allowed greater competition and innovation. Technology, especially computer and information technology including the Internet, has also enabled the industry to transform itself, allowing it compete on volume, speed, convenience, accuracy, and efficient communication and information processing and to develop more effective systems of risk assessment and management. The global economy has created more wealth and more international flows and, therefore, more business for the industry. It has also added more complexity to the business because the industry has to deal with different clients in different countries and with different needs of banking and financial services, and it must operate under different economic, social, and political systems. The needs of banking and financial services differ with the different stages of development, and therefore, satisfying the needs of worldwide clients is a growing challenge for the globalizing industry.

The changing nature of the business of the banking industry and the environment in which it operates has brought about increased uncertainty and new and unknown risks. Risk assessment and risk management have become a much more critical core competence for the banking industry than ever before. The risks and consequences of bank failures and financial crises have become one of the byproducts of globalization. These concerns are not limited to bankers and their clients; they are also concerns of governments of globalizing economies, international financial institutions, global corporations, and the international community in general. As the experience of the Asian financial crisis clearly showed, failures in the banking system of one country affect the economic interests of businesses and households in many other countries. Therefore, managing banking and financial crisis is now accepted as an integral part of managing globalization. This means that newly globalizing developing countries must develop the human capital and institutional capacity for managing banking and financial crises.

The purpose of this chapter is to discuss the challenges facing globalizing developing countries and transition economies in managing and restructuring their banking systems and dealing with financial crises. I begin with a discussion of banking as a strategic industry and draw a distinction between securities-market and bank-loan capitalism. I then discuss the anatomy and causes of banking and financial crises, focusing on both macroeconomic and microeconomic factors. Following that, I discuss strategies for strengthening the banking system, both within the country as well as the role of the international financial institutions. Lessons of experience are drawn for the benefit of other globalizing developing countries.

BANKING AS A STRATEGIC INDUSTRY

Industrial and developing countries are attracted to globalization because of its promise of more economic development, which involves expanding the productive capacity of the economy. It means producing new and more goods and services; undertaking research, development, and commercialization of innovations brought to market by entrepreneurs; and adding capital and investment in the economy. All of this costs money and must be financed. Banks are important institutions because they help transform savings into investments. How well a country manages to finance economic development depends on how effectively its banking and financial industry manages to mobilize and utilize domestic and foreign savings and other financial resources to finance investment rather than consumption. Therefore, an effective banking and financial industry is absolutely crucial for sustaining economic development.

For any given country, there are basically three ways of financing investments and capital formation: selling equity interests by issuing stocks and shares, borrowing by issuing debt instruments such as bonds and other securities, and using the banking system to create credit in the form of bank loans. The first two methods of financing development are widely used in industrial economies with well-developed capital markets. This type of finance is called "securities-market capitalism" because of its dependence on the securities market for its investment financing. It is also quite speculative and highly risky.

The third type of financing investment and capital formation is called "bank-loan capitalism" because of its heavy reliance on banks to extend loans to businesses rather than raising money through the securities market. Bank-loan financing is particularly attractive to developing countries with underdeveloped securities markets in which businesses have little or no opportunity to raise the financing needed for development. It is also a method that was extensively used in Japan and, with modifications, in Korea and Taiwan.[1] One of the problems with most developing countries is that the level of domestic saving is much less than what is required to finance investment, and therefore, a country must find a way to obtain additional financing. One of the options is to allow the banking industry, with the help of the central bank, to extend credit investment to priority sectors or projects. Close coordination exists between the banks, the central bank, and the macroeconomic planners who insist on "policy lending" and directing the loans to priority investment projects of their choice. This coordination becomes particularly easy when the banking sector is dominated by state-owned banks whose corporate governance is closely controlled by the same government that sets the policy-lending priorities. This financing arrangement is particularly attractive to nationalists because it minimizes the extent of foreign borrowing for capital formation, thus keeping the national foreign debt low.

Critics of bank-loan financing—those who are against treating the banking sector as a strategic industry—argue that it is inflationary, creates crony capitalism, misdirects investment funds, and crowds out the more deserving entrepreneurial investments, which may not be considered a priority by government policy lending. Bank credit expansion always entails the risk of inflation, especially if the additional liquidity is used for consumption, government expenditure, or failed projects. It is less inflationary if, as Joseph Schumpeter would argue, the bank credits are used to produce more goods and services for the economy.

Policy lending tends to create bad bank loans because investment decisions are based on government priorities rather than the business merits and risks of a particular project. Credit tends to go to state-owned enterprises (SOEs) or projects owned by those close to government decision makers. Once the initial loan has been made, subsequent loans become almost automatic as banks try to protect their initial investments, thus exposing themselves to greater risks. The integrity of the banking system becomes seriously compromised when banks expose themselves to greater risks by continuing to extend credit to money-losing businesses or SOEs.

Supporters of consideration of banking as a strategic industry and the use of bank loans for capital formation argue that this is a necessary stage in the development of developing countries. Without the advantage of fully developed capital markets and with low levels of savings, developing countries should take advantage of their banking industry to create the necessary additional financing for development. Proponents also argue that most developing countries do not have the right macroeconomic environment to attract long-term investment from abroad. The only form of capital developing countries can attract in the early stages of globalization is short-term capital, which is highly speculative. In fact, the rapid buildup of short-term debt has been blamed as a key factor in the financial crisis that rocked Mexico in 1994–1995, East Asia in 1997–1998, Russia and Brazil in 1998–1999, and Turkey and Argentina in 2001–2002. Therefore, in order to protect themselves from financial crises, newly globalizing developing countries are advised to limit their exposure to foreign short-term debt.[2] Available evidence seems to suggest that for the newly globalizing developing countries and transition economies bank loans and the judicious and disciplined use of banking as a strategic industry for capital formation may be inevitable and even desirable, especially in the early stages of development. However, each country must develop a banking system and financial services industry that is most suited for its economic, political, social, and cultural realities and strategic directions.

THE ANATOMY AND CAUSES OF BANKING AND FINANCIAL CRISES

Banking and financial crises are not new. They inflict industrial and developing countries alike, and they are not about to go away. Just as today's financial systems have been transformed to become more expanded and diversified—driven by globalization, deregulation, new business instruments, and computerized transactions—so, too, have the banking and financial crises become more frequent, costly, and pervasive. According to the Bank for International Settlements (BIS), during the 1980–1996 period, at least two-thirds of the IMF member states experienced significant banking sector problems.[3] Incidents of bank crises have increased every ten-year period for the past fifty years of the twentieth century. For example, there were more bank and financial crises in the world in the 1980s and 1990s than in the 1970s, and the 1970s had many more than the more tranquil periods of the 1950s and 1960s. Likewise, bank crises have become increasingly more severe, costly, and globally pervasive. For example, Argentina's 1980–1982 crisis is estimated to have had a direct cost of 57 percent of GDP, and Mexico's crisis lasted more than twelve years.[4]

Banking and financial crises are particularly serious for developing and transition economies for several reasons: First, they have serious and potentially far-reaching consequences for the local economy, as well as the social and political governance of the country. In poor countries with few resources and weak governance systems and institutions (P2), banking and financial crises can lead to serious political instabilities, with the result that appropriate macroeconomic and microeconomic policy options cannot be implemented and sustained. Even in relatively strong developing countries (BEMs) such as Mexico, Malaysia, and Thailand, these crises have caused lasting economic and political difficulties at all levels of society. Second, the fallout of these crises on other countries is of serious concern because international financial markets are highly integrated and are becoming increasingly more integrated. For example, at the end of 1995, banks in the BIS reporting area (mainly industrial countries) had outstanding claims against developing countries of more than U.S.$717 billion. During the 1990–1995 period, developing countries issued bonds of more than U.S.$133 billion. Portifolio equity flows into developing countries in the 1990s approached U.S.$128 billion. At the time of the Mexican crisis, nonresidents held about 80 percent of the peso bonos held outside the banking system. With this level of integration and interdependence, a banking and financial crisis in one country creates economic, political, and social problems for other countries. Third, a banking and financial crisis in developing countries and transition economies is important because of the impact it has on these countries' confidence in liberalization and globalization. For most of the newly globalizing and democratizing countries, political and public support is soft at the best of times. Banking and financial crises put the reformers on the defensive, and if satisfactory solutions are not found in good time, there is a danger that gains in economic and political reforms can be reversed. It is in this context that one understands why in the early 1990s the Clinton administration moved quickly to commit the U.S. government to providing a U.S. $40 billion bailout to Mexico's banking and financial crisis. This was in the interest of the United States, Mexico, and the global economy. It is also in this context that, for example, the Halifax Summit of the G8 industrial countries, in June 1995, called for new initiatives for strengthening market supervision and regulation, including more effective risk management.

The Anatomy of a Financial Crisis

A financial crisis is characterized by three distinct and related phases: speculative boom, loss of confidence, and failure and collapse. During the speculative boom phase, key market participants develop a very optimistic view of the economy's overall prospects and upgrade economic expectations. This is followed by rapidly increasing profit expectations, and large capital gains are taken for granted. There is a surge in "perceived wealth" creation, and normal investment risks are greatly underestimated. In expectation of continuing prosperity, household and business consumption grows too fast, accompanied by growing demand for credit to finance consumption and capital investment and to acquire assets such as real estate, stocks, bonds, land, office buildings, and so forth. The value of assets soar, and the high asset valuation drives the economy as the assets are used as collateral for more credit. In this phase, the economy is characterized by high investment, strong demand, high prices, growing private wealth, and a little bit of "irrational exuberance." Banks are more than willing to extend credit in order to cash in on the boom and race ahead of the curve, driven by their Keynesian animal spirits to build up their loan portfolios at an even more frantic pace. In this stage, risk management for these banks is like an oxymoron.[5]

The speculative boom can be triggered by several factors, individually or in combination. It can be caused by discovery of valuable natural or mineral resources, a surge in productivity in one or several sectors of the economy, or significant positive gains in terms of trade. It can also be caused by significant political events such as the fall of the Berlin Wall and the collapse of Communism in the Soviet Union, giving rise to high expectations for the new world order. The fall of dictators or the end of oppressive regimes can also give rise to the speculative boom. Whatever the cause, the speculative boom does not last forever.

The second phase of a banking and financial crisis is loss of confidence in the economy. Economic uncertainty begins to set in as key macroeconomic indicators such as interest rates, exchange rates, wages, and inflation are misaligned. Investors start looking for the smallest excuse to trigger massive sell off of tradable assets such as stocks and bonds. This is accompanied by drastic shifts in relative portfolio values, which negatively affect financial institutions' balance sheets as the market value of bank assets begins to fall sharply. The banks' real exposure to risk is high as the leverage of the banking system expands to unsustainable levels. The banks' balance sheets begin to show red with growing amounts of bad loans and doubtful assets. There is no more confidence in the economy, and the country's political and governance systems are on trial. This is what basically happened in Southeast Asia in the mid-1990s.[6]

The third phase is financial failure and possible total economic collapse. As lack of confidence becomes generalized across all productive sectors of the economy, the crisis in the banking system becomes public knowledge. Banks' balance sheets are now loaded with nonperforming dead loans and unrecoverable collateralized previously overvalued assets. Foreign investors run for cover, not only by stopping to invest in the economy but by moving their investments elsewhere. The supply of foreign funds to financial institutions becomes infinitely inelastic. Therefore, the promise of higher interest rates (price) is no longer enough incentive to attract or retain foreign investment (demand). The results are high interest rates, widespread bank failure, a credit crunch, a sharp fall in the exchange rate as the value of the local currency heads to the basement, and overall economic decline.

The structure and anatomy of the banking and financial crisis is potentially useful for both conceptual understanding and practical initiatives. Conceptually, it can be used as a framework for the study of each of the three stages, their antecedents, causes, and consequences. Knowledge acquired can be useful as a basis for providing informed advice to policy makers, managers, investors, and other stakeholders. The information can also be used for practical initiatives. For example, macroeconomic policy makers could use it to introduce policy initiatives most likely to mitigate against the negative consequences of each of the phases of the crisis. Managers of banks and other financial institutions can use the information to develop and apply new control and risk management strategies that protect them from the excesses of the boom-bust economic cycle. International financial institutions can use the framework to advise newly globalizing economies of the potential challenges and dangers of the crisis before it becomes reality. International investors can use the information to avoid, or at least minimize, irrational panic behavior such as massive selling of investments and assets, even when the country's macroeconomic fundamentals are basically sound. Finally, reform-minded political and civic leaders can use the framework to prepare for the next fight.

It is during the boom phase when things appear to be going well that preparations need to begin for the downturn. Public education is particularly important because the investing public, and citizens in general, need to understand the nature and behavior of an open economy, as well as the individual and collective initiatives that must be taken to survive the various stages of the crisis. The best strategy for managing a banking and financial crisis is to be proactive—by anticipating the phases I have outlined and taking preemptive policy and practical steps to prevent or mitigate against the avoidable negative consequences. Waiting until the crisis is full-blown is risky and it costs too much.

The Causes of Banking and Financial Crises

In its simplest form, the general theory of banking is relatively easy to understand. Banks are financial intermediaries, which means that they bring depositors and their savings together with borrowers and charge a fee for the service. A typical bank's balance sheet is made up of liabilities of mainly short-term deposits (savers can withdraw their deposits at short notice) and assets made up of both short-term and long-term loans to business and consumers. When the value of their assets fall short of their liabilities, banks become insolvent, which precipitates a banking crisis. The value of a bank's assets may drop because borrowers become unable or unwilling to service their debt. This is part of the credit risk that banks must manage effectively in order to remain viable and profitable. If public confidence in the banking system is shaken and if the deposits are not sufficiently insured, there may be a run on a particular bank or the whole banking sector, as depositors rush to withdraw their funds before the bank(s) declares bankruptcy. Banks operate on the premise that depositors can get access to their money quickly and efficiently. Therefore, maintaining public confidence is one of the most important requirements for building an effective banking system.

Table 7.1 provides a list of countries that have experienced banking crises along with the duration of the crisis and cost. The table includes BEMs, industrial countries, and the P2 least-developed countries. The table shows that banking crises do not discriminate: both industrial and developing countries are susceptible to bank crises. The table also shows that the developing countries pay a higher percentage of their GDP because of banking crises than the industrial countries. For example, the banking crisis cost Chile 42 percent of GDP as compared to 8 percent for Finland. It cost Côte d'Ivoire 24 percent of GDP as opposed to 3 percent for the United States. There is also evidence in the table suggesting that banking crises tend to last longer for developing countries than for industrial countries. This was particularly true of countries such as the Philippines (1981–1987), Tanzania (1988–1994), Papua New Guinea (1989–1994), Senegal (1983–1988), Nepal (1988–1994), and Uruguay (1981–1985). For these countries, the average duration for the banking crises is 5.4 years. Excluding the United States, which is a special case, the average duration of the banking crises for the industrial countries is 3.0 years. The evidence from Table 7.1 suggests that the greater severity and longer duration of the banking crises in developing countries, especially the P2 least-developed ones, may be symptomatic of the inherent weaknesses in their respective macroeconomic policy environment and microeconomic institutional capacities as compared to the BEMs and industrial countries.[7]

Exhibit 7.1 lists some of the causes of banking and financial crises.

Exhibit 7.1
Causes of Banking and Financial Crises

- Macroeconomic volatility: external and domestic.

- Increasing bank liabilities with large maturity/currency mismatches.

- Lending booms, asset price collapses, and surges in capital inflows.

- Inadequate preparation for financial liberalization.

- Heavy government involvement and loose controls on connected lending.

- Weakness in accounting, disclosure, and legal framework.

- Distorted incentives of bank owners, managers, depositors, and supervisors.

- Exchange rate regimes.

Source: Compiled from Morris Goldstein and Philip Turner, "Banking Crises in Emerging Economies: Origins and Policy Options," BIS Economic Paper 46 (Basel: Bank for International Settlements, October 1996).

As shown in Exhibit 7.1, the causes are macroeconomic such as volatility, exchange rate regimes, and the quality of the country's national integrity and regulatory system (NIRS), including banking regulatory and supervisory institutional arrangements and performance. They are also microeconomic, focusing on the structure, behavior, and performance of the banks and other financial institutions.

Macroeconomic volatility can be caused by factors internal and external to the economy because in an open economy the banking and financial crisis can be triggered by events outside the country. Volatility can be brought about as a result of several factors: a weak macroeconomic environment characterized by slow GDP growth and high inflation, vulnerability to certain capital outflows, low liquidity in the banking sector, and poor governance as manifested by weak regulatory and supervisory institutions. In most developing countries and transition economies, the banking sector operates in an externally and internally volatile environment, and there is a general reluctance by these countries to address the fundamental causes of the volatility, for example, by diversification, insurance, or higher bank capital. There is a tendency for banks to underestimate their real exposure to business risks, especially during a period of speculative boom, and to lend rather recklessly to inadequately secured debtors. This is accentuated by large-scale capital inflows, which are ultimately intermediated by the banking system. An excessively short-term orientation of the financial system magnifies the normal bank problems of liquidity–maturity mismatches so that the bank's balance sheet short-term assets are inadequate to meet short-term liabilities. Most developing countries do not have a well-developed domestic long-term bond market, although many have access to the international bond market in good times. This means that the only realistic option open to them is to raise short-term debt as the source of financing reform and development. As I have already noted, excessive short-term debt causes its own financial crises. As well, the market for bank assets is very limited in developing countries. Regulatory and supervisory human capital is limited, and the institutional framework for managing, supervising, and reforming the banking and financial system is weak and often lacks the political support and independence it needs.[8]

At the microeconomic level, there is need for more efficient management of the banking sector, more prudence, and more ethical conduct. Weaknesses in accounting, disclosure, supervision, and the legal framework allow banks to break the rules, for example, by capitalizing bad loans, engaging in inside lending, maintaining low levels of capital, overvaluing their assets, and keeping dangerously low levels of credit. Where state-owned banks dominate the banking and financial sector, they can get away with breaking the

TABLE 7.1
Banking Crises for Selected Countries: Duration and Cost

1. Big Emerging Markets (BEMs):	2. Industrial Countries:
India 1991-94 Indonesia 1992-94 Mexico 1982-94 Malaysia 1985-88 Philippines 1981-87 Turkey 1991-94	Finland 1991-94 Israel 1983-84 Japan 1992-94 Norway 1987-93 Portugal 1986-89 Sweden 1990-93 USA 1981-93
3. Least Developed (P2):	4. Cost as percentage of GDP:
Colombia 1982-85 Guyana 1993-95 Kenya 1993 Sri Lanka 1989-93 Mali 1987-89 Nigeria 1991-94 Nepal 1988-94 Papua New Guinea 1989-94 Senegal 1983-88 Tanzania 1988-94 Uganda 1990-94 Uruguay 1981-85 Venezuela 1993-94 South Africa 1985	Argentina 57% Chile 42% Uruguay 33% Côte d'Ivoire 24% Venezuela 18% Spain 17% Mexico 15% Bulgaria 14% Hungary 10% Finland 8% United States 3%

Source: Compiled from Asli Demirguc-Kunt and Enrica Detragiache, "The Determinants of Banking Crises: Evidence from Industrial and Developing Countries," Policy Working Paper 1828 (Washington, DC: World Bank Development Research Group and IMF Research Department, September 1997), 35; World Bank, *World Development Report* (Washington, DC: World Bank 1997), 68.

rules in the name of promoting policy lending and fulfilling their role as a strategic industry. Even when reforms are undertaken, implementing financial liberalization is difficult if a strong and effective regulatory and supervisory system is not already in place. Incentives can also play an important role. If the investors—bank owners and managers—are not fully exposed to the risks of their investments, they are likely to take on excessive risks. As well, bank supervisors need personal incentives and institutional protection in order to overcome the pressures from bank owners and their political friends for any delay in enforcing the implementation of corrective measures. As a general rule, state-owned banks tend to receive political protection from full compliance with the banking rules and regulations. Every country needs a politically independent, institutionally strong, and operationally professional central bank; however, many of the P2 developing countries do not have one.

- Maintain a comprehensive and effective monitoring system: use liquidity as an early warning system, enhance use of external auditors, and emphasize the importance of private rating agencies.

- Maintain a system for competent handling of banking failures: appropriate bankruptcy rules for banks, early remedial actions, clarify responsibilities in crisis management, determine in advance distribution costs of crisis among various stakeholders, ensure availability of timely and accurate information, avoid disruptive bank closures, keep government involvement in banking to a minimum, protect the payment system.

Source: Summarized in part from Ruth de Krivoy, "Crisis Avoidance," in *Banking Crises in Latin America*, ed. Ricardo Hausmann and Liliana Rojas-Suarez (Washington, DC: Inter-American Development Bank, 1996), 171–192.

It is necessary to maintain sound macroeconomic policies with sustained commitment to reform especially in times of crisis. As well, it is important to have an effective institutional infrastructure for coordinating fiscal and monetary policies and their sustained and consistent implementation. There must be effective coordination between the central bank and the government. The central bank needs high-level political support without being politicized; it also needs effective leadership, management, and operational professional efficiency. The central bank as an institution as well as its leaders and its professional staff must enjoy the highest possible level of support and confidence not only within the banking and financial industry but also in the general public both at home and abroad.

Among the microeconomic policy options for managing banking and financial crises, effective banking regulationary and supervisory systems and their consistent and professional implementation is key. This is a more specialized subsystem of the NIRS discussed in an earlier chapter. Here, the objective is to maintain the integrity of the national banking and financial industry by setting the rules for sound and safe banking and by supervising the industry to ensure proper and uniform compliance. The country must maintain a comprehensive and effective monitoring system. This can be done, for example, by using liquidity indicators as an early warning system and by using independent and respected outside sources of assessment information such as external auditors and private rating agencies. In many developing countries, especially the P2 category, quality accurate and timely financial information is hard to come by. State-owned banks are particularly susceptible to delays in producing independently audited financial statements or using modern technology to enhance financial accountability and transparency. These systemic weaknesses must be overcome in order to mitigate against the incidents of banking failures or financial crises.

In an operational sense, banks are like any other business: their success or failure can be discerned through close examination of their financial statements, especially the quality of their assets and liabilities, as well as their income statement. It is particularly important to focus on the quality of the industry's assets, avoid overvaluation of assets, prevent inside lending, and periodically perform on-site inspections. The industry should avoid speculative bubbles and massive short-term debt. It should ensure cross-border home country consolidated supervision to cover cross-border transactions. The industry should have a system in place to deal with bank failures, which should include a comprehensive legal and administrative framework for handling bankruptcies, early remedial actions, sharing of costs, clear responsibilities, and timely and accurate information. It is also important to avoid disruptive bank closures, keep government involvement at a minimum, and protect the payment system.

The NIRS should assist the country in ensuring that the owners, investors, managers, and professionals in the banking industry are "fit and proper." It is not enough to have the required capital to start a banking business. It is not even enough to have the necessary industry managerial and professional knowledge and experience. Those entrusted with the privilege of owning and managing banks must show a higher level of prudence and ethical conduct than entrepreneurs in other sectors of the economy. Most countries have a system of screening new applicants to keep out crooks and the incompetent, but the industry has an obligation to maintain a system of monitoring its members, and to maintain high levels of prudence and ethical conduct.

Exhibit 7.2 also includes a suggestion that newly globalizing developing countries should implement the Basel Committee Banking Accord. This is because in a highly interdependent world no single country can go it alone. Therefore, the international financial institutions have become critical in providing assistance to member countries in their efforts to avoid or manage banking and financial crises. The following paragraphs describe the philosophy and provisions of the Basel accord and its relevancy for newly globalizing developing countries and transition economies.

The Basel accord is the product of the work of the Bank for International Settlements, headquartered in Basel, Switzerland, and thus the name. It is based on the philosophy that an effective banking system needs healthy competition, discipline, and sufficient capitalization. The accord was originally designed for international banks mainly operating in industrialized countries, and it is constantly being revised and simplified to meet the needs of developing countries and transition economies.

One of the recommendations of the Basel accord is that regulators should establish and insist on a higher capital–asset ratio. Originally, it was proposed that bank capital should be at least 8 percent of a bank's total assets. However, this has been found to be too rigid and inadequate for developing countries. In 1997, the World Bank recommended that the ratio for globalizing developing countries should be at least 20 percent. Work is continuing to revise and improve on the original 1988 accord. For example, in January 2001, the Basel Committee on Banking Supervision issued revisions to the accord aimed at getting away from a "one-size-fits-all" set of rules governing banks' capital requirements. According to the new rules, the level of required capital will be determined not only by credit risk but also by market risk and the overall quality of management of each bank, including the development of an internal capital assessment process that continually adjusts required capital levels in accordance with changes in market risks. The accord also requires the individual banks to make public the methodology they use for calculating capital levels and for assessing credit and market risks. This would be particularly useful for developing countries where investors and depositors often lack accurate and timely information for sound investment decisions.

In cases in which the banks are undercapitalized, as is often the case in developing countries, time must be allowed to provide opportunities for recapitalization. Banks should use the boom times to increase their capitalization by use of retained earnings. They can also attract new capital from new domestic or international investors. As part of liberalization and reform, the government should generally avoid active involvement in the recapitalization of private banks. Those which cannot attract enough capital for sufficient capitalization should be either restructured through mergers or acquisitions or allowed to close. Strengthening the banking system takes effort, time, and planning and sustained implementation of reform. It invokes building human capital, institutional infrastructure, and political support. It is a slow evolutionary process that takes into account not only the banking principles as outlined in the Basel accord but also the economic, political, institutional, and social realities of the country and its banking and financial industry. Reflecting on all these issues, Andres Blanche, president of Banco Credit Lyonnais in Chile, observed:

> If . . . the agencies charged with bank regulation and supervision have grossly inadequate human, physical, and financial resources; if they lack authority and prestige; if they do not receive in timely fashion the information they need to fulfill their responsibilities; and if in addition they are vulnerable to political pressure and influence, they will be in no position to introduce and implement a large number of reforms simultaneously. Under these conditions, even if these reforms were established by law or decree, they would not be sufficiently enforced in practice.[9]

One of the institutional questions relating to banking regulation and supervision corresponds to the appropriate location of banking supervision. In most of the developing countries, banking supervision is located within the central bank; in other countries, it is part of the ministry of finance. It has been suggested that banking supervision should be an independent professional agency at arms' length from the administrative and political control or influence of the government. Therefore, locating banking supervision either in the central bank or the line ministry may compromise its professional independence, stature, influence, and public confidence. It has been suggested that in order to clarify and distinguish the three roles of supervision and regulation, monetary policy (central bank), and fiscal policy (ministry of finance) they should have separate institutional arrangements. On the other hand, poor countries with weak institutions have limited resources for institutional building and coordination. Separating banking supervision from already established institutions may simply make it weaker and more vulnerable to manipulation by more powerful individuals and institutions.

Banking supervision remains a serious problem for most of the P2 developing countries. In 1988, a management resource audit was undertaken for the central Bank of Uganda, which among other things is responsible for the country's banking supervision. The audit found that, over the years and in response to the country's political and economic problems during the 1970s and early 1980s, the bank's mandate had been considerably expanded. Besides the traditional central banking regulatory, supervisory, and advisory functions, the bank had taken on a nonbanking national corporate development role in areas in which it had no competitive advantage. The audit also found that the central bank suffered from managerial and professional brain drain as well as institutional decay. It was simply not able to fulfill its mandate, including effective regulation and supervision of the banking industry. At the same time, as the new National Resistance Movement government was initiating political and economic reforms, more small, often undercapitalized and poorly managed commercial banks were mushrooming in the country. At one time a small country with a small commercial sector, Uganda had more than twenty independently owned commercial banks and near-bank financial institutions. Dominated by the state-owned Uganda Commercial Bank, the country's banking industry was seriously undercapitalized, poorly managed, and received little or no constructive regulation or supervision.[10]

It is not surprising that by 1991 the country was experiencing a full-scale banking and financial crisis, which lasted for most of the 1990s (see Table 7.1). In 1994, more than half of the banks incurred losses with a large negative core capital. Aggregate nonperforming assets were in excess of 50 percent of total loans. The banks generally lacked financial discipline and administrative efficiency, thus causing high intermediation costs. The Bank of Uganda continued to experience institutional weakness for most of the 1990s, especially in the area of banking regulation, supervision, and debt management.

The government of Uganda spent most of the late 1990s managing the banking and financial crisis, and its aftermaths, and restructuring and strengthening the banking system. With the help of the international financial institutions and the major donor agencies, the government responded by privatizing its own Uganda Commercial Bank, forcing the closure of targeted and nonperforming banks and strengthening the supervisory capacity of the central bank. Still, major challenges remain, and there is the danger of future banking financial crises on the horizon.[11]

Lessons from China

China is one of the fastest growing BEMs, attracting billions of foreign direct investment (FDI) and gradually opening up its economy. By the late 1990s it was generally believed that China was at a crossroad between making and implementing important policy decisions relating to its banking and financial industry, or heading toward a possible severe and costly banking crisis. The international community is concerned because of China's size, membership in the WTO, and the possible economic, financial, and political consequences of a large-scale banking crisis for the rest of the world. Therefore, in March 1999, the People's Bank of China (the country's central bank) and the BIS jointly organized an international conference to identify China's policy options and reform initiatives for strengthening its banking and financial system.

Exhibit 7.3 summarizes the conference's deliberations, identifies issues important for China, and spells out specific reforms the country must initiate quickly in order to avoid the impending banking crisis. It also provides a summary of the conference's lessons of experience from China, which are particularly relevant for other emerging and globalizing countries. For example, the conference dealt with issues relating to the bad and doubtful loans and assets commonly found in the banking industries of such countries. Equally important is the need to understand the new credit and market risks arising from liberalization and the challenge of developing new tools of managing such risks. The conference recommended that China, and similar countries, make sure that the restructuring of its banking system is accompanied by the development of a deeper national capital market for both equity and debt.

Exhibit 7.3
Strengthening the Banking System in China:
Lessons for Other Globalizing Economies

Background: China is one of the fastest growing BEMs, attracting increasing sums of FDI, and is a full member of the WTO. As it continues to liberalize its economy, the quality of its banking system becomes of national strategic importance. In recognition of the need for urgent action, the BIS and the People's Bank of China (central bank) organized a joint conference in Beijing on March 1–2, 1999. The purpose of the conference was to share experiences from within and outside China and to provide expert advice to China's policy makers.

Important Policy Choices: In his opening address, Governor Dai Xianglong outlined three main challenges facing China: the need to maintain a healthy, stable macroeconomic environment; the nature and quality of supervision of the financial system, consistent with the country's specific circumstances; and the need to address proactively the new risks arising from the country's developing financial industry. The conference traced the roots of the bad debts that weigh heavily on the country's banking system and identified the following key issues: the true size of bad debts in China, whether enough public funds were being devoted to dealing with the true scale of the problem, how the bad loans are to be financed, whether enough competition is being injected into the banking system, and what can be done to reduce the taxation of banks. It was recommended that restructuring of the banking system should be accompanied by the development of a deeper national capital market for both debt and equity.

Reforming the System: Reforms are needed both at the national macroeconomic centralized level and the microeconomic local or institutional decentralized level. Among the strengths, China was praised for strong action by the state (governance), dynamic economic growth rates, and high rate of private savings. The conference recommended that measures should be taken to encourage the development of small- and medium-size private business, strengthen the financial system, and reform SOEs. It was suggested that policy lending should be removed from China's state banks to allow them to operate on a commercial basis. Microeconomic issues discussed included: determining the appropriate framework for financial supervision and using the state development bank to mitigate policy-oriented risks by improving its screening and project appraisal methodology and the need for an effective national and sectoral risk management system.

Principles for Successful Bank Restructuring: The conference was told that the regulatory structure should fit the country's stage of economic development. The following principles were emphasized: the need to separate money and credit creation from finance of public sector deficits, the need for not-too-gradual (get-on-it-quick) reforms, and the need for a strengthened supervisory system that should precede any significant opening up of the external capital account. China has enough fiscal resources to strengthen the bank's balance sheets, and its debt/GDP ratio is low. Yet, banks should be advised to avoid maturity mismatches and should balance long-term loans with long-term sources of financing. Resources should be made available to remove bad and doubtful loans from the bank's balance sheets.

Methodology for Supervision of the Financial Sector: Four major issues were discussed: unsound governing mechanisms of many financial institutions, the need to educate investors about financial risks, the quality and influences of supervisory staff, and the mechanism for problem institutions to exit. Implementation of the Basel Committee's "Core Principles of Effective Bank Supervision" was the most acute problem to be addressed because supervisory agencies needed to be autonomous. Any insurance scheme had to be designed to minimize moral hazard risks.

Management of Banking Crises: China was warned of the dangers of undue delays in dealing with bad loan problems and the need to act quickly on at list six important issues: ownership structure of financial institutions, guarantee of household bank deposits, means for disposing of bad assets, stopping loss of SOEs that produce bad loans for the banks, developing a transparent system that includes dealing with foreign creditors of failed institutions, and undertaking effective corporate restructuring. Although foreign financial institutions could contribute much to China's reform initiatives, fear was expressed that the privatization of state banks could lead to foreign domination of the banking sector, raising sensitive political and social issues. In closing, a senior Chinese official summed it all as follows: "China tomorrow can be better only if we think harder, learn harder, and respond quickly."

Source: Based on "Strengthening the Banking System in China: Issues and Experience," Conference Policy Paper 7. Beijing, China, March 1–2, 1999. Available: http://www.bis.org/publ/plcy07.htm.

STRATEGIES FOR STRENGTHENING
THE BANKING SYSTEM

The root causes of banking and financial failure and crises are multiple, interrelated, and persistent. Accordingly, the policy options and practical solutions must be multiple and co-ordinated with determination and perseverance from all stakeholders. Exhibit 7.2 summarizes some of the common macroeconomic and microeconomic policy options for mitigating against banking and financial crises.

EXHIBIT 7.2
Policy Options for Mitigating against Banking and Financial Crises

Macroeconomic and Political Initiatives

- Sound macroeconomic policies: monetary stability, real growth, effective coordination between fiscal and monetary policy.

- Sustained commitment to economic reforms: establish government accountability in the market, support market-oriented policies.

- Close coordination between the central bank and the government.

- Ensure political and public support for formulation and implementation of policies and reforms.

- Sustain the reforms even in times of crises.

- Effective banking regulations and supervision: setting the rules for sound and safe banking, supervision to ensure proper compliance, monitoring to optimize the results.

- Cross-border capital flows: avoid massive short-term debt.

Microeconomic Initiatives

- Avoid speculative bubbles.

- Focus on bank asset quality: avoid inside lending, revisit asset valuation criteria (for example, market value), encourage on-site inspections.

- Implement the Basel Committee Banking Accord: work closely with the international financial institutions.

- Ensure home country consolidated supervision.

- Fit and proper for banking; skills, prudence, ethics

China needs to initiate and sustain reforms both at the macroeconomic and microeconomic levels. At the macroeconomic level, it needs to sustain macroeconomic stability, encourage privatization through the development of small- and medium-size entrepreneurial enterprises, and reform its SOEs. It was also suggested that policy lending should be discouraged. At the microeconomic level, recommended reforms focused on the need to separate money and credit creation from finance of public sector deficits, strengthen the supervisory system before opening up the external capital account, and to make additional resources available to remove bad and doubtful loans from the bank's balance sheets. In this case, China may find Chile's experiences (discussed in the next section) in managing and reforming its banking and financial crisis particularly relevant. Particularly important was the recommendation that as far as reforming and strengthening its banking system China could not afford to procrastinate. The longer the banking and financial problems are allowed to linger and simmer, the more intractable and costly they become. These lessons of experience suggest that the country's political, industry, and civic leaders must gather strength and embark on a comprehensive and one-way journey of reform whose destination is the strengthening of the country's banking system and the avoidance of banking and financial crises. This is the common challenge for all globalizing countries.

Lessons from Chile

For most globalizing developing countries and transition economies, it is almost inevitable that sooner or later they will experience some form of banking failure or financial crisis. While strategies for crisis avoidance are highly recommended, it is prudent for globalizing countries to develop core competencies and institutional capacities for crisis management in banking and finance. The lessons of experience drawn from China were identified by Chinese and international banking experts *before* a crisis struck. Here, I draw on lessons of managing a banking and financial crisis in Chile *after* a crisis. By putting the two sets of lessons together, newly globalizing countries can learn and acquire the strategies for managing banking and financial crisis proactively (before) and reactively to an ongoing crisis.

Exhibit 7.4 provides fifteen important steps taken by the Chilean authorities to manage the banking crisis and strengthen the country's banking and financial system. Chile had one of the most severe and costly banking crises, lasting from 1981 to 1993 and costing more than 40 percent of GDP. The program of reform started in 1982, but was revised in 1984 to make it more serious and disciplined. Like other developing countries, Chile had three types of commercial banks: foreign-owned, state, and private domestic. The private domestic banks had the weakest balance sheets, with more bad loans, and, therefore, used the recovery program more extensively than other types of banks. Chile's primary objectives were to:

1. restore the integrity and confidence of the banking system to both the domestic Chilean public and foreign investors;
2. return the commercial banking sector to profitability through recapitalization, restructuring, and professional discipline imposed by an effective system of regulation and supervision;

3. reduce Chile's overall indebtedness and vulnerability;

4. develop a national institutional capacity for managing and guarding against similar future crises.

EXHIBIT 7.4
Key Components of Chile's Measures to Strengthen
Its Banking and Financial System

1. Banks were prevented from capitalizating interest on loans to borrowers who were in default.

2. Stockholders of risky institutions were forced to bear part of the cost of restructuring the banking system.

3. Mandatory restructuring of about 50 percent of the loans of the banking system was imposed, and the principals of restructured loans were indexed to reflect the rate of inflation, and banks were forced to pay predetermined real interest rates.

4. Commercial banks were permitted to place loans with the central bank in return for a long-term bond.

5. The banks were required to purchase a central bank security with the funds received from the transfer of restructured loans to the balance sheet of the central bank.

6. Banks were required to buy back loans sold to the central bank.

7. With the exception of a few small banks, the reform program did not include sale of banks with depleted capital to new owners nor did it include a government takeover of failed banks. Existing banks were bailed out for recapitalization.

8. In the absence of markets for bank assets, the country had to seek funds from multinational agencies to finance the restructuring program.

9. Resources for the bank restructuring program were channeled through the central bank to the commercial banks to a maximum of 87 percent of total loans in 1985.

10. The central bank borrowed money from domestic commercial banks to finance the restructuring. This reduced the amount of credit available to private domestic borrowers.

11. The central bank absorbed the credit risk of lending to impaired banks by acting as intermediary between banks lending funds and banks borrowing funds.

12. The central bank absorbed the foreign exchange risk for the banks. Many foreign currency loans held on the balance sheet of banks (liabilities) were converted into indexed peso loans to relieve borrowers of foreign exchange risks. Therefore, foreign currency liabilities were funding indexed peso assets.

13. The central bank issued foreign currency bonds to the banks while offering them loans denominated in indexed pesos.

14. After 1985, the nonbanking sector became a significant source of funding for the restructuring program. Although most of the money came from the country's mandatory pension system, it was a sign of evidence of improving domestic confidence in the economy, the reform program, and the banking system.

15. By the late 1980s, Chile achieved a stable banking system, with deposits increasing relative to GDP. It took eight years to work itself out of bad loans. It was not until 1992 that banks became net lenders to the central bank.

Source: Compiled from Liliana Rojas-Suarez and Steven R Weisbrod, "The Do's and Don'ts of Banking Crisis Management," in *Banking Crises in Latin America*, ed. Ricardo Hausmann and Liliana Rojas-Suarez (Washington, DC: Inter-American Development Bank, 1996), 119–151.

As the measures shown in Exhibit 7.4 clearly indicate, the central bank played a pivotal role in managing the crisis and strengthening the banking system. For example, after preventing the commercial banks from capitalizing bad loans and forcing bank owners to bear part of the cost of restructuring, the central bank provided funds from which the troubled commercial banks could borrow to meet their current liquidity obligations. The central bank acted as the conduit for funds to the commercial banks and acted as both facilitator and confidence builder for the banking and financial sector. It also absorbed the banks' foreign exchange risk by converting their foreign currency loans into indexed peso loans. The banks received foreign currency bonds from the central bank and loans indexed in the local currency.

Chile went through a period of both severe banking crisis and high levels of indebtedness. Inflation could not have eliminated Chile's bad loan problems because a large portion of bank liabilities to foreigners were denominated in foreign currency (see Table 7.2).

It took time, determination, and political will, but eight years later the banking system was sound again. By 1992, the commercial banking sector became a net lender to the central bank. Compared to Argentina, Chile is credited for its more effective, disciplined, and sustaining strategy for managing itself out of a very serious banking and financial crisis. Two economists from the Inter-American Development Bank summed it up nicely when they observed:

TABLE 7.2
Chile's Fiscal Deficit and Long-Term Foreign Debt
(Percentage of GDP)

Year	Fiscal Deficit	Long-term Foreign Debt
1979	4.8	37.7
1980	5.4	35.4
1981	2.6	4.07
1982	-1.0	62.6
1983	-2.6	82.0
1984	-3.0	99.5
1985	-2.3	122.6
1986	-0.9	114.9
1987	0.4	95.1
1988	-0.2	72.4
1989	1.8	52.8
1990	0.8	51.9
1991	1.5	46.0
1992	2.2	38.6
1993	1.9	38.0

Source: Compiled from Liliana Rojas-Suarez and Steven R. Weisbrod, "Do's and Don'ts of Banking Crisis Management," in *Banking Crises in Latin America*, ed. Ricardo Hausmann and Liliana Rojas-Suarez (Washington, DC: Inter-American Development Bank, 1996), table4.1, p.129.

As Chile's bank restructuring demonstrates, adequate real funding can buy sufficient time to prove to domestic investors that bank liabilities will be honored. To obtain this result, a program must encourage borrowers to meet their commitment and must provide incentives for bank managers to return their banks to solvency. However, even carefully devised programs succeed only if public policies promote low inflation and macroeconomic stability. When investors become convinced that their domestic financial assets are safe, they will be willing to provide a good portion of the real funds needed for a successful restructuring program.[12]

The International Financial Institutional Architecture

It is not possible to strengthen the world's banking and financial systems without the active involvement of international financial institutions. Two of the most important lessons from the financial crises of the 1980s, and more so in the 1990s, in Asia, Latin America, and elsewhere are that while these institutions were part of the solution (and perhaps part of the problem) they were nowhere to be seen when they were needed. It has been suggested that at the height of the Asian crisis the international financial institutions did not know what to do and how to respond. It has also been pointed out that informed, firm, and more expeditious response from these institutions would have significantly reduced the severity and costs of these crises.

It is with this background in mind that it is important to understand why the 2000s started a frantic search for the proper international financial institutional architecture to bring about financial stability in the global economy and to try to tame the excesses of "casino capitalism."[13] In 1995, the Halifax Summit of the G7[14] leaders called for a review and update of the global financial institutions and rules to deal with the growing and increasingly complex and highly integrated world of capital markets. This was followed by various search activities by the G10, G22, and G26—all groupings of countries dominated by industrial countries and looking for ways to strengthen the international financial institutional architecture. At the same time the three leading international financial institutions—the World Bank, the IMF, and the BIS—were busy redefining their changing roles in the context of emerging global financial and capital markets challenges. Likewise, regional organizations such as the OECD, the European Monetary Union, the ASEAN, and regional development banks in Asia and Latin America have become deeply involved in the search for improved and locally more acceptable institutional arrangements. Many proposals have been put forward, some radical and others moderate, but to date, few practical and universally acceptable solutions have been found.

The Open-Market Trilemma

In an open-market economy, policy makers pursue three goals: independence, confidence, and liquidity. Independence is the country's ability to pursue independent macroeconomic policies such as setting interest rates to stimulate or cool off the economy. Confidence is the ability to protect exchange rates from destabilizing speculation and to encourage investment flows—a sign that the country is open for business. Liquidity is the ability to borrow money from abroad through the free flow of capital. This requires keeping international capital flows free. Unfortunately, these three goals are incompatible, and it is only possible to achieve two of these goals at a time. Yet, the central task of the international political economy is to seek balance in the integration of these three goals.

At the national level, policy makers would expect the international financial institutions to promote those three goals by fostering capital market integration, ensuring that international capital markets are regulated and supervised, and, at the same time, respecting national sovereignty. Obviously, these three goals are incompatible for the following reasons: First, maintaining national sovereignty (independence) in a world of free capital means forfeiting market regulation and support. Second, creating regulations and an international lender of last resort (liquidity) implies overriding national sovereignty. Third, the only way a country can regulate and support its financial markets (confidence) while maintaining national sovereignty (independence) is by controlling capital flows. Therefore, the central task the national policy makers assign to the international financial institutions is intrinsically impossible to perform in its totality because open-market conditions create for them not a dilemma but a trilemma.

The first step in dealing with the trilemma is for a country or group of countries to choose among the incompatible goals. For example, the industrial countries choose stable exchange rates (confidence) and liquidity. To achieve these two goals, a country needs to establish a currency board or join a monetary union like many European countries have done. This obviously requires giving up some independence.

In a world of freely mobile, fixed, but adjustable exchange rates, pegs are unstable because they would sooner or later be tested by currency speculation. The only way a country can maintain both confidence and independence is by restricting capital flows. This is the combination of goals that policy makers of the immediate post–World War II era had chosen under the original Bretton Woods regime of fixed rates. For twenty-five years of the Bretton Woods agreement, the global financial institutional architecture was based on a system of fixed exchange rates and strict capital controls. However, during the 1960s, international investors gradually began to evade the fixed exchange rate regime of capital controls. International capital flows increased, and countries were forced to choose between ability to maintain macroeconomic policies (independence) and exchange rate stability. In 1971, the system of fixed exchange rates broke down, and industrial countries chose to maintain independence by forfeiting fixed exchange rates. Since 1971, the world's major currencies including the U.S. dollar, the yen, and the European currencies have all floated. However, by creating the euro, European countries have revisited the trilemma one more time. Specifically, they have reversed themselves by giving up exchange rate flexibility entirely. This is a different way of dealing with the trilemma.

In general, developing countries have addressed themselves to the trilemma rather differently. Even after 1971, developing countries maintained tight controls on capital flows. Therefore, they initially dealt with the trilemma by choosing independence and confidence, thus forfeiting liquidity. During the 1980s and more so the 1990s, as international capital flows increased, some developing countries, especially the BEMs, like industrial countries before, chose greater capital mobility. As more countries face the choice between exchange rate stability and policy independence, most are moving toward exchange rate flexibility. For example, in 1976, about 86 percent of developing countries pegged their currency to a single currency such as the U.S. dollar, the French franc, the British pound sterling, or a basket of currencies. By the end of the 1990s, only about 45 percent of the developing countries still had pegged exchange rates. For the most part, these are the category P2 poor countries, which are experiencing difficulties with liberalization and globalization. While the more successful globalizing developing countries are steadily gravitating toward flexible exchange rates, just like industrial countries, the least-developed poor countries are still stuck with pegged exchange rates. Reflecting on the recent financial crises and pegged exchange rates, a recent Asia Development Bank report observed: "The Asian financial crisis, as well as recent crises in Brazil, Mexico, and Russia, hit countries with pegged exchange rates and heavy inflows of foreign capital. They were a direct result of the open economy trilemma. Thus at the heart of the debate on improving the international financial architecture is the thorny question of which of the three goals to give up."[15]

Proposals for Strengthening the International Financial Institutional Architecture

Numerous proposals have been put forward—all aimed at reforming and strengthening the international financial institutional architecture. Many more are likely to be proposed in the coming years before some kind of global consensus emerges. This reflects both the diversity of opinions and interests, especially between and within industrial and developing countries, and the complexity and dynamic nature of the issues associated with global finance and capital markets, as well as national sovereignty and sense of independence. Following, I present and discuss five proposals most likely to form the basis for the evolution of a global consensus: controlling capital flows, improving regulatory standards, rethinking exchange rate regimes, creating an international lender of last resort, and "bailing in" the private sector.

Controlling Capital Flows

National policy makers are proposing that the international financial institutions should solve the trilemma by controlling capital mobility. Two arguments are made in favor of this proposal: First, it is suggested that countries can gain free trade in goods and services without, at the same time, opening up their financial markets to foreign competition. In this case, capital mobility is seen as an "extra," not integral to free trade. Second, the theoretical benefits of free-trade capital flows such as increased capital investment do not occur in practice because the efficiency gains that a country obtains from opening up foreign capital are more than offset by increasing uncertainty and greater risks of financial crises. This is particularly so for the less-developed developing countries where financial markets, which are operating under imperfect information, tend to overshoot, thus bringing these countries more risks than rewards.

However, experience shows that there are serious practical problems of administering controls as people and businesses try to evade the capital controls. For example, importers are known to over invoice their shipments in order to smuggle capital out of the economy. As economies grow and become more open, capital controls foster corruption and restrict the growth of trade. This has been the experience in Africa, Latin America, and Asia—in countries where capital controls have been the preferred choice of dealing with the trilemma. As was demonstrated from the lessons of experience from Chile and the conference on China, financial liberalization must be carefully sequenced so that it is done in tandem with economic liberalization and institutional strengthening.

Improving Regulatory Standards

Poor regulation and supervision and enforcement and compliance thereof are major sources of banking and financial crises. Therefore, the international financial institutions have concentrated on promoting improved standards and building human and institutional capacities for the development and effective implementation of national banking and financial regulatory and supervisory systems. It has been suggested that the IMF should issue regular transparency reports for its member states, and that regional institutions such as the Asia Development Bank should establish surveillance and monitoring capabilities to complement the work of international financial institutions.

There are a number of professional private sector organizations working on improving international standards. For example, the International Accounting Standards Committee, with more than one hundred countries represented, formulates international accounting standards. The International Federation of Accountants and the International Organization of Supreme Audit Institutions formulate auditing standards and issue auditing guidelines. The Committee of the International Bar Association is working on bankruptcy laws and insolvency guides. The International Corporate Governance Network deals with issues of corporate governance. Still, more work needs to be done to translate all this effort into practical realities in the professional practices of many developing countries.

There is a need for more decentralization of most of this work so that the private sector plays a more active role in the development, updating, and enforcement of the regulatory standards. For now, much of the work is done by international financial institutions and the economic line ministries of industrial countries. Global corporations, developing country institutions, NGOs, research and academic institutions, and subnational governments should be coopted into many of the working groups and standing committees.

The G7 has proposed the establishment of a financial stability forum—a meeting of financial and banking policy makers, finance ministers, and representatives from international financial institutions. The forum would provide members with the opportunity to share experiences, improve the exchange of information, and coordinate reform initiatives. This is a good idea that should be extended to BEMs and other groups of developing countries facing similar trilemma challenges.

Rethinking Exchange Rate Regimes

As experience from Asia and elsewhere has demonstrated, pegged but adjustable exchange rates are difficult to sustain in a world of increasing capital mobility. Sooner or later, such exchange rates are tested by a speculative attack, forcing the country to raise interest rates and cut its budget. By creating the illusion of permanent currency stability, such exchange rate regimes reinforce the incentives for banks and other financial institutions and business firms to borrow from abroad without hedging. Because of these problems, most economists recommend that a globalizing country must either rapidly and irrevocably tie its currency to another by adopting a currency board or entering into a currency union or it must allow its currency to float. Fixed exchange rates are no longer a realistic option for globalizing economies.

Industrial and developing globalizing countries are attracted to flexible exchange rates for several reasons: First, countries with flexible exchange rates are less likely to suffer from sudden crises of investor confidence. Serious currency crises are generally associated with the collapse of fixed exchange rates. As well, countries that experience a sudden depreciation of a floating currency suffer less macroeconomic distress. Second, a flexible exchange rate gives the government more room to act as lender of last resort to its banking and financial industry when in need. Third, flexible exchange rates allow a country more autonomy with respect to its macroeconomic policies.

Yet, flexible exchange rates are not popular with all developing countries. A developing country with significant policy autonomy may have trouble gaining credibility in international financial markets. Countries with floating exchange rates often have to keep interest rates high in order to develop and sustain investor confidence. For example, in mid-1998, Mexico's peso fell by 20 percent in response to turmoil in Asia and Russia. At the time, Mexico's interest rates were considered much higher than those of Argentina, a country that has a very tough currency board. If this can happen to Mexico, imagine what would happen to weaker economies such as Jamaica, Ghana, or Sri Lanka.

The ultimate choice of a currency regime depends on a country's size, history, political economy, and geographical location. Europe has adopted the euro and, therefore, floating exchange rates. Latin America is seriously considering dollarization, with Argentina leading the drive. In Asia, however, there is resistance to a regional currency union. Instead, individual countries will adopt or retain their own exchange rate regimes but will attempt to achieve close coordination through ASEAN and the Asia Development Bank. There is a growing movement toward flexible exchange rates in Asia, especially by members of ASEAN. Africa remains cautious about flexible exchange rates. Even relatively strong or well-performing economies such as South Africa, Zimbabwe, Ghana, and Uganda have seen the value of their currencies plunge in relation to the U.S. dollar or other hard currencies.

Creating an International Lender of Last Resort

In principle, this is one of the least controversial proposals. It is calling on the international financial institutions to play a role similar to national central banks when the banking and financial institutions are facing liquidity problems. Already, the IMF plays the role of lender of last resort in a limited way: by providing countries in financial crisis limited liquidity in return for policy reform (conditionality). The proposal would likely be extended to banking and financial institutions in member states.

The idea of lender of last resort is that the lender should lend freely, charge a fee or impose a penalty, and receive good collateral from the borrower who is experiencing liquidity problems. This means that the lender of last resort should be able and willing to discriminate between potential borrowers who are suffering from short-term liquidity problems and those who are fundamentally insolvent. The latter should be allowed to fail.

The IMF is not able to act as lender of last resort for all member states and their financial institutions. It cannot assume the role of the central bank in every country. Even if it were able to distinguish between local institutions, which are illiquid from those which are insolvent, it would be hard-pressed to force problem institutions to close. Furthermore, the IMF does not have the money to act as lender of last resort in an expanded capacity. It has no mandate to print money, unlike some central banks (limited only by fixed exchange rates). Even with recent initiatives such as the increase of the IMF's capital and the creation of the "New Arrangements to Borrow"—an emergency credit line from donor countries to the IMF—the IMF would still have limited resources.

Other proposals have been put forward and are currently under discussion. These include Japan's proposal for the creation of regional currency mechanisms to complement the IMF and G7's goal of setting up a contingency financing facility for qualified countries to set up a precautionary credit line with the IMF. It has also been suggested that regional monetary funds should be established. Japan has proposed the need for the establishment of an Asian Monetary Fund. For the moment, national central banks and, in a limited way, the IMF remain as the accepted lenders of last resort for financial institutions and countries, respectively, experiencing financial crises. Any future proposals will have to work with the existing institutional architecture, which seems to be working, as was the case in Chile.

"Bailing In" the Private Sector

This proposal is aimed at minimizing moral hazard and spreading the burden of a financial crisis by making sure that private investors and bankers bear some of the cost of restructuring. Argentina and Mexico have successfully pioneered an approach whereby private sector credit lines are set up before the crisis. For example, Argentina negotiated U.S.$6.7 billion worth of repurchasing arrangements with international banks. Against the collateral of domestic bonds, these arrangements give Argentina access to capital in the event of financial crisis. In a sense, they are a form of private lender of last resort. These types of arrangements have wide applicability in other BEMs and globalizing developing countries. Recall that the conference on China's banking and financial strengthening raised issues of moral hazard and raised questions about the financing of the restructuring. For other developing countries, especially of the P2 category, these arrangements can work, especially if multilateral development banks guarantee some portion of the risk involved, thereby encouraging private banks to participate.

Regional Approaches to Financial Crisis Management

There is increasing interest among experts and political leaders of globalizing countries for the development of regional solutions to global problems. Part of this is due to the inherent duality of globalization, which on one hand promotes internationalism and, on the other hand, the preservation and strengthening of local institutions and culture. It is also partly a response to the way the existing international financial institutional architecture, led by the Bretton Woods institutions, has managed the economic and financial and banking crises during the last quarter of the twentieth century. For example, the way the World Bank and the IMF managed the structural adjustment programs in response to the economic crises of the 1980s in Africa and elsewhere and the way they responded to the financial crises in Asia, Latin America, and Central and Eastern Europe left many citizens dissatisfied. As more developing countries and transition economies develop their own human capital, political leadership, and local institutions, they begin to search for more indigenous solutions to the management of globalization and its consequences. This is good and should be supported by the international community.

In the case of managing financial crises, regional approaches have the following advantages. First, it is believed that regional institutional arrangements would be better suited to provide member states with early warning systems than the global institutions. If the globalizing countries received clear and unequivocal early warning signals of an impending crisis and if the regional institutional architecture worked in close collaboration with the national institutions, the country would be much better prepared to manage the crisis and reduce its severity and costs. Second, regional institutions have the potential to overcome official procrastination and get the regulators and supervisors into action immediately. This problem was noted in the discussion regarding China's preparedness for action—the need for not-too-gradual reforms (see Exhibit 7.3). Third, regional institutions can be a source of additional resources to complement the international institutions. These resources could be financial, which are needed because neither the IMF nor the World Bank have enough capital to finance all financial crises for all globalizing countries. Perhaps more significant, regional institutions are better suited to mobilize nonfinancial resources in preparation for a coming crisis. These resources may be in the form of broad-based political leadership, support, and commitment; local institutional support from the private sector including civil society and the business community; trade unions; or a regional pool of experts mobilized to come together to share information, expertise, and lessons of experience. It is generally believed that local knowledge, often embedded in local tradition, culture, and institutions, is best understood and utilized by those from within the community rather than foreigners.

A fourth reason for advocating a regional approach is one of acceptance and credibility. Regional institutions, staffed by regional nationals and providing properly contexualized information and advice, are more likely to receive local acceptance and credibility than foreigners whose message and intentions are sometimes suspected by the local leadership. Unlike the international institutions, regional institutions would have the opportunity to work more closely with the national stakeholders to enhance local understanding, acceptance, and ownership of the reform initiatives. They would be more likely to avoid a "one-size-fits-all" approach or blueprinting solutions to locally complex contextual problems. Where capacity gaps have been identified, regional institutions would be more likely to complement less expensive national initiatives to develop the necessary human capital and strengthen the relevant institutions. They would be more politically in tune with national and local governments and governance systems. Although these arguments clearly demonstrate that regional approaches have comparative advantages, they are not meant to supplant but complement the international financial architecture. Therefore, there would have to be close coordination among the international, regional, national, and local institutions for the effective management of banking and financial crises.

Regional approaches are not without criticism. They are opposed on the grounds that they are duplicative and undermine the work of the international financial architecture. They detract from the search for truly global solutions to global problems. In a highly interconnected world, regional solutions are ineffective because what happens in one region affects and, in turn, is affected by what happens in others. The Asian crisis clearly showed how regions are highly interdependent when Latin America and Russia became victims of events beyond their control. Therefore, it is argued that regional approaches do not promote openness, competitiveness, and globalization; rather, they are protectionists and harbingers of narrow nationalism and isolationism.

It is also feared that regional institutions would be "soft" on countries in crisis and that rather than helping them to make tough decisions and enforce discipline they would create a false sense of security. For example, the IMF extends loans under strict reform conditions, making the IMF very unpopular in many liberalizing countries. It is not clear if regional institutions would be able and willing to take the same wrath in cases in which stern measures are warranted. The proposed Asian Monetary Fund was supposed to extend assistance to member states in crisis without conditions. This would have the potential of raising the moral hazard and not forcing the investors, owners, and managers to pay their fair share of the costs of the financial crisis.

Under Japan's leadership, and with strong support from Malaysia, Asia has taken practical initiatives to create such a fund. Exhibit 7.5 provides the background, proposed role, and funding proposals for the proposed Asian Monetary Fund. As George Soros and others have observed, Prime Minister Dr. Mahathir of Malaysia resented the way Asia, in general, and Malaysia, in particular, was treated by the international financial institutions and capital markets during and after the crisis.[16] Therefore, he became a leading advocate for alternative institutional arrangements including a regional monetary fund or currency union. However, as evidence in Exhibit 7.5 suggests, Asia's economic and political complexities and diversity has meant that to date only modest steps have been accepted. The situation is not likely to change dramatically in the near future.

Exhibit 7.5
Asian Monetary Fund: Proposal for a Regional Approach

Background: In September 1997, Japan proposed the creation of the Asian Monetary Fund (AMF) as a regional and locally sensitive and responsive institutional complement to the IMF, in the way the Asian Development Bank complements the World Bank. After all, Western Europe has its own comprehensive regional financial institutional architecture: the European Monetary Union. It was argued that regional institutions such as the AMF, as part of the new emerging financial architecture, will help to enhance financial markets and minimize their systemic risk.

Role: The AMF would perform four complementary functions:

1. Serve as an early warning system by forewarning member states of impending crises using detailed knowledge of problems from each country.

2. Use regional peer pressure to ensure speedy, comprehensive, and disciplined country response to the crisis.

3. Draw on its local knowledge and regional location to assist individual countries in developing local understanding, commitment, and ownership of the crisis and its management.

4. Provide ongoing financial and nonfinancial resources as a line of defense for the management of regional crises.

Funding: Japan originally proposed funding for the AMF of U.S.$100 billion, half of which they would contribute and the other half to come from the richer regional members such as China, including Hong Kong, and Taiwan and Singapore. This amount was considered necessary to provide sufficient liquidity to forestall speculative attacks on the region's currencies. This proposal was turned down at the fifth Asia–Pacific Economic Cooperation (APEC) meeting in Manila. During the 1998 IMF–World Bank meeting, Japan returned with a more modest proposal, under the "Miyazawa Plan," which proposed a U.S.$30 billion package. Half the money was to facilitate short-term trade financing, the other half was to promote economic recovery by financing medium- and long-term projects. Japan's Import–Export Bank, the World Bank, and the Asia Development Bank would provide the money. In October of the same year, at the APEC meeting, Japan and the United States, supported by the Asia Development Bank and the World Bank, launched a U.S.$10 billion Asian growth and recovery initiative, targeted for the crisis-affected countries in the region.

Next Steps: Apart from Western Europe, no other region has a comprehensive regional financial institutional architecture for crisis management and prevention. Besides Asia, other regions such as Eastern Europe, South America, and North America could be prime candidates for experimentation. Regional trading blocks and associations such as NAFTA, CARICOM, and ASEAN could provide the institutional platform by which regional financial institutional arrangements could be developed.

Source: "Is There a Case for an Asian Monetary Fund?" in Asia Development Bank, *Asian Development Outlook* (Manila: Asia Development Bank, 1999), 44.

Preparing for the Coming Crises

It has been estimated that in any given year, there is a 10–15 percent likelihood of a financial, banking, or currency crisis in globalizing developing countries and transition economies. In 2001, it was mainly Turkey and Argentina; in coming years, other globalizing countries will most likely fall victim. Therefore, it is important that policy makers for these countries take effective measures to reduce the risks of these crises. While reforms of international financial architecture and continuing improvements in macroeconomic policies and banking systems are the best protection against these crises, countries can complement them with safeguards. Safeguards are domestically initiated short-term financial measures aimed at reducing the possibility of the occurrence of financial crises.

There are two types of safeguards: controls on capital flows and measures that improve a country's access to international liquidity. Controls are preventive measures designed to prevent crises, whereas access to international liquidity measures are curative in that they are designed to help contain the crises when they occur. Controls on capital include Chilean-type taxes on inflows, quantitative controls on the banking sector's international short-term liabilities, and restrictions on capital outflows. Although traditional sources of vulnerability such as large budget deficits, excessive international borrowing, and overvalued currencies remain significant, the safeguards are primarily targeted for new sources of vulnerability such as financial sector liberalization and capital account opening and short-term capital flows. These short-term safeguards are each associated with several advantages and disadvantages. For example, they impose a cost to the domestic economy by restricting the quantity of foreign borrowing or by raising its price. Capital controls and liquidity enhancement safeguards are not easy to implement. In the case of capital controls, Chilean-type reserve requirements are hard to implement because they require comprehensive coverage of all inflows to be effective. Prudent controls require careful monitoring to ensure compliance, and controls on outflows, if made permanent, can lead to evasion and corruption. As for liquidity enhancement, using reserves to cover short-term debt requires a country to develop a strategy for managing foreign reserves. Contingent credit lines, on the other hand, are relatively easy to implement as a short-term strategy for accessing international liquidity, as long as the country enjoys strong creditworthiness—real or perceived.[17] Countries must use these safeguards with care and due consideration with regard to the associated costs and the country's particular circumstances.

Protecting the Poor

For newly globalizing developing countries and transition economies, it is reasonable to assume that sooner or later one of the three types of crises—financial, currency, banking—will occur. Therefore, it is prudent for policy makers to put in place a comprehensive emergency management plan covering not only economics but, equally important, political and social preparedness. One area becoming increasingly important is the development of policies and programs to protect the poor and the country's other most vulnerable groups such as children, orphans, the unemployed, the elderly, the poorly educated, and other demographically determined vulnerable groups. Although crises hurt both the poor and the non-poor, the poor suffer more because of their limited savings and because they have limited access to social and market insurance. World Bank studies estimate that each percentage-point decline in growth from an adverse economic shock raises the poverty rate by 2 percentage points. For example, it is estimated that in 1993 Argentina's national population below the poverty line was 17.6 percent. If in the same period, the country's GDP declined by an estimated 4 percentage points, the national population below the poverty line would rise to over 25 percent. Obviously, the effects would be different in urban and rural areas because poverty rates tend to be higher in the former.[18]

Governments and the private sector can protect the poor by taking several preparatory and mitigating policy initiatives. Governments can ensure that the national and subnational budgets protect spending, which benefits the poor the most. This includes spending on primary education, nutrition and health care, water and sanitation, rural development including infrastructure, and housing. Government and large employers can expand food subsidy programs for the poor or develop targeted programs to avoid subsidies leaking to the non-poor. For example, instead of providing subsidized meals to all employees, employers could provide nutritional programs to expectant mothers and young children under five years old.

Governments, working in partnership with the private sector, should develop and put in place social and welfare programs for the poor before the crisis rather than as part of crisis management. Recommended programs include scholarships for poor children, public works programs, cash transfers, food-related transfers and subsidies, social and fee waivers for various essential services, and retraining and relocation programs for displaced workers. Local NGOs should be encouraged to focus their programming on the needs of the poor. Employers could also develop more creative methods of managing surplus labor, such as various forms of job sharing, rather than mass layoffs. Whatever strategies or combinations thereof a country decides to apply to mitigate the effect of the coming crisis for its poor and other vulnerable groups, it is always important to remember that prevention is better than cure.[19]

NOTES

1. In defense of bank-loan capitalism in Japan and newly industrializing countries, see Terutomo Ozawa, "Bank Loan Capitalism and Financial Crises: Japanese and Korean Experiences," in *Deepening Integration in the Pacific Economies*, ed. Alan M. Rugman and Gavin Boyd (Cheltenham, UK: Edward Elgar, 1999), 214–248.

2. Short-term debt owed by developing countries to foreign banks rose from U.S.$176 billion to U.S.$454 billion between 1990 and 1997. According to an IMF study, this was a key factor in the financial crises of several developing countries and transition economies. See Uri Dadush, Dipak Dasgupta, and Dilip Ratha, "The Role of Short-Term Debt in Recent Crises," *Finance and Development* 37, no. 4 (2000):54–57.

3. For more technical discussions, see Morris Goldstein and Philip Turner, "Banking Crises in Emerging Economies: Origins and Policy Options," BIS Economic Paper 46 (Basel: Bank for International Settlement, October 1996). On January 16, 2001, the Basel Committee issued revised capital requirement rules, updating the proposals issued in June of the previous year. These rules cover the three important areas of minimum capital requirements, regulatory supervision, and disclosure. Final consultation with various stakeholders was to be completed within a year. The rules are expected to take effect in 2004. See "Sweeter Basel," *The Economist*, January 20, 2001, p. 18; and "Stronger Foundations," *The Economist*, January 20, 2001, pp. 67–68. Also see, Omotunde E. G. Johnson, ed., *Financial Risks, Stabilization, and Globalization* (Washington, DC: IMF, 2002); and Wilbert O. Bascom, *Bank Management and Supervision in Developing Financial Markets* (London: Macmillan, 1997).

4. World Bank, *The State in a Changing World:World Development Report* (Washington, DC:World Bank, 1997).

5. Ibid., 68.

6. The anatomy of the banking and financial crisis is described by a former Chilean finance minister. See Edwardo Aninat, "Chile," in *Banking Crises in Latin America*, ed. Ricardo Hausmann and Liliana Rojas-Suarez (Washington, DC: Inter-American Development Bank, 1996), 229–233.

7. George Soros, *The Crisis of Global Capitalism* (New York: Public Affairs, 1998), chaps. 6 and 7.

8. Asli Demirguc-Kunt and Enrica Detragiache, "The Determinants of Banking Crises: Evidence from Industrial and Developing Countries," Policy Research Working Paper 1828 (Washington, DC: World Bank Development Research Group and IMF Research Department, September 1997).

9. Cited in Ricardo Hausmann and Liliana Rojas-Suarez, eds., *Banking Crisis in Latin America* (Washington, DC: Inter-American Development Bank, 1996), 196.

10. Moses N. Kiggundu and George Sekinobe-Musoke, "Management Resource Audit of the Bank of Uganda," School of Business Working Paper (Ottawa: Carleton University, 1988).

11. Moses N. Kiggundu, "Management in Uganda," in *Management in Emerging Countries*, ed. Malcolm Warner (London: Thomson Learning, 2000), 228–236.

12. Liliana Rojas-Suarez and Steven R. Weisbrod, "The Do's and Don'ts of Banking Crisis Management," in *Banking Crisis in Latin America* (Washington, DC: Inter-American Development Bank, 1996), 138.

13. "Casino capitalism" is a pejorative term used to refer to the open-market-economy equivalent of bank-loan capitalism as discussed previously. It is called "casino" because of its speculative nature. See Ozawa, "Bank Loan Capitalism," 214.

14. The G7 group of industrialized countries is also called G8 when Russia is included. The original seven are: the United States, Japan, Germany, France, the United Kingdom, Italy, and Canada. This group has been very active in developing proposals for strengthening the international financial institutions. In 1995, it coined the term *financial architecture*. The G10, set up in 1962, includes eleven industrial countries because Switzerland joined later. It is a group of finance ministers and central bank governors and concentrates on the supervisory and regulatory aspects of banking. It works closely with the BIS. G22 is an ad hoc group of the G8 plus some BEMs. It was set up by the United States in April 1998 and has at least three working groups focusing on enhancing transparency, accountability, and strengthening financial systems, as well as managing international financial crises. At the request of some of the small European countries, the G22 was expanded to G26. It is important to note that the poor, less-developed category P2 countries are barely represented in any of these G groupings, except the G77, which opposes globalization. This exclusion is punitive. See Asia Development Bank, *Asian Development Outlook* (Manilla: Asia Development Bank, 1999), 37.

15. The quote and discussion about the trilemma and the proposals for strengthening the international institutional achitecture are based on ibid., 38.

16. The Soros–Mahathir violent dialogue on currency speculation illustrates the frustration and inherent conflicts and contradictions between Western capitalistic values as practiced by the Bretton Woods institutions and the global capital markets and Malaysian values, culture, and political economy as exposited by the Malaysian prime minister. See BBC News Report, September 20–21, 1997.

17. For a more detailed discussion of short-term safeguards and their applications, see World Bank, *Global Development Finance: Analysis and Summary Tables* (Washington, DC: World Bank, 2000), 97–117.

18. The 2000s have started with a renewed focus on poverty alleviation, especially with the publication of the *World Bank Report: Attacking Poverty* (Washington, DC: World Bank, 2000/2001).

19. Paul Krugman and Anthony J. Venables, "Globalization and Inequality," *Quarterly Journal of Economics* 110, no. 4 (1995):857–880; Nancy Birdsall, "Managing Inequality in the Developing World," *Current History* 98, no. 631 (1999):376–381; and Geoffrey J. Bannister and Kamau Thugge, "International Trade and Poverty Alleviation," *Finance and Development* 31, no. 4 (2001):48–51.

CHAPTER 8

Globalization and Debt

Debt is one of the most contentious and emotionally charged issues in the debate about globalization and development. It has become more of a moral crusade than a question of global political economy. It is also technically complex, involving dynamic interplay of the weak (debtors) and strong (creditors), under the influence of global and domestic macroeconomic and microeconomic forces, geopolitics, history, and governance systems at home and abroad. It has generated a series of intractable problems with no easy solutions. Accordingly, although all world leaders, including the Pope and Nelson Mandela, have called for the elimination of debt, technicians have not found solutions satisfactory to both debtors and creditors. Part of the reason for this lack of consensus is that debt does not exist in a vacuum. Rather, it must be understood within the broader context of national governance and economic management as well as the global political economy, especially the international financial architecture. The debt problem is intimately related to openness and the capacity or lack thereof for competitiveness and beneficial globalization. Those countries unable or unwilling to take advantage of globalization have the highest debt burden.

In this chapter, I discuss the measurement of the debt burden and how countries are classified according to how much debt they owe in relation to their capacity to meet the debt obligations. I then discuss the relationship between debt and poverty and show that the poorest countries of the world also suffer from the biggest debt burden. This explains the world's indignation about debt and provides fodder for anti-globalization forces. Next will be a discussion on debt–equity swaps or conversion, domestic debt, and alternative solutions to the debt problem. The chapter ends with a discussion of capacity development for debt management. As was the case with trade, investment, banking, and finance, it is also the case that the countries with the most serious debt problems are lacking the human capital and institutional capacity for effective debt management.

MEASURING THE DEBT BURDEN

Debt is not a unitary concept; rather, there are many different types or aspects each with different effects and implications. For example, debt can be external or domestic, public or private, short term or long term, and debt can be dead or productive. External debt is owed to outsiders, usually denominated in foreign currency with implications for foreign reserves and exchange rates, whereas domestic debt is usually owed to residents and is denominated in the local currency. Most of the discussions about debt tend to focus almost exclusively on external or foreign debt. However, as I will discuss, attention must also be given to domestic debt because of its direct implications on the country's budgetary, fiscal, and monetary policies and policy options. Public debt is owed by the government; private debt is owed by private corporations, agencies, institutions, and private citizens. Public debt should include debt owed not only by the national government but also by subnational governments, state-owned enterprises (SOEs), and other public institutions. Together, they constitute the consolidated public debt profile, which gives a much more accurate picture of the total public debt burden. Private debt can become public if the debtor—such as banks, financial institutions, or business corporations—become illiquid or insolvent and the government must step in to rescue the ailing debtors.

The debt problems of Asian countries provide an example of private debt with serious public implications. During the boom years, the private sector corporations and banks contracted most of the new external debt. Rapid financial market and capital account liberalization during the 1990s made possible large-scale private sector external borrowing; and during the year before the crisis, a large exposure to short-term bank borrowing was built up due to lower interest rates on foreign borrowing than on domestic loans. When the crisis finally hit these economies, governments, with the help of the international financial institutions, assumed some of the liabilities of these private loans.

How is the debt burden measured? Although there are several ways of measuring the debt burden and classifying countries, the one presented here is most widely used by the international community. The World Bank classifies indebtedness based on two ratios: They calculate the ratio of the present value of total debt service to GNP and then the ratio of the present value of total debt service to exports. These two ratios reflect the country's indebtedness in terms of two important aspects of its potential capacity to service its debt obligations: exports and GNP. Exports are important because they reflect the country's capacity to earn foreign exchange and service its foreign debt. GNP is the measure of the country's capacity to generate income and therefore meet its obligations—domestic or foreign. Therefore, countries with poor export portfolios, declining terms of trade, or low or negative overall economic growth face the most serious debt burdens.[1]

If either ratio exceeds a critical value, the country is classified as "severely indebted." The critical values for this category are 80 percent for debt service to GNP ratio and 220 percent for the debt service to exports ratio. If the critical value is not exceeded but either ratio is three-fifths or more of the critical value (that is, 48 percent for the present value of debt service to GNP and 132 percent for the present value of debt service to exports), the country is classified as "moderately indebted." If both ratios are less than three-fifths of the critical value, the country is classified as "less indebted." Countries are also classified as "low income" if 1998 GNP per capita was U.S.$760 or less and as "middle income" if 1998 GNP per capita was more than U.S.$785 but less than U.S.$9,360. This produces a 2 × 3 matrix that classifies countries by income and debt burden.

Table 8.1 provides a matrix classifying 137 countries for which data were available to calculate the two important ratios. Before analyzing the data, it is important to point out that the classification system, although widely applied, should be used with caution. If a

TABLE 8.1
Classification of Low- and Middle-Income Countries by Debt Burden, 2000

	Income Classification	
Indebtedness Classification	Low Income (GNP per capita less than U.S.$760)	Middle Income (GNP per capita between U.S.$761 and U.S.$9,360)
PV/XGS less than 132 percent and PV/GNP less than 48 percent	Less-indebted low-income countries (9)	Less-indebted middle-income countries (41)
PV/XGS less than 220 percent but higher than 132 percent or PV/GNP less than 80 percent but higher than 48 percent	Moderately indebted low-income countries (18)	Moderately indebted middle-income countries (24)
PV/XGS higher than 220 percent or PV/GNP higher than 80 percent	Severely indebted low-income countries (34)	Severely indebted middle-income countries (11)

Severely Indebted Low-Income Countries
Angola, Burkina Faso, Burundi, Cameroon, Central African Republic, Comoros, Congo (Republic of), Côte d'Ivoire, Democratic Republic of the Congo, Ethiopia, Guinea, Guinea-Bissau, Indonesia, Lao (People's Democratic Republic of), Liberia, Madagascar, Malawi, Mali, Mauritania, Mozambique, Myanmar, Nicaragua, Niger, Nigeria, Rwanda, São Tomé and Príncipe, Sierra Leone, Somalia, Sudan, Tanzania, Uganda, Vietnam, Zambia

Severely Indebted Middle-Income Countries
Argentina, Bolivia, Bosnia and Herzegovina, Brazil, Bulgaria, Ecuador, Gabon, Guyana, Jordan, Peru, Syrian Arab Republic

Note: PV = present value of total debt service; XGS = average exports; GNP = gross national product. Figures in parentheses indicate the total number of countries belonging to that group. Due to the technical nature of the calculation of debt burden indicators, readers are advised to consult the original source for detailed technical explanations.

Source: Compiled from World Bank, *Global Development Finance 2000: Analysis and Summary Tables* (Washington, DC: World Bank, 2002), app. 1, tables A1.1, A1.2, pp. 142, 143.

country has values close to the critical values, a small change in these values could trigger a change in indebtedness classification, even if the economic fundamentals have not changed. This happened with the original classification of highly indebted poor countries (HIPCs) when countries such as Malawi were excluded when in fact their indebtedness did not differ significantly from those on the original list. Malawi was eventually added to the list.

As well, these ratios do not represent an exhaustive set of useful indicators of external indebtedness. For example, they do not necessarily capture the debt-servicing capacity of countries where government budget constraints are key to debt-service difficulties. Member countries of the franc zone of West Africa, which allow the use or free conversion of a foreign currency, can face government budget difficulties related to servicing external public debt but are not necessarily reflected in balance of payments data. For other countries, the servicing of domestic public debt may be a source of fiscal strain not reflected in balance of payments data. Moreover, the fact that the external debt is rising does not necessarily mean that the country is experiencing difficulties with debt servicing. If the debt is being used productively to create wealth, add value, and generate income (productive, not a dead loan) or if the country has otherwise improved its debt-servicing capacity, the increase in the debt may not be associated with payment problems. Therefore, these ratios should be used in the broader context of a country's specific analysis of debt sustainability.

DEBT AND POVERTY

Table 8.1 shows the relationship between poverty and national indebtedness. Of the sixty-one low-income countries, thirty-four of them (or 55.7 percent) are classified as severely indebted, and only nine of them (or 14.7 percent) are less indebted. On the other hand, of the seventy-six middle-income countries, only eleven of them (or 14.5 percent) are classified as severely indebted, and forty-one of them (or 53.9 percent) are classified as less indebted. These findings are not surprising. The poor countries with low or negative economic growth and weak export sectors do not have the capacity to effectively utilize foreign capital, and over time, debts become increasingly burdensome because there is no local capacity to service them.

The combined inability to earn foreign exchange and raise sufficient government revenue through improved economic activities means that these countries are forced to borrow in order to meet basic budgetary requirements. This creates for them a debt–borrow–debt vicious cycle that they cannot break out of. Table 8.1 lists the thirty-four countries that suffer from this debt trap and are classified as severely indebted. They are the least-developed countries, are highly indebted (HIPCs), and belong to the P2 category. Over thirty of them are in sub-Saharan Africa, but all regions of the developing world are represented. They include post-conflict countries such as Vietnam, Rwanda, Liberia, Mozambique, and Ethiopia. They also represent countries that were struggling during the 1980s and 1990s with the implementation of structured adjustment programs (SAPs) and, therefore, needed to borrow heavily to finance macroeconomic and institutional reforms. As was shown in the previous discussion, these are the countries which have not managed to attract and retain high-quality foreign direct investment (FDI). While a number of them are working hard to liberalize their economies—Indonesia, Uganda, Mozambique, Nigeria—the majority remain relatively closed and unable or unwilling to participate fully in the global economy. When world leaders and anti-globalization protesters call for the elimination of the debt burden, they are mainly thinking about these poor countries and their citizens who survive on no more than a couple of dollars a day.

For example, Shridath Ramphal, co-chair of the Commission on Global Governance and former secretary-general of the Commonwealth, blames severe indebtedness on child poverty, ill health, ignorance, and high rates of infant mortality in these countries. More than one-third of children in the heavily indebted poor countries have not been immunized, and about one-half of the people in these countries are illiterate. Others have argued that severe indebtedness for poor countries is associated with poor governance, corruption, lawlessness, and abuse of human rights.[2]

More recently, the relationship between debt and poverty has been extended to transition economies of Central and Eastern Europe. In January 2000, the European Children's Trust issued a report entitled the "Silent Crisis" in which they found that poverty in the region had increased tenfold since the breakup of the Communist system. At least 50 million children were reported to live in "genuine poverty" with about 40 million of them in the former Soviet Union. Overall, 160 million people (or 40 percent of the total population) were thought to live in poverty. As of February 2002, the seven former Soviet Union States of Armenia, Azerbaijan, Georgia, Kyrgyzstan, Meldova, Tajikistan, and Uzbekistan together had a combined government and government guaranteed external debt of more than U.S.$11 billion. The five worst hit—Georgia, Kyrgyztan, Meldova, Armenia, and Tajikistan—had an average ratio of debt to GDP of 73.5 percent. The report blames the state of poverty in Central and Eastern Europe on these countries' growing indebtedness and calls on the international community to help by easing the debt burdens.[3]

Debt and Middle-Income Countries

Globalizing middle-income countries with access to international capital markets have experienced significant increases in their indebtedness. In countries such as Korea, Malaysia, and Thailand, the debt crisis was largely due to fast external liberalization of the financial sector. In other countries such as the Russian Federation and Brazil, the debt problems mainly resulted from the difficulties of raising government revenues enough to reduce the growing government budget deficits. The new international financial context, with its high speed of contagion of crisis from one country or region to another, requires that countries undertake drastic adjustment measures, including sudden large increases in interest rates and currency devaluations. The net effects of all this is a significant lack of policy flexibility by the debtor countries.

As Table 8.1 shows, Indonesia is the only big emerging market (BEM) country listed as a severely indebted low-income country; and Argentina and Brazil are listed as severely indebted middle-income countries. Indonesia, with its large population and relatively low per capita income level, has experienced dramatic deterioration in living standards, resulting in serious political and social disorder. Its debt burden gets worse as its economic growth slows down, exports decline, or terms of trade worsen, and internal strife reduces the capacity to collect government revenues. Macroeconomic stabilization in Indonesia remains incomplete, and economic recovery is still out of reach. The country is yet to address itself sufficiently to firm-level debt problems. Indonesia's case provides a good example of a country where governance problems are related to the persistence of the debt crisis, giving rise to rising levels of unemployment, lost productivity, and deepening poverty.

Brazil suffers from a long-standing fiscal imbalance. The cumulative federal financing gap has been made up by domestic debt. Most of the debt is short term and is on variable interest rates. In November 1998, Brazil signed a three-year standby agreement with the IMF. Still, the government was forced to float its currency—the real—in January 1999. Brazil, unlike Indonesia and Russia, still maintains access to international capital markets. It has arrangements with foreign bank creditors to roll over its short-term credit, and it successfully launched an international sovereign bond issue. Brazil's banking and financial sector is much healthier and is institutionally stronger than that of Indonesia or the Russian Federation.[4]

In the case of the Russian Federation, the biggest challenge is with effective fiscal management. The country suffers from a narrow tax base that is characteristic of developing countries. Like developing countries, the federation also relies heavily on commodity exports, especially oil and gas, for tax revenues. In addition, there are institutional weaknesses in the country's public administration and management, and the net result of all this is that the country does not generate sufficient tax revenue to meet its expenditures. Therefore, it must borrow both internally and externally to make up for the shortfall in revenue. Domestically, the government raises money by issuing bonds through the ministry of finance. In 1989, the government had to raise money on the Eurobond market at increasingly high interest rates. Higher interest rates owing to monetary tightening under an IMF SAP accentuated the domestic debt burden. By August 1998, the government could not meet maturing domestic debt payments and announced a ninety-day moratorium on payment of various debt obligations. A combination of devaluation and default on domestic debt devastated the already weak domestic banking sector, which had invested heavily in government bonds and other debt instruments.

Unlike Brazil, Indonesia, and the Russian Federation, two other BEMs—Korea and Thailand—have had different experiences with the debt crisis. According to the World Bank's classification of 2000, Korea was classified as a less-indebted middle-income country, and Thailand was classified as a moderately indebted middle-income country. Although both experienced the Asian financial crisis and had to borrow large sums of foreign capital to finance the restructuring, they are not severely indebted. For both countries, macroeconomic stability has been largely reestablished, with exchange rates and interest rates falling to more sustainable levels. The economies turned around with positive economic growth. Although debt restructuring at the firm level remains a serious challenge to sustainable broad-based growth, both countries have taken steps to strengthen their banking and financial sectors. As well, their export sectors are performing much better than those of Indonesia or the Russian Federation.[5]

A close look at the debt problems of the low-income countries and the case studies briefly described for the middle-income countries leads to some observations and conclusions. First, as already pointed out, debt and poverty are positively correlated: More low-income countries are categorized as severely indebted than middle-income countries. This may explain the moral indignity associated with debt and globalization. Ordinary citizens find it hard to understand why, during the 1990s, poor countries were transferring more money to the IMF and the World Bank than they were receiving. Nor can they understand why the Paris Club—a group of rich creditor countries—cannot simply write off all bilateral and overseas development assistance (ODA) debt. Second, the evidence suggests that countries are able to reduce the severity of their indebtedness by maintaining good governance, economic growth, liberalization, and openness. Successful globalization increases the country's capacity to sustain indebtedness. A country, like a corporation, can borrow more, but only if it is doing economically well and is well governed so as to retain public confidence, its debt-carrying capacity increases, and the severity of its indebtedness declines or remains the same. This is what happened to the more successful Asian BEMs after the financial crisis.

The third observation is that countries unable to sustain good governance and economic management and those unable or unwilling to effectively liberalize and achieve greater levels of openness suffer from severe indebtedness. Therefore, effective globalization would help these countries to reduce the severity of their indebtedness. Finally, the thirty-four low-income severely indebted countries, including most of the HIPCs for which the World Bank has created special concessionary debt payments arrangements, need special assistance beyond debt repayment in order to significantly and permanently reduce the severity of their indebtedness. For these countries, severe indebtedness is a symptom of deeper structural and institutional problems, which must be addressed simultaneously with any debt relief initiatives. The most effective and nonpatronizing way of assisting these countries in overcoming the severity of their indebtedness is for the international community to work closely and in partnership with them so that they can build up the capacity for good governance, economic management, liberalization, openness, and debt management. If the total indebtedness for each of these countries were to be completely written off without at the same time developing and sustaining any of these capacities, the relief would be, at best, temporary, and sooner or later, they would each find themselves in similar or worse conditions of indebtedness.

DEBT–EQUITY SWAPS

The prolonged debt crisis of developing countries has always been associated with active searches for different strategies for solving the crisis. At the beginning, emphasis was on rescheduling debt payments to give debtor countries more time and to provide them with additional financial resources to meet their current and future obligations. By the mid-1980s, the emphasis shifted from rescheduling debt to finding ways of reducing the debt principal itself. This was particularly critical for the then heavily indebted countries of South America, especially Mexico, Brazil, and Argentina—the most indebted "Big Three." In March 1989, the "Brady Plan" was announced that, among other things, introduced debt–equity swaps aimed at significant reductions in the debt loads of participating developing countries. This section discusses the meaning and purpose of debt–equity swaps and their impact on the debt load and political economies of the participating countries.

Debt–equity swaps, also known as debt–equity conversion, refers to a process or processes by which a debt instrument of a debtor country, denominated in foreign exchange, is converted into an equity investment in that country. For example, if Brazil borrows $100 million from an American bank, the loan can be converted into debt–equity swaps whereby the American bank, or other investors, converts the market value of the loan into equity shares of a Brazilian company.

The process of converting debt into equity varies from country to country. In a simplified form, here are the common steps. To begin with, an investor wishing to invest in a debtor country through the debt–equity swaps submits a proposal to the debtor government. Once the proposal is approved, the investor purchases the debt of that country, often owed to an international bank. The price paid is less than the face value of the debt instrument, calculated to reflect the market expectations concerning the likelihood that the debt will be serviced according to the original schedule. The more severely indebted a country is, the less likely it is to service its debt according to schedule and, therefore, the lower the price the investors pay for the debt–equity swaps. Once the sale is complete, it is presented to the central bank for redemption in the local currency. The central bank pays somewhere between the face value and the secondary market value of the paper. Investors then use these funds to make their investments.

The debt–equity swap programs were popular in the 1990s and were tried in one form or another by many countries, including Argentina, Bolivia, Chile, Colombia, Costa Rica, Jamaica, Mexico, Nigeria, the Philippines, and Yugoslavia. Different countries were attracted to debt–equity programs for different reasons, but the common objectives included reduction of the burden of external debt; stimulating FDI and the flow of technology and skills; encouraging the return of "flight capital," that is, capital held abroad by residents; channeling investment into debtor country priority areas such as export sectors or depressed regions; capturing a part of the discount at which the debtor countries' debt instruments are traded in the secondary market; and supporting the privatization of SOEs.

To maximize the benefits and minimize the costs of debt–equity swaps, debtor countries develop a policy framework and detailed guidelines for their implementation. The guidelines generally define the eligible investors, purpose for the investments, priority sectors or geographical areas for the investments, restrictions on profit remittance and capital repatriation, and requirements for new money inflows. Regarding eligibility, an important issue is whether the debtor country allows nationals and foreigners to participate in the program. In some countries, only foreign investors were allowed to participate; others allowed local residents in order to encourage the repatriation of flight capital. This would be beneficial to African countries where about 70 percent of the region's private capital is estimated to be invested overseas.

Chile and the Philippines allowed participation of their nationals. At first, Mexico restricted participation only to foreigners during the first phase of the program (1986–1987) but opened it up in 1990 to allow both domestic and foreign investors to participate in the auction system. Likewise, Venezuela first allowed only foreigners when it started the program in April 1987 but opened it up to include national investors in March 1989.[6]

In assessing the policy framework for debt–equity swaps, governments consider four factors: additionality, round-tripping, inflationary impact, and discrimination against one's nationals. Additionality relates to the question of whether debt–equity swaps bring in additional investment or simply provide a subsidy to investments that would have been made anyway. Round-tripping refers to the process whereby foreign currency is brought in from outside or purchased from the parallel market in order to acquire foreign debt obligations at a discount, which are subsequently redeemed in local currency and then converted back into foreign currency and taken out of the country. Round-tripping means that the debtor country receives no additional capital investment as a result of the debt–equity swap program. Inflationary impact refers to the fear that redemption of the debt instrument in local currency would lead to a significant increase in the supply of money and create inflationary pressures in the debtor country's domestic economy. Finally, there are the constitutional, legal, political, and moral questions of developing a national program that benefits or subsidizes foreigners but excludes one's own fellow citizens.

Several participating countries stipulated that investments could not be entirely financed through debt–equity swaps. Argentina, for example, required that 30 percent of the total investment cost had to be in the form of new money. Until 1987, the requirement was that a swap had to be matched dollar for dollar by new money. In Mexico, swaps could only be used to finance up to one-half of the price where public assets were being privatized. In Peru, only 70 percent of the local cost of a project could be funded with swap proceeds. The Philippines had varying new money requirements ranging from 0–60 percent depending on the priority attached to the investment project and the fees paid to the central bank. In Venezuela, a maximum of 30 percent of a project could be financed through a swap, except for investments in tourism where the maximum was 60 percent. These various stipulations clearly show that debt–equity swaps have adequate flexibility to allow each debtor country to design a program most appropriate for its debt reduction and capital investment policy framework.

What was the impact of the debt–equity swap programs for the various macroeconomic indicators of the participating countries? The results, as they relate to debt reduction, FDI, return on flight capital, impact on balance of payments, and privatization, are discussed in the following paragraphs. These variables were selected for review because of their importance to macroeconomic stability and growth, especially for globalizing countries. As a group, they represent the component elements of a policy framework that a debtor country could use to manage and reduce its indebtedness and to stimulate macroeconomic investment and growth.

The extent to which debt–equity swaps contributed significantly to debt reduction varied from country to country. In the case of Brazil and Mexico, swaps yielded relatively small debt reductions amounting to about U.S.$9.5 billion and U.S.$4.1 billion, respectively. However, for Chile, the reductions were more significant. The difference is due to the different priorities given to the debt–equity swaps as a policy instrument for debt reduction. Chile stood out as the only country where the reduction of debt was assigned the highest priority in implementing its debt–equity swap program. This shows that the debt–equity swaps can significantly reduce the national debt if given high priority by the debtor country.

Debt–equity swap programs can also contribute to FDI inflows for the debtor country. A 1993 U.N. report investigating the affects of debt–equity swaps in Brazil, Chile, Mexico, and the Philippines concluded that debt–equity swaps were a significant vehicle for FDI, accounting for from one-fifth to four-fifths of total flows. However, the net contribution to FDI varied widely across countries.[7] Table 8.2 provides summary statistics of the effects of debt–equity swaps for the Philippines and four South American countries. The debt–equity swaps contributions as a percentage of total FDI for the period 1985–1989 ranged from a low of 20 percent to a high of 80 percent. Once again, Chile

TABLE 8.2
The Effects of Debt–Equity Swaps on Foreign Direct Investment
(Millions of Dollars)

	Total foreign direct investment inflow		FDI through debt–equity	FDI through debt–equity swaps as a percentage
Country	1980–1984	1985–1989	Swaps 1985–1989	Total FDI 1985–1989
Argentina	2,195	3,66	731	20
Brazil	10,499	7,687	4,529	59
Chile	1,210	3,947	3,160	80
Mexico	7,497	10,098	3,052	30
Philippines	196	2,306	473	21

Source: United Nations, _Debt–Equity Swaps and Development_ (New York: United Nations, 1993), table 1.3, p. 3.

seems to have benefited most from the debt–equity swap program's contribution to the country's inflow of FDI. Brazil came in second with 59 percent, but Table 8.2 shows the country's total FDI inflow fell from more than U.S.$10 billion during the 1980–1984 period to just more than U.S.$7 billion during 1985–1989. It has been suggested that if it were not for the debt–equity swap program, Brazil would have suffered a bigger decline in FDI inflow than it did in the late 1980s.

The findings relating to the positive contributions of debt–equity swaps to FDI for participating countries are relevant for newly globalizing indebted developing countries. These countries need policy instruments that help them reduce their indebtedness as well as attract and retain FDI. Therefore, debt–equity swaps or variations thereof could provide the basis for the development of a policy framework that could address the twin problems of debt and shortage of FDI.

Debt–equity swaps were also attractive to participating countries because of their promise to reverse flight capital. In countries where both foreigners and local residents were allowed to participate, the program provided opportunities for the repatriation of capital. Available evidence suggests that this indeed was the case in Chile and Argentina. Between 1985 and 1990, nationals accounted for 29 percent of total debt–equity swaps in Chile. In the Philippines, nationals accounted for 45 percent of authorized debt–equity swaps. The government of Chile responded to the threats of round-tripping by controlling the volume of debt–equity swaps held by nationals and by closely monitoring the parallel exchange rate. In 1988, for example, the gap between the official and the parallel rates widened, and the central bank responded by scaling back the quota for nationals and by temporarily suspending the auctions. As well, local residents were given more incentives to hold on to their investments and to discourage round-tripping. Likewise, the government of the Philippines instituted various administrative procedures to control round-tripping and to keep the investments made by Filipino investors in the country.

The lessons from Chile and the Philippines are potentially useful for indebted newly globalizing countries with significant investment capital held abroad by nationals. There are many developing countries whose nationals have decided to export their investment capital abroad. This includes countries with a history of political conflicts, poor governance, high-level corruption, parallel exchange rates, and those with extensive rich natural resources such as oil and gas, diamonds, wildlife, and other easy to smuggle exports. In fact, both Chile and the Philippines needed to attract capital back home because they each had a period in their history when they experienced heavy losses due to flight capital as a result of internal political conflicts. Many post-conflict countries in Africa, Asia, Eastern Europe, and South America can draw lessons from the debt–equity swap programs and begin to attract capital back home. Countries that could benefit from a deliberate policy of return of flight capital include Nigeria, Colombia, South Africa, Sierra Leone, Angola, Uganda, Vietnam, Sri Lanka, China, and the Democratic Republic of the Congo.

Because most newly globalizing developing countries are always concerned about balance of payments, it is important to examine the impact of a particular debt–equity swap program on the country's balance of payments. In theory, one would expect both positive and negative effects. On the positive side, savings in interest and amortization on debt liquidated through swaps could make a big difference to the capital account. Return of flight capital is also positive. If the program is used to boost exports, that too has a positive impact on balance of payments. On the negative side, however, swap-financed investments may lead to future claims on foreign exchange for the repatriation of profits, dividends, and capital. This may be compounded by purchases on the parallel market for round-tripping. These variables together interact differently in different countries to produce the net effects on balance of payments. Therefore, each country must study its own particular circumstances and develop a program that maximizes the positive impact on its foreign exchange reserves. The evidence from Brazil, Chile, and Mexico suggests that, on the whole, debt–equity swaps have positive effects on the country's balance of payments situation. Argentina, faced with a contracting economy and serious balance of payments problems, decided to use debt–equity swaps to manage its external debt problems. In November 2001, the Emerging Markets Creditors Association, formed the previous year to give foreign bondholders more bargaining power, threatened to take legal action against the government of Argentina's debt–equity swap operations on behalf of foreign creditors.

The privatization of SOEs is a major issue for practically all globalizing developing countries and transition economies. The debt–equity swap programs were attractive to participating countries, in part, because they were expected to facilitate the process of privatization. It should be noted that once a government has accepted privatization as part of its overall macroeconomic reform program it has many options by which the privatization of its assets could be implemented. Debt–equity swaps are just one among many different options. Where nationals are allowed to participate in the swap program, privatization becomes politically easier to sell domestically because of local participation and ownership. On the other hand, the swap program may be criticized for subsidizing foreigners when they are buying national assets. However, from a financial point of view, debt–equity swap programs merit serious consideration as a tool for privatization of ailing SOEs. This is particularly important for severely indebted countries facing serious budgetary constraints.

In summary, debt–equity swap programs provide useful lessons of experience for today's severely indebted developing countries and transition economies. When used as a tool within the broader policy framework of macroeconomic reform and management, they make several positive contributions to the country's financial situation. As expected, debt–equity swap programs reduce the country's debt load, but they also attract FDI and flight capital back home. With additional capital investment, the country can finance economic development, achieve higher levels of economic growth, and increase exports, thereby enhancing its capacity to sustain debt. As well, the debt–equity swap programs, overall, have positive effects on the country's balance of payments situation, and they help with the financing of the privatization of SOEs. Although debt–equity swap programs were popular more than ten years ago, the basic lessons of experience are still useful for today's severely indebted newly globalizing developing countries and transition economies.

The HIPC Initiative

During the 1980s and 1990s, debt problems and debt relief for developing countries became one of the most controversial and emotionally charged issues in international relations and the debate against globalization. Several initiatives were, therefore, undertaken at the national and multilateral levels and by international financial institutions to find solutions to the debt problems. In addition to the Paris Club, the individual creditor countries of Europe, North America, and Japan developed various strategies aimed at reducing the debt burden of the developing countries.[8] The key issue was whether these initiatives should be aimed at debt relief or whether debt for the least-developed countries should be completely cancelled. The fight for cancellation of debt was lead by, among others, Ann Pettifor, director of Jubilee 2000/UK; Archbishop Oscar Rodriguez of Honduras; and the president of the AFL-CIO, John Sweeney, as well as other labor and environmental movements. They put tremendous pressure on the international community to act quickly and find meaningful solutions for the poor debtor countries.[9]

In 1996, in response to these and other pressures, the World Bank and the IMF introduced the HIPC debt initiative. The purpose of this initiative was to reduce the debt of the HIPCs to sustainable levels and to renew their prospects for growth and to free up resources for poverty alleviation and social development. Only the poorest countries, those which are eligible for highly concessional assistance from the International Development Association—the part of the World Bank that lends on highly concessional terms—and from the IMF's Poverty Reduction and Growth Facility (previously the Enhanced Structural Adjustment Facility) qualify for the HIPC initiative. Also, poor countries qualify if they still face unsustainable debt situations even after the full application of traditional debt relief mechanisms such as the Paris Club agreement. As is often the case with the World Bank and the IMF, there were conditions attached to the initiative. Specifically, to be eligible, countries had to undertake sustained implementation of integrated poverty reduction and economic reform programs. Although the idea of debt cancellation was rejected, the link between debt relief, poverty alleviation, and economic liberation and management provides a sound long-term approach to debt and development. This was the first comprehensive approach to reduce the external debt of the world's poorest, most heavily indebted countries, and it represented an important step forward in placing debt relief within an overall framework of poverty reduction and social development.

In its initial phases of implementation, the HIPC initiative was slow, complex, and ineffective. A 1999 U.N. report reviewed the initiative and concluded, "The debt 'hangover' of many developing countries, and particularly of the heavily indebted poor countries (HIPCs) has not been resolved, despite important and significant measures and initiatives adopted by creditors at the national or multilateral levels."[10] In response, the World Bank and the IMF, in consultation with creditors, debtor countries, and various pressure groups, have revised and modified the initial proposal several times over. Most of the new provisions of the enhanced HIPC initiative relate to how and when countries become eligible, methods used to calculate a country's debt sustainability, coordination among all creditors, and the creation of the HIPC Trust Fund. The changes were designed to make it easier for countries to qualify, to increase the amount of debt relief they receive, and to ensure that additional revenues are channeled toward poverty reduction and social services. The HIPC Trust Fund was created to ensure that funds are made available for the World Bank and the IMF to meet their cost of the HIPC initiative.

Frustrated by the lack of progress, the Executive Committee on Economic and Social Affairs of the United Nations made proposals for an enhanced initiative on HIPC debt relief. Exhibit 8.1 provides a summary of the main recommendations by the United Nations. In addition to making it easier and faster for countries to qualify, these proposals also call for cancellation of ODA debt for HIPCs; increasing ODA (aid) to these countries; more involvement and collaboration with debtor countries, NGOs, and the private sector; and sale of IMF gold to finance debt relief.

Exhibit 8.1
U.N. Proposals for an Enhanced Initiative on HIPC Debt Relief

- Review the list of HIPCs in order to ensure that all poor countries facing debt-servicing difficulties will be considered under the initiative.

- Shorten the time frame for implementation to three years so that final debt relief can be provided after the first track record of three years of Enhanced Structural Adjustment Facility programs.

- Apply less restrictive eligibility criteria, notably by reducing the thresholds of debt-to-exports and debt-service-to-exports ratios. (Be guided by the fact that over the recent period 1990–1997, HIPCs were able to service debt, on average, for up to 18 percent of their exports and that their nominal debt stock, excluding payments arrears, was still equivalent to 300 percent of

exports.) For certain countries facing very severe foreign equivalent exchange constraints, the thresholds could be lower than
the general eligibility level. The aim should be to provide a real
exit from debt rescheduling.

- Set a ceiling for the share of fiscal revenue allocated to external
  debt service and provide additional debt reduction if necessary
  to meet the benchmark. Twenty-five percent of fiscal revenue
  allocated to external debt service is an excessive burden for
  HIPCs.

- Cancel HIPCs' ODA debts and extend at least 80 percent debt
  reduction on other official bilateral debts to all HIPCs; consider
  full cancellation of bilateral official debts for post-conflict
  countries, countries affected by serious natural disasters, and
  countries with very low social and human development indicators. Paris Club debt eligible for reduction should also include post-cutoff-date debt.

- Provide full funding of the initiative through partial sales of IMF
  gold, a new general allocation of special drawing rights and additional bilateral contributions to multilateral trust funds for
  debt relief.

- Take steps to reverse the current trend of declining ODA and
  budget new aid funds for social and human development projects and poverty reduction and adopt procedures to release resources for HIPC relief without impinging on regular ODA
  budgets; debt relief should not be given at the expense of ODA.

- Provide a link between debt relief and poverty reduction, with
  debtor countries determining their own national priorities. In this
  respect, increase collaboration with NGOs and the private sector
  to raise funds for debt relief and development projects in HIPCs.

Source: United Nations, "Finding Solutions to the Debt Problems of Developing
Countries," Report of the Executive Committee on Economic and Social Affairs
(New York: United Nations, May 20, 1999), 23.

HIPC Initiative: Progress at the Millennium Year

How much debt relief has been achieved through the HIPC initiative and other measures? To address this question, I chose the year 2000 to review what has been achieved so
far for two reasons: First, it is almost fifteen years since the initial HIPC proposal was made
in the fall of 1986. Second, it marks the end and the beginning of a new decade, century, and
millennium. This makes it symbolically important, but it also provides a baseline for future

performance of this or other debt relief initiatives. Data for the year 2000 should be compared in the future with achievements in the year 2010 and 2020 to assess the long-term impact of current debt relief initiatives. Since indebtedness is a long-term problem, it must be addressed by long-term strategies, and these must be assessed on a long-term basis.

On December 22, 2000, Horst Kohler, managing director of the IMF, and James D. Wolfensohn, president of the World Bank Group, issued a joint statement in Washington, DC, about milestones achieved for debt relief for the poorest countries. It was then announced that twenty-two countries, eighteen of them in Africa, were approved as eligible for HIPC assistance. The total amount of debt relief for these countries was estimated at U.S. $34 billion—an average of U.S. $1.54 billion per country. These countries were expected to see their foreign debt reduced by almost one-half on average, and combined with other debt relief programs such as the Paris Club of creditor countries, the approved countries were expected to see their debtors fall, on average, by about two-thirds. It was also reported that while facing serious challenges such as the AIDS epidemic the twenty-two countries have committed themselves to continuing economic reform and to applying the debt relief resources to poverty reduction and investments in social and human development. The World Bank–IMF statement also pledged to continue to work hard to increase the number of eligible poor countries and called on the international community, especially the creditors, to support the HIPC initiative and for donor countries to increase their ODA levels.

Figure 8.1 provides a status report of the grouping of the heavily indebted poor countries as of the end of 2000. Of the forty-one designated HIPC countries, thirty-seven carried officially unsustainable debt burdens and only four—Angola, Kenya, Vietnam, and Yemen— were classified as sustainable cases. This means that at the beginning of the new millennium almost all of the world's poorest countries were carrying debt loads for which they had no means by which to meet their debt obligations. As pointed out earlier, these are the same countries experiencing difficulties in terms of gainful participation in globalization.

Of the thirty-seven unsustainable cases listed in Figure 8.1, twenty-two countries were approved to receive HIPC assistance, thirteen were waiting approval, and two—Ghana and the People's Republic of Lao—decided not to seek debt relief. This includes the conflict-affected countries such as Burundi, Myanmar, Sierra Leone, Sudan, and the Democratic Republic of the Congo, whose internal governance and economic management systems make it hard for them to meet the HIPC eligibility criteria. If it took almost fifteen years for the World Bank–IMF to approve HIPC assistance for twenty-two of the relatively easier countries, how long will it take to approve the remaining fifteen hard cases to approve?

In November 2001, the World Bank and the IMF agreed to U.S. $3 billion in debt relief for Tanzania under the HIPC initiative. This followed similar debt relief for Bolivia, Mozambique, and Uganda. These initiatives reduced the external debts for Mozambique by 73 percent and by 54 percent for Tanzania. According to the World Bank projections, Tanzania's debt obligations as a percentage of government revenue would decline from 19 percent in 2001 to about 7.7 percent in 2011.[11]

It is also important to examine in some detail the actual benefits of the twenty-two approved countries from the HIPC initiative. Table 8.3 provides data for each of the twenty-two countries in terms of net present value (NPV) debt reduction and nominal debt service relief. The total committed debt relief for the twenty-two countries is more than U.S. $20

FIGURE 8.1

Grouping of the Heavily Indebted Poor Countries (Status as of the End of December 2000)

41 HIPC Countries

Angola*	Central African Republic*	Democratic Republic of the Congo*	Guinea-Bissau*	Lao, People's Democratic Republic of	Mozambique	São Tomé and Príncipe
Benin	Chad	Gambia, The	Guyana	Malawi	Myanmar*	Sierra Leone*
Bolivia	Congo*	Ghana	Honduras	Mali	Nicaragua	Somalia*
Burkina Faso	Côte d'Ivoire	Guinea	Kenya	Mauritania	Niger	Sudan*
Burundi*	Ethiopia**		Liberia*		Rwanda*	Tanzania
Cameroon			Madagascar		Senegal	Togo
						Uganda
						Vietnam
						Yemen
						Zambia

4 Sustainable Cases[1]

Angola
Kenya
Vietnam
Yemen

37 Unsustainable Cases

Benin	Côte d'Ivoire	Guinea-Bissau	Lao, People's Democratic Republic of	Myanmar	Senegal
Bolivia	Central African Republic	Guyana	Liberia	Nicaragua	Sierra Leone
Burkina Faso	Democratic Republic of the Congo	Honduras	Mauritania	Niger	Somalia
Burundi	Gambia, The	Madagascar	Mozambique	Rwanda	Sudan
Cameroon	Ghana	Malawi		São Tomé and Príncipe	Tanzania
Chad	Ethiopia	Mali			Togo
					Uganda
					Zambia

22 Decision Point Countries through End of 2000[2]

Benin	Honduras	Rwanda
Bolivia	Madagascar	Senegal
Burkina Faso	Malawi	São Tomé and Príncipe
Burundi	Mali	Tanzania
Cameroon	Mauritania	Uganda
Chad	Mozambique	Zambia
	Nicaragua	
	Niger	

Post-2000 Decision Point Countries

Conflict Affected (9)

Burundi
Central African Republic
Democratic Republic of the Congo
Congo
Liberia
Myanmar
Sierra Leone
Somalia
Sudan

Others (4)

Chad
Côte d'Ivoire
Ethiopia**
Togo

At Government Request not Seeking Debt Relief

Ghana
Lao, People's Democratic Republic of

*Conflict affected.

**Cessation of hostilities signed on June 18, 2000. A peace agreement was signed with Eritrea on December 12, 2000.

[1]These countries are expected to achieve debt sustainability after receiving debt relief provided under traditional mechanisms.

[2]Countries that reached their decision points under the original HIPC framework (that is, prior to the endorsement of the enhanced HIPC framework during the annual meetings of the World Bank and IMF in September 1999).

Source: World Bank Web site: www.worldbank.org.

TABLE 8.3
Debt Relief Committed under the Enhanced HIPC Initiative
(Status as of the End of December 2000—in billions of U.S. Dollars)

Country	NPV Debt Reduction		Nominal Debt Sevice Relief [3]
	Committed Debt Relief	Percentage Reduction [1,2]	
TOTAL	20.3	47 [4]	33.6
AFRICAN COUNTRIES	14.6	46 [4]	25.1
Benin	0.3	31	0.5
Burkina Faso	0.4	46	0.7
Cameroon	1.3	27	2.0
Gambia	0.1	27	0.1
Guinea	0.5	32	0.8
Guinea-Bissau	0.4	85	0.8
Madagascar	0.8	40	1.5
Malawi	0.6	44	1.0
Mali	0.5	37	0.9
Mauritania	0.6	50	1.1
Mozambique	2.0	72	4.3
Niger	0.5	54	0.9
Rwanda	0.5	71	0.8
São Tomé and Príncipe	0.1	83	0.2
Senegal	0.5	19	0.9
Tanzania	2.0	53	3.0
Uganda	1.0	48	2.0
Zambia	2.5	63	3.8
LATIN AMERICAN COUNTRIES	5.7	49 [4]	8.5
Bolivia	1.3	45	2.1
Guyana	0.6	54	1.0
Honduras	0.6	18	0.9
Nicaragua	3.3	72	4.5

[1]Calculated on the basis of NPVs of debt and assistance committed.

[2]Cumulative reduction, including traditional debt relief, is estimated at about two-thirds.

[3]Estimates based on HIPC initiative assistance in NPV as approved by the executive boards of the IMF and the World Bank.

[4]Weighted average based on debt stocks in NPV terms.

Source: World Bank and IMF staff estimate.

billion or a weighted average of 47 percent. Nicaragua benefits the most with a debt reduction of U.S.$3.3 billion or 72 percent, and Senegal benefits the least with a reduction of
only U.S.$0.5 billion or 19 percent. While these sums look rather small, they are relatively
significant for these poor countries. For example, Mozambique's committed debt relief is

U.S.$2.0 billion. In 1998, that country's GNP was estimated at U.S.$3.6 billion; therefore, the debt relief is more than 55 percent of annual GNP. Moreover, all the relief is in foreign exchange, which impacs directly on the country's foreign reserves and its capacity to finance imports for economic and social development.

In summary, some progress has been made both quantitatively and qualitatively. In quantitative terms, more HIPC countries have been approved for assistance from only four in 1997 to twenty-two by the end of 2000—a more than fivefold increase. This has translated into more debt relief to the tune of almost U.S.$35 billion, thus making more money available to those countries to finance economic reform, poverty alleviation, human and social development. Eligible rules have been simplified and relaxed to make it easier for countries to qualify for HIPC assistance. Through the HIPC Trust Fund, more money has been made available for the World Bank–IMF to meet the current and future costs of HIPC debt relief and assistance. More creditors are actively involved in debt relief initiatives of their own similar to the HIPC initiative of the Paris Club agreement.

Qualitatively, progress has been made by making the debt problems of developing countries everybody's problem and a top priority on the global agenda. The persistent work of the United Nations and its specialized agencies such as UNICEF and the UNDP, international NGOs, religious leaders in both the north and the south, trade union and environmental movements, and other anti-globalization protesters have made a significant qualitative difference. They have forced creditor nations and the international financial institutions to pay more attention to the debt problem of poor countries. These pressures are likely to continue partly because the calls for debt cancellation have not been heeded and partly because the poorest countries are likely to remain heavily indebted. The international financial community, including the IMF, supports the development of a global bankruptcy plan to protect heavily indebted countries along the lines of the U.S. Chapter 11 bankruptcy protection framework.

In the long run, the full impact of the HIPC initiative will depend on each country's capacity not only to manage debt but, more important, to develop and sustain good governance, economic reform and management, and effective integration into the global economy. Heavy indebtedness is simply a symptom of deeper structural and systemic problems. Only those countries able and willing to overcome these problems will, in the long run, remain less heavily indebted.

Domestic Debt

Like the HIPC initiative, most of the concerns about developing countries' indebtedness focuses on the external debt and pays little or no attention to the domestic debt. This bias, though not warranted, is easy to understand. Focusing on the external debt puts pressure on the creditors who are mainly the rich donor countries, global corporations, or international financial institutions. For example, the "Dump the Debt" campaign, calling for the cancellation of debt owed by the poor countries, targets the Western creditors as the villains and the debtor countries as the victims. The external debt receives more attention because it has wider and more obvious implications for international capital flows and the debtor country's ability to pay for imported goods and services needed for development. External debt is often associated with conditions imposed by outsiders, and so it evokes resentment and nationalist sentiments within the debtor country. Finally, focusing on the external debt deflects attention away from the domestic debt and debtor country's internal fiscal and monetary management problems or lack of economic discipline and accountability.

To provide a balanced approach, I will briefly discuss domestic debt: what it is, its importance for the domestic economy, why it has been going up for most of the poor indebted countries, and the need to take an integrated approach to understanding and managing the national debt.

Public domestic debt is the debt a government incurs through borrowing in its own currency from residents of its own country. To obtain a consolidated public national debt, the definition includes not only central government debt but also debt owed by local and municipal governments, SOEs, and agencies and institutions whose borrowing is guaranteed by the central government. The domestic debt, unlike foreign debt, does not increase new resources available for development; rather, it is a tool for the transfer of resources from the private to the public sector within a country. The only time when the domestic debt contributes to the total resource pool is when foreign investors buy government securities in the local currency. In that case, government obligations to the foreign investor is in its local currency. Governments use a number of instruments to borrow in the domestic economy. These include treasury bills, government notes and bonds, loans, promissory notes, overdrafts or advances from the central bank, and savings certificates. Domestic creditors to governments are typically the central bank, the commercial banks, financial institutions such as insurance and trust companies, pension and provident funds, private companies, and individuals.[12]

Excessive government borrowing is bad for the economy because the debt burden can slow down the economy and lead to inefficient distribution and utilization of resources between the major sectors of the economy. If the cost of servicing the debt is a big part of the budget, as is the case with many heavily indebted countries, this leaves little flexibility to finance development and social services. Government borrowing may also crowd out the private sector so that resources are limited for the productive sector of the economy. By borrowing excessively from the central bank—basically printing money—the government can unleash inflationary pressures, which may later become difficult to control. Public debt also constitutes a mortgage or financial obligation on future generations who must pay higher taxes in order to meet debt obligations as they fall due. Excessive domestic debt can also negatively affect a country's credit rating, raise interest rates, and make it more expensive to borrow in the domestic market. In the extreme case, unsustainable debt levels can precipitate an economic crisis. For these reasons, debtor countries must be concerned about both external and domestic debt—they both have consequences.

For most developing countries, there is an intimate relationship between external indebtedness and domestic debt. The external debt crisis is one reason why domestic debt has been growing for the debtor countries. Debtor governments have had to squeeze domestic demand in order to generate surpluses on the current account of the balance of payments in order to service large external debts. This reduces income levels in the form of wages and profits and lower tax revenues. Many have structural problems in their tax collection systems, and as they liberalize the economy, they may have to pay higher interests rates to service the domestic debt. With many loss-making SOEs, government financial obligations increase, and when revenues are low, the only option is to borrow domestically. As was shown in the list of HIPC countries, about one-third of these countries experience internal or regional conflict or are just emerging out of such conflicts. These conflicts are costly and force governments into deficit spending and excessive borrowing. Once again, we see the relationship between indebtedness, foreign or domestic, and the quality of governance and economic management of the debtor country.

To avoid excessive domestic borrowing, the government must have the human capital and institutional capacity for domestic debt management. Most indebted developing countries lack both. As well, unlike developed countries, developing countries do not have fully developed domestic financial markets. Where financial markets are underdeveloped, the instruments for both debt management and monetary control are primitive. There is always conflict between borrowing cheaply for the government and keeping inflation down. Yet, for most developing countries, these two potentially conflicting functions of debt management and monetary policy are institutionally under the control of the central bank.

To optimize the objectives of debt management and monetary policy, the government must develop an institutional capacity to coordinate the two. Because these countries operate in an environment of unstable budgets and inflationary pressures on undeveloped financial markets, both debt management and monetary policy must also support the common objectives of stabilization and market development. Specifically, domestic debt management must take on an integrated approach. In addition to selling government debt, it must also be concerned with the liquidity needs of the economy, control of inflationary pressures, the development of money and capital markets, protecting the interests of the private sector in terms of its access to credit, encouraging domestic saving, and harmonizing the relationship between foreign and domestic debt. Heavily indebted countries cannot become debt free or less indebted until they have developed and can sustain the human capital and institutional capacity for debt management within the broader context of macroeconomic reform and management. Those interested in debt relief should also be interested in making sure that the debtor countries they assist with reducing indebtedness are also assisted to develop and sustaining the competencies and capacities for integrated debt management.

CAPACITY DEVELOPMENT FOR DEBT MANAGEMENT

By now, it is quite clear that the widely published international initiatives of debt relief are necessary but not sufficient to solve the debt problems of developing countries and transition economies. What each of these countries needs, in addition, is the development of a national debt management institutional capacity that enables them to deal with their debt problems, systematically taking an integrated and long-term perspective for maintaining sustainable debt levels.

Table 8.4 identifies the key functions and related competencies which a newly globalizing developing country and transition economy would need to develop and maintain a national system of effective debt management. The seven functions identified in the table are managerial, technical, administrative, and professional. They are based on the

TABLE 8.4
Key Functions and Competencies for Debt Management

Functions	Related Competencies
Debt Policy Formulation	• Formulate debt management strategy and objectives; decide on volume, type of instruments, timing, frequency, and selling techniques; develop benchmark debt structure. • Integrate debt management into the country's macroeconomic strategy.
Planning Fiscal Requirements	• Make projections of government borrowing requirements in the context of fiscal and monetary targets and debt sustainability.
Development of Markets for Government Securities	• Develop primary market organization (new issues), organize distribution channels and selling procedures, supervise operations. • Including auctions, subscriptions, and so on maintain close contacts with the market. • Develop secondary market organizations, actively manage secondary sales of government's outstanding portfolio, develop these markets, maintain contacts, intervene in markets, encourage dealing and dealer system. • Manage issuance/redemption by providing administration of new and old issues, for example, delivery and redemption of issues.
Assess Debt Sustainability	• Review the theory, current practices, and models of assessment of debt sustainability. Simulate economy using various models. Compare with the World Bank–IMF methodology. • Choose method of assessing debt sustainability most appropriate for the country and link debt sustainability to budget deficit, interest rates, and growth rates. Use judgment or rules of thumb to define debt sustainability. • Advise on how to avoid persistent fiscal deficits, and how to deal with a debt hangover.
Coordination, Administration, and Accounting	• Ensure effective coordination between debt and monetary management: department of finance, central bank and accounts general's office. • Maintain an accounting system for debt operations, manage administrative systems for debt holders and stock, servicing of government debt, maintaining a register of all government debt instruments.
Establish and Maintain Debt Management Information Systems	• Digitize the national debt management information systems. • Establish efficient payments systems, trading procedures, and smooth clearing and settlement systems.
Undertake Human and Institutional Development	• Set up and maintain an appropriate institutional structure, including debt review committees, to ensure proper coordination of fiscal, monetary, and debt management operations. • Create a knowledge-based learning organizational environment. • Establish and maintain learning and training opportunities for management and staff at the central bank, ministry of finance, and contractual service organizations (captive funds), or external/domestic debt management portfolio. • Management, debt issues, marketing and sales management. • Provide competitive compensation and incentives to all staff and management to ensure human resource retention and development.

Source: Compiled in part from Commonwealth Secretariat, *Effective Domestic Debt Management in Developing Countries* (London: Legal Advisory Services Division, Commonwealth Secretariat, March 1999).

assumption that the country has in place or is in the process of developing corresponding governance systems with effective executive political leadership with sound legal and administrative systems, including a national integrity and regulatory system as discussed in Chapter 2.

The managerial functions required for the development of an effective debt management capacity include institutional development, policy formulation, coordination, supervision, and networking. In cases in which they do not already exist, new institutional arrangements such as a debt management unit, a joint monetary and debt management coordination committee, and securities marketing organizations may have to be established. The newly created debt management organizations must be accorded proper authority and adequate resources to attract and retain competent staff and to discharge their responsibilities including providing high-level advice to government. It is also important to ensure that these new organizations do not operate in isolation but are institutionally, managerially, and operationally coordinated with other institutions within the ministry of finance, the central bank, and other central agencies such as the accounts general's office, the legislature, and the executive branches of government. This requires, among other things, staffing senior positions with highly qualified and widely respected nationals.

Table 8.4 also shows that debt management is highly technical and requires qualified and experience professionals. Some of the critical areas of competencies include macroeconomics with specialization in budgeting, taxation, and public finance; quantitative skills including modeling and simulation; accounting; business and public administration including corporate finance and marketing and sales management; computer science including programming, software development, and systems operation and maintenance; and human resource management including institutional analysis and development, change management, learning, training and development, and motivation and compensation management. It is also important for the debt management institutional infrastructure to have middle- and lower-level staff capable of providing technical and administrative support in a professional and computerized environment. Important areas of support include data collection and analysis, records management, library and Internet research, reports and publications, computer systems maintenance and upgrading, and administrative and secretarial services.

Very few heavily indebted countries would have the required mix and level of competencies for effective debt management. Therefore, the international community must help by providing technical assistance and other forms of capacity development. Donor countries could work together in partnership with the government and the private sector to develop and implement a debt management improvement strategy. The international financial institutions have the expertise and obligation to help the newly globalizing developing countries develop and maintain debt management competencies and institutional capacities to achieve sustainable debt levels. International NGOs should also become actively involved. In fact, it would be highly commendable if organizations such as Jubilee 2000 would channel some of their efforts and resources into assisting heavily indebted poor countries build and sustain their debt management institutional capacities as part of the overall global strategy for solving their debt problems.

Debt Management and the Computer

Debt management is essentially about managing data and information. A major part of the responsibility involves data collection, analysis, communication, storage, retrieval, and updating and maintaining an institutional corporate memory. Data must be transformed into information, knowledge, insight, wisdom, advice, and informed policy formulation and implementation. The best way of managing data and information is to use the computer and to digitize as much of the information as possible. In an earlier chapter, I discussed how managers can draw on the organization's digital nervous system to develop innovative solutions to old problems. It is, therefore, imperative that the proposed debt management organization must work in a computerized, digitized, Internet-connected environment to be effective. Since most countries will be building their debt management units from scratch, it may be easier to establish a computerized environment than work with already established units in the public sector.

Exhibit 8.2 provides a brief description of an international initiative designed to improve debt management by using standardized computer software. The computerized debt Recording and Management System handles both domestic and external debt, generates forecasts, produces reports, helps managers in their formulation of debt management advice and policy recommendations, and has built-in capacity for upgrading and modifications. This system provides a useful start towards the development of a totally digitized debt management environment, which should be the ultimate objective for any effective debt management organization for debtor countries.

EXHIBIT 8.2
Effective Debt Management Using Computer Software

Over the years, the Economic and Legal Advisory Service Division of the Commonwealth Secretariat has made considerable efforts to improve debt management capacity in member countries. The program of assistance comprises policy advice for debt management and technical assistance through the provision of the in-house developed Commonwealth Secretariat Debt Recording and Management System (CS-DRMS) software, which includes both external and domestic debt modules. The software has become a model of good practice in debt management and is in use at more than seventy sites in forty-nine countries, including seven outside the Commonwealth.

The domestic debt module in the system allows users/countries to record various instruments of domestic borrowing: standard loans, Treasury Bills, Treasury Bonds, government stocks and savings, and deposit certificates. The system is able to generate forecasts of debt service, monitor arrears, and assist in guiding debt policies including borrowing strategies. The software provides useful domestic debt reports to guide economic managers in decision making. Over the years, however, there have been major developments in domestic debt markets encompassing a new range of debt instruments, including those for specifically targeting different types of investors—retailers and wholesalers—instruments to diversify the maturity structure of domestic debt, and facilities to promote secondary trading of debt instruments. As markets become sophisticated, new systems need to be introduced that can assist in formulating dynamic benchmark debt portfolios, transforming them through numerous debt management techniques. The CS-DRMS was modernized. CS-DRMS 2000+ has greatly enhanced functionality in the area of domestic debt management.

Source: Commonwealth Secretariat, *Effective Domestic Debt Management in Developing Countries* (London: Legal Advisory Services Division, Commonwealth Secretariat, March 1999), box 5, p. 33.

In summary, there are three aspects to the debt problems facing developing countries and transition economies: street demonstrations, debt relief, and capacity development for debt management. During the 1980s, and increasingly the 1990s, Western efforts have focuses on the first two. Although street demonstrations and international campaigns have succeeded in keeping the debt problems of the poorest countries on top of the international community's agenda, they have not been able to persuade Western creditors to completely cancel these countries' debts. Moreover, total debt cancellation may have been used as a pressure tactic rather than a realistic goal. Initiatives by the Paris Club members and the World Bank–IMF HIPC Initiative have combined to reduce the debt load of developing countries by about U.S. $50 billion, but more remains to be done. By the end of 2000, only twenty-two countries out of the forty-one designated HIPCs had qualified for HIPC assistance. Moreover, these two strategies—street demonstration and debt relief—are short-term solutions, not unlike the moral equivalent of giving people a meal instead of teaching them how to fish. While focusing on reducing these countries' stock of debt, they have done little to prepare them to take care of their future debt problems.

The critical and long-terms aspect, which has been largely neglected, is making sure that every debtor country develops and sustains its capacity for effective debt management. This is the moral equivalent of teaching people how to fish and ensures that, in the future, countries will have the capacity to maintain sustainable debt levels. For the next ten years or so, capacity development for debt management must become the next front for the battle against unsustainable indebtedness.

NOTES

1. For technical details of changes in the measurement of debt systainability, see World Bank, "Debt Burden Indicators and Country Classifications," in *Global Development Finance: Analysis and Summary Tables 2000* (Washington, DC: World Bank, 2000), 141.

2. Shridath Ramphal, "Debt Has a Child's Face," in *The Progress of Nations 1999* (New York: UNICEF, 1999), 26–33.

3. See "Study Finds Poverty Deepening in Former Communist Countries," *The New York Times*, October 12, 2000, p. A3.

4. This discussion draws on United Nations, "Finding Solutions to the Debt Problems of Developing Countries," Report of the Executive Committee on Economic and Social Affairs (New York: United Nations, May 20, 1999), p. 5–28.

5. See United Nations, *Debt–Equity Swaps and Development* (New York: United Nations, 1993).

6. For detailed debt relief proposals by G7 members—Germany, (the Cologne debt initiative, January 1999), Great Britain (The Mauritius Mandate, September 1997), the United States (Conference on U.S.–Africa Partnership, March 1999), France (host of the Paris Club), Japan, and Canada—see United Nations, *Funding Solutions*, 19–21.

7. United Nations, *Debt–Equity Swaps and Development*, chaps. 2, 3, 4, 6.

8. "Dump the Debt," April 10, 2000, demonstration on the Mall in Washington, DC. Organized by the Jubilee 2000 Coalition and attended by thousands of people. Available: www.worldbank.org.

9. United Nations Report, *op. Cit*, 1999:7.

10. World Bank News Release 2001/1905, December 2000. Available: www.worldbank.org. Based on Commonwealth Secretariat, *Effective Domestic Debt Management in Developing Countries* (London: Legal Advisory Services Division, Commonwealth Secretariat, March 1999). For a theoretical framework policy makers can use as a guide to debt management, see Alessandra Missale, *Public Debt Management* (Oxford: Oxford University Press, 1999).

11. World Bank, *Background Press Briefing: Heavily Indebted Poor Countries (HIPC) Initiative* (Washington, DC: World Bank, December 18, 2000). Available: www.worldbank.org. In March 2001, following the election of a new government, Ghana agreed to apply for HIPC debt relief after pressure from the British government and despite Japan's opposition.

12. Commonwealth Secretariat, *Effective Domestic Debt*, chap. 1.

PART III
Globalization and Society

CHAPTER 9

Globalization and Health Services

The General Agreement on Trade in Services (GATS) was negotiated as part of the Uruguay Round and was put in force in January 1995. The agreement, which provides the framework within which firms and individuals can conduct international trade in services, is regarded as one of the single most important and controversial developments in the (global) multilateral trading system since the General Agreement on Tariffs and Trade (GATT) came into being in 1948. GATS contains two parts: the framework agreement containing the general rules and disciplines for members and the national "schemes" by which individual countries make specific commitments on access to the domestic markets by foreign suppliers.

Services are particularly important for developing and transition economies for several reasons: First, the service sector, as a percentage of GDP is growing for both developed and developing countries. In 2000, services accounted for more than 60 percent of global production but only 20 percent of global trade. Therefore, most of the trade in services is domestic, and in many developing countries, especially the least-developed countries, it is still subsistence. Therefore, the service sector provides these countries with a great potential for developing gainful global trade. Moreover, developing countries, with large supplies of cheap labor and endowed with attractive natural and weather conditions as well as social and cultural attributes, have many potential areas of comparative advantage in services. Global trade in services is growing due to a combination of factors including deregulation, introduction of new transmission technologies such as electronic banking and telehealth, rising incomes, and changing consumer preferences. During the period since the inception of GATS and despite restrictions in trade in services, there have been significant economic benefits to WTO members in the form of increased production, income, employment, and trade. The services most actively traded include telecommunications, social services (health, education), financial services, hotels and tourism, construction, transportation, and professional services (for example, consulting, accounting and auditing, security, and so on).

GATS, in particular, and international trade in services, in general, generate a lot of controversy and provide fodder for the anti-globalization movement. Those opposed to GATS have argued that the accord has the potential of restricting governments in terms of their ability to protect or subsidize public services and the local social service sectors such as health, education, and welfare. They also argue that GATS accelerates the privatization or deregulation of public social services, especially those most important for the poor and most vulnerable groups. It is also feared that GATS could force countries to export water, electricity, and other utilities against their long-term national interests. There is also the fear that commitments made by governments under GATS are irreversible. Nationalists have argued that GATS dispute settlement mechanisms undermine national sovereignty and democratic decision making. The WTO secretariat has refuted these and other claims as false.[1]

Despite the controversy and opposition, progress has been made. Under article 19 of GATS, member states agreed to launch successive rounds of service negotiations in order to achieve higher levels of liberalization. The first round of negotiations started as scheduled in January 2000, not more than five years from the date GATS came into force in 1995. In March 2001, members agreed to the "Negotiating Guidelines and Procedures" for the new round and discussed sector-specific proposals submitted by individual countries.

At Doha, Qatar, the fifth Ministerial Conference agreed that future GATS negotiations should be aimed at promoting economic growth for all trading partners and the development of developing and least-developed countries. The conference also reaffirmed the "Negotiating Guidelines and Procedures" previously adopted by the Council for Trade in Services in March 2001, as the basis for continuing GATS negotiations. Member countries were required to submit initial requests for specific commitments by June 30, 2002, and initial offers by March 31, 2003.

The conference recognized the progress made to date under article 19 and the large number of proposals submitted by members on a wide range of service sectors, several horizontal issues, and on the movement of natural persons. Horizontal commitments refer to provisions that apply to foreign suppliers of any service that has been scheduled by a member country. The issue of movement of natural persons is particularly important for developing countries and transition economies. These countries realize the potential growth opportunities for international trade in services. They also expressed dissatisfaction with the original GATS commitments made under the Uruguay Round when they were not adequately represented. The Doha conference, in an attempt to redress this dissatisfaction, agreed to reopen negotiations relating to the movement of natural persons to achieve higher commitments from the developed countries. Developing countries and transition economies would like to see restrictions removed so that their citizens have better access to the service sectors of the rich countries. This chapter deals with one of the service sectors: health.

THE GROWING AND CHANGING DEMAND FOR HEALTH SERVICES

In most countries, the health services sector is one of the largest in the economy. On average, countries spend 2.5 percent of GDP on public health, but this rises to 6.0 percent for high-income countries. European countries spend even more; for example, Germany spends 8.1 percent of GDP, France 7.7 percent, and Sweden and Switzerland 7.2 percent and 7.1 percent, respectively. These figures, which do not include private expenditures on health, translate into billions of dollars every year. For example, in 1998, the U.S. public expenditure on health was 6.6 percent, which translates in total annual expenditure to more than U.S. $520 billion. This is more than the size of the telecommunications sector of these countries. Even poor countries spend relatively high on health as compared to other sectors of the economy. Moreover, the health sector is very labor intensive and, therefore, provides employment to people ranging from the most specialized surgeons to unskilled hospital workers.

In practically every globalizing country, the demand for health services is both growing and changing—it is growing because of demographic changes, and it is changing because of government policy, globalization, economic growth, advances in science and technology, new health challenges, and the changing definition of health, illness, and wellness. The aging population in developed countries, rising incomes, population growth, and a relatively young population in developing countries and transition economies combine to unleash growing but differentiated demand for global health services. As incomes rise, the demand for health care increases, and the type of health-care goods and services needs to be changed. This is particularly so in the big emerging markets and other economically fast-growing developing countries.

According to a recent U.N. study, the world population is projected to grow from about 6.1 billion in 2000 to 9.3 billion by the year 2050.[2] Most of the growth will be concentrated in developing countries, with a share of 90 percent of the total population, especially in Asia and Africa. Africa, in spite of HIV/AIDS, is expected to increase its population threefold to 2 billion people by the middle of the twenty-first century. This will represent three times the projected population of Europe. On the other hand, the population of Europe and Japan is expected to decline over the same period. This will create a situation of aging wealthy nations seeking labor and developing countries with a surplus.

Increasingly, governments have accepted and legitimized the role others play in the health services sector, including the private sector, both domestic and global. In its 1999 *World Health Report*, the WHO accepted the position that the private sector provision of publicly financed services is compatible with government responsibility for health for all, providing it is done within the framework of a clear regulatory role of governments.[3]

The nature of health services is also changing because of emerging global health challenges for the twenty-first century. New and previously unknown diseases are emerging and old diseases are reappearing with no known cure or effective treatment; diseases associated with environmental pollution and lifestyles, and biological terrorism—regional conflicts are also causing new medical and public health challenges.

In countries where the population is affluent, informed, and relatively healthy but aging, the expectations from health services are changing. Health services are not meant only for the sick. People do not seek out health services only when they are sick; rather, they seek out these services because they want to stay healthy, and they are willing to pay for it. Therefore, wellness, rather than sickness, becomes the primary objective of the health services delivery system. This opens the door for healthy people seeking health services to remain healthy, live longer, and enjoy life. Therefore, in thinking about health services for international trade, policy makers and entrepreneurs in developing countries must go beyond the traditional sickness-based diagnosis—treatment—discharge cycle. They must see health services broadly—as an integral part of wellness and good living. In this way, they can develop a wide range of nonspecific health tradable goods and services and package them in ways that appeal to this emerging market.

OPPORTUNITIES FOR DEVELOPING COUNTRIES

In the context of globalization, developing countries have the opportunity, responsibility, and challenge to reform and restructure their health services sector to make them efficient, effective, affordable, responsive, and universally accessible. More important, globalization provides these countries the opportunity to rethink their national strategies for industrial development and international trade. As a labor-intensive industry, health services offer developing countries opportunities to develop and sustain new areas of global competitiveness. It is also relatively easy and manageable to access the global economy and global society. Investing in health is an effective avenue to poverty alleviation. Trading in health services provides poor countries and their governments the resources they need to improve health services for all and raise overall standards of living through quality international trade. To develop successful export strategies, health services operators must benefit from optimal use of forward and backward linkages between domestic production and the foreign markets of health-care services.

MODES OF TRADE IN HEALTH SERVICES

There are four modes of trade available to countries wishing to trade in health services: movement of natural persons, movement of consumers, establishing commercial operations, and cross-border trade. Each of these modes offers different opportunities and challenges to different countries and their current and future potentials for developing countries.

Movement of Natural Persons

This is the temporary movement of health services personnel from one country to another to work as health services providers. It is facilitated by the fact that health care is labor intensive, some countries experience labor shortages, and the training of medical and health personnel is based on universal scientific knowledge, making it possible, for example, for Indian- or Nigerian-trained personnel to work in Germany or the United States with a minimum of reorientation or retraining. Health-care professionals seek employment abroad for a variety of reasons, including better working conditions, opportunities for professional development, and exposure to new technologies not readily available in their home country. They may also be part of the national strategy for international cooperation and global trade. The movement of health-care professionals can remove shortages in the receiving countries, and remittances can improve the standard of living in the countries of origin.

This mode of trade in health services is particularly attractive to developing countries. The most sought-after professionals are doctors and nurses. It is estimated that on a global scale more than 68 percent of all migrating physicians are from developing countries.[4] Asia provides the greatest number of health-care professionals to the rest of the world. For example, India uses the category of service providers working abroad as the most important mode of trade in health services. More than 50 percent of Indian doctors trained abroad do not return, and in the mid-1990s, there were more than 60,000 doctors of Indian origin working in the United Kingdom and 35,000 in the United States.[5]

China has used this mode since the early 1950s, sending doctors and other medical personnel to developing countries in Asia, Africa, the Middle East, and Latin America as part of its Cold War foreign policy and international cooperation. In 1993, China had medical teams working in more than forty countries. The top-five recipients of Chinese medical teams were Algeria, Yemen, Tunisia, Morocco, and Tanzania. In more than thirty years, China had sent more than 15,000 medical personnel providing both Chinese traditional medicine (CTM) and Western medicine. China, like Cuba, sends doctors, pharmacists, and nurses abroad. Increasingly, the dispatch of these medical teams to developing countries has become part of trade in medical services.[6]

More recently, the international movement of health service professionals has become more dynamic and complex, not limited to developing countries alone. For example, the United Kingdom exports junior nurses to the United States and imports them from Commonwealth countries such as Nigeria. South Africa loses doctors and other internationally qualified professionals to the United Kingdom, Canada, Australia, and the United States but imports them from sub-Saharan African countries and Cuba. Therefore, for many of these countries, the outflow of nationals should be compensated by the inflow of foreigners.

Unfortunately, there are winners and losers in the health services trade using the movement of natural persons. Winners are countries that organize the movement of health professionals such that they create export earnings and ensure that the personnel return to their home countries with better skills, knowledge, and experience. Cuba and China have been particularly successful at doing both, in part because the movement of persons is strictly controlled by the state. The lowest-income countries are among the losers, suffering from a net brain drain because they have very limited capacity to import and retain highly qualified health professionals. In India, the shortage of state-of-the art medical equipment and infrastructure may explain why medical doctors choose to remain abroad. South Africa is also increasingly losing its capacity to attract and retain medical professionals. A combination of deteriorating working conditions, high levels of crime in urban areas, HIV/AIDS, regional conflicts, aggressive recruitment campaigns from abroad, and a lack of a national health management strategy may explain the country's inability to trade successfully in health services.

Movement of Consumers

Instead of health professionals going abroad, trade in health services is provided to foreign patients and other health services consumers. This mode covers a wide range of patients seeking health services in foreign countries, including travelers looking for specialized services not readily available in their home country; travelers taking advantage of a favorable climate and combining health care with other pursuits such as business, vacation, education, and so on; people seeking convalescent care; travelers seeking better services at lower costs; and elderly persons looking for a better quality of life and a lower cost of living. Countries using this mode of trade must ensure that the services are internationally competitive in quality, cost, or uniqueness to continue to attract a critical mass of foreign paying patients.

In the past, most patients used to travel to developed countries, especially Europe and the United States, for medical service. Increasingly, developing countries are providing competitive services either regionally or on a global scale. The developing countries most active in using this mode of trade include China, Cuba, Jordan, Egypt, India, Singapore, and South Africa. Jordan and Egypt have become major suppliers of quality health services to other Arab States in Africa and the Middle East. Cuba provides both regional services to the Caribbean and Latin American countries and, internationally, to other developing countries (see Exhibit 9.2 on page 279). South Africa is a major supplier of medical services to the rest of sub-Saharan Africa; and Singapore serves Southeast Asia and beyond.

Foreign patients come to China mainly for CTM. At first, this involved only overseas Chinese, but increasingly, others come from Europe, Africa, the Middle East, and the United States. Some of China's clinics combine CTM with Western medicine, and patients who have been failed by the latter are glad to try alternative treatment from China. There are certain procedures and treatments in which China claims world leadership, including microsurgery, ophthalmology, dentistry, orthopedics of spine and limb deformations, and early diagnosis and treatment of liver cancer. In addition to being attracted to CTM, patients come to China when Western medicine fails, when they cannot afford Western medicine in expensive countries, or for special treatment in the areas in which China is known to excel.

As for the other developing countries wishing to attract foreign patients, retirees constitute one of the growing and most promising potential markets. As the world population gets older, first in the developed countries but increasingly in the developing countries as well, there will be more people seeking wellness and health services. It is estimated that by the year 2015, 15 percent of the U.S. population, 24 percent of Japan's population, and 17 percent of the European population will be sixty-five years of age or older.[7] The combined total of people sixty-five years and older for these three will exceed 100 million people. Those who are retired and have the time and money to travel will seek the best and most cost-effective services wherever they are offered. With increased globalization, free trade in services, and use of technology such as the Internet, it will be increasingly attractive for people to travel abroad in search of quality health care. Older people need a lot of care and tend to stay in hospitals longer. Therefore, those developing countries which develop the capacity to provide quality care to the elderly will be likely to succeed in trading in health services. Countries in the tropics, with warm climates that are attractive to the elderly, can use their natural advantages to develop competitive tradable services. By combining health services with other attractions such as tourism, art, culture, and education, retirees will more than likely stay longer in search of a better life. This is an area in which developing countries can develop a globally competitive service culture and attract foreigners to buy health and related tradable services.

Establishing Commercial Operations

In the past, most countries restricted foreign operations in the health services sector. With globalization, liberalization, and private sector participation, more foreign operators are now allowed to open shop as a way of permitting competition, providing better services, reducing costs, and reducing the pressure on the public health system. New technology allows foreign operations, with a minimum of front-end investment. The target consumers are often host country nationals, but they could also be home country nationals or third country nationals. Foreign operations can be established by the public sector through a government-owned agency and private sector operators such as global corporations, professional associations, or joint ventures combining private and public sector participation in both the home and the host countries. The operations can take the form of standing hospitals, clinics, dispensaries, health insurance, health-care consulting, management or research contracts, education, or project-by-project operations. Entrepreneurial firms do not need to be in the health-care field to establish commercial operations; they can invest in auxiliary services for the health-care industry such as laundry, food, housekeeping, transportation, and laboratory work.

Management contracts and licensing are common methods for foreigners to establish commercial operations in hospital services. Pharmaceutical companies are particularly attracted to these foreign commercial opportunities as a way of diversifying investments and developing potential new business. Managed care is commonly used in setting up foreign operations. Under managed care, the financing and delivery of medical services are combined through contract arrangements linking together service providers, hospital administration, and insurance companies. Managed care includes health maintenance organizations, preferred-provider organizations, and point-of-service financing and service delivery. Managed care systems are competitive because they take advantage of scale and specialization.[8]

Not surprisingly, the countries most active in establishing foreign operations in health services are the same ones most active in providing or receiving foreign direct investment (FDI). This is not surprising because the factors that attract FDI also attract investments in health services abroad. Therefore, the developed countries control a significant share of the market. Increasingly, developing countries are becoming competitive, especially China and Cuba.

China has set up foreign operations specializing in CTM. Initially, these operations targeted overseas Chinese who remain closely tied to Chinese culture no matter where they live, have become increasingly wealthy and, therefore, are able to spend on health services, and are a highly globalizing group.[9] Because of the increasing presence and influence of Chinese culture, China has opened commercial operations in more than twenty countries in Africa, Europe, and Asia, as well as the United States. Other facilities have been opened in countries where China has large construction contracts and exports workers to these countries. By combining health services with construction services and public administration in terms of foreign relations, China has managed to develop, package, and successfully market its unique brand of medical services, specializing in acupuncture and moxibustion. It has been argued that other developing countries could develop their own brands of traditional or alternative medicine and market them globally. For example, India has a large internal demand for alternative medicine, which could be developed and exported to other countries. Likewise, the native populations in Mexico, Canada, Brazil, Malaysia, and other developing countries could develop their traditional and alternative medicines and export them to the rest of the world.

Once again, the poor countries would appear to be limited in their capacity to establish foreign health services operations. However, they, too, can benefit in several ways. First, by liberalizing the health services sector, they allow private sector operators to participate. Foreign private operators would bring in investment, technology, and management know-how, thereby contributing to sector-specific improvements and overall economic growth. Domestic private sector participation would inject needed competition into the sector, stimulate entrepreneurship, and contribute to private sector development. Joint ventures with local operators and global corporations, drawing on indigenous knowledge and local natural conditions, can mobilize the resources necessary to develop local tradable health-care goods and services for the global market. In the end, it is possible to achieve "parento optimal," whereby nobody is worse off, but someone is better off.

Cross-Border Trade

This is the most recent and underdeveloped mode of trade of health services, especially for developing countries; it also has the greatest potential for those countries able and willing to build the necessary technological infrastructure. Cross-border trade uses advanced telecommunications to deliver health-care services to patients across national borders. It draws on the emerging and related developments in health informatics, telehealth, telemedicine, and tele-education.

Telemedicine is the delivery of medical care using interactive audio, visual, and data communications, including diagnosis, treatment, consultation, and research. Increasingly, it is being widely used within national boundaries, especially between specialized health-care facilities and outlying health-care providers. The same technology can be used across national borders to support international trade in health services. It can also be used for health services administrative functions such as processing insurance claims in developing countries where labor costs are lower. Telemedicine is attractive because it significantly cuts costs and because it improves accessibility of the best and most technologically advanced medical services to patients in countries where they are not readily available. To benefit from the cross-border health services trade and to be able to commercially take advantage of the opportunities of telehealth and telemedicine, countries must make strategic investments in telecommunications and build a competitive infrastructure capable of supporting and sustaining comparative export advantages.

Exhibit 9.1 provides examples of applications of telemedicine in various developing countries.

Exhibit 9.1
Examples of Telemedicine Applications in Developing Countries

Africa: Teleconferencing links have been established among institutions in Canada and select African countries to support continuing medical education and to enable health workers in Africa to benefit from the latest medical knowledge and advances.

China: International direct dialing fax services provide information to overseas customers on marketable services, facilities and prices.

- Chinese research institutions are connected by computers to international networks, facilitating information exchange with foreign institutions.

- In coastal areas—Guangdong, Fijian, Guangshi Provinces— cross-border telediagnostic services are provided to patients in neighboring territorial countries by telephone or fax.

- Domestic hospitals provide diagnostic databases to Chinese clinics and medical personnel overseas by computer connections, Internet.

Gulf States: WorldCare, a private U.S.–based company, provides telemedicine services to hospitals in Arab Gulf States.

Jordan: King Hussein Medical Center and Amman Surgical Hospital have established satellite links to the Mayo Clinic in the United States for second opinions on diagnoses and treatments.

Mexico: Satellite-based links allow specialists in more than twenty hospitals in Mexico City to support general practitioners, in general, and rural hospitals in the Chiapas region. Services include teleradiology, telepathology, and teleconsultation.

Saudi Arabia: TeleMedicine, a global corporation service, links King Faisal Specialist Hospital and Research Center with leading American hospitals led by the Massachusetts General Hospital. The links are used for routine diagnoses and second opinions from American medical specialists. Emergency cases are supported with international video teleconferencing.

Singapore: Telemedicine is part of the National IT2000 Strategy. The national broadband network is used to support telemedicine using dynamic images, conferencing, and so on. International telemedicine links are made for second opinions in diagnoses and treatments, as well as training, education, and professional development. Singapore General Hospital is digitally linked with Stanford University Hospital.

Source: Compiled from Simonetta Zarrilli and Colette Kinnon, eds., *International Trade in Health Services: A Development Perspective* (Geneva: WHO/UNCTAD, 1998), especially chaps. 5 and 12.

Africa has the least-developed telemedicine applications; Singapore has the most effective. China has a range of applications from simple fax messaging to complex computer connections with international networks. Jordan, Saudi Arabia, and the Gulf States use telemedicine to maintain links between their respective hospitals and world-class medical facilities in the United States. These links allow providers in the developing countries to access the best diagnostic and treatment experts in the world. In return, patients, especially from neighboring countries, travel to these countries for treatment with the knowledge that they have the technology and know-how to access the best medical specialists in the advanced countries. In this way, these countries can use telemedicine to develop tradable services, not through cross-border trade but by attracting foreign patients—that is, the movement of consumers.

Singapore's applications of telemedicine are particularly effective because they are strategic. Telemedicine was not developed in isolation but is a part of the national IT2000 strategy. Therefore, it draws on and takes advantage of the national information technology infrastructure and digital nervous system developed and maintained for the national strategy. The international telemedicine links maintained between the Singapore General Hospital and overseas medical centers allow operators to get second opinions on diagnoses and treatments. They can also be used to support local training, education, and professional development. As a result, telemedicine becomes a tool for the achievement of various national objectives. It supports international trade in health services, it turns medical brain drain into a brain gain by providing attractive working conditions for doctors and other medical professionals, and it provides local entrepreneurs the opportunity to develop goods and services to support, maintain, and upgrade the telecommunications infrastructure.

BARRIERS AND RESTRICTIONS
TO TRADE IN SERVICES

While globalization creates opportunities for developed and developing countries to expand international trade in services, barriers, challenges, and trade restrictions must first be overcome. The developed countries control the biggest, most diversified, and fastest-growing market in international trade in services. Yet, services such as health and construction, areas in which developing countries have a competitive advantage, are not open to free trade. Developing countries also have challenges to overcome. Most of them have health services that do not meet the basic needs of their citizens. Therefore, it is hard for them to talk about health as a tradable service when it hardly meets citizens' expectations as a public service. There are also legal and constitutional limitations. For example, the 1988 Brazilian Constitution forbids foreigners from owning hospitals or clinics. Other countries, including Mexico, India, and Malaysia, have similar restrictions that discourage private sector investment in restricted services.

One of the challenges facing developing countries wishing to participate in international trade in health services is fear of the brain drain. Most developing countries are losing significant numbers of highly trained and experienced medical professionals, mainly to the developed countries. The poor, low-income countries are hit particularly hard by net outflow of highly qualified human capital. For example, in Ethiopia between 1984 and 1994, more than 55 percent of the pathology graduates from Addis Ababa Faculty of Medicine left the country. In 1985, Ghana's medical school graduated a total of sixty-five doctors; by 1997, only twenty-two remained in the country—a 66 percent brain drain. A 1989 study found that "more Iranian doctors live in NewYork City than in all of Iran."[11] The brain drain is not only across borders. Where the public sector operates side by side with the private sector, there is a tendency for professionals to be more attracted to the private sector, leaving the public sector with more serious staff shortages. For example, in India, only 10 percent of medical doctors work in the public sector, and even then, they are allowed to work part time in the private sector in order to earn extra income.

It has been recognized that lack of state-of-the-art medical equipment and a poor telecommunications infrastructure serve as serious barriers to international trade in services such as health, banking, and tourism. For example, many developing countries are unable to take advantage of opportunities of cross-border trade due to lack of equipment, infrastructure, and qualified personnel. Telecommunications and computer technologies in support of telehealth, telemedicine, tele-education, and informatics are particularly critical for globalizaing developing countries because of their potential advantage of improving the delivery of domestic health services, as well as promoting various modes of international trade in health services.[12]

Another area of potential relevancy for the development of health services in developing countries, both for domestic applications and international trade, is healing, especially drawing on indigenous knowledge systems. For more than two hundred years, European settlers in the Americas (Canada, Mexico, the United States, Central and South America) working for the police, schools, and church organizations physically, emotionally, and sexually abused the native population, especially children, women, and the elderly. This left the victims with permanent scars and affected their ability to function effectively as contributing members of society. In January 1998, the government of Canada acknowledged past mistakes and issued a "Statement of Reconciliation" with an action plan to deal with the many and complex problems the native communities face. It also provided a $300 million (Canadian) grant for the establishment of the Aboriginal Healing Foundation to be used by native communities seeking traditional systems of treatment and healing.[13]

Sadly, it is not only the North American native population in need of healing. Regional conflicts, civil wars, dictatorships, and genocidal regimes that have bedeviled the world since the end of World War II have left many people in different parts of the world badly scarred, and in need of healing. In Africa—from Algeria to Zimbabwe, Nigeria to South Africa, the Great Lakes Region and the Horn of Africa—there are many in need of healing. In Asia, one can think of Cambodia, Vietnam, Afghanistan, Sri Lanka, and, more recently, Myanmar, East Timor, and Indonesia. In the Middle East, the Balkans, the former Soviet Union, Latin America (for example, Chile, Argentina, Nicaragua, Haiti), and even Northern Ireland, there are millions of individuals, families, and communities in need of healing. In the United States, terrorist attacks in Oklahoma City, Washington, DC, and New York City and abuses of children in Catholic churches have touched thousands of individuals, families, and corporations now in need of healing. Six months after the events of September 11, 2001, CNN reported that according to a study published in the *New England Journal of Medicine*, more than 150,000 New Yorkers were suffering as a result of the psychological effects of the attacks (CNN, March 28, 2002). Yet, current reforms and restructuring of health-care services, both in developed and developing countries, do not include the development of diagnostic and treatment procedures and technologies for individual and community healing.

The first country to develop effective healing procedures as an integral part of health-care services will have a potentially large domestic and international market. Obviously, this will require expensive research and development, which many developing countries cannot afford. Countries such as Canada and South Africa, which have experimented with different approaches to healing, could pool their resources and undertake the necessary research and development.[14] The United Nations and other international organizations could also be interested because peace, reconstruction, and development are proving difficult in post-conflict countries without first giving people genuine healing opportunities. This is another example in which two sectors working together—health and peacekeeping—may prove more beneficial to the globalizing world than working separately.

Perhaps the single greatest challenge developing countries face in their efforts to participate fully in international trade in health services is restrictions in trade. These restrictions apply in services, in general, and health services, in particular. At the moment, there are multilateral agreements governing trade in services. GATS does not oblige WTO members to open a specific sector, such as health or education, to foreign suppliers nor to lift all trade restrictions. Members are free to specify any trade barriers they intend to retain by simply specifying so on a schedule of commitment. Although more than one-half of WTO members have included one or more aspects of health services in their GATS schedules of specific commitments, trade restrictions still remain. These restrictions negatively affect the freedom of movement of natural persons: both the health professionals seeking employment abroad and patients seeking visa and entry permits to foreign countries for medical treatment. As well, temporary entry and stay of independent health-care personnel are generally not covered by GATS commitments. Although many countries have flexibility in their immigration laws to allow freer movement of health-care professionals, enforcement of these laws are generally restrictive, and flexible arrangements tend to be made on bilateral bases. Consequently, many professionals, especially from developing countries, experience difficulties in obtaining entry and work permits and are often forced to work illegally in Europe and North America.

Other restrictions include economic needs test requirements, refusal to accredit or recognize foreign professional qualifications, nationality or residency requirements, subnational licensing requirements, foreign exchange controls restricting repatriation of earnings, and discriminatory regulations governing the payment of fees and expenses. Economic needs tests are carried out to determine if there are no qualified nationals available for employment before foreign applicants are considered. These tests act as qualitative or quantitative quotas and, therefore, restrict free trade in health services. Difficulties associated with accreditation or recognition of foreign health professionals are very serious, especially in countries such as Canada, the United States, and Australia, where individual provinces and states govern and control both training and certification. In Canada, there are thousands of foreign-trained health professionals who are not allowed to practice because the provincial governing bodies do not recognize their qualifications. At the same time, serious personnel shortages exist, especially in the remote areas of the country and in the poorer provinces. Mutual recognition of qualifications, supported by more standardized education, training, and certification of health professionals on an international level, would help overcome some of these restrictions.

Insurance constitutes a serious source of trade restriction because, in most countries, insurance policies are not portable across national boundaries. This means that patients are not free to seek health services anywhere in the world and expect their insurance company to cover the expenses. This is a serious impediment to international free trade because these restrictions can be used as effective nontariff barriers to trade. In some cases, patients can request permission to travel abroad from their insurance providers, but this can cause undue delays, especially when time and timing are critical for diagnosis and treatment.

It is in the long-term interests of globalizing developing countries to negotiate and conclude a fair and responsive agreement along the lines of GATS. The agreement should, among other things, provide for freer movement of health services personnel and consumers, full portability of health insurance, mutual recognition of qualifications, freedom to establish commercial operations, and a general liberalization of both the domestic and the international health services sectors. Portability of health insurance is particularly important because not allowing it substantially restricts free trade in health services.

CUBA AND INTERNATIONAL TRADE IN HEALTH SERVICES

Exhibit 9.2 describes the strategy Cuba used to become a world leader in international trade in health services. It is an example of how a developing country can benefit from trade in health services.

Exhibit 9.2
Cuba's Strategy for International Trade in Health Services

Background: Compared to other Caribbean countries, Cuba is relatively isolated. It is not a member of the World Bank or the IMF and has no full diplomatic relations with the United States. It gets very little FDI. Still, over the years, the country has managed to develop potentially competitive international trade portfolios in health services.

Objectives: With the government playing the lead role as policy maker, regulator, provider, and exporter, the strategy aims to achieve the following objectives: (1) making the country a "world medical power" and using health services as an instrument of international cooperation, especially with the G77 countries; (2) sending medical personnel abroad, especially to developing countries with serious shortages; (3) attracting foreign patients to specialized clinics providing high-quality health care at internationally competitive prices; (4) providing education and training to foreign students, using the specialized clinics for training; (5) providing

Cuban medical professionals the opportunity for professional development by working overseas and dealing with tropical diseases no longer active in Cuba; (6) linking health care with tourism; and (7) ultimately becoming the leading regional exporter of health-care services.

Strategies: Cuba specializes in trading services associated with diagnosis and treatment of skin diseases (cancers), which Western doctors regard as incurable. Services are targeted at G77 countries with no specialized services of their own. For targeting rich paying customers, Cuba uses SERVIMED, a state-owned corporation that packages and markets health/tourism services and works closely with tour and travel operators in Europe, Asia, Canada, and even the United States.

Results: In 1995–1996, more than 25,000 patients and 1,500 students went to Cuba for treatment and training, respectively. Income from foreign patients amounted to more than U.S.$25 million.

Limitations: Language limitations for non-Spanish-speaking clients, limited telecommunications infrastructure and services for telemedicine, no direct access to the U.S. market, Communist regime turning off some potential customers, fall of the former U.S.S.R., and continuing economic difficulties with Russia.

Source: Based on information in "Export Strategies in the Health Services Sector," in *International Trade in Health Services: A Development Perspective,* ed. Simonetta Zarrilli and Colette Kinnon (Geneva: WHO/UNCIAD, 1998), 28.

The strategy takes an intersectoral approach, linking health with tourism and international cooperation. Drawing on the experiences of the Cold War period, Cuba took advantage of its influence and leadership among the G77 group of developing countries and turned them into a market for its health services. The strategy also takes advantage of the country's natural endowment such as climate (warm, semitropical, with dry winters and wet summers), coastlines with beautiful beaches, the ocean, and a wide variety of wildlife. The strategy also combines modes of trade in health services, emphasizing those for which Cuba has a comparative export advantage and leaving out those for which it does not. Specifically, Cuba's international trade in health services uses the movement of natural persons and movement of consumers. It does not attempt to establish commercial operations abroad nor use cross-border trade. With a relatively undeveloped telecommunications infrastructure, Cuba would not be competitive trying to provide cross-border health services.

The strategy is also effective in that drawing on the principles of niche marketing, Cuba's health services for export chose to specialize in skin diseases rather than providing a wide range of services. The selected areas of specialization are in high demand and have relatively little competition, especially from other developing countries. Finally, by using state power, authority, and influence, Cuba, unlike many developing countries such as Jamaica, has managed to limit its brain drain through the movement of natural persons. Cuba, like China, carefully screens its medical personnel for foreign assignments and sends them out and back in teams. Group pressure keeps them cohesive and connected to their home country. As well, most of them are sent to countries in Africa where they would not like to settle permanently.

The strategy is not without problems, limitations, and challenges, however. There are cultural and language barriers, especially for non-Spanish-speaking clients and those outside Latin America. Due to long periods of isolation, relatively few Cubans speak international languages other than Spanish. Yet, for most developing countries, potential clients speak English, French, Arabic, Portuguese, Chinese, and German, but not Spanish. Cuba's political ideology, and its long-standing political feud with the United States, limit its ability to market its services to one of the biggest, richest, and fastest-growing markets in the world. As more developing countries develop their own capacity for international trade in health services and as some of them become regional leaders, Cuba faces increasing competition. For example, South America is now taking patients from Africa who would otherwise go to Cuba. Even within South America, MERCOSUR (the regional common market) has set up "tarjeta MERCOSUR," which allows exchange of patients across member states through the services of associate cooperatives. This, too, creates more competition and reduces the potential pool of patients from the region that would otherwise go to Cuba for treatment. Ultimately, however, the long-term prospects of Cuba's international trade in health services depend on whether the country will liberalize its political economy and join, as a full participant, the global economy and global society. If the Free Trade Area of the Americas were to conclude a free-trade agreement that includes services, the developing countries of Central and South America as well as the Caribbean would benefit. Cuba is not a member of this regional grouping.

NOTES

1. For basic information about GATS, see "An Introduction to the GATS" (October 1999); "The General Agreement on Trade in Services (GATS): Objectives, Coverage, and Discipline;" and "GATS: Fact and Fiction" (February 2001). All available on www.wto.otg.

2. United Nations, *World Population Prospects: The 1998 Revision* (New York: United Nations, 1998). Also visit the Population Reference Bureau Web site: www.prb.org.

3. See World Health Organization, *World Health Report 1999: Making a Difference* (Geneva: WHO, 1999).

4. This section draws on various parts of *International Trade in Health Services: A Development Perspective*, ed. Simonetta Zarrilli and Colette Kinnon (Geneva: WHO/UNCTAD, 1998).

5. See Indrani Gupta, Bishwanath Goldar, and Arup Mitra, "The Case of India," in *International Trade in Health Services: A Development Perspective*, ed. Simonetta Zarrilli and Colette Kinnon (Geneva: WHO/UNCTAD, 1998), 213–236.

6. See Xing Houyuan, "The Case of China," in *International Trade in Health Services: A Development Perspective*, ed. Simonetta Zarrilli and Colette Kinnon (Geneva: WHO/UNCTAD, 1998), 189–211.

7. See, for example, "Marketing to the Old: Over 60 and Overlooked," *The Economist*, August 10, 2002, pp. 51–52.

8. Health maintenance organizations are tightly structured and require patients to use participating doctors except in case of emergencies. Preferred-provider organizations are networks of health-care providers who accept discounted payments in exchange for guaranteed payments. Point-of-service financing and delivery systems are more restrictive than preferred-provider organizations. See J. K. Iglehart, "Health Policy Report: Physicians and the Growth of Managed Care," *New England Journal of Medicine* 331, no. 17 (October 1994):1167–1171.

9. For discussions of the role and importance of the overseas Chinese in globalization, see Henry Wai-chung Yeung and Kris Olds, eds., *Globalization of Chinese Business Firms* (London: Macmillan, 1999); and Evelyn Hu-DeHart, ed., *Across the Pacific: Asian Americans and Globalization* (Philadelphia: Temple University Press, 1999).

10. According to the *Gale Encyclopedia of Alternative Medicine*, moxbustion is a technique used in CTM in which a stick or cone of burning mugwort is placed over an inflamed of affected area of the body in order to stimulate and strengthen the blood and the body's life energy.

11. See Orvill Adams and Colette Kinnon, "A Public Health Perspective," in *International Trade in Health Services: A Development Perspective*, ed. Simonetta Zarrilli and Colette Kinnon (Geneva: WHO/UNCTAD, 1998), 35; and Moses N. Kiggundu, *Managing Organizations in Developing Countries: An Operational and Strategic Approach* (West Hartford, CT: Kumarian, 1989), 172.

12. For more information on telemedicine, visit the Telemedicine Information Exchange at www.tie.telemed.org.

13. For background materials, see Government of Canada, *Gathering Strength: Canada's Aboriginal Action Plan* (Ottawa: Government of Canada, 1997). For information on the Aboriginal Healing Foundation, visit the Web sites: www.inac.gc.ca and www.ahf.ca.

14. Canada's Aboriginal Healing Foundation and South Africa's Truth and Reconciliation Commission have much in common as strategies for individual and collective healing by victims of the state over a long period of time. For South Africa's needs for healing, see Antjie Krog, *Country of My Skull* (Johannesburg: Random House, 1998).

CHAPTER 10

Globalization and Culture

During the 1990s, it was feared that globalization was bad for cultural expression and development—that it would drive out weak or less competitive cultures, sacrifice cultural diversity and creativity, and impose a universal monocultural world. It was also feared that alternative models of development based on different cultural, historical and institutional backgrounds would be suppressed due to the fall of Soviet-led Communism, the ascendance of capitalism, and increased Western influence. These fears were deeply felt and eloquently expressed in the 1995 UNESCO report produced by the World Commission on Culture and Development, which, among other things, warned the world that globalization would bring about cultural harmonization and destroy cultural diversity and creativity.[1] In a very perverse way, some cultural relativists have attempted to explain away terrorist attacks on U.S. interests on globalization and Western cultural dominance.

However, available evidence suggests that these fears were largely exaggerated. Globalization can be, and in most cases has been, good for cultural diversity and development. By contributing to liberalization, rising incomes, increased use of technology, better education, and global migration, globalization helps to create multiple environments in support of cultural and interactive diversity. It allows people to experiment with alternative models of development, while at the same time borrowing ideas and practices from other cultures and institutions. It provides people with the opportunity to enjoy freedom for their own culture and, at the same time, be exposed to other cultures. It allows weaker and smaller cultures to coexist alongside the big and powerful cultures. It allows minor or provincial languages and remote cultures to connect with other cultures.

Globalization thrives on diversity and, therefore, enhances respect and appreciation for differences and promotes reciprocity as well as shared values among nations, communities, institutions, organizations, and individuals. It facilitates cultural creativity through the free flow of ideas and interchanges among different cultures. It builds a culture of peace through mutual understanding and respect. Trading nations or communities and those in constant interchange are less likely to go to war and, in fact, are more likely to find peaceful and culturally appropriate approaches to conflict management. During the Cold War, the NATO alliance managed to remain strong, in part because member states were also active trading partners. On the contrary, the Warsaw Pact remained weak because there was little meaningful trade among the members. Therefore, it can be predicted that for the U.S.–led international coalition against global terrorism, only those countries with close trading or investment relationships with the United States are likely to sustain their membership through thick and thin.

Globalization also empowers nations and communities to fight cultural imperialism or chauvinism by helping them to define who they are, where they come from, and where they are going. Globalization and technology help communities develop cultural networks free from state or hierarchical controls, regulations, or limitations. It also helps to demystify cultural differences by facilitating intercultural connectedness, interactions, and hybridization. Therefore, when properly managed, globalization can be good for cultural creativity, diversity, and development.

Similarly, culture is good for globalization. In fact, a monocultural world would not be good for globalization because diversity stimulates creativity, innovation, and the capacity to manage change. It also enhances competitiveness so that multicultural societies are more convivial, accumulate more positive social capital, and are better equipped to fight political oppression, assimilation, and economic dependence. Therefore, cultural diversity is here to stay, which is good for globalization. Still, governments and communities must maintain the right policy environment and institutions to ensure positive and mutually reinforcing relationships between culture and globalization. They must support individual cultural creativity, democratic institutions to facilitate participatory cultural expression, political structures open to culturally diverse voices and interests, and entrepreneurs to help transform cultural talents into commercially viable cultural assets. This requires individual and collective creativity, leadership, and partnerships within and between the public and private sectors, at home and abroad.

CULTURE AND COMMERCE: OPPORTUNITIES AND CHALLENGES FOR DEVELOPING COUNTRIES

The cultural industry is varied and diverse. It includes music, painting, sculpture, theater, film, video, the new media, books and magazines, crafts and beading, carpeting and matting, jewelry, ethnic dress/clothing, food, games, and sporting events. Although its size is difficult to estimate, it is known that the cultural industry is a very important part of the national economy, especially for the developed countries and, increasingly, the emerging markets. For example, in the United States, culture, dominated by audiovisual production, accounts for approximately 6 percent of GDP, and employs approximately 1.5 million people. In the early 1990s, culture accounted for more than 3 percent of GDP. In Japan and other European countries, culture is a significant contributor to the national economy. Unfortunately, most developing countries have not been able to develop their cultural industries to the same levels of contribution to their respective economies. Most of the cultural output is locally produced and consumed at subsistence or near-subsistence levels; the government or other public agencies with no mandate or capacity for commercialization control the others. Yet, most developing countries are multicultural with lots of potential for cultural creativity and commercialization. Therefore, it is suggested that every newly globalizing developing country should review its cultural industry with a view to producing international tradable cultural goods and services for the global economy and global society. In addition to serving purely domestic social, community, and political purposes, culture and the cultural industry can be used as a positive instrument for economic development and international trade and to enhance cooperation and understanding among peoples and nations.

In most developing countries, culture is regarded as a public good, and the state is the custodian of national cultures. The different levels of government have exclusive, or almost exclusive, responsibility for historic heritage, monuments, popular culture, language, music and dance, traditional celebrations, games, and sports. It amounts to nationalization of the cultural industry; it is also the unfortunate consequence of cultural elitism because the government, with limited resources and narrow sectoral vision, resorts to elite accommodation and marginalization of the small, powerless, and isolated cultural communities. Government control of the industry, in addition to stifling cultural creativity and competitiveness, accentuates tensions and even open conflicts between cultural integrators—those who wish to develop new hybrid cultures—and the purists or nationalists who support cultural isolation and supremacy. One way of overcoming these obstacles is to open up the cultural industry: allow more freedom for individual cultural creativity, promote entrepreneurship by giving the private sector more opportunities to participate, and foster public–private partnerships.

In other developing countries, especially those with a colonial post, culture was used by oppressed or marginalized groups to express passive political resistance, opposition to assimilation, and popular mobilization of community resources and political support. Independence movements in countries such as Algeria, Indonesia, and Kenya and more recent liberation movements in Ethiopia, Mexico, South Africa, Rwanda, and Zimbabwe all used music, dance, and other cultural media to mobilize local community support and to fight for freedom and redress. These groups, with very limited resources or access to modern technology, were very creative and imaginative, producing very powerful and captivating cultural products that contributed significantly to their success. Similar cultural creativity and imagination still exists among artists in these communities, although they have been largely neglected after independence. The opportunity and challenge for these developing countries is to draw on the same cultural talent and potential to enable local artists to produce equally captivating cultural products, however, this time not for liberation, but for commercialization, international trade, and globalization.

MUSIC AND INTERNATIONAL TRADE

Music is used here as an example of international trade in the cultural industry. It is used to illustrate the potential opportunities available to developing countries and transition economies both nationally and in the global economy. Music was chosen for several reasons. First, it is the most common form of cultural expression. Every day, people create and enjoy music in every corner of the world. It is widely produced and consumed in every community, and it is the bond that binds humanity. Second, it is one of the easiest cultural commodities to commercialize and export. It is both local and global. Consumers do not have to understand the language of the creator to enjoy and pay for the music. Third, developing countries have a potential comparative advantage in the production and trading of music. Most developing countries are multicultural and multilingual; therefore, they have a richer and more diverse cultural platform for making music. They have many traditional communities still making "pure" ethnic music and, therefore, lots of opportunities for hybridization and deregionalization. They produce music different from Western music, and thus they have the opportunity to attract young musicians and music lovers in the world looking for unique or different musical experiences. Fourth, music was chosen because from an entrepreneurial standpoint the music industry provides plenty of potential niches for small- and medium-size enterprises (SMEs) to participate in the cultural industry. With a relatively small capital investment, entrepreneurs can get started, beginning with live entertainment and local tours before venturing into more complex and capital-intensive operations such as recording and export. Therefore, countries with limited resources should consider the music industry as one of the most attractive entry points in the economic development of the cultural industry.

Table 10.1 provides a summary of the global music market and its dominant players. Section (a) provides a regional breakdown of the percentage share of music recording sales for the ten-year period 1991–2001. As expected, Europe, North America, and Japan dominate the market. Together, in 1991, they accounted for more than 90 percent of the world share of music recording sales. The other regions, Asia (excluding Japan), Central and South America, and Austria, together accounted for less than 8 percent of the global market. This suggests that any country wishing to get into the business of exporting music must be able to penetrate the market of the "Big Three." However, over the years from 1991 to 2001, the percentage share of sales for the Big Three was estimated to have declined from more than 90 percent to a bit more than 75 percent. On the other hand, the market share for Asia (excluding Japan) and Central and South America was estimated to grow from a bit more than 5 percent in 1991 to more than 20 percent. Even Africa's share of the market was expected to grow from 0.5 percent to more than 2 percent. The economic growth enjoyed by these developing regions and the resulting rising consumer incomes help to explain the increasing importance of the music industry for developing and transition economies.

The strategic implications for the summary findings in Table 10.1 for developing countries are clear. First, the data point to the growing economic potential of the music industry within the developing and transition economies. This potential should provide incentives for local entrepreneurs and investors to participate in the commercialization and export development of the local music industry. Second, dominance of the export market by the Big Three is declining as other developing countries and emerging markets are becoming more important. Therefore, countries in the process of developing their music industry for export should also target other developing and emerging markets. For example, African music, properly hybridized and packaged, would do well in export markets in Brazil and other developing countries in Central and South America. Likewise, music exports from North Africa could find attractive markets in Asia and the Middle East. Young people constitute the single biggest market for export music. Most of these developing countries have relatively young populations with rising disposable incomes, which makes them increasingly important for the music industry.

Section (b) of Table 10.1 provides data on the sale of popular music for selected developed and developing countries, big emerging markets (BEMs), and transition economies. For each of the twelve listed countries, the table provides the sales of national popular music

Table 10.1
Summary: Global Music Market Information

a) **Regional Percentage Share of Music Recording Sales**

Region	1991	1996	2001[e]
Europe	38.1	33.7	30.1
North America	34.4	33.2	28.1
Japan	18.8	17.0	18.6
Asia (excluding Japan)	3.2	5.7	11.6
Central & South America	2.4	6.3	7.3
Australia	2.1	2.4	1.7
Africa & Middle East	0.5	1.7	2.1
Other	0.5	0.1	0.5
Total	100.0	100.0	100.0

b) **Sales of National Popular Music as a Percentage of All Popular Music (1996)**
   (Selected Countries)

Country	Percentage	Country	Percentage
Indonesia	81	France	47
Bulgaria	80	Hungary	29
Turkey	78	South Africa	23
Ghana	71	Canada	10
Brazil	66	New Zealand	9
Nigeria	65	Switzerland	7

Note: [e] = estimate.
Source: Compiled from David Throsby, "The Role of Music in International Trade and Economic Development,"
in *World Culture Report: Culture, Creativity, and Markets* (Paris: UNESCO, 1998).

as a percentage of all popular music sold in the country in 1986. It is a measure of how well
each of the country's popular music does in its own domestic market. The results are quite
encouraging for most of the developing countries wishing to commercialize their music. For
example, in Indonesia, of all the popular music sold in the country in 1986, 81 percent was
national popular music, and only 19 percent was foreign. The percentages are also high for
Bulgaria (80 percent), Turkey (78 percent), Ghana (71 percent), Brazil (66 percent), and
Nigeria (65 percent). For these countries, their own music provides a significant domestic
market to attract a profitable music industry, with a critical mass of artists, investors, and

competitive SMEs. It also provides a basis for developing exports either directly or through joint ventures with global corporations. The domestic market for the BEMs—Brazil, Indonesia, Turkey, and even Nigeria—is big enough to attract foreign direct investment (FDI), providing the investment climate is attractive.

Table 10.1 also reveals export opportunities for developing countries. The data for the developed countries shows that they consume more foreign music. For example, in 1986, France's share of its national popular music as a percentage of all popular music consumed in the country was 47 percent. This means that more than one-half of France's market for popular music went to foreign popular music producers. The table shows similar results for other high- and middle-income countries: Hungary (29 percent), South Africa (23 percent), Canada (10 percent), New Zealand (9 percent), and Switzerland (7 percent). This means that these countries offer sizable market opportunities for developing and emerging economies to export their popular music. Since the population in these countries is already consuming large volumes of foreign popular music, chances are foreign music from developing and emerging economies would be equally attractive. This is particularly likely to be the case if the music is hybridized and marketed through global distribution channels.

Hybridization, the cross-cultural enrichment of art and music, brings the industry to a crossroad between culture and commerce. It makes monocultural art and music attractive to the global economy and global society and enriches both poor and rich countries alike. For example, the Americanization of Latin America is increasingly being matched by the Latinization of the United States. Examples of traditional music benefiting from hybridization include gamelan (Indonesia), salsa (Latino), Congolese (Democratic Republic of the Congo), calypso (Caribbean), morna (Cape Verde), rai (Algeria), and rap (African American).

COPYRIGHT PROTECTION AND ANTIPIRACY STRATEGIES

The greatest challenge facing the cultural industry the world over is the development of an effective and enforceable system of copyright protection and antipiracy strategies. Copyright is central to the cultural industry because it protects the rights of the creative artists and the business entrepreneurs who invest in the industry. It allows the rights holders to control the copying, distribution, broadcasting, exhibition, or other commercial uses of their works. It provides the economic incentive for the creation and dissemination of music, art, films, books, computer software, paintings, and other works of art. It defines the commercial "rules of the game" and helps maintain integrity in the cultural industry. Piracy is the violation of copyright protection. It is the unauthorized copying, manufacture, distribution, and sale of copyrighted works of art. In the past, piracy used to be determined in terms profit motive or personal gain. However, as the Napster case has shown, the perpetuator is guilty even if there are no direct financial benefits received.[2]

Cultural piracy is a serious global problem. According to the International Federation of Performing Industries, an international lobby organization representing the recording industry in more than seventy countries, in 1998, the global pirate music market topped 2 billion units, with an estimated value of U.S.$4.5 billion. In the same year, Peter Tufo, then

U.S. ambassador to Hungary, in a speech at the "Intellectual Property Rights Protection" held at the International Law Enforcement Academy attended by more than fifty Central and East European law enforcement professionals, estimated that the total annual cost of piracy in the five countries of Eastern Europe—Hungary, Poland, the Czech Republic, Slovakia, and Romania—was more than U.S. $700 million.[3]

Table 10.2 lists seven countries with the most serious piracy problems in 1995. For each country, the table provides data on the relative importance of piracy in both the domestic and the global markets. For example, while Russia's piracy accounted for 16.9 percent of total world private sales, at home, more than 60 percent of the country's sales were pirated. Even the United States, one of the most vocal antipiracy countries, is not free from piracy. It's own piracy accounts for 13 percent of global private sales and 2.3 percent of its own domestic market. With such a big domestic market, 2.3 percent translates into hundreds of millions of dollars. China is often singled out as one of the perpetrators of piracy in the cultural industry. As the table shows, most of this is in the domestic market where almost one-half (48 percent) of the country's sales are pirated. As the Chinese economy continues to grow and as incomes rise and given its huge population, the domestic market becomes significant. This explains why most international antipiracy strategies are directed at China and other BEMs, where the market for cultural goods and services is expected to grow faster than in the industrialized countries. Since China is a full member of the WTO, the antipiracy campaign will intensify, and the government will be obligated to take firm steps to strengthen its antipiracy integrity and regulatory system and enforcement mechanisms.[4] India and Pakistan are also important markets for cultural piracy. India's large population, rising incomes, and a growing high-technology industry in need of computer software make the country particularly important for antipiracy strategies. Table 10.2 shows that Pakistan has the most piracy-dominated domestic market with almost all (93.8 percent) of the country's sales being pirated.

Taken together, the data in the table suggests a strong relationship between cultural piracy and the quality of the country's national integrity and regulatory system as discussed

TABLE 10.2
Major Music Piracy Markets (1995)

Country	Piracy as % of Country Sales	Piracy as % of World Private Sales
Russia	61.8	16.9
United States	2.3	13.0
China	48.5	7.8
Brazil	10.1	5.5
Mexico	22.2	4.0
India	23.0	3.8
Pakistan	93.8	2.9

Source: Compiled from David Throsby, "The Role of Music in International Trade and Economic Development," in *World Cultural Report: Culture, Creativity, and Markets* (Paris: UNESCO, 1998), table 12, p. 200.

in an earlier chapter above. Specifically, countries with weak integrity and regulatory systems experience more serious problem of cultural piracy than those with relatively strong and enforceable systems. If this is true, then organizations such as the U.N. World Intellectual Property Organization (WIPO) should pay more attention to strengthening member states' national integrity and regulatory systems rather than focusing almost exclusively on treaties, whose domestic enforcements remain weak.

WORLD INTELLECTUAL PROPERTY ORGANIZATION: RELEVANCE FOR DEVELOPING COUNTRIES

In 1974, the WIPO was created as a specialized agency of the U.N. system, with a mandate to ensure that rights holders of intellectual property are duly protected worldwide, and that creators, inventors, and authors receive their due recognition and rewards. By providing international copyright protection, the WIPO encourages human creativity in science, technology, literature, and the arts. By providing a stable environment for the marketing of intellectual and cultural products, it promotes commercialization and international trade. As of 2001, the organization's program of work included:

1. development of international intellectual property law,
2. providing simplified and cost-effective global protection systems and services,
3. extending technical assistance to member states,
4. maintaining an arbitration and mediation center,
5. seeking out and maintaining cooperative partnerships with other U.N. agencies and private sector organizations,
6. giving out awards to honor individual creators or inventors who made significant contributions to their countries.[5]

Here, the interest in the WIPO is to find out if the organization can be of assistance to developing countries in the process of developing their cultural industries, and whether they can count on the WIPO as a strategic partner as they prepare for various challenges ahead associated with globalization. The organization assists developing countries, especially the least developed (P2) to develop and maintain their intellectual property infrastructure. This is done using a variety of collaborative strategies. Working with governments of WTO members, the WIPO assists developing countries in modernizing and extending national intellectual property offices and assists them in bringing their intellectual property legislation and administration into line with the provisions of the Agreement on Trade-Related Aspects of Intellectual Property Rights (TRIPs). This helps to promote international trade in culture, and to strengthen the national integrity and regulatory system for copyright protection. Since July 1998, the WIPO has maintained a joint initiative with the WTO aimed at helping developing countries meet their TRIPs obligations—paying particular attention to the least-developed countries—originally scheduled to be met by 2006.

The WIPO also assists developing countries in developing their human capital and strengthening their institutions. This is done in several ways: First, through the WIPO Worldwide Academy, various learning opportunities are made available to developing countries to acquire the necessary knowledge, skills, and competencies to enable them to realize the full benefits of the national, regional, and international intellectual property systems. Targeting mainly policy makers, advisers, and development managers, the programs include new training and teaching techniques, distance learning using the Internet, and use of modern public-access media to disseminate knowledge of intellectual property to the general public. In 1999, the WIPO provided training—more than 200 courses, seminars, and other learning opportunities—to more than 14,000 people from more than 125 countries.

Second, the WIPO assists developing countries in integrating into the Internet environment and acquiring the technical capacity for the electronic delivery of information and services. This allows these countries to exchange commercially valuable information at the international level, including quick and easy access to information about global changes in markets, technology, cultural interchange, and copyright protection. The WIPO is also helpful to developing countries because it provides models for striking a balance between the interests of rights holders and the potential users and clients. For example, it has developed a program for the formulation of appropriate responses for encouraging dissemination and use of online intellectual property such as music and films, while at the same time ensuring the protection of the rights of the creators and copyright owners. It also provides dispute resolution mechanisms relating to online services. These models are potentially useful for countries progressing through commercialization, entrepreneurship, and export of cultural products and services. They are also useful for attracting FDI and global corporations.

Third, the WIPO helps developing countries in developing effective enforcement mechanisms to combat illegal activities including piracy and counterfeiting. This is done by developing tailor-made, nationally focused action plans based on each country's specific needs and capacities. These multiyear capacity development programs are particularly useful in Africa, the Arab States, the Pacific, and parts of Asia, where national intellectual property systems need a lot of international support.

Perhaps one of the lasting benefits for developing countries using the WIPO as a strategic partner, is emulating the collaborative ways by which the organization works with its various principal constituencies. As of June 2000, 175 states were members of the WIPO. In addition to the usual divisions between developed and developing countries, some of these member states are not yet members of the WTO. Yet, the WIPO has to provide services to all its members regardless of their level of globalization.[6] Although only states can become members of the WIPO, the organization regards the private sector as one of its principal constituencies. As well, the WIPO works closely with NGOs and draws on their expertise as consultants in the field. The organization's strategy of developing and maintaining collaborative working relationships with various players from its principal constituencies provides a useful model for newly globalizing developing countries. Although the WIPO cannot do everything for all countries, it is beneficial to include the organization as a strategic partner in the development of a country's cultural industry for globalization.

NOTES

1. World Commission on Culture and Development, *Our Creative Diversity: Report of the World Commission on Culture and Development* (Paris: UNESCO, 1995). Also see Prime Mininster Tony Blair's speech to the Labour Party Convention, October 2, 2001. Available at www.politics.guardian.co.uk.

2. Napster was founded in May 1999 by university student Horatio J. Napster as a free Internet service, nerd-to-nerd file sharing, allowing users to trade music in MP3 (Metallic-a-Peeved) format. This created controversy as users, mostly young people, hailed Napster for democratizing the music industry, while at the same time rights holders accused him of piracy. In December 1995, American record labels sued Napster for illegal distribution of copyrighted music. In July 2000, a U.S. district judge issued an injunction against Napster. Napster appealed. In February 2001, Napster was ordered to shutdown. The controversy continues: With or without Napster, the uneasy interface between technology and the law in the cultural industry continues. See "Music File-Swapping: Napster R.I.P.: The Ex-King of Illegal File-Swapping Expires, But Its Clones Are Thriving," *The Economist*, September 7, 2002, p. 56.

3. For information about the International Federation of Performing Industries, visit www.ifpi.org. Also see Ambassador Tufo's remarks at "Intellectual Property Rights," April 28, 1998 (same Web site).

4. For China's growing economic power, see "China's Rising Power: Enter the Dragon," *The Economist*, March 10, 2001, pp. 23–25. Also see Seth Faison, "Copyright Pirates Prosper in China," *The New York Times*, February 26, 1996. For details of International Federation of Performing Industries' antipiracy strategy, visit http://www.ifpi.org/antipiracy/strategy/html.

5. Detailed information about the WIPO can be found on the organization's Web site: www.wipo.org and related sites.

6. Countries such as Cuba, Sudan, Iran, and Iraq are members of the WIPO but not the WTO.

CHAPTER 11

Globalization, Labor, and Employment Practices

In this chapter, I discuss the effects of globalization on labor and employment practices in developing countries and transition economies. I begin with a general survey of the global employment situation during the 1980s and 1990s before discussing major changes in employment practices in these countries owing to globalization and its drive for greater enterprise competitiveness. I also discuss the importance and challenges of human resource development for globalizing countries to become competitive through training, development, and a commitment to lifelong learning. I then discuss the advantages and disadvantages of imposing extensive labor standards on developing countries and emerging economies, with a brief discussion of child labor. I conclude the chapter with a discussion of the human and institutional competencies and capacities these countries need to develop to be able to manage labor and industrial relations and employment standards and practices for effective and equitable globalization. In general, while globalization has had positive effects on labor and employment practices, these vary across countries, sectors, industries, enterprises, and types of workers. Besides globalization and technological change, significant effects on labor and employment practices can be attributed to other factors such as growth-oriented macroeconomic policies, labor, employment, management practices, and industrial relations systems and practices.

THE GLOBAL EMPLOYMENT SITUATION

According to the ILO in Geneva, during the 1990s, the global employment situation was depressed—just as it had been during the 1980s. The ILO described a world characterized by high levels of unemployment, falling employment, rising poverty, and increasing social tension. It estimated that out of a world labor force of 3 billion people, 140 million, or 4.7 percent, are fully unemployed. While this does not seem like a high rate of unemployment (see Table 11.1 on page 295), another 25–30 percent, or an estimated 900 million people, were underemployed. Moreover, the East Asian crisis is estimated to have added another 10 million unemployed workers worldwide. The situation was particularly harsh, with high risk of exclusion from meaningful labor force participation, for many vulnerable groups

including the unskilled and poorly educated, young people with no previous work experience, the long-term unemployed, older displaced workers, workers with disabilities,
women, and ethnic and minority groups. The report concluded with a call for action: "In
sum, the employment situation in the world remains largely grim and the pressing need to
find new ways to overcome barriers to employment poses a common and urgent challenge
for countries around the globe."[1]

Is globalization to blame for the world's grim unemployment situation? Not entirely. It is
true that global economic integration and increased travel have resulted in increased competitiveness at the national and enterprise levels, forcing producers to find ways to cut costs, improve efficiency, and raise productivity and profits. To attract and retain foreign investments,
countries and companies have had to pay much more attention to labor costs than they have in
the past. Consequently, the globalizing countries experienced more frequent and severe labor
adjustments during the 1980–2000 period than during the previous twenty years.

In addition to globalization, two other factors explaining the world employment situation are technological change and national policy initiatives. Technological advances in
information and computer technology, telecommunications including the Internet, biotechnology, transportation and logistics, and new forms of production, management, and work
organization brought about significant changes in the nature and structure of the required
labor force, especially in globalizing countries that are consistently open to new ideas and
outside influences. A combination of economic global integration and technological advances and the shift from protected import-substitution to competitive export-oriented industries brought about a drastic change in the demand for labor from a large number of
cheap, unskilled workers to more educated, skilled, flexible, and trainable employees. In
those countries where the economic structure shifted from predominantly agricultural or
manufacturing to the service sector, there were sharp changes in the demand for more educated and skilled workers. In fact, one of the prerequisites for a country's ability to take full
advantage of the benefits of globalization is the quality of basic education and workplace
skills and capabilities in the general population.

Perhaps the most important factor for determining the level and quality of employment
during the 1980–2000 period was the national or regional macroeconomic policies and the
vigor with which they were being implemented and sustained. Globalizing regions, developed and developing countries, and transition economies experienced different levels of
unemployment based on the particular labor, employment, and industrial relations systems,
policies, and practices they pursued. Those countries which, in addition to liberal macroeconomic reforms, pursued policies promoting flexible labor markets and employment
practices, decentralized industrial relations systems, and judicious enforcement of labor
standards focusing on "core human standards," fared much better in terms of employment
creation and lower levels of unemployment. On the other hand, countries with rigid labor
and employment laws, regulations, and policies experienced higher levels of unemployment
because they were not able to attract and retain as many new jobs.

Table 11.1 provides data on unemployment rates during the 1980–2000 period for select regions and transition economies. The table compares unemployment rates for Europe
and the United States for 1987 and 1997. In Europe, the unemployment rate remained high
(more than 10 percent) and did not change much. In the United States, it was significantly

TABLE 11.1

Rate of Unemployment: Selected Regions and Countries 1980–2000

Region/Country	Unemployment rates (percentages)	
	1987	1997
Europe	10.4	10.5
United States	6.2	4.9
Latin America & the		
Caribbean	5.7	7.4
Asia and Pacific	1987	1996
Indonesia	2.6	4.1
Malaysia	7.3	2.5
Philippines	9.1	7.4
Thailand	5.9	1.1
Pakistan	3.1	5.4
Sri Lanka	14.1	11.3
Central & Eastern Europe	1993	1996
Bulgaria	16.4	12.5
Czech Republic	3.8	3.9
Hungary	11.9	9.9
Poland	14.0	12.3
Russian Federation	5.5	9.3
Africa	1989	1995
Algeria	17.0	23.8
Mauritius	5.0	6.0
Egypt	6.9	11.3
Europe	1987	1997
Netherlands	9.6	6.3
Sweden	2.1	8.0
France	10.6	11.7
Spain	20.5	20.8

Source: International Labour Organization, "Employability in the Global Economy: How Training Matters," *World Employment Report 1998–99* (Geneva: International Labour Organization, 1999), tables 1.1, 1.6, 1.7, 1.11, 1.12. Available: www.ilo.org.

lower and declined even more during the 1990s. Since both Europe and the United States are globalizing regions of the world, the most plausible explanation for the significant differences in unemployment rates is the differences in their respective labor and employment policies, regulations, and practices. In general, the United States pursues a much more flexible labor market and employment practices than Europe.

Table 11.1 also shows, within Asia and the Pacific, the differential effects of different national policies on the levels and changes of the unemployment rates for the years 1987 and 1996 (before the Asian crisis). Malaysia and Thailand recorded the lowest levels of unemployment in 1996. They also had the most flexible and decentralized labor markets, employment practices, and industrial relations systems. For both Thailand and Malaysia, as well as other middle-income countries that achieved 5 percent or more per capita growth between 1986 and 1994, wage negotiations are decentralized at the enterprise level. None of them have national-level, regionwide, sectorwide, or industry-wide centralized bargaining or collective agreements for wages and other conditions of service. While they have active unions, they are organized enterprise by enterprise. While trade union leaders complain that it is difficult to organize workers enterprise by enterprise, this process provides the necessary flexibility, especially for new enterprises, to negotiate affordable labor contracts. Therefore, it creates attractive conditions for start-up small- and medium-size enterprises (SMEs), which are often the leading job-creating sector of a growing open economy. The globalizing countries enjoying low levels of unemployment provide a policy environment in support of flexibility in wage negotiation, in hiring and firing, and low rates of taxation. Countries experiencing high unemployment rates provide the opposite: rigid employment practices, centralized collective bargaining, and high rates of taxation.[2]

Table 11.1 provides more evidence of the importance of labor market policy and practices for explaining differences in unemployment for different countries in Central and Eastern Europe, Africa, and Europe. The Czech Republic experienced significantly lower levels of unemployment during the 1990s than Bulgaria, Poland, or the Russian Federation. Likewise, in Africa, Mauritius recorded significantly lower levels of unemployment rates than Algeria and Egypt. In Europe, the same is true of the Netherlands as compared to Spain. In all these cases, the countries with the lowest unemployment rates pursued pro-growth macroeconomic policies within the context of flexible labor markets. For example, Mauritius has a decentralized industrial relations system in which wages and other conditions of service are negotiated at the enterprise level. On the other hand, Algeria, Egypt, and Spain—all high unemployment countries—have rigid employment practices, and employers have little or no flexibility in wage negotiations, firing and hiring of staff, and other changes in employment practices. The evidence strongly supports the argument that policy change and labor market flexibility explain the differences in unemployment rates across regions and countries of the world.

GLOBALIZATION AND EMPLOYMENT PRACTICES

Newly globalizing countries must undertake corresponding changes in their labor, employment, and industrial relations laws, regulations, systems, and practices. These changes must be effective at the macro (national), meso (industry, sector, region), and micro (enterprise) levels. The overall objective of these changes is to help the globalizing country move away from a rigid and regulatory regime to an increasingly flexible, open, facilitative, and participative labor and industrial relations system while at the same time providing appropriate protection for the workers. Among other things, the new labor and industrial relations system must (1) encourage and support macroeconomic reforms and growth; (2) promote the effective use of technology, labor market flexibility, and high productivity growth; (3) foster the development of competitive export-oriented entrepreneurial private sector firms and discourage import-substitution, subsidy-dependent industries; (4) re-examine and, where necessary, make changes to the roles, structures, and functions of trade unions, employer associations, workers, governments, and other key actors in the country's industrial relations system; (5) establish effective collaborations and partnerships with government, employers, and workers' organizations to bring about and sustain required changes in the workplace in areas such as work organization, job design, skills development, technological changes, and employee participation, motivation, and commitment; and (6) develop appropriate policies and programs for dealing with the social consequences of globalization such as unemployment, deskilling, child labor, social justice, treatment of vulnerable groups, environmental protection, and so on.

For newly globalizing countries, the two most important newcomers to the industrial relations system are global corporations and entrepreneurial small- and medium-size indigenous private sector firms (SMEs). Global corporations bring in foreign capital, new technology, and management know-how. They create permanent jobs, pay better, tend to be more socially responsible if working within a high integrity governance system, and create business opportunities for the local SMEs. They prefer an industrial relations system characterized by flexible labor markets; decentralized collective bargaining; low taxation; clear and fairly enforced laws, rules, and regulations; and a sizable pool of educated and trainable labor. Experience from the fastest-growing globalizing countries strongly suggests that SMEs are more competitive with a decentralized industrial relations system in which wages and conditions of service are negotiated collectively, or individually, at the enterprise level. This is particularly important for the growth of entrepreneurship and indigenous private sector development because it allows new enterprises to set affordable conditions of service.

A newly globalizing country must reexamine its industrial relations system as it relates to the trade union movement, its role, and organization, and relationships with government, employers, the work it represents, civil society, and the international community. For the most part, developing countries and transition economies have highly politicized trade unions organized nationally by industry, sector, or regions. They have tended to pursue employment policies designed to protect existing jobs and improve the working conditions of those already employed, rather than work for the development of an enabling environment for new job creation. South Africa provides an excellent example. In 2000, the unemployment rate among blacks was almost 50 percent. During the struggle for independence, the trade union movement worked very closely with the African National Congress and other anti-apartheid forces, and when independence came, union leaders gained new power and influence, which they used to push for improvements in wages and other conditions of employment. Consequently, wages for union workers in the formal sector in the major cities are three times the wages of nonunionized workers in the informal sectors in Soweto and other townships. The unions lobbied the new government to pass the Wages Act and the New Industrial Relations Act so that these wage differentials are protected geographically and by sector. This has the unintended consequence of condemning the vast majority of black workers to the informal sector and makes it difficult for new enterprises to join the formal sector because the wages are more than they can afford. The new industrial relations system, designed to right past ills and to protect workers' rights to employment, appears to have the unfortunate effects of labor market rigidity and killing jobs for the unemployed majority.

Changes at the Enterprise Level

For newly globalizing economies, some of the most fundamental changes take place at the enterprise level, affecting production processes, human resource management, and overall enterprise management. Managers, employers, and owners of these enterprises seek to enhance competitiveness through attitudinal and behavioral changes; modern labor policies, legislation, and institutions; compensation and incentive systems linked to enterprise, group, and individual performance; a pool of skilled trainable and adaptable labor; flexible forms of work organization and management; and cross-cultural management and adaptation.[3]

Behavioral and attitudinal changes are required on the part of management, workers, union representatives, and government officials from regulatory agencies. These changes must reflect a deliberate policy of getting away from conflictual modes of industrial relations and human resource management practices to more collaborative and participative practices. The managers must refrain from exercising restrictive and hierarchical close supervision and learn to manage using flexible, participative, consultative, and collaborative styles. Workers need to have a positive and competitive attitude toward work and be well informed and involved in the decisions affecting their work, jobs, and lives. Both management and workers need ongoing feedback on how well they, their coworkers, and the whole enterprise are doing and what they need to do to maintain or enhance competitiveness. There must be closer coordination between industrial relations practices, including the terms and conditions of work as negotiated in the collective agreement and the personnel policies and human resource management practices within the enterprise.

In terms of modern labor policies, legislation, and institutions, the changes should be aimed at maintaining harmony in industrial relations and avoiding work stoppages (strikes or lockouts) by emphasizing conflict prevention rather than resolution and by being proactive in addressing enterprise-level labor and industrial relations problems, disputes, and grievances. Collaborative approaches to industrial relations practices such as alternative dispute resolution methods and interest-based bargaining should be tried and, where appropriate, institutionalized. Perhaps one of the most profound changes is the pressures for increased enterprise efficiency and effectiveness and the corresponding demands by managers and entrepreneurs to link wage increases to clearly identified performance criteria, not only at the enterprise level but right down to the individual managers, supervisors, and employees. This differs significantly from the old methods of wage determination based on seniority, which is what unions prefer, and job content as determined by job analysis and job evaluation, which is the traditionally favored approach by personnel administration. Enterprises interested in developing performance-based compensation systems should have in place management systems and practices that establish clear performance criteria and management, attract and retain competent staff by providing a component of compensation over and above regular pay, reward sound performance without significantly increasing labor costs, and maintain labor force flexibility so that the enterprise can quickly make labor adjustments in response to the economic/business cycle and its own poor performance.

Flexible forms of work organization and management are particularly common among competitive global corporations. These include job redesign, away from highly specialized individual jobs to broader, higher-value, and capabilities jobs requiring cross-training and multiskilling; flat and learning organizations with emphasis on cross-functional coordination and the application of lessons of experience related to superior performance to the work of individual managers and workers in other parts of the organization; and rationalization of enterprise operations. Rationalization can take different forms, including identifying core functions—those which are related to the core mission and business objectives—outsourcing, downsizing, forming strategic alliances, and benchmarking. All these changes are designed to keep the enterprise competitive and, therefore, require a strategic approach to both industrial relations and human resource management. All this is aimed at improving enterprise productivity and global competitiveness.

Skills and Competencies for Global Competitiveness

Globalization thrives on individual initiatives. In the old, partially closed systems of political economy, the emphasis was on the state, the party, the church, or monopolistic enterprises as the drivers of development and progress. Globalization is much more people-centered. Its success ultimately depends on many able and willing individuals taking risks and the initiative, learning, working hard, and persevering in order to create value, enjoy the fruits of their efforts, and contribute to the country's overall improvements in living standards. Of course, institutions are still important, but without a critical mass of individuals with the commitment, motivation, skills, and competencies, no country can succeed in the global economy or global society. In this section, I highlight the importance for newly globalizing countries to develop and maintain—within their societies—quality education, skills, and competencies for global competitiveness.

During the 1980s and 1990s, when more countries were responding to the challenges of globalization, it became clear that human capital development is a major engine of economic growth. Differences in living standards both within and between countries could be explained in differences in the level and quality of education and workplace skills and competencies. Countries, cities, or parts thereof with a critical mass of educated and skilled people have the advantage of being able to understand and exploit new and emerging opportunities of globalization. They can adapt more quickly and efficiently to new ideas and technology, acquire new competitive skills, establish productive relationships with outsiders, and create new opportunities in response to the changing circumstances around them. In this regard, successful globalization means that the country has the capacity to identify the right opportunities for the right people, with the right educational levels, skills, and competencies, producing the right goods and services, at the right time, place, and price for the world economy.

How does a newly globalizing country develop the necessary skills and competencies for global competitiveness? While the particular strategies differ depending on a country's history, culture, demographics, and political economy, there are some common basic elements that can be applied to many globalizing developing countries and transition economies. Following are some of the key elements.[4]

1. Basic education is necessary but not sufficient. The population should be literate and numerate. It should be able to function not only in its local languages but also in at least one of the international languages. It should be computer literate as well. Yet, given the rapid

and continuous pace of change in the demand for new skills, skill sets, and qualifications, the globalizing country must emphasize continuous training and a culture of lifelong learning for its population. For this reason, countries and donors focusing only on universal primary education without, at the same time, enhancing the population's competitive skills and competencies and providing opportunities for lifelong learning are not building long-term competitive capabilities. Low-quality primary education for the masses does not prepare a country for global competitiveness or build a learning society.

2. Successful globalizing countries need an effective system of portable skills. The term *portable skills* is used here to refer to the transfer of skills from family and school to work and from work to work. In the first instance, the globalizing country must have an educational system with successful transition from school to work. This depends on three things: a solid, high-quality basic education; the development of sound analytical, cognitive, and behavioral skills and the ability to communicate ideas and solve problems individually and in groups; and close working relationships between the schools, their communities, and the prospective employers through activities that expose students to the practical realities of work. This can be done through apprenticeships, vocational training, coops, work–study arrangements, and staff exchanges between employers and training institutions.

The second reference to portable skills—from one work situation to others—is important because globalization involves a process of "destructive construction," which is destroying old industries or jobs and creating new ones. Therefore, the globalizing country's labor force should have the capacity to move from the jobs of declining industries to the emerging and growing sectors. This is determined by the workers' potential for learning and the quality of enterprise training and work experience they get. The more general and theoretical training—emphasizing principles and general applications—the workers receive, the better they become at transferring skills across jobs. Cross-training, multiskilling, and exposure to various jobs facilitate transfer. Narrow, highly specialized, job-specific training does not facilitate skills transfer across jobs, enterprises, or industries.

3. A globalizing country needs a general population and labor force with the education, training, and mind-set for flexibility in adapting to new technology and changing workplace demands and expectations. Just as enterprises must be flexible in order to remain competitive, the labor force must also remain flexible in order to be employable. Workers with a higher education and a better level of skills and competencies tend to adjust better and more effectively to the changing workplace requirements. Young workers also tend to be more flexible than older workers. Yet, older workers have more work experience with valuable corporate memory. Therefore, to be successful, a globalizing country needs a mixture of young and experienced workers. There is also evidence to suggest that diversity at the workplace is associated with creativity and more effective group problem solving.

4. Newly globalizing countries need to review and modernize their educational and training institutional infrastructure to reflect changing labor market demands. The new institutional infrastructure must be characterized by responsive and flexible partnerships. All the institutions involved in education and training must be responsive and flexible. Close working relationships, partnerships, or strategic alliances should be encouraged between and among academic schools and training institutions; between schools and employers, the trade unions, and the workers; and the government must play a leadership role in areas

such as policy development, strategic funding, and facilitating the development of effective partnerships among the major stakeholders.

A case can be made for the development of a global (or regional) system of training for skills and competencies for the global economy. Before the recent wave of globalization started, most of the countries developed their educational and training policies and institutions independently of other countries. Citizens were educated and trained for the national labor market. Those who left were regarded as a brain drain or statistically insignificant loss. Although labor is still much less mobile than capital, highly educated people with portable skills and experiences are highly globally mobile. With increasing globalization, labor will become much more global as well. The skills and competencies for global corporations and international organizations are also becoming more global in terms of the intrinsic requirements for effective job performance. Governments of globalizing countries also require public servants who are globally apt and experienced.

As well, the third sector—NGOs, community organizations, traditional institutions, and so on—cannot provide effective leadership to civil society without acquiring the skills and competencies required to deal with others in the global society. Therefore, it makes sense for newly globalizing countries to get together and investigate the opportunities for the development of a global training, learning, and skills development system whereby local, national, and regional institutions will be linked together globally. Global corporations and the world's leading education and training institutions can play an important role in providing resources and expertise for the development of the global learning and skills development system. Already, American and European education and training institutions are extending their services to the global market, but these are very limited and targeted only to those who can afford the exorbitant training costs. The proposed global training system should be more inclusive and affordable and be aimed at creating opportunities for citizens of marginalized globalizing countries to acquire globally competitive skills and competencies.

5. Most developing countries have a sizable and economically active informal sector. This sector creates business and employment opportunities for millions of people, especially those with less formal education, skills, and competencies needed in the formal sector. No discussion of education, training, and skills development is complete without paying serious attention to modernizing the informal sector and making it globally competitive. According to the ILO in Geneva, initiatives should be taken by globalizing developing countries to increase incomes, productivity, and working conditions for the informal sector. These initiatives include upgrading traditional apprenticeship systems; increasing access to new technology through training and extension services; increasing operational linkages and developing strategic alliances between the informal sector and the emerging SMEs; increasing networking to arrange for cost-effective training and skills development for the informal sector; and rethinking the mix, packaging, and delivery of services to the informal sector including training, credit, extension services, technology transfer, infrastructure development, and government services. Newly globalizing developing countries need an efficient modernizing informal sector to serve the economy not only as an engine of growth but, equally important, as a cushion or insurance policy for the rest of the economy, especially during periods of economic crises.

6. Globalization creates and highlights the plight of vulnerable and marginalized groups who are unable to participate or take full advantage of the opportunities of globalization. Although these groups can be found in every country, developing countries and transition economies have higher percentages of the excluded population. The typical vulnerable groups include the poorly educated and unskilled; young people with limited education and no previous work experience; displaced, often older, workers; women; people with disabilities; and ethnic and minority groups. Education, training, and skills development provide effective tools against exclusion. Newly globalizing developing countries and transition economies must develop policies and programs specifically targeted to their vulnerable groups.

Programs for education, training, and skills development for vulnerable groups have four basic objectives: integration into the labor force either as employees or self-employed persons; providing resources, opportunities, and skills for independent living; providing social and welfare services to enable workers to live with dignity; and respecting workers' human rights and protecting them from abuse and exploitation by other more powerful members of society.

In most globalizing countries, women provide the bulk of the increase in labor supply. By opening up education, training, and skills development opportunities and by providing supportive working conditions and a good environment, women can become more active participants in the global economy. By providing child care and other family services, flexible maternity leave, and enforcing antidiscrimination laws, women's employment opportunities, especially in the sectors in which they are underrepresented, can be greatly enhanced. In most newly globalizing developing countries, women need better access to education and training in mathematics, science, information and communication technologies, management, and entrepreneurship.

LABOR STANDARDS: GOOD OR BAD?

The ILO was created in 1919 primarily for the purpose of adopting and helping enforce standards to cope with the problems of labor conditions involving injustice, hardship, and privation. In 1944, the Declaration of Philadelphia was incorporated into the ILO's constitution, thus broadening its mandate to include more general, but related, social policy, human and civil rights, and general conditions of work. Therefore, labor standards have been around much longer than the current wave of globalization. Yet, with globalization, labor standards have become very controversial especially between the advanced countries, on one hand, and the developing countries and transition economies, on the other hand. The controversy is directly related to international trade and competitiveness, with overtones for human and civil rights as well as social justice.

The case for strict enforcement of labor standards is advanced by the ILO and supported by the WTO with strong backing from the industrialized countries. They argue that by not enforcing labor standards, emerging economies, developing countries, and transition economies are able to produce internationally tradable goods and services below cost and, therefore, gain unfair cost advantage over their competitors who pay to have the standards fully enforced. It is also argued that enforcement of standards protects vulnerable workers from abuse and exploitation from the powerful owners of capital and their agents. The abuse and exploitation takes many forms, including low wages with no benefits; slavelike working conditions; endangering workers' health and safety; and depriving workers of their human and civil rights especially in terms of the right to support and belong to a union, the right to collective bargaining, and the right to refuse to work in unhealthy and unsafe environments. Exploitation can also be targeted to vulnerable and voiceless groups such as children, migrant workers, and the poor, uneducated, and unskilled job seekers. The history of industrialization is a history of abuse and exploitation of the weak by the powerful. Therefore, governments and the international community have a duty and a responsibility to provide and enforce labor standards to protect workers from abuse and exploitation.

Developing countries see it differently. While accepting the need to protect workers from abuse and exploitation from unscrupulous employers, they argue that the current labor standards go too far, cost too much, and are not related to their cultural, social, or economic realities. In terms of international trade, the elaborate and costly labor standards take on the form of nontariff protectionism by the advanced countries. Emerging economies and developing countries are most competitive in labor-intensive industries such as agriculture, textiles, tourism, and other services. Labor standards have direct upward effects on labor costs and, therefore, raise the cost of production for these countries. By insisting on strict observation of labor standards and by threatening boycott if they do not observe them, advanced countries and the international organizations are undermining the developing countries' capacity to compete and participate in the global economy.

The debate about human and civil rights and social justice is much more complicated because it includes issues related to national political and governance ideology and systems, local cultural values and practices, national sovereignty, and international law. For example, over the years, different industrial relations systems and employment practices have evolved in different countries with varying degrees of effective protection of workers' rights. It is also necessary to consider labor standards in the broader context of society's economic realities and political and cultural development. Poor people are more likely to give up some of their political rights in order to improve their economy and personal standards of living. As well, most traditional societies in developing countries do not have the same history of human and civil rights as practiced in the rich advanced societies. Therefore, it is reasonable to expect that as these economies grow and societies advance they will be less willing to continue giving up their political rights and, instead, insist on more strict enforcement of labor standards. In fact, this is already happening in many emerging markets and developing countries where the emergence of a critical mass of educated middle-class citizens has created conditions for the population to demand political reform and respect for human rights. Since workers and trade unions are always part of this middle-class pressure group, there is a tendency for the reforms to focus on workers' rights and improved wages and working conditions.

Are labor standards good or bad for developing countries? The answer is yes and no. They are good because they provide appropriate protection for the workers and attempt to ensure international standards of treatment. They are bad because they impose hardships on the developing countries. The international community should not impose minimum conditions of work or even institutional arrangements for collective bargaining on newly globalizing developing countries; this would cost a country an unreasonable amount of money and would produce few benefits to the population. Imposing standards on others is morally wrong and smacks of imperialism. As well, there is no empirical evidence to support the view that these standards are significantly beneficial to the targeted groups, the total labor force, or the general population.

Still, the international community has a role to play in protecting workers and their rights. Instead of developing and enforcing blanket uniform labor standards for all countries with widely different economic, political, social, and cultural realities, efforts should be directed to the development of core human standards. These core human standards would cover a smaller range of items and limit itself to widely acceptable human standards such as protection against slavelike conditions, freedom of association and collective bargaining, protection from unhealthy and unsafe workplaces, and protection of vulnerable groups, such as children, from abuse and exploitation. These core human standards should be strictly enforced. However, they should not include "non-core" human standards such as minimum wages, conditions of work, the right to hire or fire, or the type of acceptable industrial relations system. One of the problems with existing labor standards is that they are not adequately enforced by governments of most of the developing countries. This is partly because most of these governments lack the human capital and institutional capacity for effective enforcement and partly because they see them as an externally imposed obligation over which they have no local control, influence, or ownership.

Globalization, Wages, and Income Distribution

Globalization has been blamed for depressing wage levels and accentuating differences in income distribution among rich, developing, and least-developed countries. Differences in income, wealth, and opportunity has been escalating since the 1980s, and grew worse in the 1990s. According to the UNDP's *Human Development Report 2000*, in 1999 the combined wealth of the world's 200 richest people was U.S.$1 trillion, while the combined incomes of the 582 million people living in the forty-three least-developed countries was only U.S.$146 million.[5] Income distribution problems arise, in part, within income classes or between different skill and competence levels but not between economies, which grow more or less rapidly as a result of globalization.

At the enterprise level, union wages are driven down by the openness of the world financial system. Capital mobility poses limits on trade unions' wage demands in light of high elasticity of demand for labor. According to the Stoker–Samuelson theorem, increased globalization lowers the relative wages of unskilled labor in the advanced countries and raises the relative wages of unskilled labor in developing countries when the two groups of countries begin to trade together. However, labor economists are not sure of the validity of this theorem or the conditions or contingencies under which it may or may not hold. What is clear is that besides globalization and trade, wages for unskilled labor are pulled down by technological change and the large supply of unskilled job seekers in most of the developing countries.

It is predicted that most globalizing developing countries will continue to experience high unemployment and downward wage pressures for unskilled labor. A number of factors account for this: First, demographically, these countries have an almost unlimited supply of young, unskilled, inexperienced job seekers. A typical developing country's population distribution is about 40 percent under fifteen years of age. In ten years' time, this young cohort will have left school and joined the already crowded ranks of the unemployed job seekers. In the short and immediate term, there is little policy makers can do to stem this flow. Second, the overall demand for unskilled labor is not growing. While the East Asian economies made their miracles based on cheap unskilled labor and while such opportunities still exist in the traditional labor-intensive industries such as construction, agriculture, and textiles, the new economy is increasingly dependent on skilled rather than unskilled labor. Third, many of the newly globalizing developing countries have poor-quality education, especially in the rural areas where the majority of the population lives. For example, in East Africa, as the education systems expanded and grew fast to accommodate increasing numbers of students, the quality of education went down. This is particularly so in the government-supported public systems and the rural areas. A recent Canadian International Development Agency report on Uganda's education system confirms my impressions. It found that the results of a random national sample of third-grade students showed a significant decline in performance. On the mathematics test, the number of students who achieved a satisfactory score declined from 48 percent in 1996 to 31 percent in 1999. In English, the scores declined from 92 percent to 56 percent. On the reading test, only 11 percent of the sample achieved a satisfactory score in 1999. The results were even worse in rural areas, with Kampala (the major urban area in the country) outperforming all other regions.[6] Therefore, with or without trade and globalization, poorly educated, unskilled workers—the majority of the labor force in many globalizing developing countries—will continue to be disadvantaged in the labor market.

Child Labor

Child labor is a multidimensional and often emotional problem blamed on globalization. It has taken on an international dimension, although its meaning and implications vary across regions, countries, and sectors and between urban and rural settings. Like many other socioeconomic problems, child labor is not entirely caused by the current wave of globalization. Stories of child labor and child abuse in the workplace date back to the early days of the Industrial Revolution, first in England, then in mainland Europe and North America. Globalization has made the problem worse and more visible, and therefore, newly globalizing developing countries must respond to the challenge by developing realistic policies, systems, institutional arrangements, programs, and enforcement mechanisms to protect their children from workplace abuses and exploitation.

According to the ILO, by the year 2000, there were some 250 million children 5–14 years old who were involved in economic activities in the developing countries. This is approximately 8.3 percent of the total estimated global labor force of 3 billion people. Close to one-half of them—120 million—carry out these economic activities on a full-time basis, while the other half combines working with schooling. These figures do not include children who perform "noneconomic" activities such as domestic or family services on a full-time or part-time basis without pay. In terms of gender, approximately three-quarters of the child labor force are boys. On the other hand, more girls than boys perform the noneconomic unpaid domestic work.[7]

The distribution of child labor varies by region, industry, occupation, and urban–rural setting. In absolute terms, Asia (excluding Japan) has the highest density of child labor with 61 percent of the world total (about 152.5 million) as compared to 32 percent (80 million) for Africa, 7 percent (17.5 million) for Latin America, and a small number for other developing regions of the world. In relative terms, however, Africa has the highest child labor participation rate, with about two children out of five, or 41 percent of the total number of children 5–14 years old, involved in paid economic activities. Since the largest number of working children is in Asia and since Asia leads the developing world in globalization and trade, the link between child labor and globalization is easy to make. Yet, Africa, which is much less globalized, also has a serious and growing child labor problem.[8]

Child labor participation is directly related to underdevelopment. The less developed a country is, the greater the proportion of the child population who work. In most cases, these countries have a wide range of economic activities that require extra hands but no specific skills. Accordingly, the least-developed countries have most of the child labor in basic industries such as agriculture, whereas the emerging markets have moved them to more "advanced" jobs in service and simple manufacturing. For example, in Cambodia, close to 90 percent of child labor is in agriculture; but in the Philippines, an increasing number of children have moved from agriculture to wholesale and retail trade, restaurants, and hotels.

Although statistics are always hard to validate for clandestine and sometimes illegal activities such as child labor, Table 11.2 provides the best estimates from a number of developing countries. By far, the largest number of working children, both boys and girls, are in agriculture, hunting, forestry, and fishing. This is because agriculture is labor intensive, requires no specific skills or previous working experience, takes place in rural areas where most of the children live, and is hard to regulate by labor inspectors often found in urban areas in the offices of the ministries of labor. Other sectors in which children are heavily employed are manufacturing, wholesale and retail trade, restaurants and hotels, transport and communications, and community, social, and personal services. Contrary to popular belief, construction is not a heavy employer of child labor. This may be because of the heavy lifting required, increased mechanization and required skill levels, or simply better labor inspection on construction sites as compared to agricultural plantations. Likewise, mining and quarrying— despite their rural, isolated locations—do not employ large numbers of children.

Table 11.2 also gives statistics for the distribution of injuries by industry and gender. Children are more susceptible to injury or illness from work than adults; they are physically tender, mentally not fully mature, and are more likely to take undue risks at work. In the advanced countries, young drivers (16–21 years old) are involved in more driving accidents than other driver age groups. Similar factors are in play with children in the labor force in developing countries. According to the statistics (see Table 11.2), the largest number of injuries occur in agriculture and related industries. Other sectors of high injury rates for child labor include wholesale, retail, restaurant and hotels, manufacturing, construction, transport and communication, and community, social, and personal services. The injuries and illnesses vary in seriousness and include punctures; broken or complete loss of body parts; burns and skin disease; eye, hand, and hearing impairment; respiratory and gastrointestinal illness; fever; headaches; and other illnesses associated with exposure to excessive heat or harmful chemicals. Both the distribution of injuries by sector and the type of injuries

TABLE 11.2

Distribution of Economically Active Children 5–14 Years Old in Developing Countries, by Region, Industry, Injuries, and Gender

Distribution	Both Sexes	Boys	Girls
I. Region			
World (estimate in millions)	250	140	110
World (in percentages)	24.7	27.0	22.0
Regions	%	%	%
Africa	32	56	44
Asia (excluding Japan)	61	54	46
Latin America & Caribbean	7	67	33
Oceania (excluding Australia and New Zealand)	0.2	57	43
II. Industry	%	%	%
1. Agriculture, hunting, forestry and Fishing	70.4	68.9	75.3
2. Mining and Quarrying	0.9	1.0	0.9
3. Manufacturing	8.3	9.4	7.9
4. Construction	1.9	2.0	1.9
5. Wholesale, retail, restaurants and Hotels	8.3	10.4	5.0
6. Transport, Storage and Communication	3.8	3.8	-
7. Community, Social and Personal Services	6.5	4.7	8.5
III. Distribution of Injuries	%	%	%
1. Agriculture, hunting, forestry and Fishing	70.2	75.8	57.2
2. Manufacturing	4.7	4.3	5.8
3. Construction	2.9	4.1	0.3
4. Wholesale, retail, restaurants and Hotels	13.4	8.3	-
5. Transport, Storage and Communication	2.6	3.8	-
6. Community, Social and Personal Services	4.9	2.5	10.2

Source: Complied from various tables from Kebebew Ashagrie, "Statistics on Working Children and Hazardous Child Labor in Brief," ILO Working Paper Series (Geneva: ILO, April 1998). Available: www.ilo.org/public/english/comp/child/stat/stats.htm.

reported are similar to studies of occupational health and safety in the more advanced countries. For example, agriculture, construction, transport, and personal services continue to be the major sources of occupational accidents in industrial countries. Most of the injuries are to the back (due to lifting), fingers, hands, arms, legs, eyes, feet, and other exposed body parts.

In an ideal world, there would be no child labor. In the real world, children have always been and perhaps will continue to be part of the labor force. The international community, through the United Nations, bilateral donors, and NGOs, is working very hard to eradicate or at least reduce the incidence of child labor. In November 1999, the ILO celebrated the coming into force of the "Worst Forms of Child Labor Convention," which was adopted by the International Labor Conference in June 1999 and has since been ratified by more than forty countries. The convention came up with proposals to protect children against the worst forms of child labor. These proposals included research activities; development of international guidelines; capacity building and institutional development in labor ministries and employers' and workers' organizations; advocacy and awareness-raising campaigns; assistance in developing legal instruments to combat discrimination and stigmatization and offer social protection, training, and workers' educational programs; sensitization activities targeted at employers and their organizations; and care and support initiatives.

Since child labor cannot be completely eliminated, especially in the short run for the newly globalizing least-developed countries, one of the short-term protective measures should be improvements in health and safety targeted at the countries and industries with the largest participation of child labor. Most industrial accidents can be prevented through education and proper enforcement of basic safety rules and regulations: using proper safety devices (for example, clothes, boots, eyeglasses), using proper work procedures and supervision, following good housekeeping practices, complying with the law regarding reporting of accidents and injuries, avoiding carelessness or horseplay, and providing proper training and staffing. Proper incentives at the enterprise, industry, and national levels can bring about required changes in behavior. International campaigns such as labeling of goods that are not produced with child labor could also reduce abuse and exploitation. This has proven to be effective in international environmental campaigns such as "dolphin-friendly tuna." The trade union movement, as a business organization and champion of social justice, can play a leading role in eliminating or reducing child labor in developing countries and improving the health and safety of the workplace for all employees, both young and old.

CAPACITY DEVELOPMENT

In addition to reviewing the global employment situation as of the year 2000, this chapter has discussed the effects of globalization on employment practices, required skills and competencies for global competitiveness, labor standards, and child labor. It has emphasized the need for globalizing countries to maintain flexible and responsive labor and employment practices; a collaborative, decentralized, and facilitative industrial relations system; cost-effective and technologically adaptable enterprise management; and a regulatory system that provides effective protection of workers including protection of children from abuse and exploitation. All this requires capacities and competencies. It requires human capital in the form of knowledge, skills, competencies and motivation, and institutional capacities within government, the trade union movement, the business sector, and civil society in general.

Most of the newly globalizing developing countries and transition economies do not have the necessary capabilities and institutional capacities for the effective management of the required changes in labor and employment practices. For example, in the Asian countries with the worst cases of child labor, a major part of the problem is the inability or un-willingness by the authorities at the different levels of society to enforce existing laws, rules, and regulations for the protection of children against abuse and exploitation by employers. As the ILO has stated in various field missions, the ministries of labor in most developing countries are often institutionally weak because they do not get the same priority as high-profile ministries such as finance and economic planning. The trade union movements tend to be politically active but professionally and organizationally weak, and most of the work-ers, especially in the informal sector and those employed by family and SMEs, are often un-organized. Even professional associations for trades and professionals are often small and organizationally weak. There are very few community-based organizations or NGOs spe-cializing in labor and employment, especially in the context of globalization. Very little em-pirical research has been done on the relationship between globalization, labor, and employment practices. Accordingly, policy makers are forced to make policy without local knowledge or to accept advice from outside. At the enterprise level, while global corpora-tions have the resources and expertise to introduce and manage the required changes in labor and employment practices, the other parts of the business sector—the SMEs and the informal sector—have very limited capabilities and capacities to do so. Even the global cor-porations often need to adapt their technology, products, services, and management know-how to the changing local conditions. Therefore, it is quite clear that developing countries and transition economies need to develop and sustain a wide range of knowledge, skills, and competencies as well as institutional arrangements to be able to manage labor, employment, and industrial relations in accordance with the requirements for globalization.

Table 11.3 provides a summary of the required capacity development for managing labor and employment under globalization. The five key areas of required capacities and capabili-ties are policy management and coordination; reform of the country's industrial relations sys-tem; development of competitive knowledge, skills, and competencies; enterprise-level innovations; and effective protection of workers including all the vulnerable groups. The table also provides examples of lead institutions corresponding to specific required capacities and the functions they must perform effectively. If these institutions are unable or unwilling to perform the required functions, initiatives must be undertaken to address the perfor-mance gaps. For example, it is important for the newly globalizing country to formulate new policies regarding labor and employment practices. In this regard, the government must take the lead in consultation with other stakeholders in the private sector. This requires political will and technical and administrative capabilities in the cabinet (executive), parliament (leg-islative), line ministries such as labor (technical and administrative), and local and interna-tional research institutes for knowledge and information. If any of these is lacking, then the government, in partnership with the international community and the local stakeholders, should take the necessary steps to address the identified capacity gaps.

When the government is so weak that it does not have the capacity to assess its own ca-pacity requirements, the international community through bilateral donors and specialized U.N. agencies such as the ILO and the WTO should provide the necessary resources and expertise. The international labor movement can also play a developmental role by work-ing closely with the weak, poor countries to strengthen their capacities for the manage-ment of labor and employment practices. Global corporations have extensive resources

TABLE **11**.3
Capacity Development for Managing Labor and Employment under Globalization

Required Capacity	Lead Institutions	Illustrative Functions
1. Policy: Management and co-ordination	• Cabinet • Parliament • Ministry of Labor • Research Institute	• Policy formulation & implementation • Policy co-ordination at home/abroad • Research: Labor & employment • International representation
2. Reform of Industrial Relations System	• Ministry of labor • Trade Unions • Employer Organizations • GC; SMEs;ISO	• Changing laws, rules & regulations • Promoting industrial relations collaboration, not conflict • Strengthening collective bargaining at enterprise level • Facilitating flexible & responsive, competitive labor markets
3. Development of Competitive Skills and Competencies	• Academic and Training Institutions • Ministry of Education • GC;SMEs;ISO • Technology Vendors • Employer and Trade Union Organizations	• Developing cost effective programs for continuous training, portable skills, & life long learning • Close co-ordination among training, employer & employee organizations • Development of global learning system
4. Enterprise Level Innovations	• GC;SMEs;ISO • Ministry of Industry • Business/Manage-ment Consulting Firms • Employers and Trade Union Organizations	• Introducing cost effective production processes & management systems • Developing culture of technological innovation & global competitiveness • Effective enterprise level collective bargaining
5. Effective Protection of Workers	• Ministry of Labor • Trade Union and Employer Organizations • Mass Media • Local/traditional Authorities • ILO;WTO;UN; NGOs	• Judicious enforcement of labor standards & worker protection • Protection of children from abuse & exploitation • Education, advocacy, training, sensitization, social protection, international campaigns, incentives, etc.

Note: ILO = International Labour Organization; WTO = World Trade Organization; UN = United Nations; NGOs = nongovernmental organizations; GC = global corporations; SMEs = small- and medium-size enterprises; ISO = informal sector organizations.

and expertise in this area, and they, too, should be involved in assisting these countries build the necessary knowledge, skills, competencies, and institutions. For example, they are very good in the development of competitive knowledge, skills, and competencies as well as managing enterprise-level innovations and collective bargaining. Therefore, they can help these countries in their efforts to build the capacities they need in these areas as well as reforming their industrial relations system. International research institutions can also help the local research institutes to develop and retain the competencies they need to undertake labor and employment research needed for globalization. All this would need mobilization, coordination, and effective utilization. Therefore, in terms of sequencing, it makes sense to begin by strengthening the human capabilities and institutional capacity of the ministry of labor, the workers' organizations, and civil society in general.

NOTES

1. This discussion draws on the *World Employment Report: 1998–99* (Geneva: International Labour Organization, 1999), 4. Available: www.ilo.org.

2. See Jeffrey Sachs, "Globalization and Industrial Relations in Asia," Public Lecture for the ILO, Geneva, January 2001; this is also available on the ILO Web site. Also see Matthew J. Slaughter and Philip Swagel, "Does Globalization Lower Wages and Export Jobs?" Economic Issues Paper 11 (Washington, DC: IMF, 1997).

3. For a detailed discussion of globalization and industrial relations in Asia, see David Macdonald, "Industrial Relations and Globalization: Challenges for Employers and their Organizations" (paper prepared for the ILO Workshop on Employers' Organizations, Turin, Italy, May 5–13, 1997). Available on the ILO Web site.

4. See ILO, "How Training Matters," in *World Employment Report 1998–99* (Geneva: ILO, 1999), 201–224. Also see Jane Knight and Hans de Wit, "An Introduction to the IQRP Project and Process," in *Quality and Internationalization in Higher Education* (Paris: OECD, 1999), 45–59.

5. United Nations, *World Development Report 2000* (New York: UNDP, 2001), 82. Also see Nancy Birdsall, "Managing Inequality in the Developing World," *Current History* 98, no. 631 (November 1999):376–381.

6. Data obtained from "Support to the Universal Primary Education of the Government of Uganda using the Sector Wide Approach," Project Approval Document (Hull, Quebec: Canadian International Development Agency, Government of Canada, January 2001).

7. This discussion draws on Kebebew Ashagrie, "Statistics on Working Children and Hazardous Child Labor in Brief," ILO Working Paper 7, 1–14. (Geneva: ILO, 1997; revised April 1998). Available: www.ilo.org/public/English/comp/child/stat/stats.htm. For an update, see ILO, *A Future without Child Labour: Global Report under the Follow-up to the ILO Declaration on Fundamental Principles and Rights at Work* (Geneva: ILO, International Labour Conference [90th Session], 2002), pt. 1.

8. See Jens Andvig, Sudharshan Canagarajah, and Anne Kielland, "Issues on Child Labor in Africa," Africa Region Human Development Working Paper Series (Washington, DC: World Bank, September 2001). Available: www.worldbank.org/childlabor.

CHAPTER 12

Globalization and the Environment

In this chapter I discuss the dynamic, complex, and often controversial relationships between globalization and the environment. I begin with a brief discussion of the state of the global environment as of the end of the twentieth century and then focus on the impact of globalization on the environment. After discussing the significance of the big-eight environmental countries (E8), I turn to an examination of the impact of business enterprises and the environment, looking separately at the contributions of the global corporations and the local business sector. I also discuss the relationship between poverty and the environment, focusing mainly on those poor countries and communities marginalized by globalization, but suffering from environmental degradation. I end the chapter with a discussion of the changing role of the state and the need to build partnerships, capabilities, and capacities for environmental management for all developing countries and transition economies. Environmental challenges are so complex and interdependent that no one country or institution can go it alone. It will take collective will and collaborative effort and persistence for the individual communities, countries, regions, and the international community to gather strength and take the necessary practical steps to maintain a healthy balance between the twin goals of globalization and sustainable development. This explains, at least in part, why the international community has given broad-based support to the Kyoto Accord.

THE EARTH'S ENVIRONMENTAL REPORT CARD: 2000

Most environmental doctors, advocates, and caregivers agree that the earth is, and has been for some time, in ill health. They also agree that if present trends of global production and consumption continue, the earth's health will not improve and may get worse. Sustainable development remains an honorable but elusive global goal. In June 1997, the U.N. General Assembly Special Session (UNGASS), also known as "Earth Summit +5" or "Earth Summit II," met in New York five years after the Rio Earth Summit of 1992 to review the environmental health of the earth and to develop a plan of action for the future. Background technical reports prepared for UNGASS concluded that by most measures of environmental conditions worldwide, the earth's conditions have worsened since 1992, and that the present trends and patterns of behavior are not sustainable.

The United Nations Environment Programme (UNEP) 1997 *Global Environment Outlook* report confirmed the worsening conditions of the earth, noting that:

1. Greenhouse gases are being emitted at levels higher than the stabilization goal agreed on under the United Nations Framework Convention on Climate Change.
2. The use of renewable resources, such as land, fisheries, forests, and freshwater, is beyond their natural capacity for regeneration and, therefore, unsustainable.
3. Rapid, unplanned urbanization, especially in coastal areas and in developing countries, is placing major stress on adjacent ecosystems, and causing social and political conflicts and war.
4. Changes in global biogeochemical cycles are leading to widespread acidification, changes in hydrological cycles, and the loss of biodiversity, biomass, and bioproductivity.[1]

One of the causes of the earth's ill health relates to the world production and consumption of energy. Energy in all its forms powers the world in ways often hazardous to the earth. For example, most of the world's energy comes from oil, coal, and natural gas—fossil fuels that emit an estimated 22 billion tons of carbon dioxide into the earth's atmosphere each year. The U.S. Department of Energy estimates that if present trends continue the emissions could rise 55 percent by the year 2020. Population growth and economic development among the developing countries make this a very likely scenario. A jump in carbon dioxide and other greenhouse gases could boost smog, ozone depletion, and global warming. Coal has more carbon than any other fuel. When burned, it produces carbon, mercury, lead, and sulfur. Yet, China and India, the most populous countries in the world, are predicted to account for the greatest increase in the use of coal by the year 2020. By the year 2000, the United States was the leading user of coal, consuming 25.5 percent of the total, followed closely by China at 24 percent and India at only 7 percent. The United States also led the world in per capita gasoline use at 459 gallons, followed by Canada at 308 gallons, Germany at 140 gallons, Japan at 113 gallons, Russia at 55 gallons, and China at only 10 gallons. Since China and Russia are expected to significantly increase their per capita gas consumption, more emissions are expected in the earth's atmosphere.

As expected, the consumption of energy is unevenly distributed among the regions of the world. North America leads the world in energy use, taking an estimated 29.8 percent, followed by developing Asia at 19.3 percent; Western Europe at 17.3 percent; Eastern Europe and the former Soviet Union at 13.3 percent; Japan, Australia, and New Zealand combined at 7.0 percent; the Middle East and South/Central America each at 5.1 percent; and Africa at only 3.1 percent. According to the International Energy Agency, world consumption of end-use fuels will rise from 5,808 million tons of oil equivalent in 1997 to an estimated 9,117 million tons of oil equivalent by 2020, an increase of 57 percent. The combined contribution of the three fuel sources of world energy—oil, gas, and coal—is not expected to change very much from the current total of 78 percent. Likewise, the total contribution to world energy use from electricity and other renewable sources is expected to remain relatively small at 17–20 percent.[2]

The world reactions to the earth's health problems have been loud and overwhelming. Individuals, communities, national and subnational governments, businesses, NGOs, private and public institutions, and the international community are each in their own way responding to the earth's plight with the one clear objective of stopping a bad situation from getting worse and, hopefully, bringing about sustainable improvements. Of course, the strategies and tactics differ from demonstrations and boycotts to scientific and technical studies and interventions to international negotiations and initiatives. Although there is no global consensus on the best way to deal with global environmental challenges, especially among the advanced industrial countries, the emerging economies, and the poor developing countries, the United Nations has made some reasonable suggestions. Meeting in New York in February 1997, delegates of the United Nations Commission for Sustainable Development (UNCSD) agreed that in order to address the earth's environmental ill health five areas needed particular attention:

1. Combatting poverty and growing inequality within and among countries because poverty and environmental degradation are closely related, especially in the developing countries and transition economies;

2. Freshwater, especially the need to bring clean water and sanitation to the hundreds of millions of people who lack access to these basic needs; the UNCSD also highlighted the need for a global long-term strategy to deal with problems of dwindling freshwater resources in places such as the Middle East and California and increasing pollution of water supplies in many parts of the world;

3. Climate change and the need for a clear global strategy to improve global atmosphere because air pollution remains a major world problem at regional and local levels;

4. Forests and the urgent need to establish an effective ongoing process to promote sustainable management of forests worldwide, especially to newly globalizing developing countries whose forest resources are at risk;

5. The oceans and the importance of strengthening international cooperation and political impetus to halt the severe decline in fish stocks, resulting from commercial overfishing in many parts of the world.

While the UNCSD focused on poverty, freshwater, climate change, forests, and oceans as the critical issues for achieving global sustainable development, members of the OECD and their trading partners from developing countries and transition economies took a slightly different approach. Also meeting in November 1997, OECD members and representatives from the Dynamic Non-Member Economies (DNME)[3] of Asia and Latin America discussed the relationships between globalization and the environment and came up with the following suggestions:

1. the need for both OECD and DNME members to access and share information and technical knowledge about the environment and the environmental impacts of development within and among countries;
2. the role of environmental standards and the extent to which they can be
   harmonized;
3. the linkages among trade, investment, and the environment and the extent
   to which common rules and standards are appropriate;
4. the role of environmentally sound technologies and the extent to which
   globalization can further facilitate its transfer and effective utilization.

The difference in emphasis between the UNCSD, on the one hand, and the OECD–
DNME member states, on the other hand, is quite instructive and points to the "self-interests"
approach by which the winning globalizing countries respond to environmental issues. While
the U.N. approach starts with consideration of the needs of the poor, and mostly losing globalizing countries, the OECD–DNME approach almost completely ignores the immediate
needs of the extremely poor and globally excluded countries. It is not surprising that consensus about the agenda for "Earth Summit +10" in 2002 remains elusive.

THE IMPACT OF GLOBALIZATION ON THE ENVIRONMENT

Globalization is changing the nature and context of environmental problems and solutions at the local, municipal, national, regional, and international levels. There are new
concerns about the formulation and implementation of environmental policies and
strategies and the ability and willingness of various players to exploit new opportunities
to pursue sound environmental practices in the context of globalization. There is no
doubt that globalization has both direct and indirect effects on the environment. Some
of these effects are positive, others are negative. The net effects vary across regions, countries, communities, industrial sectors, types of institutional players, and over time. Globalization's effects on the environment are likely to be long term, whereas most of the
current environmental policies and initiatives take more of a short- and medium-term
perspective. Therefore, it is difficult to convince the major players to adopt a strategic approach because policy makers are more influenced by current realities rather than future
possibilities.

While the future is not necessarily all doom and gloom, it is not rosy either. Like most
complex and dynamic world issues, the truth is probably somewhere in between. Globalization is not the harbinger of as much environmental abuse and degradation as critics and
protestors claim. Yet, the world has not found effective processes, structures, and mechanisms for addressing current and future environmental challenges, especially resulting from
globalization. The interdependent nature of the environmental problems requires increasingly collaborative approaches and creative solutions by all participants in the global economy. This has not been easy because the two main actors—global corporations and
nation–states—often act in pursuit of self-interests. Pressure from domestic politics and

shareholders limits the extent to which governments and corporations can and will embrace collaborative approaches to solving global environmental problems.

Exhibit 12.1 lists ten key contemporary issues concerning the relationship between globalization and the environment. These relate to questions of governance; economic competitiveness; international trade and investment; sectoral economic policies; technological change; business policy and strategy; labor and employment; environmental policies and their enforcement; skills, competencies, and capacities; and the strategies and behavior of individual private sector organizations. Perhaps progress or lack thereof in developing effective governance systems for global environmental management, technological change, poverty alleviation, and the strategic behavior of the private sector will ultimately collectively determine the net impact of globalization on the environment. Even in the rather complex and uncertain context of the globalization–environment relationships, governments have a very important role to play locally, nationally, and internationally. Therefore, every globalizing developing country must develop and sustain the political will and the technical and institutional capacity for effective environmental policy formulation, management, and enforcement.

Exhibit 12.1
Contemporary Key Globalization–Environment Issues

1. *Environmental Governance:* What kind of changes will be required locally, nationally, regionally, and internationally to deal effectively with environmental effects of globalization? How can multilateral approaches be encouraged to help solve "prisoners' dilemma" problems?

2. *Economic Competitiveness:* What is the best way to achieve an optimal balance between competitiveness and sustainable development?

3. *International Trade and Investment:* What is the net effect of international trade and investment on the environment? Are developing countries creating "pollution havens," and do environmental standards play a significant role in the location decisions of global corporations? Is industrial flight a serious problem?

4. *Sectoral Economic Policies:* How should these policies be adjusted to reduce or increase the negative or positive consequences of globalization on the environment or the economy?

5. *Technological Change:* How can technological innovation, adoption, and diffusion become much more widely used to solve environmental problems, and what role might environmental technologies play in mitigating the environmental impact of globalization?

6. *Business Policy and Strategy:* How do business enterprises formulate and implement corporate policies and strategies, and what significance do they attach to environmental issues, especially in the context of a more globalized economy?

7. *Labor and Employment:* What are the effects on total employment and the structure and composition of labor resulting from changes in environmental policies induced by economic globalization? How can collaboration of multilateral institutions on environmental issues limit the negative effects on labor and unemployment?

8. *Environmental Policies:* What effects do different environmental policies, regulations, and their enforcement or lack thereof have on the globalization process? What effects do they have on the quality of the environment?

9. *Skills, Competencies, and Capacity:* What knowledge, skills, competencies, and capacities do the major actors and stakeholders in the globalization–environment nexus, especially in developing countries and transition economies, need to perform their roles and functions effectively in the best interests of both globalization and environmental protection?

10. *Local Businesses:* Since globalization increases the importance of the local business sector, what sort of policies, programs, and incentives should be introduced to ensure that these enterprises remain both economically competitive and environmentally clean and green?

Source: Compiled in part from *Globalization and Environment: Preliminary Perspectives* (Paris, OECD, 1997), 15–17.

THE BIG-EIGHT ENVIRONMENTALLY IMPORTANT COUNTRIES

As one would expect, all countries are not equally important in terms of their effects on the environmental health of the earth. Eight countries—the big-eight, or E8—have had, and are expected to continue to have, an increasingly important role in shaping future global environmental trends. These countries, listed in Table 12.1, are Brazil, China, Germany, India, Indonesia, Japan, the Russian Federation, and the United States. Together, they account for 54.4 percent of world population, 58.6 percent of world economic output, and 60.8 percent of world carbon emissions, but they contain only 36.9 percent of the world's total nationally protected areas such as forests, parks, and other wildlife preserves. The industrial countries in this group—Japan, Germany, and the United States—influence environmental trends and the health of the earth through their high levels of production and

TABLE 12.1
The Big-Eight Environmentally Important Countries

Country	Share of World Population 1999 million	%	Share of Gross World Product 1999 $billion	%	Share of World Carbon Dioxide Emissions 1996 mmt.	%	Nationally Protected Areas 1996 000SqKm	%	Annual Deforestation 1990-95 SqKm	%
1. United States	273.9	4.6	8351.0	28.6	5301.0	23.4	1226.7	14.4	-5886	-
2. Russian Federation	146.5	2.4	332.5	1.1	1579.5	6.9	516.7	6.0	0	-
3. Japan	126.6	2.1	4078.9	13.9	1167.1	5.1	25.5	0.3	132	-
4. Germany	82.0	1.4	2079.2	7.1	861.2	3.8	94.2	1.1	0	-
5. China	1249.7	20.9	980.2	3.6	3363.5	14.8	598.1	7.0	866	-
6. India[1]	997.5	16.7	442.2	1.5	997.4	4.4	142.9	1.7	- 72	-
7. Indonesia	207.0	3.5	119.5	0.4	245.1	1.1	192.3	2.2	10,844	10.7
8. Brazil	168.1	2.8	742.8	2.5	273.4	1.2	355.5	4.2	25,544	25.1
Total	3250.3	54.4	17,126.3	58.6	13,788.2	60.8	3151.9	36.9	-	-
World Total	5974.7	100.0	29,232.1	100.0	22,690.1	100.0	8,543.5	100.0	101,724	100.0

[1]India's population passed the 1 billion mark in early 2001.

Note: mmt = million metric tons.

Source: World Development Report 2000/2001:Attacking Poverty (Washington, DC: World Bank, 2001), tables 1, 9, 10.

consumption, as well as their dominance in technological innovations, including those directly relevant for environmental management. They are also very active and influential in all multilateral organizations working in the areas of globalization (for example, WTO) and the environment (for example, OECD, UNCSD, UNEP). What these countries do both at home and internationally and how they decide to leverage their economic strength, technological superiority, and geopolitical power and influence will have significant effects on the relationships between globalization and the environment.

The other countries of the E8—Brazil, China, India, Indonesia, and the Russian Federation—are big emerging markets (BEMs) and transition economies. They have a significant impact on the environment because of their large populations, rapid economic growth, and rich biodiversity. They are expected to maintain high levels of economic growth and significant increases in production and domestic consumption, thus increasing stresses on the earth. They have significantly large pockets of poor regions, communities, or populations. Since there is a negative relationship between poverty and the quality of the environment, these countries can be expected to contribute to environmental degradation. At the same time, urbanization is growing in these emerging and transition economies. For example, the urban population as a percentage of total population grew from 1980 to 1999 from 66 percent to 81 percent for Brazil, from 20 percent to 31 percent for China, and from 22 percent to 40 percent for Indonesia. Urbanization is associated with environmental problems, especially in poor and fast-growing economies where services such as sanitation, housing, and clean water do not keep pace with urban population growth.

These five countries also have extensive coastal areas, oceans, freshwater, forests, minerals, and other natural resources. Globalization makes these resources attractive for development and exploitation for global production and consumption. The UNCSD has already identified coastal areas, oceans, freshwater, forests, and mineral resources as critical for the future of global environmental protection. Therefore, what these countries do individually and collectively, the policies and environmental governance systems they develop, the enforcement mechanisms they use, the role they play in the multilateral economic and environmental negotiations, and the success with which they effectively balance economic growth and sustainable development will have far-reaching effects on the world management of the globalization—environment relationships and, ultimately, the health of the earth.

Table 12.1 also provides some interesting country comparisons relevant for environmental protection. For example, the data in the table show that there is no direct relationship between economic output and carbon emissions. Russia accounts for 1.1 percent of world output but 6.9 percent of carbon emissions. The corresponding figures for India are 1.5 percent output and 4.4 percent for emissions. On the other hand, while Japan accounts for 13.9 percent of world output, it contributes 5.1 percent of carbon emissions. Germany's output is 7.1 percent with carbon emissions of 3.8 percent, and the U.S. output is 28.6 percent with carbon emissions of 23.4 percent.

These statistics point to several observations. First, the emerging and transition economies need to improve their production processes to reduce carbon emissions per unit output. Since they are expected to significantly increase their total production as their economies grow, if they continue to use the same or similar highly polluting technologies and production processes, they will harm the global environment and the earth's atmosphere much more than the industrial countries have done so far. Second, the evidence also points to the fact that the technologies exist to reduce carbon emissions while still maintaining high levels of economic output. This is what Japan and Germany have attempted to do. Through international collaboration and environmentally friendly technology transfer, adoption and diffusion can be facilitated to help the productive enterprises of the globalizing developing countries and transition economies to reduce environmental pollution while remaining globally competitive. In proportional terms between output and carbon emissions, the data suggest that the United States has a lot of room to improve in reducing carbon emissions per unit output to get closer to its competitors: Japan and Germany.

Table 12.1 also shows the share of protected areas for the E8. While China, the Russian Federation, and the United States show significantly higher percentages of protected areas as a percentage of the world total, the other countries, including Brazil and Indonesia, show small percentages (6.6 percent of the world is covered by protected areas). Japan and Germany do not have the territory to allocate more land to protected areas, but Brazil, China, Russia, and many developing countries in Africa and Latin America do. If the globalizing world took the view that these protected areas are not only national assets but also common goods for the earth, then the rich countries with no territory of their own should spend money to help the poor countries with territory to allocate and manage more protected areas. For example, Japan, Germany, or any of the industrial rich countries with limited territory could take out a one-hundred-year lease of part of the forests or wetlands in Africa or Latin America on condition that the land remains as a protected area for the duration of the lease. The recipient countries would use the money to promote liberalization and economic development and to build capabilities and capacities for effective globalization. The leasing country would also provide technology, technical know-how, and managerial expertise for better environmental management systems of the country or countries whose territory is being leased. These are the kinds of collaborative and creative solutions that will be required in the future for the effective management of the complex and dynamic relationships between globalization and the environment.

The challenges of sustaining global forests illustrate both the problem and the need for international partnerships and collaboration. Led by Brazil (Table 12.1), most of the emerging and developing countries in the tropics are losing their forests faster than they can regenerate. Brazil and Indonesia alone account for more than 35 percent of annual global deforestation. Other big losers include Bolivia (2,245), Mexico (1,961), Malaysia (1,545), Thailand (1,272), Myanmar (1,496), Tanzania (1,245), Paraguay (1,261), Zambia (1,021), and Angola (1,021). These figures, which are the annual rate of deforestation in square miles, suggest that the world forests are becoming victims of globalization because the emerging and developing countries and the global corporations who harvest the forests have failed to balance short-term economic gains with long-term needs for sustainable development. However, this need not be so.

Several advanced countries, including Canada, Sweden, France, Greece, and the United States, already have in place environmental management systems that allow them to harvest forests for economic benefits while at the same time adding to the slate of available forests for the future. The technology and managerial expertise for sustainable forest management exists among the enterprises in the forest products enterprises, the governments that regulate the industry, and the various private and public institutions including colleges, universities, and community-based organizations. The interests of globalization would be best served by the creation of collaborative mechanisms whereby this technology and management expertise would be effectively transferred, adopted, and utilized by the government and private sector operations in the emerging and developing countries.

Forests are not only a national resource, they are also a global resource. They renew the air we breathe, moderate the global climate, recycle atmospheric moisture, stabilize soils, serve as a large bank of genetic diversity, and provide materials for commercial and traditional medicines, and they are the principal habitat for millions of plants and animal species, many of which are endangered. They also sustain the economies of many communities by providing important products to the global economy such as lumber and panel boards for construction materials, pulp and paper for packaging and writing material, and firewood for fuel. By denying the developing countries effective access to and utilization of the technology and management expertise for sustaining global forests, global corporations and advanced countries are not serving the interests of globalization. They may not be serving their own long-term interests, either. Balancing the long-term interests of a global economy, the global environment, and the global society calls for new governance systems and collaborative institutional arrangements among all private sector players in advanced and developing countries.

BUSINESS AND THE ENVIRONMENT

Business enterprises are the agents of globalization in terms of trade, investment, and industrialization. What they do or do not do, how they do it, and where they do it in pursuit of globalization affects the economic fortunes of globalizing developing countries and transition economies as well as the environmental health of the earth. Here, I distinguish between two different types of business enterprises: the global corporations (also known as transnational corporations) and the local business sector of the globalizing host country, often made up of state-owned enterprises (SOEs), small- and medium-size enterprises (SMEs), and, in the case of developing countries, the informal sector. Each of these types of business enterprises poses different challenges and offers different possible solutions to the understanding and management of the globalization–environment relationships.

Global Corporations and the Environment

Global corporations operate worldwide and, therefore, exert considerable influence, good and bad, over many aspects of environmental quality in the home and host countries, as well as globally. Although individual countries, are primarily responsible for the protection and management of the quality of their environment, global corporations play an important role because (1) they have resources other players do not have including leading-edge environmentally friendly technology, economic power and influence, and technical and managerial expertise gained from different environmental regimes; (2) they often have non-equity relationships with other players, especially in the host country including backward and forward linkages, which afford them additional opportunities to influence environmental decisions and actions; (3) they have a strategic global image to project, protect, and preserve and worldwide informed and critical shareholders and stakeholders to report to; and (4) foreign direct investment (FDI), which is mostly provided by global corporations, tends to be concentrated in a few countries and a few sectors. Many of these sectors such as oil and metal refining, cement, chemicals, pulp and paper, mining, and agriculture are known to be heavy polluters.

To what extent are global corporations responsible for the world's environmental problems resulting from globalization? The evidence is not as clear-cut as public perception might lead us to believe. Global corporations have been responsible for some of the world's worst cases of pollution, industrial accidents, and environmental degradation, but they are also increasingly becoming a positive force in the effective management of environmental systems globally and in specific globalizing developing countries and transition economies.

On the negative side, global corporations are the primary producers—and often the intermediate consumers—of chlorofluorocarbons (CFCs), which are the principal cause of stratosphere ozone depletion and account for at least 15 percent of greenhouse gas emissions. One chemical company alone—E. I. du Pont de Nemours and Company (Dupont)—accounts for 25 percent of world production of CFCs. It has also been estimated that the twenty largest global pesticide manufacturers accounted for 94 percent of world agrochemical sales in 1990. Global corporations have also been accused of transferring pollution-intensive industries such as chemicals, petroleum and coal products, metal, and pulp and paper from the advanced countries where environmental regulations are strictly enforced to developing countries and transition economies where they can negotiate for lower environmental standards. Indeed, the share of these pollution-intensive industries as a percentage of FDI ranges from 20 percent to 25 percent. Sometimes, global corporations have been known to use local subcontractors in pollution-intensive industries in order to avoid responsibilities for environmental standards. This is the race to the bottom.

Studies in Malaysia, the Philippines, and other Asian countries found that global corporations often adopted lower environmental standards in their operations than they did in their home (advanced) countries. Studies have also found that entire sectors, which are slowly disappearing from OECD economies, account for a growing share of the exports from developing countries. The studies concluded that environmental standards seem to be at least partly responsible for promoting the exodus of basic industries from the developed to the developing countries.[4] Environmentalists and other critics have argued that instead of promoting technology transfer for development, global corporations have, in the past, engaged in eco-dumping. According to Conservation International, an American NGO based in Washington, DC, operations by oil global corporations caused the spillage of an estimated 19 billion gallons of toxic waste between 1972 and 1989. In India, Union Carbide and the Bhopal gas disaster and Dupont's transfer of its nylon 6.6 plant from the militant state of Goa to the more business-friendly state of Tamil Nadu are given as examples of environmental crimes by global corporations operating in emerging and developing countries.[5] In the early 1990s, the World Bank seemed to give tacit approval to the policy of encouraging more "dirty" industries to migrate to the emerging economies and developing countries.[6]

In addition to having significant and direct environmental effects in the host country, global corporations, through FDI, can have transboundary environmental effects. For example, in Southeast Asia, Toyota has plants in Thailand, the Philippines, Indonesia, and Malaysia producing different parts, components, and subsystems of the automobile. Thailand specializes in diesel engines, stamped parts, and electrical equipment; the Philippines in transmissions; Indonesia in gasoline engines and stamped parts; and Malaysia in steering gears and electrical equipment. These parts are exchanged among the four countries, and their production, packaging, transportation, storage, and use affect the nature and levels of pollution in these countries and in the region as a whole.

It has been argued that "pollution havens" exist in developing countries because of pressures from both the global corporations and the host country government. Government officials are under pressure to attract FDI in order to maintain high levels of economic growth. Global operations are under pressure to use the most effective methods of production in order to remain globally competitive. These competitive pressures create conditions of "willing buyer and willing seller" between the host government and the global corporation, forcing them to negotiate down environmental standards. In the early stages of industrialization, some of the BEMs such as Chile, Thailand, Malaysia, Indonesia, and Brazil were suspected of compromising environmental standards in order to attract FDI. India provides some examples. For example, in the early 1990s Dupont transferred the location of the proposed nylon plant from the state of Goa to Tamil Nadu. It was suspected that Tamil Nadu gave economic considerations priority over environmental concerns in order to win the investment.[7]

On the positive side, there is increasing awareness and empirical evidence pointing to the contributions global corporations make to the effective management of the environment. Global corporations have relatively fewer adverse effects on the environment of the host country and its natural systems than the local enterprises. Many factors explain this:

First, most well-managed corporations integrate environmental considerations in their corporate strategy and business planning. Since they have superior financial, managerial, and technological resources, they can exercise leadership in environmental protection and management. They can draw on technology used in advanced countries with strict environmental standards to improve the production, processes, handling, transportation, storage, and packaging of goods in emerging economies and developing countries. They exercise dominant influence in the innovation of new products including redesigning, packaging, use, and disposal. Their dominant position in product design and development provides important channels for affecting environmental quality. They have the resources to hire and retain more technically and professionally qualified managers and operators. Moreover, the technology they bring to deal with host country environmental challenges is reinforced by superior management skills and lessons of experience gained elsewhere in their global operations.

Second, global corporations can develop effective channels for the transfer and utilization of productive (competitive) and environmentally sound technologies worldwide. For example, many manufacturing facilities operated abroad by American companies have been found to be significantly cleaner than plants operated by local entrepreneurs. By introducing new pollution control technologies, by training technicians in pollution control, by sharing technical data, and sometimes by building joint waste treatment facilities with local authorities, U.S. global corporations have often had a positive impact in reducing industrial pollution in emerging markets and developing countries.

Third, global corporations often have a special relationship with the host government and, more increasingly, with the various interest groups in the wider community. Global corporations are often treated as guests, care about the quality of the relationship they maintain with the host government and the local community, have a global image to project and protect, and are often subject to home country regulations on social and ethical responsibilities. In the final analysis, it is in the long-term strategic interest for global corporations. They have the means to do so, and the costs of doing otherwise are high. Shareholders and society, in general, demand high levels of environmental accountability from the executives of global corporations.

Recent experiences suggest that most global corporations do not support the pollution-haven hypothesis whereby they seek out and move operations to developing countries with the lowest environmental standards. There are good reasons for this. Experience shows that those countries with weak environmental standards also tend to have weak national integrity and regulatory systems. They also tend to be associated with political instability, uncertainty about future regulations, and corrupt officials. Reputable global corporations would not want to do business under these conditions. Companies seeking pollution havens tend to be running away from problems in their home country. These may be financial, technical, or managerial problems, or they may be industrial relations problems and conflicts with trade unions and employees. Such companies do not do well, and eventually they are forced out of business by better competition. The lesson for developing countries is clear: Global corporations seeking environmental exemptions are not good at business, they are not good for the economy or society, and they are not good for the environment.

Local Business and the Environment

The enterprise sector of globalizing countries is largely made up of the global corporations and the local businesses. In the previous section, I discussed the role global corporations play in affecting the quality of the global environment. In this section, I focus on the relationship between the local business sector and the environment in the context of globalization. The local business sector in developing countries and transition economies is typically made up of the SOEs, SMEs, and the informal sector. The relative size of these three subsectors varies across countries and sectors, but with globalization, it is expected that the industrial sector will be increasingly dominated by SMEs, with fewer SOEs. Here, I focus on SMEs and the role they play in environmental protection and management.

In any competitive economy, SMEs play a significant role in production and employment. In the EU, for example, they account for 99.8 percent of business enterprises and provide 95 percent of total turnover and employment. As a result of globalization, SMEs have become more important players in the industrial sectors of emerging economies and developing countries. In Thailand, they make up more than 98.6 percent (1991) of the total number of industrial enterprises; in Indonesia (1993), 97 percent; and in the Philippines (1988), 98.7 percent. In Taiwan and Thailand, SMEs account for more than 70 percent of the workforce. In most countries, SMEs also play an important role in upgrading indigenous enterprises from the informal sector and contribute significantly to the share of exports. In the case of Taiwan, SMEs account for 55 percent of total exports. Many global corporations maintain close strategic and operational business alliances with SMEs.[8]

Given their increasing importance in the economies of developing countries, what is the environmental record of SMEs? Hard to say, but according to available evidence, not good. The pollution load generated by SMEs is significant because of their large numbers and the diversity of waste discharged. It has also been found that SMEs do more harm to the environment than global corporations. A number of factors account for this: First, unlike global corporations, SMEs do not have the resources—capital, technology, and human resources—to invest in and operate pollution control and environmental management systems. They lack the resources to access and effectively utilize modern productive and environmentally sound technologies. They tend to operate on smaller margins and, therefore, are limited in their ability to pay for the cost of environmental control and management.

Second, SMEs are large in number but low in individual visibility. They can easily hide their environmental sins, and they do not have a high-profile image to protect. Because they are small, they can easily get in and out of business or reappear under new identity in order to avoid detection and punishment. Government and other regulatory agencies have a hard time monitoring, catching, and holding them environmentally accountable. As well, in many newly industrializing and globalizing countries, SMEs have a special relationship with government and local authorities. If they are the only or biggest employer in the community, the authorities may relax environmental standards for them in exchange for guarantee of continuing operations and employment. Since SMEs do not have the same leverage as global corporations to negotiate special environmental exemptions, they are more likely to engage in clandestine operations in order to remain competitive. For example, they have been known to install pollution control equipment but turn it off during the production process in order to cut costs or because they cannot afford the services of the technical operator or maintenance.

In those countries where it has been recognized that SMEs are unable to balance their short-term business financial interests with the medium- and long-term environmental interests, the strategy has been to help them rather than prosecute or demonize them. Help has been coming from different levels of government, community organizations, global corporations, and the international community. Governments are helping SMEs in various ways including providing information on cleaner technologies and environmental management systems. They are also working with local communities to create environmental awareness in the general population and to use civil society as pressure groups for environmental protection. The international donors and financing agencies are also paying more attention to the environmental impact of the projects they support and allocating some of the resources to enhance the capabilities and capacities of SMEs in the area of environmental protection and management. For example, in the 1990s, USAID sponsored a project in the Philippines targeted at the country's SMEs and the environment. The Industrial Environmental Management Project provided training for 140 SMEs in cleaner production and waste minimization methods. The objective was to help these enterprises identify low and no-cost ways to reduce their pollution through process improvements and positive financial payback. Therefore, the project provided the kind of incentives most entrepreneurs would find attractive. By March 1996, the SMEs had invested U.S.$25 million on environmental management, achieved annualized net benefits of U.S.$31.4 million, reduced pollution by 33 percent against targets of 5–10 percent, and reduced water use by 43 million cubic yards per year; and 98 percent of the participating SMEs had adopted new waste management systems. These results show that with the right incentives SMEs, like global corporations, can adopt environmentally sound business practices.

Perhaps the greatest influence on the behavior of the SMEs toward the environment comes from global corporations. As they increase the amount of business they do with them, global corporations are also putting pressure on the SMEs they do business with to "clean up their act." The global corporations are using various business, operational, and management practices to raise SMEs' environmental awareness and to develop the necessary capabilities and capacities for environmental management. Global corporations provide SMEs with the resources—technology, operational and managerial know-how, information on certification, and so on—they need to become and remain environmentally responsible. Through a variety of business practices known as "green purchasing," global corporations can impose and enforce strict environmental standards more effectively than governments can. For example, they can use environmental surveys and audits to select or deselect SME suppliers depending on their record of environmental practices. They can give the problem SMEs deadlines to conform to certain environmental standards or be permanently excluded as suppliers. They can insist that as a condition of continuing business relationships, SMEs should obtain environmental certification such as ISO 1400 as well as quality assurance ISO 9000. In some cases, global corporations implement "product stewardship" agreements in which they undertake to collect, transport, and dispose of materials or byproducts from the SME suppliers who lack the capacity to handle such materials.

Global corporations have been particularly instrumental in developing strategic alliances with SMEs in emerging economies and developing countries with the view of making them economically competitive and environmentally responsible. In his 1995 book, Jordan Lewis gives an example of the global corporation—SME collaboration by Apple Computer and its Asian suppliers. Apple Computer was faced with the challenge of eliminating CFCs in its products. Working closely with its suppliers, the company developed a new process for circuit board production that eliminated the need for cleaning. The new production process reduced pollution at the suppliers' factories, eliminated production bottlenecks, and increased productivity both for Apple Computer and its suppliers.[9]

There is need for more of these collaborative arrangements—forward and backward linkages—and they should be supported by the international community including providing tax credits for global corporations, which enhance the capacity of the developing countries to protect and manage their environmental systems. SMEs, which have been assisted by global corporations, should also be encouraged with similar incentives to help other SMEs, as well as the weaker operators in the informal sector. Through regional, multilateral, or south–south collaborative arrangements, SMEs from one developing country can provide environmental technical assistance to other SMEs in another developing country. For example, SMEs with environmentally sound farming practices (for example, plantation, pig farming, irrigation, fertilizer applications, ranching) from Asia and Latin America can twin with SMEs in Africa to share and exchange information and to learn from one another. Global corporations can still play a role by facilitating these international exchanges. These initiatives are more likely to succeed and be taken more seriously if conducted by and for private sector enterprises rather than governments or multilateral organizations.

GLOBALIZATION, THE ENVIRONMENT, AND THE POOR

The relationship between poverty and the environment is well established. Poor countries and their people and communities suffer from more environmental degradation than rich countries. Many factors account for the positive relationship between poverty and environmental degradation including ignorance, overpopulation, dependency on the subsistence economy, the inability to adjust to climate changes, wars and domestic conflicts, and poor or weak governance systems at the national and subnational levels. The question of interest here is how does globalization effect the environment–poverty relationships?

The effects of globalization on the relationships between poverty and the environment are complex, multidimensional, dynamic, often long term, and can be either positive or negative. On the positive side, globalization can provide channels facilitating the exchange of ideas, including lessons of experience and better methods of technology transfer, and environmental management systems and practices. For example, since most of the poor are in the tropics, globalization can facilitate the transfer and adoption of the best practices on how to balance economic development and environmental protection from Central America to Asia and Africa. This can be done either through global corporations active in these regions, international organizations, scientific institutions, governments, NGOs, or even SMEs.

Globalization can also promote openness, good governance, and economic growth—all of which help mobilize local resources, capabilities, and capacities for better environmental awareness and protection and regeneration. Openness through globalization makes it possible for the international interest groups to expose the polluters and put pressures on them to bring about positive changes.

With globalization, the international community has become much more active in protecting the interests of the poor and those least able to defend themselves against the more powerful global interests. Within the scientific community, efforts are underway in the search for development alternatives, which are more environmentally sustainable and more diverse. Since globalization facilitates both integration in the world society and differentiation at the national or local levels, it can serve as a positive force in the search for community-based balance and trade-offs between economic growth and sustainable development. International organizations have been particularly instrumental in bringing the environmental message to the poor and helping to find effective and locally acceptable solutions. For example, there are serious environmental problems associated with oceans and coastlines. Many poor countries share coastal and ocean resources. Globalization has brought about increased recognition of the importance of these resources to global sustainable development and of specific related issues such as climate change, sea-level rise, and food from the sea. Environmental concerns have been expressed by the international community through various agreements and instruments including the United Nations Convention on the Law of the Sea (UNCLOS), the U.N. Conference on Environment and Development (UNCED), the U.N. Conventions on Biodiversity and Climate Change, the 1995 U.N. Agreement on the Conservation and Management of Straddling Fish Stocks and Highly-Migrating Fish Stocks, the Global Programme of Action on land-based sources of marine pollution, and the 1995 Kyoto Declaration and Plan of Action, which deals with the sustainable contribution of fisheries to food security. At the same time, globalization has contributed to the increased realization by the international community of the potential value of ocean and coastal resources to developing countries and transition economies. For example, considerable potential value has been transferred to these countries by the creation, under UNCLOS, of two-hundred-nautical-mile exclusive economic zones, in which coastal developing countries, including small-island states, have jurisdiction over their offshore resources. This has brought valuable economic and social assets under the potential control of these countries, while confronting them with new challenges, responsibilities, and opportunities for their conservation and protection.[10]

On the negative side, globalization can accentuate the environment–poverty relationship in many different ways. A combination of rapid economic growth, urbanization, and population growth contribute to pollution and environmental degradation. Quite often, globalization leads to faster economic growth than the development of the local capacity for effective environmental management and protection. Globalization provides ready markets for polluters and environmental abusers, especially in agriculture and natural resource industries, most commonly developed for newly globalizing poor countries. Deforestation in countries including Bolivia, Myanmar, Nigeria, and Paraguay, caused by the increasing demand for forest products and the demand for clearing the land for higher-value exports (for example, soybeans, ranching), is directly linked to the rate of economic globalization. In

Chile, for example, native forests are being eliminated to plant exotic trees for timber, pulp, and paper. These monospecific plantations are associated with several negative side effects to the native ecosystems and hydrological systems, resulting in loss of biodiversity and other forms of environmental degradation. The destruction of ecosystems is also associated with river sedimentations, causing floods, geological hazards such as landslides, and new plant and animal diseases, all directly or indirectly linked to economic globalization.[11]

In South America, the maquiladora industrial strategy has been associated with environmental problems. This is the practice whereby foreign firms, usually global corporations, carry out part or all of the phases of the production process in another country. The host country, usually a developing or emerging market, extends free-port status to the plants located within its borders so that the parent company does not pay taxes on the raw materials, partly finished products, or other outputs crossing the border in either direction. The country of origin also agrees to charge customs duties only on the net value added outside its borders. The overall objective of the maquiladora incentive system is to promote globalization of trade by encouraging industrial development in the host developing country. The best-known example of maquiladora plants is between Mexico and the southwestern United States, especially Texas, New Mexico, California, and Arizona. Maquiladora plants also exist in Costa Rica, Guatemala, and the Dominican Republic.

Maquiladora-type industrial establishments can be harmful to the environment because of a lack of environmental standards and effective enforcement in the host country. In the case of the U.S.–Mexican border, the semi-desert ecosystem has been subjected to a larger and growing population and economic activities beyond its natural carrying capacity for water, energy, and other industrial and urban services.

Many poor developing countries suffer from internal conflict, civil war, and protracted wars with their neighbors. While there is no direct relationship between war and globalization, many of these conflicts have been sustained by illegal economic activities supported by the global economy. This has been the case particularly in countries such as Afghanistan, Angola, Congo, Sierra Leone, and Colombia where the sale of diamonds, gold, and drugs to the West has financed rebel movements in these countries. Experience from these countries points to the sad fact that the environment remains one of the lasting victims of war. For example, in Angola, forests have been burned, animals have been hunted indiscriminately, and mines and other explosive devices have been buried in many parts of the countryside. These warlike conditions contribute directly to the weakening of the state and the inability of the government to develop and sustain an effective environment management system and protection. For example, in Nigeria, a combination of poor governance and economic crisis has badly affected the natural environment. The uncontrolled population growth, especially in and around the major urban areas of Lagos and Ibadan, has caused the country to lose its forests and wildlife, and the coastal waters and rivers are increasingly becoming contaminated. In fact, most of the West African coastal areas are suffering from environmental degradation because the governments are unable or unwilling to provide effective environmental protection. Likewise, on the East African coast, countries such as Tanzania and Mozambique do not have the capacity to protect their exclusive economic zones from unauthorized foreign fishing boats from Russia, Asia, the Middle East, or Mediterranean countries.

A number of solutions have been proposed to address problems in poor countries where environmental degradation has worsened due to globalization. It is important to maintain appropriate environmental standards in all developing countries and between developing and developed countries. It is also important for advanced countries to ban the export of hazardous industries to poor countries. For example, in the early 1990s, the government of Denmark made it illegal for one of its companies—Dansk Sojakagefabrik Industries—to ship a mercury cell chlor-alkali factory to Pakistan. The country wanted to avoid the costly disposal fees, which would have been charged in the European Community. Transparency is also important: Global corporations and SMEs in developing countries and transition economies provide information about their operations so government inspectors and environmental interest groups can identify and expose the polluters. The individual countries, supported by the international community, should enforce the principle of making polluters and users of polluting goods and services pay for the full costs of environmental damage and cleanup. Global corporations and other potential polluters should also be persuaded to apply the precautionary principle so they are required to adopt measures against possible environmental hazards even if full scientific evidence is not available. Perhaps the most effective long-term solution is for the poor countries to develop their own human capital and institutional capacity to manage and protect their environments while, at the same time, pursuing policies in support of globalization and economic growth and sustainable development, which is so necessary in the context of globalization and yet so difficult and challenging for the poor.

CAPACITY DEVELOPMENT FOR THE ENVIRONMENT

It goes without saying that preserving the health of the earth is humanity's most important and challenging responsibility for the twenty-first century. Globalization, or no globalization, if the earth's atmosphere becomes so polluted and the environment so degraded that it fails to continue to sustain the various interdependent forms of life as we know them, our collective future is doomed. In February 2001, the U.N. agency for climate change issued another warning about the impending dangers of global warming. It was further suggested that countries, communities, and governments should make preparations to deal with the emerging effects of climate change. These include floods, storms, and hurricanes in low-lying areas; drought and famine in Africa; landslides in mountainous areas; and the spread of diseases to plants, animals, and humans as tropical diseases move and survive in the increasingly warmer temperate zones.[12]

Since globalization reinforces worldwide interdependence, it should be used as a powerful and positive force for improving the health of the earth and the management of the environment. It should provide the mechanisms for mobilizing resources for public awareness and concern, political will, technical and managerial expertise, and international cooperation. It should be used as the channel of communication so that the main actors understand that the environment is everybody's first business. Above all, it should be part of the long-term solution by assisting countries and their communities to build human capital and institutional capacities for effective environmental management and protection.

In most developing countries and transition economies, there is a mismatch between the speed at which the economy is globalizing and the national capacity for sustainable development. This imbalance will get worse if the next round of trade negotiations is successfully completed and more developing countries participate more actively in the global economy. Therefore, efforts to acquire knowledge, skill, and expertise, as well as institutional capacities, must be directed toward the elimination of this gap. It is unrealistic to expect communities to abandon economic growth and all its material benefits in order to protect the environment. Therefore, the challenge for the newly globalizing countries and transition economies is to develop human capital and institutional capacities for balancing the specific needs for economic growth and the demands for sustainable development.

Unfortunately, for most developing countries, the prospects for sustainable development are not good. Public awareness and concern about environmental hazards is generally low, and there is little or no domestic pressure for the government to act. In most of these countries, the ministries of the environment are new and weak, lack technical and managerial expertise for environmental management, and enjoy little or no stature at cabinet tables. At the subnational level, local municipal authorities do not have the resources to build and maintain an effective environmental management system or enforcement mechanisms. Although in some of the BEMs such as India, Mexico, and South Africa, local NGOs and community-based organizations have linked up with their international counterparts to fight for environmental protection; in the poorer developing countries, the NGOs and civil society remain weak, unorganized, and dependent on international funding and technical and managerial resources. The indigenous private sector—made up of the SMEs, SOEs, and the informal sector—has not been effectively mobilized as a partner in the fight against industrial pollution and environmental degradation. The local educational and research institutions do not conduct much research on the relationships between globalization and the environment, except in a few isolated cases in which the international organizations provide the lead and the resources. Domestically, it would appear that the demand for such knowledge and information is rather low, except when used by international researchers and their organizations. In summary, as they begin to address serious environmental problems, most developing countries and transition economies are faced with weak physical and institutional infrastructures, as well as low levels of social and political awareness and support.

The efforts to build the national capacity for the environment must start with the state. By state, I do not mean only the central government authority but also local, municipal, provincial, and district authorities, as well as the private sector. In dealing with environmental issues in the context of globalization, the state in developing countries and transition economies faces complex, dynamic, and interrelated issues requiring difficult economic, social, political, and cultural trade-offs. These trade-offs can only be made and effectively implemented in a collaborative atmosphere in which all the key stakeholders are involved. Therefore, in addition to building competencies and capacities for environmental policy, the state must institute a system of collaborative environmental management and protection. Once the proper policies and robust legal framework are in place and the regulatory agencies are professionally staffed and properly resourced, then the government must build public–private partnerships for effective implementation of policies and enforcement of regulations. By involving all the key stakeholders and by making sure that both the policies and regulations are based on the best available technical information and realities on the ground, it becomes relatively easy to develop the necessary capacity to integrate environmental policies and action plans with policies and programs about trade, employment, urbanization, liberalization, industrialization, and even democratic development. Environmental policies and regulations must be linked to the country's national integrity and regulatory system, and the different levels of government, with help from the media and other members of civil society, must promote transparency, accountability, information flow, and dialogue as well as fight corruption, especially among the private sector polluters and environmental abusers such as the SMEs, SOEs, and global corporations.

Like globalization, the environmental agenda is driven by international forces. Therefore, the state needs to build and sustain the skills, competencies, and institutional capacities to deal effectively with the rest of the world on its most important environmental issues. This can be expensive and time consuming because there are so many environmental organizations and international conferences that keeping up with them would be beyond the resources available to most developing countries. Therefore, the state must take a strategic approach in dealing with the international community in matters of environmental management. Starting with a comprehensive policy analysis, the state should identify its environmental priorities, develop a plan of action, and then seek out alliances and partnerships with international organizations relevant for the identified priorities and tasks associated with the plan of action. For example, if a globalizing emerging economy is facing problems of environmental enforcement from its SME sector, it may be strategically more effective to develop international alliances with select global corporations with experience in the relevant sector(s) and a good environmental record. It may also be advisable to work closely with other economies in the region or elsewhere facing similar situations. For example, in Asia, Singapore has a reputation of having the most consistent and effective record of enforcement.

As the World Bank rightly pointed out, the state must match its role with capacity by clearly defining what it must do, and develop the skills, competencies, and institutional capacity to do it. Then, it must improve its performance in terms of efficiency, effectiveness, accountability, and transparency.[13] Unfortunately, there are many poor states that do not have the capacity to define what role and responsibility they must take regarding the environment. Most of the forty-three highly indebted poor countries discussed in a previous chapter, the conflict and post-conflict states, and the least-developed countries (P2 type) fall into this category. For these countries, the international community has both a moral and a practical obligation to help them define the role and responsibility they must play and then develop the capabilities and institutional capacity to do them efficiently and effectively. The World Bank, the WTO, the United Nations, the OECD, and bilateral donor agencies have a very important role to play here. As well, international organizations such as Greenpeace and the World Wide Federation as well as regional and national environmental organizations based in advanced countries can make a more effective contribution by working closely, on a one-to-one basis, to help these poor countries build the capacity they need for effective environmental management. They must go beyond advocacy and protest and focus on the long-term solutions for these countries and their communities. As stated previously, global corporations are part of the problem and, thus, must be part of the solution. Just as the World Bank assists poor countries in preparing poverty reduction strategy papers and poverty reduction action plans, the same should be done for the environment. Countries with serious environmental problems such as E8s should each have an environmental protection strategy paper and a corresponding environmental protection action plan.

As the primary beneficiaries of globalization, global corporations must accept the responsibility for seeking long-term environmental problems in the context of globalization. The role global corporations can play in helping SMEs become environmentally responsible has been discussed here. In addition, they can make their resources available to help globalizing developing countries develop the knowledge, skills, and competencies they need to become effective environmental policy makers, managers, regulators, inspectors, and partners. They can improve these countries' access to the technology and know-how needed for effective protection of their environment. They can facilitate the development of working relationships, networks, alliances, and partnerships nationally, regionally, and internationally to allow for exchange of information and lessons of experience. They can do this directly as part of their business plans as they relate to globalizing developing countries and transition economies or they can do it indirectly through foundations and other not-for-profit environmental organizations, which they support.

All this can be achieved with determination and proper incentives. For example, global corporations could become much more involved in dealing with environmental problems associated with globalization if their shareholders insisted that they must do so and report at the annual general meetings on activities and progress. As well, they would be more active if their home country governments provided financial incentives such as tax credit for solving global environmental problems. Perhaps a global fund should be established, supported by the major beneficiaries of globalization, and funds made available to poor countries and SME polluters to finance environmental management and improvements. Likewise, government officials would become better environmental regulators, inspectors, and enforcers if there were monetary and nonmonetary incentives for them to do so. Politicians would take environmental problems more seriously if these were directly related to their fortunes at the ballot boxes.

Unfortunately, as matters stand, and despite (or because of) dire warnings about the consequences of global warming and environmental degradation, most of the world remains either ignorant or oblivious. Given that globalization is here to stay, the future of the world and its prosperity is predicated on the collective capacity to seek and maintain an optimal balance between economic growth and sustainable development. The world cannot afford to delegate responsibility for maintaining this tenuous balance in the hands of a few extreme missionaries. This is a globally shared responsibility for which we are all globally accountable.

NOTES

1. This discussion draws on *Globalization and the Environment: Perspectives from OECD and Dynamic Non-Member Economies (DNME)*. OECD Conference Proceedings (Paris: OECD, 1998), 29–37. Also see "The Global Environment: A Survey," *The Economist*, July 6, 2002, after p. 50 (special insert).

2. See "Earth Pulse: Insatiable Appetites," *National Geographic*, March 2001, pp. x–xi; and "A Survey of Energy: A Brighter Future?" *The Economist*, February 10, 2001, after p. 56 (special insert). Also visit the Web site of the International Energy Agency: www.iea.org. "The State of the Planet," *National*

Geographic 202, no. 3 (September 2002): 102–115; and "Earth's Fresh Water Under Pressure," *National Geographic* 201, no. 3 (September 2002): 2–33.

3. As of 1997, the DNME associated with the OECD were: Argentina, Brazil, Chile, Chinese Taipei, Hong Kong, Malaysia, the Philippines, Singapore, and Thailand. Therefore, the DNME and the BEMs are almost identical.

4. See Rolf-Ulrich Sprenger, "Globalization, Employment, and Environment," in *Globalization and the Environment: Preliminary Perspectives*. OECD Conference Proceedings. (Paris: OECD, 1997), 315–366.

5. These cases are discussed by Pradeep S. Mehta, "A View from the South," in *Trade, Investment, and Environment*, ed. Halina Ward and Duncan Brack (London: The Royal Institute of International Affairs and Earthscan Publications, 2000), 259–268.

6. The World Bank has never publicly supported a policy of encouraging "dirty" industries to migrate to emerging markets or developing countries. However, in the early 1990s, an internal memo written by Mr. Summers, then senior economist and executive of the World Bank, was leaked. The memo posed a question for policy discussion regarding whether it would be advantageous for dirty industries to relocate to newly industrializing countries. When the memo became public, the World Bank apologized on behalf of Mr. Summers, but there are many in the developing world who would have liked to see a more open discussion of the issue.

7. Discussed by Veena Jha, "The Role of Foreign Direct Investment: The Case of India," in *Trade, Investment, and Environment*, ed. Halina Ward and Duncan Brack (London: The Royal Institute of International Affairs and Earthscan Publications, 2000), 211–229. Also visit Conservation International's Web site: www.conservation.org.

8. This discussion draws on Burton Hamner and Teresta del Rosario, "Green Purchasing: A Channel for Improving the Environmental Performance of SMEs," in *Globalization and Environment: Perspectives from OECD and Dynamic Non-Member Economies*. OECD Conference Proceedings (Paris: OECD, 1998), 75–90.

9. Jordan D. Lewis, *The Connected Corporation: How Leading Companies Win through Customer–Supplier Alliances* (New York: Free Press, 1995). In 1999, the United Nations announced the Global Compact, a voluntary program to encourage global corporate citizenship by emphasizing human rights, fair labor practices, and respect for the environment. By January 2002, nearly forty companies around the world had signed up, wishing to unite the power of the market with the authority of universal ideals. For more on the Global Compact, visit the U.N. Web site: http://65.214.34.30/un/gc/unweb.nsf/.

10. See Canadian International Development Agency, *Strategy for Ocean Management and Development* (Hull, Quebec: Canadian International Development Agency, Government of Canada, 1998).

11. More details can be found in Danilo J. Anton, *Diversity, Globalization, and the Way of Nature* (Ottawa: International Development Research Centre, 1995).

12. At an international meeting in San Francisco in February 2001, scientists gave a bleak picture of the health of the earth and predicted dire consequences. For example, Professor Lonnie Thompson, a geologist at Ohio State University, predicted that the Kilimanjaro ice cap will melt within twenty years. Similar effects are taking place in the Andes, the Quelccaya ice cap in Peru, and the Tibetan highlands. After killing seven people in New York State in 2000, the West Nile virus is expected to move north and be able to survive the increasingly warm winters due to global warming in Canada. See Michael Smith, "Scientist Predicts End of Extinction," *The Ottawa Citizen*, February 21, 2001, p. A1.

13. For a detailed discussion of the dynamic relationship between the role and capacity of the state, see World Bank, *The State in a Changing World: World Development Report 1997* (Washington, DC: World Bank, 1998), pt. 2.

Selected Bibliography

Abdullah, A. 1996. *Going Glocal: Cultural Dimensions in Malaysian Management*. Kuala Lumpur: Malaysian Institute of Management.

Andaya, B. W., and L. Y. Andaya. 2001. *A History of Malaysia*. 2nd. ed. Honolulu: University of Hawaii Press.

Anton, D. J. 1995. *Diversity, Globalization, and the Way of Nature*. Ottawa: International Development Research Centre, 1995.

Abdor, L. 2000. *Hungary on the Road to the European Union: Transition in Blue*. Westport, CT: Praeger.

Bascom, W. O. 1997. *Bank Management and Supervision in Developing Financial Markets*. London: Macmillan.

Baume, S. K. 1996. *Entrepreneurship: A Contextual Perspective*. Lund, Sweden: Lund University Press.

Berger, B., ed., 1991. *The Culture of Entrepreneurship*. San Francisco: ICS.

Braithwaite, J., C. Grootaert, and B. Milanovic. 1999. *Poverty and Social Assistance in Transition Countries*. New York: St. Martin's.

Chambers, Robert. 1997. *Whose Reality Counts: Putting the First Last*. London: Intermediate Technology Publications.

Collins, J. C., and J. I. Porras. 1994. *Built to Last: Successful Habits of Visionary Companies*. New York: Harper Business.

Dia, M. 1966. *Africa's Management in the 1990s and Beyond: Reconciling Indigenous and Transplanted Institutions*. Washington, DC: World Bank.

DiBella, A. J., and E. C. Nevis. 1998. *How Organizations Learn: An Integrated Strategy for Building Learning Capability*. San Francisco: Jossey-Bass.

Dixit, A. K., and B. J. Nerlebuff. 1991. *Thinking Strategically: The Competitive Edge in Business, Politics, and Everyday Life*. New York: Norton.

D'Orville, D. 1993. *The Search for Global Order: The Problems of Survival*. The Tenth Session of the Interaction Council, May 28–31, 1992, Queretaro, Mexico.

Doz, Y. L., and G. Hamel. 1998. *Alliance Advantage: The Art of Creating Value through Partnering*. Boston: Harvard Business School Press.

Drucker, P. F. 1997. "The Global Economy and the Nation State." *Foreign Affairs* (September/October 1997):159–171.

———. 1999. *Management Challenges for the 21st Century*. New York: Harper Business.

Ernst, D., T. Ganiatsos, and L. Mytelka. 1998. *Technological Capabilities and Export Success in Asia*. London: UNCTAD and Routledge.

Fischer, T. C. 2000. *The United States, the European Union, and "Globalization" of World Trade: Allies or Adversaries?* Westport, CT: Quorum.

Ford, R., and D. Zussman. 1997. *Alternative Service Delivery: Transcending Boundaries*. Toronto: KPMG Centre for Government Foundation and the Institute of Public Administration of Canada.

Frese, M., ed. 2000. *Success and Failure of Microbusiness Owners in Africa*. Westport, CT: Quorum.

Friedman, T. L. 2000. *The Lexus and the Olive Tree: Understanding Globalization*. New York: Anchor Books.

Gates, B. 1994. *Business @ the Speed of Thought*. New York: Time Warner.

Gore, A. 1993. *The Gore Report on Reinventing Government: From Red Tape to Results*. New York: Random House.

Greenfield, S. M., A. Stickon, and R. T. Aubey, eds. 1979. *Entrepreneurs in Cultural Context*. Albuquerque: University of New Mexico.

Grove, A. S. 1996. *Only the Paranoid Survive*. New York: Doubleday.

Hamel, G., and C. K. Prahalad. 1994. *Competing for the Future*. Boston: Harvard Business School Press.

Hancock, M. D., and J. Logue, eds. 2000. *Transition to Capitalism and Democracy in Russia and Central Europe: Achievements, Problems, Prospects*. Westport, CT: Praeger.

Hausmann, R., and L. Rojas-Suarez, eds. 1996. *Banking Crises in Latin America*. Washington, DC: Inter-American Development Bank.

Hirst, P., and G. Thompson. 1999. *Questioning Globalization: The International Economy and the Possibilities of Governance*. Cambridge: Polity Press.

Hochschild, A. 1898. *King Leopold's Ghost: A Story of Greed, Terror, and Herosim in Colonial Africa*. New York: Houghton Miffin.

Hodges, M. R., J. J. Kirton, and J. P. Daniels, eds. 1999. *The G8's Role in the New Millennium*. Aldershot, UK: Ashgate.

Hoekman, B., A. Mattoo, and P. English. 2002. *Development, Trade, and the WTO: A Handbook*. Washington, DC: World Bank.

Hofstede, G. 1980. *Culture's Consequences: International Differences in Work Related Values*. Beverly Hills, CA: Sage.

Holmes, D. 2001. *E-Gov. E-Business Strategy for Government*. London: Nicholas Bradley.

Hu-DeHart, E., ed. 1999. *Across the Pacific: Asian Americans and Globalization*. Philadelphia: Temple University Press.

Hull, G. S. 1999. *Small Business Trickling Up in Central and Eastern Europe*. New York: Garland.

Johnson, O. E. G. 2002. *Financial Risks, Stability, and Globalization*. Washington, DC: International Monetary Fund.

Jørgensen, Jan J., T. Hafsi, and M. N. Kiggundu. 1986. "Towards a Market Imperfections Theory of Organizational Structure in Developing Countries." *Journal of Management Studies* 23, no. 4 (July):417–442.

Kallon, K. M. 1990. *The Economics of Sierra Leonean Entrepreneurship*. Lanham, MD: University Press of America.

Kaplan, D. A. 1999. *The Silicon Boys and Their Valley of Dreams*. New York: HarperCollins.

Kaplan, R. D. 1993. *Balkan Ghosts: A Journey through History*. New York: Vintage.

Kiggundu, M. N. 1997. "Capacity Development for Managing Telecommunications Reform and Restructuring: A Corporate Approach from Indonesia." *Journal of Asian Business* 13, no. 2:19–57.

———. 1989. *Managing Organizations in Developing Countries: An Operational and Strategic Approach*. West Hartford, CT: Kumarian.

———. 1999. "Civil Service Reform: Limping into the 21st Century." In *Beyond the New Public Management: Changing Ideas and Practices in Government*, 155–171, ed. Martin Minogue, Charles Polidana, and David Hulme. Cheltenham, UK: Edward Elgor.

———. 2002. "Bureaucracy and Administrative Reform in Developing Countries." In *Handbook on Development Policy and Management*, 291–302, ed. Colin Kirkpatrick, Ron Clarke, and Charles Polidano. Cheltenham, UK: Edward Elgor.

———. In Press. "Entrepreneurs and Entrepreneurship in Africa: What Is Known and What Needs to Be Done." *Journal of Developmental Entrepreneurship*.

King, K., and S. McGrath, eds. 1999. *Enterprise in Africa: Between Poverty and Growth*. London: Intermediate Technology Publications.

Kingma, K., ed. 2000. *Demobilization in Sub-Saharan Africa: The Development and Security Impacts*. New York: St. Martin's and BICC.

Krog, A. 1998. *Country of My Skull*. Johannesburg: Random House.

Krueger, A. O., ed. 1998. *The WTO as an International Organization*. Chicago: University of Chicago Press.

Landes, D. S. 1998. *The Wealth and Poverty of Nations: Why Some Are So Rich and Some So Poor*. New York: Norton.

Langseth, P., R. Stapenhurst, and J. Pape. 1997. "National Integrity System: Country Studies." EDI Working Paper 400/144/E1978. Washington, DC: World Bank, Regulatory Reform and Private Enterprise Division.

Lechner, F. J., and J. Boli, eds. 2000. *Globalization: A Reader*. Malden, MA: Blackwell.

LeVine, R. A. 1966. *Dreams and Deeds: Achievement Motivation in Nigeria*. Chicago: University of Chicago Press.

Lewis, J. D. 1995. *The Connected Corporation: How Leading Companies Win through Customer–Supplies Alliances*. New York: Free Press.

Lee, K.Y. 2000. *From Third World to First: The Singapore Story, 1965–2000*. New York: HarperCollins.

Magda, S. 1997. *Trade and the Environment in WTO: A Review of the Initial Work and Future Prospects*. Penang, Malaysia: Third World Network.

McClelland, D. C. 1961. *The Achieving Society*. Princeton, NJ: Van Nostrand.

McClelland, D. C., and D. G. Winter. 1969. *Motivating Economic Achievement*. New York: Free Press.

Mead, D. C., and C. Liedholm. 1998. "The Dynamics of Micro and Small Enterprises in Developing Countries." *World Development* 26, no. 1:61–74.

Micklethwait, J., and A. Wooldridge. 2000. *A Future Perfect: The Challenge and Hidden Promise of Globalization*. New York: Random House.

Missale, A. 1999. *Public Debt Management*. Oxford: Oxford University Press.

OECD. 1989. "Globalization and the Environment: Perspectives from OECD and Dynamic Non-Member Economies (DNME)." OECD Conference Proceedings. Paris: OECD.

———. 1997. "Environment: Preliminary Perspectives." OECD Conference Proceedings. Paris: OECD.

Peretz, D., R. Faruqi, and E. J. Kisanga. 2001. *Small States in the Global Economy*. London: Commonwealth Secretariat and World Bank.

Prakash A., and J. A. Hart. 1997. *Globalization and Governance*. London: Routledge.

———. 1998. "Political Economy of Economic integration." *Business and the Contemporary World* 10, no. 4:611–632.

Rajaee, F. 2000. *Globalization on Trial: The Human Condition and the Information Civilization*. Ottawa: International Development Research Centre.

Reynolds, D. 2000. "Globalization and Its Discontents." *One World Divisible: A Global History since 1945*. New York: Norton, 650–656.

Rifkin, J. 1995. *The End of Work*. New York: G. P. Putnam.

Rugman, A. M., and G. Boyd, eds. 1999. *Deepening Integration in the Pacific Economies*. Cheltenham, UK: Edward Elgar.

Sakong, I., and K. S. Kim, eds. 1999. *The Fifty Years of the GATT/WTO: Past Performance and Future Challenges*. Seoul: Institute for Global Economics.

Schumpeter, J. A. 1949. *Change and the Entrepreneur*. Cambridge: Harvard University Press.

Seargeant, J., and J. Steele. 1998. *Consulting the Public: Guidelines and Good Practice*. London: Policy Studies Institute.

Soros, G. 1998. *The Crisis of Global Capitalism*. New York: Public Affairs.

Srivasan, T. N. 1998. *Developing Countries and the Multilateral Trade System*. Boulder, CO: Westview.

UNDP. 1999. *Human Development Report*. 2 Vols. New York: UNDP and Oxford University Press.

UNESCO. 1995. *Our Creative Diversity: Report of the World Commission on Culture and Development*. Paris: UNESCO.

United Nations. 1993. *Debt–Equity Swaps and Development*. New York: United Nations.

————. 1999. *Finding Solutions to the Debt Problems of Developing Countries*. New York: United Nations.

————. 2000. Work of the Fifteenth Meeting of Experts on the United Nations Programme in Public Administration and Finance. E/2000/66. *Report to the Secretary General*. New York: United Nations.

Wallace, L. ed. 1999. *Africa: Adjusting to the Challenges of Globalization*. Washington, DC: International Monetary Fund.

Ward, H., and D. Brack, eds. 2000. *Trade, Investment, and Environment*. London: The Royal Institute of International Affairs and Earthscan Publications.

WHO. 1999. *The World Health Report 1999: Making a Difference*. Geneva: WHO.

World Bank. 1993. *The East Asian Miracle*. Washington, DC: World Bank.

————. 1997. *The State in a Changing World*. Washington, DC: World Bank and Oxford University Press.

————. 1998/1999. *Development Report: Knowledge for Development*. Washington, DC: World Bank.

————. 1999. *Reforming Public Institutions and Strengthening Governance: A World Bank Strategy*. Vol. 1, *Overall Strategy*. Washington, DC: World Bank.

Yeung, H. W., and K. Olds, eds. 1999. *Globalization of Chinese Business Firms*. London: Macmillan.

Yusuf, S., W. Wu, and S. Evenett, eds. 2000. *Local Dynamics in an Era of Globalization*. Washington, DC: World Bank.

Zarrilli, S., and C. Kinnon, eds. 1998. *International Trade in Health Services: A Development Perspective*. Geneva: WHO/UNCTAD.

Index

ABOUT THE AUTHOR

MOSES N. KIGGUNDU is Professor of Business at the Eric Sprott School of Business at Carleton University in Ottawa, Ontario, Canada, where he teaches courses in management and strategy, human resource management, and international business. His research interests include institutional and capacity development, cross-cultural management, and the challenges of organizing and managing for gainful globalization. He is the author of several books, including *Managing Organizations in Developing Countries* (1989), *Size and Cost of the Civil Service: Reform Programmes in Africa* (1992), and *An Analysis of Global Life Expectancy and Infant Mortality Using Health and Education Indicators* (1992). He can be reached at kiggundu@ccs.Carleton.ca.